INCEST

WORKS BY ANAÏS NIN

PUBLISHED BY THE CAPRA PRESS

The Mystic of Sex and Other Writings

PUBLISHED BY THE SWALLOW PRESS

D. H. Lawrence: An Unprofessional Study
House of Incest (a prose poem)
Winter of Artifice
Under a Glass Bell (stories)
Ladders to Fire
Children of the Albatross
The Four-Chambered Heart
A Spy in the House of Love
Solar Barque
Seduction of the Minotaur
Collages
Cities of the Interior
A Woman Speaks
The Novel of the Future

PUBLISHED BY HARCOURT, INC.

The Diary of Anaïs Nin, Volume I (1931–1934)
The Diary of Anaïs Nin, Volume II (1934–1939)
The Diary of Anaïs Nin, Volume III (1939–1944)
The Diary of Anaïs Nin, Volume IV (1944–1947)
The Diary of Anaïs Nin, Volume V (1947–1955)
A Photographic Supplement to the Diary of Anaïs Nin
In Favor of the Sensitive Man and Other Essays
The Diary of Anaïs, Volume VI (1955–1966)
Delta of Venus: Erotica
The Early Diary of Anaïs Nin, Volume I (Linotte) (1914–1920)
Little Birds: Erotica
The Diary of Anaïs Nin, Volume VII (1966–1974)
The Early Diary of Anaïs Nin, Volume II (1920–1923)
The Early Diary of Anaïs Nin, Volume III (1923–1927)
The Early Diary of Anaïs Nin, Volume IV (1927–1931)
Henry and June: From "A Journal of Love"
A Literate Passion (with Henry Miller)
Incest: From "A Journal of Love"
Fire: From "A Journal of Love"

INCEST

From "A JOURNAL OF LOVE"

The Unexpurgated Diary
of Anaïs Nin

1932–1934

With an Introduction by Rupert Pole
and Biographical Notes by
Gunther Stuhlmann

A HARVEST BOOK
HARCOURT, INC.
Orlando Austin New York San Diego Toronto London

www.HarcourtBooks.com

Some material previously appeared in *The Diary of Anaïs Nin, Vol. 1,
1931–1934*, by Anaïs Nin, copyright © 1966 by Anaïs Nin,
Introduction copyright © 1966 by Gunther Stuhlmann.

The selection by Henry Miller on pages 80–85 was first published in its entirety in Volume 7
of *Anaïs: An International Journal*, copyright © 1989 by Gunther Stuhlmann.

Excerpted letters from Henry Miller to Anaïs Nin (except for the selection on pages 80–85) first appeared
in their entirety in *A Literate Passion: Letters of Anaïs Nin and Henry Miller, 1932–1953*, edited and with an
introduction by Gunther Stuhlmann, copyright © 1987 by Rupert Pole, as Trustee under the Last Will
and Testament of Anaïs Nin. Reprinted with the permission of The Anaïs Nin Trust. The letter on
pages 116–17 was published in its entirety in *Henry Miller: Letters to Anaïs Nin,* edited and with an
introduction by Gunther Stuhlmann, copyright © 1965 by Anaïs Nin, copyright renewed 1988
by The Anaïs Nin Trust. Reprinted with the permission of The Anaïs Nin Trust.

Some of the dream passages featured throughout this book were first published in their entirety in
Volume 10 of *Anaïs: An International Journal,* copyright © 1992 by Gunther Stuhlmann.
Reprinted with the permission of The Anaïs Nin Trust.

Photographs and illustrations courtesy of The Anaïs Nin Trust.

Library of Congress Cataloging-in-Publication Data
Nin, Anaïs, 1903–1977.
Incest: from "a journal of love": the unexpurgated diary of Anaïs Nin, 1932–1934/with an introduction
by Rupert Pole and biographical notes by Gunther Stuhlmann—1st ed.
p.   cm
Includes index.
ISBN 0-15-144366-1
ISBN 0-15-644300-7 (pbk.)
1. Nin, Anaïs, 1903–1977—Diaries. 2. Authors, American—20th
century—Diaries. I. Title.
PS3527.1865Z465   1992
818'.5203—dc20   92-12441

Designed by Lisa Peters
Printed in the United States of America
First Harvest edition 1993
H J L N P Q O M K I

CONTENTS

INTRODUCTION

Incest: From "A Journal of Love" continues the story of Anaïs Nin that was begun in *Henry and June* (1986). Covering the turbulent period of Anaïs's life from October 1932 to November 1934, it complements the first volume (1966) of *The Diary of Anaïs Nin,* from which, for personal and legal reasons, Anaïs excluded so much of her love life. Now that virtually all of the people referred to in *Incest* have died, there is no cause to hold back on publishing the diary as Anaïs wished: in unexpurgated form. The material has been edited to produce a book of readable length, but nothing germane to Anaïs's emotional growth has been omitted.

Anaïs treated her diary as the ultimate confidante and wrote in it continuously from 1914 to 1977. From 1914 to 1931 she wrote without any deep emotions of love to describe. Then in Paris in 1932 she found the writer/lover she had been seeking for so long: Henry Miller. This love, the initial phases of which are described in *Henry and June,* produced a double awakening—Anaïs the woman and Anaïs the writer. This passionate awakening is well captured in the frequently wild writing to be found in the unexpurgated diary—a prose that some readers will no doubt find startlingly different from the polished, poetic prose of the expurgated diary. Recall, however, that Anaïs wrote in her diary at white heat, immediately following the events she was describing.

In *Incest* the love affair with Henry Miller continues, but it is never to have the same intensity. Anaïs has wept through the painful experience of becoming a woman, and now her "eyes are open to reality—to Henry's selfishness."

The crucial relationship explored in the present volume is that between Anaïs and her father, a famous pianist and Don Juan who divorced Anaïs's mother and married an heiress when Anaïs was a young girl. In fact Anaïs first began her diary at age eleven as letters to her father entreating him to rejoin the family. Unlike her mother and brothers, Anaïs refuses to judge her father, to see him only in black and white. She determines to "find him out." The relationship is somehow tragicomic: the father feels he is crowning his Don Juan career by attempting to seduce his daughter, but Anaïs knows she is seducing him. Later, on the advice of her psychiatrist, Dr. Otto Rank, she leaves him as punishment for abandoning her as a child.

Like the first volume of the expurgated diaries, this volume ends with Anaïs's now famous birth story. But here it appears in a new context—in a new light that starkly illuminates Anaïs's relationship with Henry Miller and her father.

When the "Journal of Love" series of Anaïs Nin's unexpurgated diaries is complete, we will have an extraordinary lifetime record of the emotional growth of a creative artist, a writer with the technique to describe her deepest emotions and the courage to give this to the world.

—RUPERT POLE
Executor, The Anaïs Nin Trust

Los Angeles
February 1992

NOTE

The text of *Incest* is taken from diary books thirty-seven through forty-six, as numbered by Anaïs Nin. Her titles for these ten books were *"La Folle Lucide," "Equilibre,"* "Uranus," *"Schizoidie and Paranoia,"* "The Triumph of Magic—White and Black Magic," "Flagellation," " 'And on the Seventh Day He Rested from His Work,' Quoted Negligently from a Book I Never Read," *"Audace,"* "The Definite Appearance of the Demon," and "Flow—Childhood—Rebirth."

Though *Incest* was written almost entirely in English, there are a number of extended passages in French or Spanish. I wish to thank Jean Sherman for her graceful translation of these passages, which are clearly noted.

—R. P.

INCEST

OCTOBER 23, 1932

I ALWAYS BELIEVED IT WAS THE ARTIST IN ME WHO
ensorcelled. I believed it was my esoteric house,
the colors, the lights, my costumes, my work. I always stood *within*
the great active-artist shell, timorous and unconscious of my power.
What has Dr. Allendy done? Discarded the *artist*, handled and loved
the core of me, without background, without my creation. I have even
been concerned over his unattachment to the artist—I have been surprised to be so seized, so *dépouillée* of artifice, of my webs, my charms,
my elixirs. And tonight, alone, waiting for visitors, I look upon this
newborn core, and I think of the gifts made to it by Hugh, Allendy,
Henry, and June. I remember the day I gave Hugh's sister, Ethel,
jewelry; and today cousin Ana Maria gives me stones for my aquarium,
and a new humorously winged fish with green wings, and she says,

"I want to go to London with you. I want to save you from June." And I lie back and weep with infinite gratitude.

I am leaving for London. My strength is new and I need to subdue the ever-recurring pain. I need many days to dull a little in my life, or to move within my journal, my story. I cannot fight off madness in a day. I have hours yet when I turn within my pain as in a furnace, and it happens when Henry says over the telephone, "Are you all right?" and I answer, "Yes." Or when the thumbtack falls off a corner of the photograph of "H. V. Miller, gangster-author," and I realize how far I have moved away from lesbianism, and how it is only the artist in me, the dominating energy, which expands to fecundate beautiful women on a plane which it is difficult to apprehend and which bears no relation whatsoever to ordinary sexual activity. Who will believe the breadth and height of my ambitions when I perfume Ana Maria's beauty with my knowledge, my experience, when I dominate and court her to enrich her, to create her? Who will believe I ceased loving June when I discovered she destroys instead of loving? Why was I not in bliss when June, the magnificent woman, made herself small in my arms, showed me her fears, her fears of me and of experience?

The *simoun* wind tonight. Things whirling. It is night and I have been strong all day. I must not weaken so just because it is night and I am tired.

When I sense that June is intensely jealous of what I have done for Henry, I tell her, "I did it all for you."

She also tells me a lie: that she wanted to see me before she saw Henry.

But I follow up my lie with a truth: I remembered being struck with great pity when I read in Henry's notes that she was working for Henry and Jean [Kronski] and that once, in a frenzy of fatigue and revolt, she exclaimed, "You both say you love me, but you do nothing for me!" I remind June of this and feel I want to do things for her. But as soon as I say this my desire dies, because I am aware that it is a self-destructive desire, that I have not enough vitality, that

I have worked enough for Henry, that I no longer want to make sacrifices. And so my spontaneity dies, my generosity becomes a lie whose coldness chills me, and I wish the three of us could admit ourselves weary of sacrifices and weary of useless suffering.

However, it is I who am working for Henry and June, but in a rebellious spirit. Aware that I have no reason to burden or punish myself, that I, at last, am absolved of guilt, and that I deserve happiness.

June expects me to say what we are going to do together tomorrow night; June is counting on my imagination; June is going to let me betray my inexperience in actual living. Now that I have her for an evening, what will I do with this evening and her? I am a writer of fantastic pages, but I do not know how to live them.

René Lalou is exuberant, forcible, loquacious, witty. He was strongly attracted to me against his own wishes, for his great equilibrium would move away from my darkness. But his physical exuberance compelled him. For the first time I was aware of my power over the sane man—slowly his flippancy and wit mellowed. I saw the crumbling of his clarity, I saw the mounting of his emotionalism. By the end of the evening he was René Lalou, the man who has Spanish blood in him.

I laughed a great deal, but I missed my love, Henry's denser, darker quality. The brilliancy of Lalou, his passion for abstraction interested me, but I missed Henry—I missed him.

Lalou talked against surrealism and then begged for my pages on June. He mocked the work of the minority and then wished to see me published where I could be more noticed than in *Transition*.

This morning I get a beautiful letter from Allendy ending, "*le plus dévoué, peut-etre,*" and I sense what deep inroads his strange devotion has made, how subtly he is surrounding me, without tragedy or sensationalism. I feel like a person who has been drugged, insane, who wakes one morning to an idyllic clarity—newborn.

What an effort to extricate myself out of darkness and suffocation, out of a great choking pain, out of inquisitional self-laceration! Allendy watching me with double love—his strange eyes and warm hands and mouth. I do not even want to *give* anymore; I want to lie back and receive gifts. June has my black cape, but with it I gave her my first fragment of hatred. I am not in her power.

Each one has found in me an intact image of himself, his potential self: Henry saw the great man he could be, June the superb personality. Each one clings to his image of himself in me for *life,* for strength.

June, having no core sureness, can only establish her greatness by her power of destruction. Henry, until he knew me, could only assert his greatness by attacking June. They devoured each other—he caricatured her, she weakened him by protecting him. And when they had succeeded in destroying each other, killing each other, Henry wept because June was dead, and June wept because Henry was no longer a god, and she needed a god to live for.

June wants Henry to be a Dostoevsky, but June prevents him from being one—unwillingly, instinctively. She wants him to sing her praises, not to write a great book. She is blameless in her destruction. It is her breathing, her life assertion, each movement of her ego which confuse, diminish, break others. She is sincere, blameless, innocent.

I have aggrandized Henry. I can make a Dostoevsky of him. I breathe strength into him. I am aware of my power, but my power is *feminine; it demands a match, not a victory.* My power is also that of the artist, so that I don't need Henry's work personally as an aggrandizement of myself. I do not need him to praise me, and as I am an artist first, I can keep my ego, my woman's ego, in the background. It does not block his work. I sustain the artist in him. June wants not only an artist but a lover and a slave.

I can relinquish the demands of my ego, capitulate to art, to creation—above all to creation.

That is what I am doing now: creating June and Henry. Alimenting them both, giving my faith. In my frailty there is the symbolism of that frail attainment they are haunted by. June sees in me the woman who has gone through hell but who remains intact—who wants to remain intact. She will not lose her self, *her ideal self.*

And Henry wants the Dostoevskian ideal. The artist. He finds the image of this artist self in me. Whole, powerful, untrammeled.

I do not need his art to glorify me. I have my own creation. June should have been an artist in order to be more selfless.

Thanks to Allendy, I can relinquish a mere victory. I love. I love them both, Henry and June.

And June, who loves me blindly, seeks to destroy me, too. My pages on her, which are a work of art, do not satisfy her. She overlooks their strength and beauty, and voices the complaint that all I have said is not true. But not for a moment am I crushed. I knew the exact value of those pages, independently of June.

My work first, then. My power as an artist shaken, and then what other power have I? My natural stimulation, my vitality, my true imagination, my health, my creative aliveness. And what will June do to them? Drugs. June offers me death and destruction. June ensorcells me—talks with her face, her caresses, lures me, uses my love of her for destruction. Double death. My freshness of body is to be destroyed so that my body may become like hers. She said, "Your body is so fresh, mine so spoiled." And so, blindly, blamelessly, innocently, she will kill my freshness, the intactness she loves. She will kill all she loves.

And whence this dark knowledge? Out of fumes, madness, champagne, intoxication of caresses, kisses, exaltation. We are in the *Poisson d'Or,* knees locked under the table, drunk with each other; and June is drunk with herself. She has told Henry that he is nothing, that he failed to be a god and failed to be a Dostoevsky—that it is she who is a god, her own god. There, the miracle is accomplished. The delusion. Henry is killed. June has again annihilated her match. "Henry," she says, "is a child." But I protest and say I believe in Henry as an artist, and then I admit I love him as a man.

It was when she asked me, "You love Henry, don't you?" that *I gave Henry my greatest gift*. My eyes dimmed with pain. I knew that by this admission Henry was saved. Henry became again a god—no one but a god, she said, could be loved by her or me. So Henry is a god. And June asks out of the innocence of her self-magnitude, "Are you jealous of Henry?"

God—I jealous of Henry's love for June, or jealous of June's love for Henry?

It is then I become fluid, dissolved, *fuyante*. I fly from the torture which awaits me like a gigantic blood squeezer, pressing my flesh between June and Henry. From this I escape by superhuman effort— to avoid self-destruction and madness. I am caught for a moment. June can see the great pain in my eyes. I have made to both my greatest offering—I give them to each other by giving to each the most beautiful image of themselves. I am only the *revealer,* the harmonizer. And as they come closer together, I give June a Dostoevsky, and I give Henry a June become creative. I am annihilated humanly only. They have both loved me.

I love June and Henry less in proportion to my rebellion against suffering. I feel that I love in them an experience that cannot destroy me—that I no longer enter wholly—because I mean to *live*.

Evening. Henry came and we talked at first with strain. Then he wanted to kiss me and I would not let him. No, I couldn't bear that. No, he shouldn't touch me; that would hurt me. He was baffled. I resisted him. He told me he wanted me more than ever, that June has become a stranger to him, that the first two nights with her he could not feel any passion. That ever since, it had been like going with a whore. That he loved me and with me alone felt a connection between his mind's image and his desire—that there was no such thing as loving two women, that I had *displaced June*. Before he had said all this I had surrendered—the closeness seemed terribly natural—nothing had *changed*. I was dazed, it seemed so unchanged. And I had thought that our connection would seem unreal and that the natural connection between June and Henry would be renewed. He cannot even become used to her body; it must be only because there is no closeness.

I looked on all this as upon a phenomenon. After this from Henry, it is possible to believe in the faithfulness of love. I look on his last pages about her return and they are empty of emotion. She has exhausted his emotions, *overplayed* them.

Then the whole thing becomes unreal to me and it seems to me that Henry is the sincerest of all, and that June and I, or I alone, am deceiving him.

There is no more tragedy. Henry and I laugh together at the multiple complications in our relationships!

I am afraid of what is happening to me. Afraid of my coldness. Has Henry exhausted my emotions, too, by his unwitting anguish about June's constant threatening of our happiness?

Or is it that often a much-expected, *too-much*-desired joy leaves one dazed and inadequate when it comes?

June tells Henry I have said that I love him. He looks surprised. He thinks perhaps I was drunk. "How? What do you mean, June?"

"Oh, simply that she loves you, not that she wants to sleep with you."

At this we laugh. But I am also upset to realize that June believes so much in my love that it was this she meant when she said, "Are you jealous of Henry?"—that I should want to eliminate Henry, hate Henry, because of my love of her. I remember our caress in the taxi last night, my head thrown back to June's kiss, she so pale, and my hand on her breast. And she never for a moment imagined today's scene. And now it is she who is duped, and now it is Henry, and now me.

And the only sincere men in the world, Allendy and Hugo, are at this moment talking together, jealous about me. Hugo unhappy.

Henry is jealous not of June but of me, jealous and fearing I should love June, or Allendy.

I feel tonight that I want to embrace *all experience*—that I can do so without danger, that I have been saved by Allendy. That I am going with June into everything and everywhere.

Letter to Henry: It was so good that we could laugh together, Henry. Anything that exists between June and me only brings out in relief my deep, deep love for you. It is as if I were experiencing the very greatest test of my love of you—the greatest *test* of all my life. And I find that I can be drunk, drugged, ensorcelled—everything that could make me lose myself—but that there is always, always *Henry*. . . . I won't hurt you anymore with mention of others. You don't need to be jealous, Henry; I belong to you. . . .

But my love for Henry is a deep echo, a deep prolongation of a self in me that is eternally double-faced. I am a double personality. There is my deep, devotional love for Henry, but already it can be easily mutated into another love. I sense the *termination* of it, as I sense, too, that Henry's love for me will end when he is strong enough to do without me.

I have done the work of an analyst—a living piece of clarification and guidance. It is true, then, what astrology has said about my strange influence on others' inner lives.

Je prends conscience de mon pouvoir—of the force of my dreams. June herself has no true imagination, or she would not need drugs; June is hungry for imagination. Henry, too, was hungry. And they have enriched me with their *experiences*. They have both given me so much. Life. They have give me life.

Allendy has awakened me by intelligence, because feeling was submerging me, life was submerging me. He gave me the strength by which I will live out my passions and my instincts without dying, as before.

Sometimes it hurts me that there should be less feeling and more intelligence. I seemed more sincere before. But if to be sincere means to throw one's self overboard, it was a sincerity of defeat. To commit suicide is easy. To live without a god is more difficult. The drunkenness of triumph is greater than the drunkenness of sacrifice.

I no longer need to *do* so much to cover the ineffectuality of my inner transmutations, to *substitute* for understanding. I need to do little, but with a great deal of strength.

Evening. Allendy is waiting for me to *break* with Henry. I see the direction of his questions. His waiting is anxious. And today I am moved by his caresses. They are wonderful.

I tell him all I owe him. He doesn't believe in any duality. Would he if he read my journals? Are not some of the phrases I write colder than what he imagines me to be?

I feel that this time I am playing with Allendy. Why? I *feel him more sincere than I am*. It moves me and frightens me. Is *he* the man I am going to *hurt—the first man—and why?* Or is this all a defense against his power? I sit here tonight and I remember his hands. They are full, but with idealistic fingertips. How they followed the outline of my body, how he buried his head on my breast, smelling my hair. How we stood up together and kissed until I was dizzy. Henry would have long ago lifted my dress—lost his head.

Then I come home in high spirits and Hugh throws me on the bed, frenzied with jealousy, and fucks me deliriously, tearing my dress to bite my shoulders. And I act pleasure, struck with the tragedy of moods which no longer fit together. Hugh's passion has come too late. I want to be in Henry's arms—*closeness*—or in Allendy's—*the unknown. And I had always wanted my dress torn!*

I feel too distinctly the departures, the meetings, the prolongations, the new sparks. In my head there is a center of diamond wholeness, control—but I look down on my emotions and they run in different directions. There is a tension of overactivity, overexpansion, a desire to attain again that high peak of joy I attained with Henry. Will I be able to melt into Allendy? I do not believe it, and *the greatest joy,* as Henry knows now, is *closeness, wholeness, absolutism in passion.*

How many *closenesses* are there in the world for a woman like me? Am I a unity? A monster? Am I *one* woman?

What is it that goes out to Allendy? The passion for abstraction, *wisdom,* equilibrium, *strength.*

To Henry? Passion—living, unwise and hot, the artist's lack of equilibrium, the melting and fluidity of the creators.

Always two men—the *become* and the *becoming*, always the moment attained and the next one divined too soon. *Too much lucidity.*

Hugh's jealousy is flaring. Jealousy of Allendy. He is going tomorrow to tell Allendy he has *won* his wife away from him—that Allendy is defeated, that Allendy has understood me very well, as well as a scientist could, but that he, Hugh, *possesses* me. Hugh knows Allendy wanted his jealousy aroused, once and for all, to display aggressivity toward man instead of complaisance and love—to save himself from homosexual passivity, by which he allowed other men to love his wife. He *knows* that all this should be a psychoanalytical *game* played for a definite purpose, but that in this case it is not a game because Allendy's feelings are involved. And so the cruel things he will say *will* hurt Allendy! And Hugh will hurt the man he loves best, to assert his manhood and love of me!

And while Hugh tells me all this, with his new clear intuition, I am silent and I am anxious that Allendy should not be hurt. I plan to go and attenuate the effect of Hugh's words—Hugh's story of the torn dress. Yet I know Allendy cannot be hurt, that he has a terrible insight which protects him. He is so *sure* that I do not love Hugh; and how surely he is waiting for me. And I admire his terrific domination of himself and of life and pain!

End of evening. The orchestra music is swelling; the room and I explode. I stand and cover my face with my arms and laugh—laugh as I have never laughed—and the laughter breaks into a sob, a loud, wailing sob. For a minute I am mad—absolutely mad. Hugh is frightened. He comes to me tender and bewildered: "My poor little pussy willow, you have been too happy. I have made you happy!"

June is my adventure and my passion, but Henry is my love. I cannot go to Clichy yet and face them both there. I tell June it is because I am afraid of not concealing our feelings from Henry, and I tell Henry it is because I am afraid of not acting well enough for June. The truth is that I look at Henry with blazing eyes and at June with exaltation. The truth is that I would suffer humanly from seeing June installed by Henry's side—where I want to be—because the closeness between Henry and me is stronger than any adventure.

Allendy is tomorrow's love. A tomorrow can be years away. I do not want to scan any spaces or distances. I let myself live. Today my nerves are shattered. But I am indomitable.

Evening. Indomitable. White gardenia from June. "*Ambre de Delhi*" for June. June. June in my arms in the taxi. It is my arm which gets strong, it is her head which is thrown back, it is I who am kissing her throat. June melts like a heavy petal. She looks at me like a child: "Anaïs, see, I am awkward. I feel small in your arms."

I see her face blurred behind the taxi window as I leave. A tormented, hungry child, desired and unsure of love, frightened, struggling desperately to wield power through mystery and mystifications.

She actually believes Henry has been dead, cannot live without her. She comes and bungles, creates artificial complications, turns one person against another, makes Henry rage himself out of his orbit, and feels that she is living, making others live, that this is drama, life. And it is all childish.

She cannot believe, except at fevered moments. She believes when I hold her in my arms. And then leaves me and struggles for complete objectivity—she and Henry talk warily, trying to seize me objectively, apart from the moments of ecstasy and vertigo.

June's perpetual cry that one cannot trust Henry with the truth. I see such a deformed picture of each in the other's eyes. I must make terrific efforts to keep my Henry and my June. And they want to involve me in conflict, to pit me against one or the other. June wants this performance, because it is another manifestation of the attention we give her; she wants us to fight for her, Henry and me. *That* would give her the moment of hatred, or passion, in which she alone believes. She cannot live in halftones, in suggestion, in truth.

My God, am I strong enough to help her?

Allendy says that I have transmuted my great need of helping and creating others into a kind of psychoanalysis. I *have* to help, to give, to create, to interfere. But I must not give *myself*—I must learn to withhold myself. And now I see that one only really *gives* by withholding one's self, because to efface the self is at once to efface egoism and possessiveness. So I give, and because I pour out less of my heart-rending feelings, I am *stronger,* I do not get lost, I keep lucid, I truly *give*.

What can I give June and Henry? Can I give them back to each other? That does not seem right to me.

June thinks Henry is stirred up when he becomes enraged, stuttering, illogical; she thinks he is alive now, whereas he was alive before she came, only deep down. Throughout her love of me there rings this note of jealousy: She wants to impede the now-certain publication of his book because it comes from me. She attacks Henry because he does not take any more advice from her. For all this I have to watch in the very moment of the greatest exaltation. When she cannot blind me she offers her body.

My only salvation is that I disarm her, I penetrate her almost without words, I dissolve her power merely by staring at her.

I cannot help seeing that she always puts herself, her ego, before her love of Henry.

Night. Henry has been here. He says one thing is clear: we need each other more than ever, and we are to be kind to the children, June and Hugh.

I was amazed to see him growing old, showing protectiveness. June is to him a pathological child—interesting as such, but stupid and empty.

Suddenly there was between us a feeling of strong alliance—a Henry changed, a Henry hurt that people should think he can only write "cunt portraits." I told him what I owe him. Because he has made me happy as a woman, he has saved me from June and dissolution, I don't want to die. I am too happy.

What a strange talk—how he takes our love as a basis from which we might move in other directions of no importance, superficial adventures. Then I told him that it was true what June has said, that he has sacrificed her to his work—made use of her as a character he needed to create—but that I will not perform for him or create any mystery, because we need the closeness, and there is no closeness with lies.

So we talked again in deep agreement—wondering why we could not disagree. No. We know why. We are undeniably close, woven from the same texture. June is dead for him because there is only June's face and June's body.

Henry then says that he can only explain my interest in June as lesbian—for June's face and body—nothing else. He knows I cannot give June either my mind or my soul. He is proud to have reached the point where he can explain my pages on Mona–Alraune to June, whereas they bewilder and confuse June.* June interprets my paragraph on the hotel room quite literally—as describing an experience with a man in a hotel room—that is, without imagination. And it is Henry, the slow German, who seizes on the symbolical meaning!

Ana Maria is wise before she has experienced life.

She is curious. She wants to know June. She tries to put herself in Eduardo's place, to imagine what he feels about me—in a man's place. I begin to explain delicately and abstractedly the *masculine attitude* in a woman—its significance and its value. I don't want her to be frightened. I want her to know.

When I talked about her to Allendy, he said, "You want to debauch her"—but he was leveling at me the obtuse accusation made against psychoanalysts: that they make people's instincts run wild. He knows the process of running wild is only a phase in the liberation, that the re-creation consolidates the being on a new level of idealism and sincerity.

As I talked to Ana Maria, I saw her limpid mind opening and escaping from her ordinary milieu. I was overjoyed when I saw her understanding *open* in a few hours, playing with the facts and images I gave her, the life I pictured. She said, "I have never talked to anyone like you before, never talked in this way."

When I arrived with violets for Tía Anaïs, Ana Maria knew they were for her. And how I liked her cry of pleasure because I arrived in the simplest costume I have yet worn: a black silky raincoat with silver buttons, a mannish black felt hat like June's. Tía Anaïs saw only a capitulation to convention. I knew it was the deep disarming of my eccentricity, an eccentricity which I wore like a mask-garment to startle, intimidate, render uneasy and strange those who frightened me.

Driving in the taxi with Ana Maria, I looked at Ana Maria's young face and asked myself, What is the greatest gift I can make her, to

---

* The "Mona–Alraune" pages, based on A. N.'s relationship with June Miller, eventually became parts of *House of Incest* (1936) and of the novella "Djuna," which appeared in the original edition of *The Winter of Artifice* (1939).

illumine life for her, or to *make the world rock for her?* That moment when the world rocks and June's head falls like a heavy flower cut off its stem—all art strains to achieve again such a moment, and the wise men plot to dilute its essence. And I hated Allendy's wisdom, and secretly I promised: If I can, Ana Maria, I will make the world rock for you!

Hugh has become an astrologer, studying at my desk. And now I am at rest with him. This new passion brings into play the best of his faculties. His new love, violent and possessive, makes of him a man of strength. I love him for the efforts he has made to dispel the vagueness and gloom—it is the essentially *passive* quality of his nature which has tormented me. Henry says Hugh has used jujitsu on me—he has used my own strength to destroy me, he has let me crash my own head against the floor when I wanted to crash *into him*. He has intelligently evaded my weight and pressure, eluded all resistance—and I have felt the void, the discipline, the absence of bouts. It is his very *faithfulness* which makes him unchanging, taciturn, restricted. But I am at rest. I will give him no more pain. I am afraid that he will *know* my work. I want to make him humanly happy. *Humanly, he is such a perfect being.* His perfection alone restricts me. His *existence* is a restriction. Perhaps my salvation, for the life I constantly renounce for Hugh is the only great discipline I have ever known. To be always thrown against the walls which enclose me has been the only element forcing me into sublimation. How long, oh God, how long can I make him happy? I dread and tremble now when Henry talks about the publication of his book and our going to Spain together. I almost hope for some catastrophe that may prevent Henry from ever telling me, "Now you follow me."

Eduardo withdrawn: offended and slighted—in his own mind—by life. In love with Allendy and knowing the futility of it. Never resigned to not having dominated me. Incapable of throwing himself, like André Gide, into a fecund and joyous homosexuality.

Bitter, cruel talk with him and Hugh in which I reveal the complete exhaustion of my pity and tenderness for Eduardo. I hate his "spirituality," of which he boasts. I hate it because it has hurt me.

He has the feeling that because he has progressed from psycho-analysis into astrology, he is living, whereas I know that Allendy interprets this as a retirement, and that even if it is an ascension in his mental development, it remains in a state of rationalization.

His personal failure, I realize now, aside from the impossibility to love, is *the short duration of his faith*. He does not give sufficient faith to achieve the miracle. There is no miracle possible without faith.

The talk was no help to him, I know. We simply threw off a hostility which is choking us both. He hates my influence on his sister, Ana Maria, and I hate to think I wasted so many years infusing faith into him.

If Allendy and I together could not save Eduardo, nobody else can do it.

Last night was my last attempt. And it was done not out of love but out of bitter resentment that *this* should be one of the men I have loved, a man I could never completely wipe out of my life. And that is what I want to do: wipe him out of my life with all my dolorous and empty past. Life is beginning *today*. Spain with Henry, perhaps; Allendy's wise love; the ruling influence of the moon, which makes me sensual and impressionable! Wisdom and sensuality—these will be my great wings, the last to save me from the nebulous, mediumistic, visionary influence of Neptune, the planet of my ascendant!

Dream: I am attending someone's wedding. I attract the attention of a tall, gray-haired man. He invites me to dinner. Talks about his love. Some women are imitating my way of dressing. Wonderful caresses from the man. Awake bathed in moisture and palpitating.

In Hugh's horoscope I find what divides us: He is chiefly mercurial, or "mental," *not subject to the moon*. His great influence is *power;* he is a king man—passion is secondary!

I am inflamed by Élie Faure's proclamations [in *The Dance over Fire and Water*]: "It is the imagination of man that provokes his adventures, and love takes here the first place. Morality reproves passion, curiosity, experience, the three bloody stages which mount toward creation."

Allendy is the man who crystallizes, balances, arrests—immobile, pure wisdom. Henry is the man who knows "obedience to the rhythm." "Rhythm," Faure writes, "is that secret agreement with the beating of our veins, the sound of our feet, the periodic demands of our appetites, the regular alternations of sleep and waking. . . . The obedience to the rhythm upraises lyric exaltation, which permits a man to attain the highest morality by flooding his heart with the giddy feeling that, suspended in the night and the confusion of an eternal genesis, he is alone in the light and desiring, seeking liberty."

O C T O B E R   3 0 ,   1 9 3 2

*T*O HENRY: YOU REPRESENT ALL THAT FAURE attributes to the great artist; it is to describe you that these lines were written. Some of those words are your own words, and that is why they inflamed you; and they inflame me. I see more clearly than ever the reason and richness of the wars you carry on; I see why I have given myself to your leadership. . . . All this is an explanation of yourself as the mold breaker, as the revolutionist, the man you describe and assert in the first pages of *Tropic of Cancer*. I would use some of those lines to defend your book. . . .

What I would like is to combine our strengths to face bigger, immense wars and dramas, to work together on that art which *follows* the drama and dominates the "unchained elements" and *dominates only to proceed, to continue,* to plunge in again, not to rest or crystallize. . . . We need each other to nourish each other. What June called your "dead period" was your reconstruction period through thought and work—in between the bloodshed. The fruitful period following the war. The period of the lyrical outburst. And perhaps when you have exhausted all wars you shall begin one against me, and I against you, the most terrible of all, against our own selves then, to make drama out of our last stronghold, of our ecstasy and romance. . . .

To Eduardo: Let us look objectively at our new relationship: There is war between us. We hate each other cordially. We hate each other because we stand diametrically opposed in emotion and attitude. Until now we had committed the error of being tender with each other because of our *need* of love. I had not the strength to wipe you out of my life when biologically, planetarily, emotionally, metaphysically, psychoanalytically, I should have. And you lacked the strength to hate me when it was the very best thing you could do. You should hate my positivism, absolutism, and sensuality, as I hate your passivity, your spirituality, and your negativity. We are healthier and stronger as honest adversaries, antitheses, than as friends. I want you to wipe me out of your life. Last night was my last interference, and it was due not to affection but to hatred: I wish the man I have loved to have been otherwise. That is egoism, not love. It is a sign that love is dead. We are both strong enough to do without each other's habit of tenderness. It was only a habit, like a marriage tie. The significance of the tenderness was dead long ago. The other night we were brave enough to concede it. I saw hatred in your eyes when you saw again a manifestation of my power (Ana Maria), and you saw me contemptuous when you mentioned "society" as an intended insult to my superb friends (Oh, Lord, what a meager insult; couldn't you find a bigger one?). I suppose you would have prevented Ana Maria from meeting D. H. Lawrence, the son of a miner? You may be surprised someday to see me marry the son of a tailor because he has genius and guts.

Mars is on the ascendant today. For you this is another mental atmospheric nebulousness; for me it is a continuation of passionate experience, either love or hatred.

People like Eduardo who cannot *move* or *live* become the great sterilizers, the great blockers in others' lives. Eduardo wants to paralyze

Ana Maria. He is frantic that he cannot exert his *negative protection* while I am exerting a positive influence of a sort.

I was able to listen the other night to "Sweet and Lovely" without a quiver. I was sitting in the *Poisson d'Or* with June! My impressionability prolongs the echoes of other loves longer than necessary—and sometimes I mistake the repercussions for a true impulse, as during the occasional reappearance of John Erskine during my life with Henry.

And now I realize this: John is the man I was at *war* with (in contrast to Henry's understanding), and I am afraid that I am going to be at war with Allendy's superwisdom. It blocks my great desire to move on, to disperse myself in passion, to spread myself by the loss of myself; it blocks the adventures desired by my imagination—dangers. Yet I know I am tied to him. At every point of equilibrium I will love Allendy. But I will descend passionately away from him into Henry's fecund chaos and confusion. I will get *inspiration* from Henry, as he did from June.

I am so extraordinarily happy. Henry's book is coming out; he is writing about Lawrence and Joyce. He sends for me, asks me to roll up my sleeves, give him help and criticism. June is a "hindrance," and suddenly she becomes a hindrance for me too. Henry and I and our work. "If only June would go to New York. I need freedom!" cries Henry.

I want to leap out of my house to him. It is a holiday. Hugh is home. I have to wait. I have never found any day so long. I am steaming too. With a filmlike rapidity I see his books, I see his gentleness, I see the dangerous, eruptive Henry, I see us both in Spain—and it is all blurred, distorted, magnified by the great driving demon in both of us, the demon of literature. June is a character, material, adventure, but this copulation of man and woman within the very furnace of creativity is a new monstrosity of a new miracle. It will upset the course of the planets, and alter the rhythm of the world, and "leave a scar upon the world."

If Neptune makes me mediumistic and overimpressionable (danger in passions, feelings sweep one away; will is relinquished!), then I realize that planetary influences affect me very distinctly and that I am absolutely attuned to them. That is why I cannot resist Allendy, who is mentally stronger than I am; but I have chosen to be hypnotized by Allendy rather than by June.

If I had no feelings I could become the most intelligent woman on earth. As soon as I am cool, my vision becomes acid and scathing. Today, listening to June's talk for two hours and reaching a pitch of exasperated boredom—so that neither her face nor body could affect me.

And then I become the dangerous woman she fears. I could write more destructively about her than Henry has. About her intelligence, which is null, the inflation of her ego. Pitilessly, I saw them. Phrases of Henry's which rankle her vanity and produce this drowning talk, irrelevant attacks, with now and then those flashes of intuition which have given Henry hope. Tonight my mind spreads high over the sky and I am not a human being. I am a serpent hissing revelations of the fatuity and vacuity of the goddess and harlot June. I would take back the very gifts I have made, to emptiness, nothingness.

Yet I was drunk. And June's eyes were still burning, and her strong neck was white, and her knees knocked against mine, but the hardness and clearness in me were immense. I could still hear Henry saying last night, "I am a steel wall."

When I met Henry in the café (before he arrived I wrote a frenzied note to him on my love of his work, asking what more I could do, understanding his strange, abstract mood, his brassiness), his eyes were black and hard. He was the *supreme egoist* expanded, artist only, needing my inflation, my help—and how I understood him. There was no sentimentality. His work only, devouring all. I had chills down my back. And his talk about June. June was completely discarded, rejected, because useless—as someday I will be, too, when he has a new need. Everybody subjected to the law of movement, annihilated. And this I understood and loved, for it seemed that I am doing the same thing on a minor scale and that the pain I cause Hugh is tragic but inevitable to all living progression.

June is not subtle enough to see that when I yield to a statement of Henry, I am like a snake who has already bitten. I retreat from a direct battle while knowing the slow effect of the poison. It is by yielding, by circuitous routes that I reach Henry's reason. I do not antagonize him, make him bristle, become emotional. And he can think—and agree or disagree with his true, undisturbed self.

June is direct and noisy. Her "discussion" is merely a disemboweling. The results are hostility and ineffectiveness.

At the same time, she is fashioning her conduct in imitation of mine. Last night, instead of spending the night out, she returns meekly to tell Henry she now understands him. And why? So that the next day she can report to me a reconciliation, a victory: "I've got Henry working and happy." How surely her woman's instincts guide her—but not far enough. She cannot sense that Henry does not want her anymore. She does not believe him when he says, "Get out, go back to New York. Leave me alone."

I don't want my relationship with June to degenerate into one of her favorite wars. Passion and compassion were good. As an enemy she is not great enough, nor dangerous enough. I am afraid it would only reveal Henry's dislike of absolutism, and mine. Neither one of us has the courage to free himself. Neither Henry nor I can hurt June. All I wanted to discover was: Does June love Henry?

I remembered the night I told Henry that if I ever discovered June did not love him I would then commit a crime to free him.

But June's lies make it impossible for me to know. Her jealousy is egotistical (a question of power, her power against mine). Her love of Henry the artist is purely egotistical (the desire for self-glorification).

The other night I was for the first time breathing their brutal world. June had been very ill—awoke in the night, shivering. June asked Henry to take her in his arms. This image of June melted me. Henry said, "I know why she was being ill. I felt sorry for her, but that's all. I was more annoyed than anything."

And when I see June, I wonder how it is that one cannot pity her—she is too strong. She has her moments of weakness, but the next morning she is again tyrannical, healthy, undefeated, marvelously assertive.

The strength of their insensitiveness about each other is new and admirable. I like to stand there and share the buffeting, to feel my own strength.

I understand Allendy's hostility. Allendy is civilization; Henry barbarism, war. Allendy is more than jealous of Henry—he hates Henry's destructive force. No two men could be more opposed to each other. And I know Allendy is *waiting for me to break with Henry*. Why does he love me?

Tonight I am again unhinged. The turmoil is so intense that music makes me weep. I have been reading Gauguin, *Avant et après*. He reminded me of Henry.

Hugh is serenely studying astrology. Beautiful serenity—unattainable. I brought him a gift of a compass. I make circles for him. I enjoy marveling at his knowledge, impenetrable to me.

On the train five pairs of men's eyes watched me—obsessively.

There is a fissure in my vision, in my body, in my desires, a fissure for all time, and madness will always push in and out, in and out. The books are submerged, the pages wrinkled; the bed groans; each pyramided perfection is burned through by the thrust of blood.

The effort I make to outline, chisel, demarcate, separate, simplify, is idiotic. I must *let myself flow multilaterally*. I have at least learned one great thing: to think, but not to think too much—so that I can let go, and so that, when events come, I have not set up an intellectual barrage against them, interfering with the movement of life by critical preparation. I think just enough to keep alive an upper stratum of surveillant intelligence, just while I am brushing my hair, patting my face, pearling my nails, and writing my journal—no more. The rest of the time I work, copy, work. And let myself slide on the impetus. I hum; I harass taxi drivers by swimming against the waves of traffic; I write Henry a note half an hour after I leave him, and coax Hugh to drive at midnight to the center of Paris to deliver the note to Fred Perlès for Henry—a love note to his work!

It is this divine slidingness which enables Henry to throw me on

June's bed and throw our talk on Lawrence and Joyce like a fishing lure into space while we roll on earth.

Hugh holds me tightly, like a big gold nugget, and his horizon is celestially hopeful because I have brought him a compass.

J'ai présagé des cercles. The circle motif in my John novel. The fascination of astrology. The circle marks the earth's turning, and all I care about is the supreme joy of turning with the earth and dying of drunkenness, to die while *turning* rather than die retired, watching the earth turning on one's desk like these cardboard globes on sale at Printemps for 120 francs. Not illumined. That is more expensive. I want to be the illumination in the globe and the dynamite which explodes on the printer's machine just before he has put a price on the page. When the earth turns, my legs open to the lava outpouring and my brain freezes in the arctic—or vice versa—but I must turn, and my legs will always open, even in the region of the midnight sun, for I do not wait for the night—I cannot wait for the night—I do not want to miss a single rhythm of its course, a single beat of its rhythm.

Dream: Hugh and I are walking in foggy night. Together. I leave him. I enter the house and lie in bed. I am aware that he is seeking me, that he is becoming frantic, that he is running madly in the fog, swimming in it. I am inert. I know I am at home. That he has not thought of looking for me in bed. I lie untouched by his despair. I am at the same time the fog. I am the night around Hugh; my body is lying on the bed. I am space around Hugh. In this space he is running, looking for me.

Morning. My tenderest love is for Hugh—something inalterable, unchanging, fixed: the child. He has the securest place, the *softest*.

I wanted to give June all I have which Henry loves, add myself to her. I cannot believe that I have taken away from her the only man who ever truly loved her.

I feel such overwhelming pity for June's primitive, hysterical suffering, for the great confusion in her mind. But it is never a suffering like mine, never pain at losing Henry, but pain at failure.

It was terrible for me to realize my strength while remembering how loyal I was all through, in my interpretations of June to Henry.

She is so vulnerable, my poor little June! I can't find anything to give her but my love, which she needs. So I invent a love for her, as a gift. I keep her alive by a simulation of love, which is pity. I listen to her inchoate talk, searching patiently for the flashes of truth, hoping she will find herself and strength in me, yet as I do this I feel like the greatest traitor on earth. She trusts me, and it is I who have deprived her of Henry.

At the same time, she does not know what I am doing for her in atonement. I am preventing Henry from telling her, from asking for freedom to marry me! Yesterday, a half hour before I meet June, I am sitting in a café with Henry and he is saying, "When the book comes out we bust up everything—no more compromises. I arrange things with June, and we get married."

I laugh it off: "I don't ever want to marry again." Then: "It would be terrible to deprive her of her last faith in two human beings."

June introduced me to Dick, a homosexual writer, who talks as Aldous Huxley writes and has the eyes of a waif. We visited Ossip Zadkine the sculptor (a character in Henry's *Tropic of Cancer*).

Dick and I recoiled from the ordeal of a new contact, each one in his own manner: he with flippancy, I with silence. But we like each other. He had been prepared to dislike me because I am Henry's friend and he abhors Henry.

Henry made a monster of June because he has a monster-creating mind. He is a madman. He suffered in June the very tortures he himself created, too, because June's love for Henry was not at all monstrous, but probably as simple as mine for her. I did adopt Henry's belief in the monstrosity of June. Now I see the human being June suffering; and I see how these two have failed to understand each other—but that June is the weakest because the contents of Henry's mind have made her insane. The contents of Henry's mind do not confuse me; they interest me objectively. They fascinate my intelligence, my imagination.

I saw the process of deformation when Henry explained my pages on June and invested me with great mystery and monstrosity. His imagination is relentless and fertile; it grasps a human being and deforms him, enhances him, magnifies, kills. It is a demon loose in the world, labyrinthian, leading to insanity. Henry could make people mad.

So far I have not lost myself; I have been stronger than June. I am insane only when I wish to be, as one gets drunk, so that I can work. Just as Henry excites himself by hatred and cruelty, I excite and stimulate myself by relinquishing the too-astringent hold of an implacable logic. I make myself spin like a top to get less lucid and more hallucinated, to listen to my *intuitions*.

I love to play with Henry this dangerous game of *imaginative deformation*. We are adequate adversaries, now that Allendy has integrated me and revealed my fundamental pattern.

Divest me of exteriorizations, theatricality, masochism, and you find a kernel, a core, an artist, a woman. But divest June of trappings and you find an ordinary beautiful woman with a feeling for illusion, sacrifice, ideals, fairy tales—but no contents.

She must remain a character, a curiosity, a freak, the illusory form of personality.

But when she weeps I feel she ought to be given an ordinary human happiness.

After all, my imagination, too, has played fantastically with both Henry and June, with this difference: I have a great need of truth, and I succumb to pity. Truth makes it impossible for me to distort, because I *understand*. As soon as I understand Henry, I cease to make a "character" of him (the underworld brute of my *second* conception of him, inflated by his books). My *first conception* is invariably true: my *first* description of Henry in the journal fits him today, and my *first* description of June is truer than my literary composition. I begin to love as a human being, and the *game* ceases.

A *character*, for a writer, is a being to whom he is not attached by sentiment. True love destroys "literature." That is also why Henry cannot write about me, and may never write about me—at least until our love is over, when I become, then, a "character," that is, a detached personality, no longer fused *together*.

I get sad when I look at Allendy's photograph—I am always *between* two desires, always in conflict. I belong to Henry and to June and to Allendy. I would like sometimes to *rest*, to be at peace, to choose a nook, a love, and engroove myself in it—to make a final selection. I can't. Certain evenings, like this, at the drooping hour, I would like to feel *whole*.

The quality of my loyalty to Hugh is easily definable: It consists in *not causing him harm*. Even in questions relating to Henry (I could force Hugh to help Henry), I remain loyal to Hugh, so much so that I will not even prevent him from achieving his own *manhood* by interfering with his new aggressivity, new avarice, cautiousness, jealousy, and possessiveness.

It is strange to watch another's love of one and remain untouched. Hugh's beautiful dreams about me. I listen to them, but I never think for a moment about them when Henry caresses me. It is absolutely true that I never think of Hugh when I am with either Allendy or Henry—or think of Henry when I am with Allendy. Some kind of sundering takes place at the moment—a temporary *wholeness*—which prevents all hesitation or paralysis. It is only afterward that the mixture reveals itself, and the conflict. I do not feel any wrong about sleeping with Henry in Hugh's bed—nor would I feel any wrong in giving myself to Allendy on the same bed. I have no morality. I know the world is horrified—not I. No morality while the harm done does not manifest itself. My morality does assert itself when I am faced with the sorrow of a human being—I would give June her Henry back if she begged me. At the same time, I am aware of the stupidity of my capitulation, for June can do without Henry much better than I can, and she is harmful to Henry. Just as it would be infinitely stupid of me for Hugh's sake to revert to my empty, restless, neurotic life of the years before Henry.

Now I experience a continous *fullness* which enables me to give Hugh fullness, too. I wish Hugh could *believe me, understand me, forgive me*. He sees my contentment, my health, my productivity. And I am still more concerned over his happiness than anybody else's.

NOVEMBER 9, 1932

SIDE-CAR BAR. JUNE IN A GAY MOOD, SHOWING Henry's feeble aspects: his childishness, his incapacity to respond immediately to the events in life, his desire to be dominated and tyrannized. I get weary of saying to myself, "Henry is different with me"; and I can't help remembering that I voiced the same complaint, although I found in Henry more of a *leader* than June can, because I have the artist-leader—the big writer who can annihilate me—and the sensualist.

NOVEMBER 10, 1932

HUGH IS PLAYING HIS GUITAR AND SINGING. *IL chante faux.* Should I mind that he sings false? He knows how to love. He sings false; he plays fumblingly; he knows how to love. I yawn. I have just found the knitting theme of my book: The thousand and one nights of Montparnasse—each night a few pages, to prevent June from taking drugs. And I will tell June everything, even about my love of Henry—*that* I will keep for the last night.

Hugh has admitted he was *jealous* of my writing—couldn't bear it, couldn't bear my activity, now balanced by his astrology! Eduardo, too. All Eduardo could do while I was working desperately on my Lawrence book was to complain that I was neglecting him. A woman. *This* Henry freed me from. I couldn't *molest* him—not him! But

I have had to be *tactful* even then. Oh, irony—tonight I'm dancing on my irony as on the chiming sparks of a dizzy star.

One of the thousand-and-one-nights tales is about kisses in taxis, a city alarmed by a psychoanalyst, Zadkine's wood sculptures, a murdered woman calling for help. And so, in my journal, I give the household accounts, the menus, the opinion of the *femme de ménage* (Emilia comments that all the señorita's friends are bald), and I hand the world a gardenia in silver paper. Fantasy for me is a form of disguise. The world forced me into fantasy, and I myself did not want to see the early-morning face of my acts. It is not only June and Henry who are here *en plus beau*.

I see calculus in Hugh's eyes, and I must note here that his fucking is superbly vehement and masterful—of a quality to satisfy a normal woman, but I am not a normal woman. Outsizes in brains, in sex. Collection of the phenomenal. I am the one woman writer who is not content with erotic literature—I live at the same pitch I write—there is a curious consistency. How beautifully I had freed myself of Eduardo, truly wiped him off. Never had the courage before to disdain. The other night, when he was here for dinner, I could look at him with steel-tempered indifference—crisp and vivifying, like a walk in the forest. As I grow less sensitive I gain *embonpoint*. No one misses my sensitiveness. Everybody enjoys the healthiness, like a vase of flowers in a room. It makes one cynical to be admired for becoming rosily invulnerable.

Syncopation—shuffling, shuffling, crooning, syncopation. This is the *one light accent* in this eighteen-year-old journal whose *accents graves*, purple lines, and salted-tear perfume will amaze the world as a masterpiece of self-torture and scorpionism. As I cut the pages of Hugh's astrology books, I swear to myself that this is a science I will never try my hand at, as I want it to be Hugh's exclusive crowing.

June said yesterday she was looking for someone to be meek for, since Henry was always the meek one (keeping his prerogative for his writing, the right to defame always in retrospection). The writer is the duelist who never fights at the stated hour, who gathers the insult like another curiosity, spreads it afterward on his desk and fights then, *alone*. Some people call it weakness. I call it postponement. What is a weakness in a man is the glory of an artist, his quality. What I spill in talk or acts rarely is restituted in writing. What is preserved, collected, is what explodes later in propitious solitude. That is why the artist is the loneliest man in the world: because he lives, fights, wars, dies, is reborn *alone, and always alone.*

Hugh says art comes from fermentation—no matter what the fermentation is about. I cannot deny that I have done my best writing *now*, while I am fermenting with victory and power.

What I have loved in music is not its austerity but that *inflation* of sound, that ampleness of notes swelling to extravagant, shattering proportions, the ensorcellment of repercussion, distention, the flow and effluvium, the majolica, the ciborium, the fall from icicles to star points, from zithers to sarcophagi, from beeswax to adders.

(I place this immediately in the book. My book and my journal step on each other's feet constantly. I can neither divorce nor reconcile them. I play the traitor to both. I am more loyal to my journal, however. I will put pages of my journal into the book but never pages of the book into the journal, showing a human faithfulness to the human authenticity of the journal!)

The jazz tonight has almost roused me to an orgasm.

Partir! No more pauses in between full living, no more dead periods!

How can I *tonight* stay in Louveciennes! Curse on sublimation. I've been flowing into writing—but I am more full of life than ever.

For Hugh it is a recrudescence of love, a recommencement. The victory over a woman which he needed to complete his assertion he has tried on me rather than on another woman, as Allendy expected. He has asserted his sexual aggressivity. He has also poured into me his need of an adventure. He wants to take me out. We go to the movies and then to a dance. We play at never having known each other before.

"I'm an astrologer," says Hugh.

"Shall I meet you *here* next time?"

"Not here. I want to travel with you. Will you come to Egypt with me?"

I cannot continue the game. I want to sob. His attitude touches and hurts me. In the car, he caresses my legs like an infatuated lover. He drives carelessly. My tenderness is deeply aroused—nothing else. But I nourish his illusion, and I am *grateful* to him for life. The cloying sweetness of it all, the cloying idealism; while behind his back I am delving into savagery, asperities, hatred, acrid living with Henry and June.

Henry is testing me to the limit. Inhuman to both June and me—hard, egotistical. As his pages come to me, my intellectual interest wavers. I need caresses. I am a woman. I am just as much woman, deep down, as June. I can't bear this stoical austerity of living. I would let *anyone* caress me just now.

Tonight I am going out with June. I will sink into a woman's atmosphere—*the constant craving for love*, the perpetual dependency on man. Signs of love, attention, telephones, little gifts, demonstrativeness, no *rival work*. That love I have now from Henry (the book is secondary, it is *for* me; astrology, too, is for me, an offering to me which I do not want, though I am making superhuman efforts to respond). I feel the distance between us falling like a diabolical ciborium, the distance eating into everything that binds us. I am afraid of my freedom. Hugo is the man I owe my life to. I owe him everything beautiful I have had; his devotion has been my stepping-stone to *all* I have today—my work, my health, my security, my happiness, my friends. He has been my one truly bountiful god. I am eternally indebted to him—to his touching and magnificent faithfulness. I could only be liberated if he were cruel, hard, mean—but now I have no justification whatsoever. He is the greatest man in the world, the man alone capable of *love* and *generosity*. *Il est facile pour les autres à donner.* For me, how easy, with my superabundance of ideas, inventiveness, art, emotions; but for him, a simple man not superabundantly gifted in art, his gifts are drawn out of a fund of deep warmth and loyalty, of pure love—not self-love!

NOVEMBER 12, 1932

*T*HERE IS A DIVERGENCE OF TIME, A DISLOCATION of rhythm between the wisdom of the mind and the impetus of instincts and the inevitability of their fulfillment. I am at peace with man, all the men who have hurt me by their weakness. My Father, Eduardo, Hugo, John, and even, to a certain extent, Henry (if Henry were strong, June would be in New York now) have more than atoned to me, and more love has been given me than denied me. I am at peace with myself, and my understanding tells me the suffering I endured through the abandonment of my Father and Eduardo's homosexuality and John's puritanism did not come from them but from my own inner composition of being, which refused to understand the natural causes of these weaknesses and refused *not to suffer*.

But on another plane, the instinct of hatred and vengefulness continues its course until it has exhausted the poison it secreted.

June and I *"déversent"* our hatred of man on the world, we insult society, conventions, *men*. We ally ourselves to vent our great disillusion, not on those we love, but on strangers, on symbols.

I see now that some of the pages I have written on June, simply and humanly penetrating, are greater as art than Henry's deformations, for understanding wounds deeper than monstrosity. About both June and Henry, I have been more *human*, more comprehending, more true; and, perhaps, I may in the end be more artistic.

June: the mandrake, a Eurasian plant (*Mandragora*) with purple flowers and a branched root resembling the human body, from which a narcotic was prepared. The mandrake of *Genesis* was—and still is—believed to have magical properties.

While we were dancing together, June was telling me how much she loved the name of the mandrake plant in German, and it is to be my name for her: *Alraune*.

When I hear June's description of her first visit to me, her timidity, her fears of meeting the "beautiful and brilliant" woman (the description given to her), and Dick's comment on my beauty and "rareness," I feel a sudden panic. I see this image of myself in these people's eyes (Osborn's, Henry's, June's, Dick's), and I am frightened as by a giant shadow. That first night, June waited for me to reveal my defects, and I made only one blunder: a flippant remark—"How American"— when her idealism sickened me. But what I marvel at is how I, coming out of my great solitude, inexperience, dream life, could meet the experience of June and Henry without blunders, charm and disarm their hardness, love and be loved by them as an equal in power and experience while I was growing each day, covering up great ignorance and innocence as I went along. No blunders in the face of continuous tests, and no loss of integrity. Adaptability without loss of myself. But this integrity I owe to Allendy!

When I praise Hugh for his human-beingness, he says he doesn't want to be a human being—*the only one among us*—as he will get lonely! (Written down per demand because I laughed so much when he said this.)

Note my trick of reading to Hugh from my journal: I see ahead what is coming, and I either substitute an entirely new passage invented on the spot or I change the name, reading "Hugh" instead of "Henry," for instance, and Hugh takes it for himself—or I alter a phrase as I read!

While he studies astrology I watch the beautiful seriousness of Hugh's mouth and I know how deeply I love him. He is my child, my son. *Noble*. I want never to hurt him. When I stand near him, I am won by his sheer nobility. He has given himself, body and soul. He is more exposed than any of us *to mortal pain. I heard him tell Allendy he would kill himself if he lost me.*

I must wrap him in security, in love. He must be protected and sheltered. All the rest of us, Henry, June, and I, have such a hard egotistical core. We give ourselves away, but the big, central ego knows how to take itself back, too. Hugh doesn't know. He is not an ego; he *is* love—the essence and symbol of a great love.

NOVEMBER 16, 1932

WHEN I WAS WITH JUNE THE OTHER NIGHT, SHE was rebellious because Henry had paid back a debt to Osborn's old mistress with the money I had so anxiously managed to send him. This had happened to her, and it was what she calls the satisfaction of his stupid masochistic conscience with a sacrifice exacted from her which incensed her—and rightly. It is nothing less than sadism. "June ought to pawn her clothes, scrub floors to pay Osborn back—this debt was on my conscience!"

I was incensed, too, by the monstrosity of this *logic*: his *conscience* in regard to a debt.

If morals enter into the question, what of his protective debt to the women he loves? No. First a satisfaction of a purely egoistical need, the immediate élan of generosity and honesty, with the money extracted no matter how—from his woman, not from his work.

At this point of my life I tried to stretch my tolerance and understanding to their *limit*. I said to myself, I have often given to Henry what I *should* have given to Hugh merely because it gave *me* a greater joy to give it to Henry at the moment. I have often given to others money which I extracted from Hugh's hard work, and of which the withholding might have saved Hugh worry. Because there was something I *wanted*. I bought the aquarium instead of buying Hugh new ties. Because I had a need.

These acts resemble Henry's, except that Henry's are less justifiable, less logical, *more* egocentric. And I have not hurt Hugh, whereas Henry would let June or me suffer *hunger* to satisfy any of his desires.

Très bien. Let Henry sacrifice people to his voraciousness and self-growth and expansion. Let him sacrifice lesser people. Let him devour Fred, whose only value in the world is his service, who can only fulfill himself through others. But June and me, no.

I was amazed at my revolt. At first merely a regret, a pain, a feeling that Henry could not do that to *me*, that he was doing it incited by his hatred of June, that June bungles with him and arouses his combative and meanest instincts. When I first heard it, I remembered the new pair of stockings given to Paulette* while I wore mended ones—and there were tears in my eyes. It seemed to me that the immediate and showy generosity was a feeble aspect—facile, not deep—and that deeper generosity was more far-reaching, more *selfless*. That Henry was showing his incapacity to love deeply—that the absence of depths aroused in the other a great *self-protective hardness*, that by an accumulation of such selfishness Henry had brought my faith to a standstill, that the very small incident of the money given to Osborn's girl had made a fissure in my confidence, that the specter of his superficiality had shown itself behind his movements, his gifts. I remembered one of June's descriptions: "He was talking to me and he seemed a far-off puppet making strange, ridiculous gestures which couldn't move me."

Oh, God, why do I always give myself to those incapable of love? Because I bear too much in myself. This is my last cry.

I feel so tired, so empty; I feel as empty as June.

I read Henry's superb pages and I know they are made of June's soft flesh, and mine.

He tells June the sacrifice she made aggrandized her and therefore there is no debt. No, there is no debt; only love, of which Henry knows

---

* In July 1932, Alfred Perlès brought a young French girl to the flat in Clichy that he shared with Miller, and Paulette stayed for several months. Upon her departure, Miller learned she was only fifteen years old. (See *A Literate Passion*, p. 109.)

nothing. What I have given Henry has also aggrandized me—there is no debt—only love lacking, the *absence of love*.

I take myself back. This is no *marriage*, no true interpenetration. It is cannibalism.

I *understood* or accepted from the first the *individual sacredness of individual wants*. When I first gave Henry and June a big sum of money and they spent it all in one night on *drink*, I was humanly hurt, but my understanding was disciplined. I gave because I wanted to—I gave them *liberty* at the same time. Otherwise I would not be giving, I would be *taking* (I give you five hundred francs, but buy food and rent a typewriter). This was the perfect, inhuman, divine *objectivity*. Later I gave love: Do what you will—use me. I love you. I want to serve you, aliment you. Henry used my love well, beautifully. He erected books with it. That was beautiful, creative. It gave me joy and, with ecstasy, strength to give more love, more aliment. But when the love and the money are shabbily used, pettily used, then the illusion, the strength, the ecstasy leaves you. Yes, I lost my ecstasy.

I send June a telegram only to tell her that she is *right* in defending herself against Henry, the enemy, only to tell her that I believe she is a far greater woman than I am because she has had more love and more faith, and I, because of my damned intelligence, see things too quickly. What it has taken June years to realize, I have realized in one by flair rather than by experience.

Hugo is truly the only man I have chiseled out of his dark chaos—Henry, too, as an artist (and perhaps as a man he came *nearer* to love than he will ever come). Eduardo and John were my failures. Though the other day Eduardo and I discarded our hatred as a childish performance and achieved a beautiful reconciliation based on absolute frankness with each other. As soon as there is understanding again, there is an elimination of conflict. He said that when I have passed through my life of sensation (Henry and June) and truly reached my Neptunian realm—which is living out passion, intuition and love on another plane—I will become a remarkable woman, full of strange magnetism!

My beautiful voyage ended in a sea of vomit. For the first time in my life I understood the sublimity of measure which I had scorned:

to be able to stand on the edge of drunkenness without drinking enough to vomit, drinking enough to enjoy one's drunkenness. It was not I who vomited; June did that for me.

It began with the drunkenness of talk, of sallies, of duels of words—*la plus belle des ivresses*—in which June did not participate. June heard Henry and me dueling with abstract intoxicants and felt lost, and so she took concrete intoxicants and soused herself in the only manner she can reach vertigo. I reached vertigo while we talked about Gide and Lalou, and while I defended my language; June reached it only when she lay inert on the floor, rolling in her vomit. My drunkenness with ideas, my effervescence, my fermentation rose keener while Henry was stupefied and June's body loosened and coarsened visibly, so visibly that even my eyes, my blind eyes, saw it. Henry toppled and fell asleep; June became a whore and I *femme de ménage*. I gave them the last sad insult of my sympathy. And I kept what is left me today, a great divorce from the animal world, which cannot live in space and must sprawl on the earth. I will only sprawl on the earth for strength, but at all other moments I move away.

My God, why did I suddenly *see* everything, why did I miss nothing, nothing? Inexorable vision. Vomit to the very last of all emptiness.

I want my solitude, my peace, my suspense in air, the balance I despised—I want to find my lightness and my joy again—expansion, song, *ecstasy*—an ecstasy without vomit, an ecstasy which is continuous, not one which fills my being with poison which I must eject afterward, all over the place where I have been dancing and singing.

The day before, I had told Allendy a lie which was only a lie caused by a discrepancy in time. I mean that it was a lie at the moment I said it, and it ceased to be a lie last night.

I went to see him in place of Hugh, who had gone to Berlin. I told him (it was so sweet, this, while in his arms) that I had broken with Henry; that I did love him, Allendy, and his life; that I accepted and understood his wisdom; that I craved strength; that I realized the pucrility of the things I had been pursuing. He was overjoyed, both as man and as analyst. His hatred of Henry flared completely, now that he felt he could express it—he showed immense hostility, contempt, jealousy, anger. He said if Henry ever did me any harm (by writing about me or using my letters) he would go and beat him with a whip!

Wonderful to see this sage in eruption. Aggressivity, jealousy, contempt. I laughed with pleasure, a feminine pleasure.

I always have the trick of vanishing. I leave Clichy—I disappear. I carry in my bag a love letter from Fred begging me not to think of him as shallow: "You are the only woman I love," and I am thinking of all the lies I told them about the evening at Lalou's house. Lalou saying at dinner, "Gide sometimes drops in." Which started me imagining a visit from Gide. I gathered all the details about Gide which the Lalous revealed and I exhibited them in the Clichy kitchen as issued from an authentic interview. I colored, without falsifying, a portrait of Gide which I feel quite adequate to make. Again, a prophetic lie, because this interview *will* take place later.

Meanwhile, the truth is that I went to the Lalous without Hugh, and that I experienced great cool joys of electrical intelligence, and more. Besides the talk, which was a bouquet of skyrockets, there was a current between Lalou and me. I was still sensually throbbing from Allendy's caresses when I arrived at this place of simple home-livingness: books, children, a roast which Madame Lalou held by the bone while she cut it. In place of Hugh we wished we might have had Joaquin. I suggested taking a taxi and calling for him, and Lalou, who is a man constantly sitting on the tip of a volcano, applauded the idea because he would go with me.

So Lalou and I are driving across the city. Our talk is very spider-weaving and deft. By the time we return there are threads between Lalou and me. And one of these threads is that his energy, his *fougue*, his vitality, has brushed against my languid and turgid flesh—the smallest brushing, the smallest detail of touch, of proximity, is like an absolute embrace which is near exploding. Lalou came very near to kissing me, and I to joyous receptivity. The intelligence kept us from too hasty a commingling, but it will happen.

It was humanly cruel of me not to return to Clichy tonight. June taunted me by saying it was tiredness, lack of stamina. I left them to a dismal, sordid stagnation, knowing Henry would think I was going to sleep with Allendy. I left them in their helpless sense of inferiority. It was cruel. Perhaps I am avenging myself; perhaps I am merely a writer, for already around the breakfast table I had lost interest in all of them, and I was yearning for Louveciennes and my journal. I came home after having slept only a few hours, and I went to bed, and I wrote. I ate my lunch, slept like a soldier, masturbated, and took up my writing again.

Catharsis? A need to empty myself. Crowded with scenes. Annoyed only because I have forgotten to record the Vilmorin scene. Pursued by fragments of phrases, so insistent. Unable, really, to *continue to live*. Cluttered. In the end I came home only to write, though my absence from Clichy tonight, I know, remains enigmatic and insulting.

I am only thinking of the Vilmorins' gigantic feudal house—labyrinthian, ancient—a universe in itself—the proud family, the incestuous love, the peculiarly flavored style of the talk between the two brothers and the sister—an incest born of harmonious intellects, knitted indissolubly by twinships of intelligence and brilliancy. And she—the pivot of this adoration, on the way to madness—an artist as intent as I on exteriorization, expression.

I carry myself to Clichy, and Henry and June get drunk because they know now I am escaping them. They know that although I am free to stay I reach a moment when of my own free will I board a train. I abandon them both. They both cling—beg—taunt—I am ready to face their hatred, their rage, their condemnation (I could never bear to be condemned); they must come to me, to Louveciennes, live my life—I don't want theirs, their ecstasies—mine are like aximite, whose crystal edge is like the edge of an ax.

June is right to consider herself a pure Dostoeveskian character—Stavrogin, who caused evil, caused crimes, and rarely acted himself—and to feel that Henry, through all his laborious work, failed to seize her.

Her efforts to explain herself, to clarify herself, failed because she is an unconscious being and, until now, incapable of analysis and synthesis. Last night a miracle took place. By some strange influence of my mind on hers, for *five hours* she talked absolutely lucidly and synthetically—the whole pattern of her life was brought to the surface. Henry's wariness of June's mind because of its emotional eclipses, I understand. I myself have experienced it. Henry realizes I have occasionally been able to translate, that I possess the linguistic suppleness to be able to talk one language with Henry and another with June. The whole self-confession was launched by a talk with Henry in which June recognized my acuity about Henry, the *further reach* of my understanding. I analyzed his lack of knowledge of himself (the rest of his lack of understanding of the world). I applied one of Allendy's fundamental themes with a clarity, emphasis, even perfection of language which were a surprise to myself. Henry said, "Now you are telling me something." June knew I was telling him everything. She was applauding, ignited with enthusiasm. I had suffered enough when I saw Allendy telling Hugh—in a more effective way—all *I* had stumblingly *told him,* arousing in him realizations I had obscurely struggled to arouse, seeing Allendy clarify all that I had fought in Hugo in the dark: his over-devotion to the bank, his masochistic handling of his own money, his feminine fear of bullies, his submission and coquetry toward men, his forced hardness toward his department, his vagueness, his lack of grip on mental and spiritual life, his unresponsiveness to my work. And so, at this moment, when I was being Allendy to Henry—that is, clearer, more forceful, wiser, and more effective—I turned several times toward June to give her the joy of recognizing that I was repeating most of what she had said. Henry was hit, affected because I aimed at his egocentricity, his overassertion of himself in his books, the absence of core that makes him live always guided by his reaction *against* another person's attitude, never out of a deep self-guidance—lives negatively, I said, and always overestimates, or depreciates, himself—and more: self-knowledge is at the root of understanding and wisdom. I attacked everything: his dependence on criticism and opinion of others (studied upon myself); his need of big minds around him (measuring himself always not from within but against something); his need of much experience, much stimulation, much talk as a substitute to a dogged wrestling with significance (Keyserling, Proust).

Then June and I were left alone. She told me I had been wonderful, splendid, that for the first time she had heard someone talk to Henry—not missing him, leveling neither too high nor too low. I had done wonderful things to her, too—all the fragments of our talks, short encounters fused into a monologue such as I always dreamed of June attaining—a June no longer talking hysterically or merely spilling over, but quiet, supple, flexible, aware, clear, and wise.

Strange, my sitting there on Henry's bed listening to her reiterations of what she was, of what she had become, of all the harm Henry had done her, and of a kind of testament she was making which puzzled me: telling me what to do for Henry and what not to do. Abdicating—why? Relinquishing without apparent cause. But all of this based on her knowledge of the dead Henry.

She mixed perfidious remarks with her generous ones—always in an effort to destroy the very man and artist for me as well as for herself. Is it protectiveness toward me which makes her say, "Tonight you showed yourself stronger than Henry. Don't let him destroy your mind and work. Remember that your work comes first." Is it feminine alliance or an envy of my *faith*—or both? Why is it that while my intellect remains wary of the distortions in her mind, my feelings believe in her feelings? I believe June and I, during this night which I will never be able to write down completely, gave each other the most generous *realizations* of each other. It seemed to me that what June had climbed to was an elimination of primitive jealousy and that the supreme test of her comprehension would be if she would permit Henry's love for me and my love for Henry.

When we had talked ourselves into a pause, a suspense, it was dawn. June came into bed with her dress on. She began to kiss me, saying, "How little you are, how little you are—I want to become like you. Why am I so awkward, so ungainly? I could break you in two." We kissed each other passionately. I fitted my body against every curve of June's body, as if melted into her. She moaned. Her embrace was around me like a multitude of arms; mine was a yieldingness which intoxicated me. I lost myself. I lost my consciousness in this bed of flesh. Our legs were bare and entwined. We rolled and heaved together. I under June, and June under me. Her light moth kisses showered on me, and mine bit her. She said, "You look beautiful just now."

I asked, "Let me see your body, let me kiss your body."

I became vaguely aware of a standstill. June said the wrong phrase: "Not yet, it isn't beautiful enough—women are so critical." I was dazed. "Women are so critical"—*at this moment,* why this awareness when we were so voluptuously lost into each other? Awareness. It awakened me.

I apologized: "I lost my head—I was drunk, June."

June watched me: "Don't worry; I wish it were I who had become drunk. It is wonderful—you can lose your head." She seemed sad, regretful. "I wish we had become drunk before. I am awkward, Anaïs, frightened."

Then she lay over me: "Besides, I want to have you all to myself. I don't want to share you. Let us go away together—where there is a lot of snow. Will you? . . ." Her voice trailed off. She kissed me violently now, but I was quiet, subdued. I had become aware. She became subdued and began playing with my hair. "I ought to strangle you." I was wholly yielding, innocent, in a sense that I felt she was not. I sensed two currents in her—a partial absence, through consciousness, from the moment. Some thought troubled her.

While we were having breakfast together, June admitted this undying self-consciousness, the loss in me she had noted with envy. She admitted knowing every word she uttered the night she was drunk, every word she uttered in fantasy or exaltation—always. We returned to the room, we lay in bed, and she began to extract confidences from me. Did I love Allendy? At this point I became wary. When I noted that her flair told her I did not love Allendy wholly, I decided to launch into a half-truth because I knew my voice, tone, and face would be more convincing in telling this half-truth. I depicted the quality of my love for Henry—while deforming completely only the facts about Henry. I kept John in mind for guidance. He was a writer who lived in New York, who was well known. That is why, I confessed, I had wanted to return to New York with June. The facts were untrue, but I knew that if I were thinking of Henry, my face, voice, and eyes could show a sufficient passion, trueness, to convince June—in contrast to the absence of passion which had revealed itself when I talked about Allendy, because when I say I love Allendy it is almost like when I say I love Hugo. It is like an admission of an ideal necessity, not a jet of clear instinct. And June could distinguish too well. June was silent. In order to give the greatest naturalness to my confession I asked her advice: Should I give up everything for this love, as she had done for Henry? I told her I had often compared my love to June's for Henry, wished to imitate her in taking the greatest risks for my greatest and only whole faith. Since I kept Henry as an image and the facts only as a barrage, I could talk in a natural way, ask questions, ask advice from June, make her an arbiter.

When I left she came to the stairs with me and we kissed again. I forgot her bracelet.

When Henry awoke late that morning, June said to him, "I know everything. I know that you love Anaïs and that Anaïs loves you. But why did you play such a comedy for me?" He denied, denied.

June left Clichy that day. Henry rushed to Louveciennes. I was asleep and the house dark. He thought I was out. He had a whole evening alone in which to decide whether he would seek out June. He went to sleep. He spent a day and two nights here. Strange hours. He wept twice over the past, but we were happy together. We plunged into work, two brilliant talks about his work, Spengler, and psychoanalysis. He awoke the next morning singing. We felt again that instant marriage which makes separation an ordeal. Hugo's return broke a delirious climax of talk and fusion.

June said she had "pulled a lesbian act" merely to discover what she wanted to discover, but that I sickened her with my lies. I said that I had intended to "pull a lesbian act" to discover whether June loved Henry. But if our love of Henry did remain the final end of all our conversations, our feelings for each other also palliated a duel which, for two other women, might have ended in death. We did not kill each other, neither individually nor in Henry. Neither June nor I fought to erase the other from Henry's being. June owns eight years of Henry's experience, and I own the Henry who works upon the experience. We have recognized each other's historical necessity, bowed to a destiny.

What I question now is which one has given the most, or least, *feeling* in her role? June seemed for a moment to have envied me my wholeness and to have been angered at her consciousness during that last night—but at other moments (when she was weeping as we walked on the dead leaves) it was she who was feeling and I who was conscious and emotionless. We have Henry's cold moments, when he probably cares more for his work than for either June or me. I had mine when I threw away June's violets and when I kissed Allendy to break the yoke of Henry's primary importance to me—an effort at defiance and independence somewhat parallel to June's two-year life with her lover in New York.

Relativity. Henry sees the scene of my talk with him in front of June as an unwitting but nevertheless instinctive final effort to make the situation absolute, to get rid of June, to define and reveal my victory. He says I showed the irrepressible joyousness and energy of the one aware of his *victory,* that it must have been clear to June. Without any scene I showed my understanding of Henry, my devotion to him, my guidance to interference in his life, simultaneously displacing June on a plane of "influence," a display which must have influenced her slowly accumulating realization of the tie between Henry and me so that *in spite* of *our* alliance, our admiration (that between June and me), my concern over her, our confidences, and in spite of June's confidence in both Henry and me, her intuition grew clear and definite and crystallized that morning. Whether any feeling for me inspired June to make an absolute surrender of Henry instead of fighting to hold him is something I will never know. Or whether in all this our feeling for each other was merely an extension of our tremendous love of Henry. I love June because she has been a part of Henry. NO—we love each other as two women recognizing each others' value. There *are* resemblances between us.

The deep joy I felt at having Henry all to myself was not deeply a joy of victory, because I saw the evolution *in Henry* which brought Henry to me, the new needs. But June, June does not *realize* the impersonality of this. June is not situated *above* all this. I am afraid she considers herself injured, tricked. She believes my love of her has been only a piece of treachery, that I have won Henry by cleverness,

42

not by love. What hurts me is her denial of this *destiny*. When Henry returned the other day, he found *my* love letter to June wrapped around the gifts I had made her: ring, earrings, bracelet; and she had written on the back, "Please get a divorce immediately." And the last morning, she had said to Henry, "I wasn't duped by Anaïs's letter to me." And, "I pulled off a lesbian act."

When Henry and I used to imagine what would happen when June returned, we never imagined *this*.

I would like June to *know*.

But June's desire to see as a defeat, an injury, an event so deeply inevitable and deep rooted, is like Henry's desire to imagine a supremely cruel June: masochism—the latent *desire to suffer*, to be humiliated; the obsession with the wound one most *fears*, as June fears cruelty, abandon. This deep, terrible fear is *now materialized by her desire of it*. She has achieved probably the greatest of her self-lacerations, while I achieved the *greatest conquering of the selfsame fear*. I am now beyond fear, and anxious over June, anxious for her, whose torments are like ghosts of mine. My little June, you do not believe; you imagine hatred and cruelty where there is only fate. You punish yourself, you punish yourself for also having loved your father. You punish yourself by destroying the love you most wanted.

NOVEMBER 26, 1932

*H*ENRY, MY LOVE, MY LOVE, HENRY, I HAVE struggled and warred to be worthy of you, to be a woman, to be strong, to be fearless. Henry, my love, my love, I deserve the deep joy I have tonight. I have loved you *against* fear and without hope of joy; I have risked the greatest wound, the most dangerous rivalry. It was not courage, it was love, love. I loved you so much I risked losing you. I disregarded tomorrow—I had no faith in victory—no *desire* for victory, yet a heartrending need of it. *I asked so little and I have been given everything!*

I tell Henry about all this and suggest we write June a letter about it, but he says that it is precisely this she will not understand—or if by a flash she does understand it, I realize now, she will not relate it to her life for more than a minute. There is no connection whatsoever between her insight and her life. If there were, she would not have repudiated me as a trickster.

Together we see clearly now a contrast: June and her great physical vitality, *absorbing* little, so that tragedy does not *kill* her; and I all mental vitality, so that I can sustain a response to Henry's creative activity.

The strange fact is the death of June's sexual vitality. Henry reveals an amazing discovery: his feeling that June was *pretending* to be aroused—like a whore. At the same time it was she who sought him out, probably for a proof of love, or in the hope of proving to herself that she was alive.

This corroborates June's own words: "I am sexually dead." But it is not, as she says, Henry who has killed her. Was she always truly *frigid* (as Allendy suspects), or did she kill herself by excess, or by masturbation? It is strange that the idea of June's onanism suddenly presents itself to my mind.

The *malefic* in June is also clear now: "If I am sexually dead, I must also *kill* Henry sexually. I will make him feel that he is losing his virility (doubt—the deathblow!)." Fortunately Henry's virility is strongly alive with me. He knows it!

Another malefic act—June leaves Henry my love letter, thinking this will destroy Henry's faith in me, not realizing that Henry knows me too well, knows what prompted that letter, and also knows that this letter was a proof of a protective love for June which she should have been able to recognize and believe in.

Meanwhile, together with the unraveling of June's twistedness, our own life flows on. When I arrive in Clichy, Henry is working on a magnificent synthesis, *Form and Language*—and I read the pages as he unwinds them from the typewriter. We talk endlessly about his work—always in the same manner, Henry flowing, gushing, spilling, spreading, and I weaving tenaciously. He ends by laughing at my tenacity.

Henry did not understand the intensity with which, as a child of eleven, I regretted the brilliant life I had lost with my Father's departure. How could I have *realized* the value of this life? How could I cling to it obstinately (pages of yearning, regrets, in the early journals)?

The realization in a child, based on flair, not on facts; I never saw my father living and talking intellectually, brilliantly—never heard the vigorous blasphemies and obscenities Mother complained of later; but it was enough to catch a glimpse of Father's face as he passed me on his way out of the house or into the parlor, that awakened, alert, vital face; it was enough to have tasted the flavor of the wall-covering books, to have heard from afar the reverberations of animated talks and music—enough to create an atmosphere which, from then on, I have wistfully sought to recapture—an atmosphere of *toughness*, substantiality (mental intellectual, artistic), lost in my life with my mother and brother in a spiritually arid American scene, lost in my attenuate-toned marriage, sought in combat with John (the exterior *voice* and *appearance* of fullness), found in Henry, in Clichy.

Incest there was, accentuated by a convergence of intellect, of artistry; and once the "deep coffers of reflectiveness" (pages on June) have absorbed all this, the profundity of the impression creates that lastingness, exactly as I am unable to throw off the little exchanges between June and me (full of lasting significance for me, and only of an ephemeral sense-impression for her). Her return of my gifts was like the flinging off of a coat, an incisiveness in gesture corresponding to an area of impressionability, not of space and depth, which inevitably create a root correlation. The need which does not bury itself into the ground strikes out, no roots. June is thus rootless, pure movement, not penetration; and that is why the *whole* does not mount like a deep-rooted edifice but bursts like fireworks, and what falls on the ground are ashes, the ashes of her sexual being, of her emotions, her loves.

Henry's daily and continuous state of responsiveness to life—his sexual activity—which I once thought an element hampering to creation, I now believe to be a quality which distinguishes him from Proust, Joyce, and Lawrence—if he can catch up with himself and complete both the recollection of the past (June) and continuity of the present, as I do on a minor scale in my journal.

It is while lying on the couch with Henry and hearing the guitar string snap that I experience emotionally the realization of the end of my love for Hugh, and not by a compilation of meditations on his yellowed letters or his wrinkled coat sleeve. It is while cooking in Clichy that I realize the meaning of my childhood, not while reading Freud's preface to a little girl's journal. This abdication of life demanded of the artist is to be achieved only relatively. Most artists have *retired* too absolutely; they grow rusty, inflexible to the flow of currents (like Allendy, who never lets himself be *washed over* as Henry does).

NOVEMBER 27, 1932

*L*AST NIGHT HENRY AND I GOT MARRIED. BY THAT I mean a particular ceremony which binds two persons until they get a divorce! I let him read most of my journal (even half of what relates to June's kisses, etc.). It was an earthquake to both. He revealed the most gentle, warm tolerance, he *exonerated* me of all things, but he condemned June. He is certain that June *did trick me.* That if it is true that she was sexually aroused (the moisture I felt with my legs), nevertheless she maintained her *whole* role; that is, she gave her body in exchange for something she wanted: to find out about Henry's betrayal.

Henry was enraged to think of the useless suffering he had experienced, to see that *truth* (though remaining mysterious) was a profound *relief* from his years of blind-bat suffering. It became horribly clear that all the experience June had hurled at him she had not really *given* to him, in the truest sense, because by *her lies* she had *cheated* him of knowledge. Henry was floundering, desperate, *bafoué, cocu,* in a maze of deformities, lost as a man and as an artist; and yesterday a *woman gave herself for the first time to him by truth.* That was marriage. Man giving woman his strength and vision, and woman giving man her strength and vision.

Henry at that moment *moved me so deeply,* reached such a secret recess of my being, that all former surrenders seemed but half gifts; and that night, in his arms, I almost wept because of that absolute *breaking up of myself,* this absolute dissolution of myself into him.

So preoccupied with loving that I failed to notice Henry's subdued response. Later his quietness did come to my mind, but not in the form of a doubt of his love—simply as a quiet wistful realization that he was slow in immediate expression (instinctively I take his love for granted), that he had exhausted a wealth of flamboyant love on June, that the past, bitter, hateful, monstrous, still occupied him more vehemently than his actual life (flare of bitterness about June's attitude more powerful than jealousy of Allendy). I went so far in my strange-mood selflessness that I even thought how good this flare of hatred was to renew his interest in his novel, to sting him into writing about this past!

It was a surprise to return to Henry and find him worried about the disproportion in emotions the other night—and me reassuring him. Yes, I knew his slowness, and I knew his lack of expressiveness, and I knew he was stunned by the revelations in my journal (the final unraveling of all his doubts about June). But when he tells that he finds I am so marvelous to talk to that he almost forgets to fuck me, I experience a strange resigned pang—this acceptance that the mind in me eclipses the woman and places passion in secondary importance. Immediately aspects of Henry's deeper love—concern—protection—worship—follow this statement, and I bow to a fatalism. I have tears in my eyes.

Henry talks of this deep tranquility he feels with me, which he has craved, needed. I tell him all women are fundamentally whores, want to be treated like whores. "You can throw in a little worship, too!"

This makes him laugh. He had been saying, "You're a great woman, and I am afraid I am going to worship you."

No defeat. No suicidal pain. Only the sadness of knowing, understanding, accepting. *Les feux d'artifice ne sont pas pour moi,* and like a child I have been fascinated by everything that glitters. June has been given all that glitters, and I men's souls, and we both feel cheated!

But I am so old now that in place of rebellion there is a kind of ironic, serious, impersonal acquiescence. I laugh again: "I will not make you a June scene and force you to admit: Do you love me, how much do you love me? and bring or wring out of you some flamboyant assertion and demonstration. I don't ask for anything yet—I get what I want!"

Joking. And a few minutes later Henry is upset by his concern over me, my life, my relationship with Hugh, my imprisonment. We are walking together and we are both in a dark mood, and he says we are two waifs, and he hates to surrender me to Hugh tonight. There is something tragic, defeated in both of us, before the curious injustices and dislocation in life. All this wealth of love given to June's face and body which should have been given to the face and body of my feelings, of my mind, of my love, to my being. But is not a new love shooting new roots in Henry for these very things in me, and why seek repetition, resemblance, rather than a new experience?

I listen to his plans: "Now I am free—and someday things will work out so that you will be free, too. I try to visualize our life. I want to *take care of you*—I don't want to lower you. It hurt me the other day to see you take the bag and go marketing; I want you to be queen, as you are in Louveciennes."

(What would Allendy say if he could hear this?)

There must always be the one who gives and the one who receives. June received from Henry and gave to Jean; Henry receives from me; I receive from Hugh, and I give to Henry . . . *L'important est d'aimer, d'aimer grandement, profondément, souvent, de se donner* . . . The answer, the response, is only a human joy—the disproportion is only a divine test of the trueness of one's love . . . *donner sans compter et sans mesurer.* Henry taught me to love. God, but I am a fortunate woman!

And Allendy—I receive from Allendy. And Eduardo received from me. Reciprocity is balance; balance is nonhuman. The acknowledgment of discrepancies, paradoxes, injustices is what makes me old. I was so old last night that I am tired today. I feel weak and broken. When I stop running and bleeding, I am sitting on a mountain of journals, also an overflow of the same cursed love.

What has June done to me that I now hate her? She is one of those who *demand* so loudly that the whole world is deafened and blinded. Instead of that, I write quietly—perhaps another way of demanding! The whole world will weep and love me when they see that my Olympian relinquishings of loves equal to mine cover a great human defeat.

Always too much seriousness! The smallest pretext to plunge into tragedy. But I know why. The pretext is inconsequential, but the need of tragedy is a deep necessity. It is the descent into coal mines, the exploration. I let myself get drowned merely to reach Atlantis. Old habit. My lead weight. My ball and chain. My compass. My barometer.

It makes me laugh.

Henry is frightened by his liberation from June—cannot quite realize it—life without his familiar pain.

Now I laugh at my *fear* of analysis. Most people's possession of *knowledge* deprives them of the *sense* of wonder, but such a sense of wonder and mystery is like the savage's fear of mysterious *fire* until he discovers the principle of it and the mastering of it. I say that after we know all there is to know, there is still mystery and wonder of a deeper kind. Example: Henry's monstrous conception of June's lesbianism. *Déroute de l'imagination.* The physical, and limited, quality of what he imagined; the sucking and gestures like those of fucking. He discovers through my journal that without the sucking or gestures there exists *a suspended world of sensations* without factual culmination, which is more mysterious and deep than what he supposed existed between June and Jean, and June and me.

Evening. We talk. I become aware that Henry is simply lost in a labyrinth of thought, self-consciousness; that he has merely paralyzed himself exactly as I used to by too much thinking. I see that my instinct is right, true, and it is *my turn* now to restore movement and life. So I laugh and we explain everything away.

Henry is saying something which reveals his *sensitiveness:* he feels that I imagine such a powerful sexual connection to have existed between himself and June that I have failed to realize that, in a sense, it was even stronger (or more *continuous,* as he described once during our summer week) with me—that as he had never before known a woman with whom he enjoyed talking for hours, he was afraid that I would take this as an insult to the *woman* and this had made him conscious. How intuitive Henry has been here in sensing my obscurest fear, a fear, however, which had disappeared entirely lately. To see Henry become mental and self-conscious amazed me. I refused his caresses, but he saw that I was ready to laugh.

What baffles me is this: According to Allendy, a fear in one being creates in the other a certain psychic equivalent. However, I am deeply sure that I have been absolutely natural—that is, enjoying our talks and not conscious of being overlooked as a woman—in fact, completely satisfied. But perhaps Henry has become aware of my fundamental sensitivity—in a general way—to my conviction that I am worth more as a mind, talent, artist than as an *animal.* But this is all old, ancient history. And the last echo of doubt.

What a struggle to be *reborn*—not to trip again, always on the *same obstacle.*

Victory is always sad. It always reveals the deformity in the imagination which had created a monster with the perverse desire to *frighten itself.* The monster killed, one finds a hill of cardboard and chicken feathers, *colle fer,* cracked pumpkins, sheets, chains.

More pages added to the diary, but pages like a prisoner's walk back and forth over the two yards' space allotted to him.

I believe Henry is now the one who seeks what he most fears—cruelty, abandon, deceit from me—that at the moment when he found me most devoted to him, he was urged diabolically to create an estrangement. I believe I am well and that I am doing all the normal acts of confident love, refusing to doubt, refusing to believe Henry wishes me to act like June. But how much danger there is in his ambivalence. And all the more because my own faith is *new* and delicate!

Dream: I am Henry. I touch my eyes and I feel their smallness, the exact touch of them (as I have felt them when I have kissed them).

I feel the contours of Henry's face with my hands—the gnomelike features and even the age. I am Henry, and I am aware that someone wants to throw me—Henry—into the sea as a prank. I have already been thrown in. I say, "Listen, don't push me in. I am tired. I may not be able to come up again." And I feel a terrible sadness.

Association: Immense pity when I noticed Henry's tiredness the other day, which disarmed me. Violent desire yesterday to have him here, protect, love him. Realization that I am again feeling too possessive, that as soon as I let go I want to live very close to Henry, enwrap him, serve him. Fear of this. Identification with Henry complete. He is a part of my own being. I suffer because he suffers.

Dream: I am in a big clinic. Joaquin has been operated upon. I want to see the doctor. I arrive at the door by an aerial route, like a mountain-suspended funicular (second time I dreamed of elevators running hung on wires). I am told doctor can only see me at seven, and even at seven there are many other people ahead of me. I am keenly disappointed. I see a list of doctors: I see the names—but I cannot remember them. I see a name beginning with *H*, and two *n*'s—I say: "Not this one, he is too expensive." I find bedbugs on the bed. Clinic like the hotel on the Mallorca shore.

Association: None—except that I have been fearing loss of Allendy, who will be angry when he discovers I love Henry.

I write while I am dressing, bathing, etc., and at the same time I am reading Allendy's *Le Problème de la destinée,* which is great.

The final word on Hugh: He is the man who *understands everything,* but passively. Henry is essentially active. There is a difference between understanding and *response*. I seek response and resistance. Henry's attacks on psychoanalysis strengthen my defense of it, and tonight, because of Henry, I begin my book on the artist and psychoanalysis. I want to be the psychoanalyst of artists.

Last night, because of L. V., the schema of my lyrical book burst into crystallization. Death. Disintegration. Perversion. Spengler's prophecies unraveled: lesbianism, June (minor themes in connection with June of lies, abortion, primitivism, psychism), incest—the de Vilmorins—Eduardo and homosexuality and paralysis, my death, holocausts. A thoroughly neurotic book including all the symptoms, phenomena, descriptions of moods, dreams, insanities, phobias, manias, hallucinations—tableau of disintegration, *franker* than Lawrence's treatment of homosexuality, than Radclyffe Hall's treatment of lesbianism, because of this conception of mine which is a reflection of Jung's attitude against Freud's—if we could understand the significance of the sexual symbol we would have the key to vast pregnancies and abortions, fecundations and impotences—*from* the sexual root, the imaginary world—as, for instance, incest does not mean only possession of the mother or sister—womb of woman—but also of the church, the earth, nature. The sexual fact is the lead weight only: The *drama* is in space. The gesture is only a symbol with enormous significance (you can even find the taste of death in copulation). All the neuroses —amplify Eduardo's fears, mine (making love in the middle of the night when half-asleep my greatest enjoyment), Henry's, June's! Accentuate each one's follies (June's fear in subway, Louise's deafness, my blindness). Character as in Grand Guignol drug addicts—*délire de persécution*—inferiority complex—theme of recurrent Johns (woman in Switzerland)—hatred—war between the sexes. A big book.

And deliverance! Henry as Rabelaisian figure—a giant—Allendy the savior—destiny—projection—image—my fight for life. The vomit scene. Making love as half the cure. Yet not absolute, either. Natasha. Louise's limping.

What is the meaning of this? Yesterday, at five o'clock, I was very busy helping Emilia with the de Vilmorins' dinner. I was at the same time combing my hair, dressing, etc. Standing in front of the bathroom mirror, I suddenly felt a tremendous *anxiety* over Henry. I wanted desperately to make him come to Louveciennes, keep him in the cave studio, ask him to work there. I even considered rushing to Paris in a taxi, calling for him, bringing him back. I had exactly an hour. It was folly. So I telephoned a telegram: "Telephone me before six or else tomorrow."

Now, Henry was out and did not get my telegram. But at seven he telephoned me because he felt the very same *anxiety* over me.

Today I had to see him—when he telephoned we arranged a hasty meeting, to discover we were all right, and both of us writing. I suggested that at that hour last night June may have been manifesting great hatred or planning a revenge. Henry and I *were* in danger. But Henry laughed at my occultism.

Is it merely our habit to imagine danger, to sense it, and to bring it upon ourselves, as Allendy would say?

Je suis affreusement inquiète.

I repeat again and again: Consciousness, intelligence, are not dangerous if one has enough emotion and enough sexuality to keep moving. The ones who are killed are those emotionally and sexually feeble (like Eduardo). Henry can bear not to be blind; his blood is thick enough. I, too.

En résumé: I am the woman who gives illusion and who is given the imagination of man. A situation the whore envies. If I were *right with myself,* as I become more and more every day, I should be supremely satisfied, since no one can reign in two kingdoms at once, and the whore reigns in reality: she gives reality. The woman in me gets ample worship, and it was only my lack of faith (the constant emphasis laid on my value), it was only my doubt, which created the need of abnormal demonstrations, the need of obscenity and violence to *destroy* the too-potent legendary element. It is like June saying she wanted to destroy Henry's worshipful attitude the first night, and so she lifted her dress!

I see the legendary aspect persisting, and I see in men the ultimate, eternal worship of illusion. How hurt Henry would be if I squatted over the bidet, if I held *my* "pussy" in my hands like a bouquet! Wisdom means giving each human being his due and playing one's role beautifully, without regrets, for one can only fulfill one's own karma, and I would probably make a poor whore!

I will have succeeded in experiencing the two kinds of attitudes within myself: the introvert and, now, the extrovert—the "tender minded" and "tough minded" (rereading two essays in analytical psychology by Jung). Must include both because "we cannot permanently allow one part of our personality to be cared for symbiotically by another" (my dependence on Henry).

Realization of the delusion of one's uniqueness when one observes the ordinary pattern of one's reactions. I discover that it is current for the patient to endow the physician with uncanny powers somewhat like a magician's or a demonic criminal's, or to see him as the corresponding personification of goodness, a savior.

Joyous evening with Henry. He has been writing about whores to dissolve his attack of self-consciousness. I submitted to his mood when he refused to talk, and we went to bed to tranquilize him. But I am so shaken and troubled in my illusion of Henry as a man without sexual consciousness. I recall Allendy's words, "You didn't choose a really earthy peasant animal man: he is tainted with literature, intellectuality."

Well, I don't want a Mellors—*I* am *too tainted* for that; I needed a match and I found one, and as a result I will suffer from *his* neuroses, inferiority complex, self-consciousness, masochism. Or rather, I did suffer and will not any longer because of all I *know*. Observed last night his terror of June knocking at the door, his anxiety over his attack of self-consciousness, just as I was saying, "Henry can bear consciousness."

I am afraid Henry and I are trying to punish ourselves for having deceived June by spoiling our joys. Last night I dreamed of punishment: that is, June returned, and called Henry, as she did the night she was drunk. He immediately answered and kissed her.

He, on the other hand, is affected by June's obsessive way of saying, "He has lost his manhood." He has doubts.

I believe a sudden, overintensive introspective life has been disturbing Henry's health, his flowingness.

This morning I almost caused a catastrophe. I was only half-aroused from my unpleasant dream about Henry and June, and in this state I thought it was Henry who was lying at my side, not Hugh. I was about to say: "Henry, I had a terrible dream." When I came to my senses, I realized I was mumbling to Hugh about my dream, and I just managed to place the dream in the proper light. How often, now, in half sleep it is Henry I feel by me instead of Hugh.

I understand this now: Henry *toujours*, either as lover or friend— a source of restlessness, creation, pain, fermentation. I belong to him by all the currents which force my destiny into tragedy, though I will not be *defeated* by my destiny. Today my joy was deep and grave, with a mature acceptance.

I stood under the attic window and looked at the stars and at Allendy's eyes, which are, for me, the firmament.

And Hugh and I laugh riotously together. Hugh says, "I'm divinely happy."

So now I am put in the ironic situation of helping others through their fears and doubts—I who am just barely cured! Henry is singing and working, flowing, and I exhaust my newborn strength on him. *Who* is the source of my strength? Allendy. And tonight I need him. I need his strength. He is my father, my god—all in one. That is all I know: that in dark moods I need him.

Reading Jung made me realize that my first feelings of power and confidence may have been partially inflation. My faith in Allendy was so exalted that it gave me a great élan—and enough élan to fight June, Henry, myself—but tonight I feel deeply tired, and so nervous that I realize what superhuman efforts of will I have been making to be strong. Allendy was so wise to suspect my confidence. So much will, so much desire not only to be strong but to strengthen others!

I should have been quiet, withdrawn, nurturing my new self carefully, not exposing it immediately to tests of all kinds, to strain, to work. Too soon. Suddenly I collapse and become child again. Allendy, Allendy.

A dream, which revealed my *activity:* I find myself in a ranch of wild animals. Some are kept in the house. I am not afraid of them. I open the door to a panther, and she is tame with me, gentle, like my own dogs. I am asked by the owners to give them a sum of money—$250,000—and I refuse very firmly, saying I know they intend to cheat me. Then I go around selling wine. I wear my simple raincoat and black hat. I decide to enter the very imposing house of the Vanderbilts. I am met by the *maître d'hôtel.* He is very affable, and he orders sixty-two bottles. I take the order down. A woman comes and is extremely interested in me. Begins to talk to me, to confide in me, to show me photographs of herself (I remember one photograph— erotic pose in flowing dress—unrecognizable). We become friendly and go out for a walk. I then confide to her that I sell wine but that I really care about writing, and I tell her about my book.

Associations: Sum of money is what Hugh used to mention as necessary for his retirement—I had wanted to help him, and instead I gave Henry, the other day, the first check I received on the sale of my [Lawrence] book, all to be spent on things he needed. At the time I remembered, with a sense of guilt, my old desire to help Hugh.

House of Vanderbilts looked like a house of de Vilmorins, which did not intimidate me as it would have before my analysis.

I know wine is *Life*.

I don't understand the friendship with woman, except that I felt I interested Louise V. the other night by my wealth of work.

All this "crisis" may be a pretext to see Allendy!

Crossroads: Arriving in Paris, overcome by desire to go and see Henry, also concerned about Allendy's severity over the telephone—because he has been wishing I would weaken and go to him in spite of my promise (to wait until Hugh is cured). Complete indecision, so rare in me. I take a taxi and give Clichy address; then, instead, I go to American Express and learn June is still in Paris, which distresses me. Again I take a taxi to Clichy address, but feel that I do not want to go on loving Henry more *actively* than he loves me (having realized that nobody will ever love me in that overabundant, overexpressive, overthoughtful, overhuman way I love people), and so I will wait for him. So I ask the taxi driver to drop me at the Galeries Lafayette, where I begin to look for a new hat and to shop for Christmas. Pride? I don't know. A kind of wise retreat. *I need people too much.* So I bury my gigantic defect, my overflow of love, under trivialities, like a child. I amuse myself with a new hat.

It isn't anymore a question of love, it is the question of passivity and activity. My activity makes others passive. I want to see Henry, and my acting on it robs Henry of the *aggressive* leadership; *and I choose that kind of man,* always. The passive man. But the irony here is that Henry is *also sexually passive*—it became clear to me today that what bewilders him is that he was accustomed to June always "mounting him," June and the whores, and that I—being thoroughly Latin and *sexually passive*—I never lead; I wait for his pleasure. And Henry is not used to this, having to take the responsibility of his desire.

This discovery was a great shock to me (adding this to his stories of being sought out, courted by women, seduced by June). I am striking something as feminine as Hugh or Eduardo almost—and what deluded me was Henry's great sensuality, but so much strikes me now; his emphasis on being fucked, his teaching me "attacks"—leadership.

All this caused a great revolt in my *femininity*. I cursed my blindness. I realized that I had not traveled so very far from my "type" of man, the weak man whose weakness kills me. I did everything to find a leader! And again I am cheated. Henry and I may "readjust" this—may find a compromise. If I can become more aggressive. But the flaw is there, the fissure. And I will not submit to it. I will not love a weak man, I will not. That sensation, so familiar to me, of being unvanquished has come back to me, terrible, awesome. And I am going to defeat my destiny. I am going to escape from this fatality.

All day I was aware of the fissure, the fissure in our harmony, doubts. Doubts. A great desire to escape. Every one of June's accusations against Henry's passivity is true. But I had counted on Henry becoming a man when confronted with a real woman—a really *passive* female. And he is baffled—baffled by my submission. He had craved it, and now he is baffled, lost. And I am in great torment, because I love him and him alone, but I must abandon him.

Defiantly I must abandon him as a lover. I do not want to be the leader. I refuse to be the leader. I want to live darkly and richly in my femaleness. I want a man lying *over* me, always *over* me. *His* will, *his* pleasure, *his* desire, *his* life, *his* work, *his* sexuality the touchstone, the command, my pivot. I don't mind working, holding my ground intellectually, artistically; but as a woman, oh, God, as a woman I want to be dominated. I don't mind being told to stand on my own feet, not to cling—all *that* I am capable of doing—but I am going to be pursued, fucked, possessed by the will of a male at *his* time, his bidding.

Je suis effroyablement triste.

And to think that at any hour I could find what I want in a *man of my own race,* and that from them I do not want it because I cannot bow before them as a mind. *Any* Spaniard will treat me as I wish to be treated sexually . . . *C'est stupide.*

ALWAYS HENRY. YESTERDAY, ABOUT FOUR O'CLOCK, when I was tormented with the desire to go to Clichy, he was telephoning me in a frantic mood, wanting to see me. Why didn't I obey my instinct?

Now I sit waiting for him, sit waiting for my beloved.

He had been going *mad,* dreaming of death, terrified by noises, unable to cross the street. His dream about me: "You were here in Louveciennes, beautifully dressed, like a princess, and the house was full of people. You were very haughty. I ate a great deal and got drunk. I felt terrible—as if you felt contempt for me. I saw Haridas (a beautiful Hindu whom Henry used to know) hovering around you. Then he comes to me and says, 'It's all finished for you, Henry; I've taken her away from you.'" Great distress. Henry asks me, "Did you deceive me Monday night? What happened Monday night?"

So we talk everything out, all that I have written, my wish to abandon him. Before I am half-finished he is kissing me, unbuttoning my dress. And we are lost in each other. And everything else falls away before our hunger for each other. Bliss. I am reading the formal testament he has made, and we are laughing over it. He leaves everything to me! He was sure he was going to die! I am kneeling before him, and we are planning that when I go to London for Christmas, he will go, too—he wants to stay near me. And he needs a holiday.

His madness of these few days moves me more deeply than Allendy's power and equilibrium. Yet I need Allendy.

Dream: Hugh and I are walking along a beautiful dark road. I am in my black chemise. I say to him, "When there is nobody on the

road, I'll lift up my chemise so that you can see my thighs as I walk."
I see the whiteness of my own body in the night. A wolf-dog passes
and he bites my hand and I cannot shake him off. Hugh cuts off a
piece of his tail, and only then the wolf-dog lets me go. We walk along,
and then we fall together down some sand dunes—wonderful airy
sliding sensation—orange sand, vaporous. We land by a dry sea. Place
looks arid, prehistorical. But I lift my eyes and see a beautiful city, all
cupolas, minarets, gold domes. I lead Hugh to it. Gorgeous vegetation.
I am met with a Louis XVI traveling chair, carried by men. Introduced
to a woman who kisses me amorously. She is beautiful, but I do not
like her. As I look at her very closely, I observe her eyes are like
Paulette's, the same tight-lidded corners—and I realize why I dislike
her.

I am not sure who I was walking with, because sensation of falling
down the sand dunes resembled sensation of joyous meltingness and
falling I experience in Henry's arms. That same vaporous, orange-
warm *glissement* between us. I have never felt with anyone that softness
of Henry's; it reminds me of a description by Lawrence.

My yieldingness to Henry is lost into the moist softness of him so
wholly that all I know is just woman and penis, as if we were within
the womb, both of us, swimming in rolling flesh and moisture which
gives that supreme silkiness, a sensation which is the climax of all one
experiences when naked in water, when touching silk, when vibrating
in orgasm. It is that nakedness, that darkness, that blinding flesh-and-
moisture feeling which *is* sex—from which I rise as from the most
magic bath. And there is *no* end—for days I am still living in flesh-
perception; for days life doesn't go to my head, it touches and surrounds
me exactly as he touches me; life is a continuation of his caresses. He
leaves the imprint of his flesh-visit on my skin, in my womb, and for
days all I know is my legs. No world in the head . . . world between
the legs . . . the dark, moist, live world.

7:30. In Allendy's salon, waiting for Hugh. I don't know what I
am doing anymore. All I know is that I don't want to lose Allendy
and so I cannot tell him about Henry. I must say I have broken with
Henry, because as soon as I am in Allendy's arms I want Allendy. And
today we kissed madly, madly. He was frenzied to let me go, repeating

he must cure Hugh quickly, quickly, so that he can see me, be with me. And each time during the rest of the afternoon that I remembered his closeness I grew dizzy.

From Allendy's place, an hour later, I went to Henry at work; my good Henry, my good Allendy—and I feeling like a devil. A devil. Henry at work. Allendy at work. My Henry cold in his spring coat. Allendy serious, Allendy loving me more than I love him, and now less wise, impetuous, finding all I said charming, whereas I know I was being a coquette. God, I hate myself. And yet I am happy, healthy; and yesterday Henry said he was singing after he left me, and I was singing. I am still singing, and I am inordinately happy. Allendy. René Allendy.

In Café Terminus. Yesterday I was drunk, and I look back on that hour I spent in the Sorbonne listening to a lecture on "The Metamorphosis of Poetry" (Allendy presenting the conference!) as upon my great divorce from the intellectual world through sensuality! Humorous. Incredible. That hour of drunkenness in Allendy's arms, the bigness, the firmness, the power in him, the intoxication of his caresses, his hand on my legs, on my breasts; and what remained most tenaciously engraved in my sense memory was that there was no pause— no break—no return to reality. When I heard the bell of the next visitor I drew away, but at the door, when I was leaving, Allendy was still kissing my eyes, the corners of my mouth, my ears, and so I left him when we were both on a height of turmoil, and this turmoil continued to eddy in me all afternoon, all night, all day today.

At the Sorbonne. The classroom atmosphere; chastity, seriousness. Allendy appears. It is the first time I see him from a distance. He is more furtive, more shy than in his office. He stoops. His victorious and sensual mouth is hidden in his beard. I cannot hear what he is saying. He is mumbling anyway, doctor, professor, scientist. What a different Allendy from mine—the Allendy who discards reality to look for a *dream,* for his exotic island dream, *le grand, le serieux, le beau* Allendy, the *oldest* of the Eduardo–Hugh web—for *they* are brothers, *all* Neptunian men, the same type fundamentally, the same image, thoughtfulness, mental activity, mysticism, romanticism, idealization, learning.

My body is battered—always a bit defeated. Fevered night, fatigue, but all I do is take all my joys with me to bed, where the heat of the log fire, the hot-water bottle, the quilt revivify me at least enough so that I can tell my story. All is well. But if I had to go to sleep without confidences! What a burden. So I shook with cold all day (Henry, my love Henry, I must get him a winter coat), and I carried my ecstasies around close to me, to be preserved drop by drop, word by word, in the journal.

If I have continued to love Henry, it means that it is not a victory I wanted, but a man I loved.

June was not superb, not generous, and not clever enough to leave in us the last scene of her departure. She had to come back and act and talk like a vulgar Broadway trollop. June! Every one of her phrases dismayed me. *Reality.* I am now "that banker woman." She tells Henry: "You've got your woman now, a mate, and now you'll see a real spider—she will devour you. She is much cleverer than you are. And she is looking for another Guiler—she is watching out for her comfort. She would not be poor with you, but she will come to you when you are rich. Of course, I knew all about it long ago. That is why I left for New York. I acted all the time. And what a foul trick she played on me—making a laughingstock of me. Do you think I ever wore her jewels? And her coral handkerchief? I used to throw them in the water closet. And the day we danced together I was trembling with hatred of her. I could have murdered her. I loathe her. She is shrewd and devilish. That last night—she sickened me with her lies. Her lies. And she is old, you'll see. You look at her now through your illusion. She is an old woman whom you have rejuvenated for a while. You look at her closely. I don't believe she ever met Gide."
And so on. Not only neurotic, abnormal, crazy, but vulgar and low-minded, stupid and destructive. Even one's crimes, one's neuroses have possibilities of beauty. June's show the face of a mean, suspicious,

money-touched Jewess. June the sieve, as I called her when Henry asked me why after twelve hours of talk she could say good-bye smiling!

Fred is anxious, thinking all this is doing something to me. He is right. I am revulsed and furious to have again embellished, trusted. The low-down gold digger and trollop. No. That is said in anger. Just a poor sport.

Where I realized the humor in all this was when she suspected I had never met Gide. But against my one story she invents a hundred to impress Henry. I have no feelings of guilt! Only laughter. And more when Henry began to say, in front of Fred, that Jean had abandoned June, had been so disillusioned by her that she had wanted to kill herself. She had written June a beautiful letter which Henry had read, telling how she pulled the trigger of the revolver twice and how it would not work. At this, Fred suddenly gets very upset: "Did Jean write that? Did she say that?" He had loved Jean and kept a great illusion about her. Henry repeated the statement.

"Well," said Fred, "That's the limit. It was I who tried to commit suicide. It was I who pulled the trigger twice. I had loaded the revolver with only five bullets, and it was built for seven. I didn't know that in that case the bullet had to be pushed forward. And Jean, Jean writes June she did all that!"

He was overwhelmed. And I was twisted with laughter—convulsed. Henry too. Oh the falsity, the falsity, the children, the children, the lying children who believe their own lies!

As I have believed my own lies, as my Father believed his own lies!

Henry, poor Henry, could not say very much against the tide of June's discourses. But last night he was a fervid lover, and I was happy—when we rested I made myself small in his arms. We were drowsy, relaxed, blissful, soft, warm. For the first time I fell asleep at that moment—no thinking—no thinking—trusting. And deep down, a sadness, a revulsion about June, a joy that Henry should be free of her—that he should be safe. I don't care what happens now. *He* is safe.

Henry *knows* he has resuscitated me—has given me life—because it is true I was dying—life was empty for me, empty intellectually and physically. But that is no reproach to me, and when Henry revived me I came to life to love him in a way few men have been loved.

DECEMBER 13, 1932

*E*VENING. JUNE TALKS AGAIN TO HENRY IN DESperate *efforts to destroy his illusion of me*. And what feminine *venom*. This is the real test of Henry's love!

Strange afternoon we had, Henry and I. June's *hitting below the belt* deprives one of wisdom, of sage qualities. One is tempted to get down to her level and fight with her words, her tools. But today I am quieter. Henry and I begin by fucking, wonderfully, in unison, nearly falling asleep. And then I know June's talk is on his mind, rankling. He tells me first that June called him a homosexual and me a lesbian.

In the back of his head float June's words. He wants to tell me because he cannot help telling me everything. He hesitates. I lie over him and plead. Then he says: "The worst June said was that you are so dead, so dead that you would have been swept off your feet by *anybody*—it happened that I came along, that's all. You wanted sensation at any cost. You are so dead that your body has no smell—no odor. That I had certainly become a homosexual when I could love a woman without breasts."

I had expected something terrible, and this did not affect me. I know why. I told Henry: "Listen, this doesn't hurt because it's so far from the truth. I'm not worried about my aliveness—nor about my seeking sensation. What hurts in caricature is when it approaches truth. What hurts me is when June attacks my physical limitations, because that is a partial truth: I could *not* have done all she did. I do not have a horse's health. *That's* true. About my aliveness—well, you know better than anyone about that. About my odor—yes—I know you noticed that—I suppose that's part of my frailty, lightness of texture, the fact that, not being fat, I don't perspire. About my breasts, since I have the body of a young girl, as you said, my breasts are in proportion." I was laughing by now, laughing with tears in my eyes. Suddenly Henry became extraordinarily serious: "Do you know that at this moment when we are talking about the worst June could say about you, *I have never felt* so acutely the *illusory quality* of you. I feel as I did the first day I came to Louveciennes, as if I did not know you at all, had not possessed you, been familiar with you. As we talked about these things and I wondered if I were blind, I felt that you are a *solid, real* woman sitting there. At the same time, like a moving picture played one reel upon another, superimposed, I see all the different faces of you, infinitely—your variety, our changeableness of roles—and yet I feel you focused there—illusion and reality together, for in reality I feel that I know you well, intimately—that I am not mistaken . . ."

I had a weird feeling of magic—a moment like in one of Barry's plays—a definite sensation of a wind passing, an unseen world hanging over us, veils, curtains, enchantment. I sat there in a trance, just looking at Henry and listening to him. I said, "At the center of the focus, there is you."

I had wet eyes—blurred—but I was *all whole* looking at Henry.

I remembered when Allendy said cruel things about Henry, when they affected me (when partly true), when not; and I understood how both of us had tried to see *through* other's eyes, to see *each other without our illusions*. And now this moment, resoldering all the year and bringing us to the first day of our encounter and the first illusion, the first dream. And yet, between us there is a year of *intimacy,* of human intimacy. Tests. I can't write. I must return to this. I am still floating.

Henry and I are parting at the door and we don't know each other. New lovers. All reality has passed over us without engulfing us. We try to open our eyes and see each other: Who are you? Are you the man who writes shit? Are you the woman who is dead, odorless, breastless?

Trying to rise up equally to meet the flow of that moment—that trance. What happened to me? I awoke from Henry's possession so ethereal—so light. All the human, fallible pain washed off, all the anger, the human feelings—all the resentment, the desire to defend myself, to attack June—all this dropped off me, dissolved. *The Ascension*—the awesome separation from human life—a pinnacle! Sainthood. My body so light, the body which had felt for a moment humiliated, defeated—now transparent, and all of me rising, rising exalted, intangible, as after the Crucifixion. After pain, this divine departure, this transcendence. It terrifies me. All the links break, all connection with the earth, all hatred and resentment, reality. I feel this passing of wind, this listening in the air, this suspense of other presences. I feel ears and eyes around me, figures, music, the rustle of leaves, the rolling of waves; I feel skies and curtains. I am floating. I am raised. I rise. I walk. I follow all this that surrounds me. I am possessed. Vertiginous ascension.

I went to bed. I fell. I fell into darkness. I said to Hugh, "I am dying." My heart seemed to have stopped beating. And this morning I have been worn-out. I don't know what all this means.

I am so happy to be able to see Allendy tomorrow. I love his strength. Henry and I get overwhelmed by life, by reality. How hurt he was that June should call him a homosexual.

What a divine fool I was whenever I believed June, when I undressed before her. What cold scrutiny she gave me. She doesn't know that Henry would love me even if I were ugly! She doesn't know what love is!

Before I went to Allendy I knew that the collision with reality had again submerged me into dreams. My eyes waver and I cannot see very well. My eyes are blurred, as if I were drunk. I talk in the car as if I were galloping on a horse, and the world totters.

In this mood I go to Allendy, and his kisses do not awaken me altogether. I tell him about my preoccupation with reality, how I feel that I miss it always. Either dreams or sensuality. No intermediate life. Dreams or sensuality. As in my writing. The overtones only, or the undertones.

Whatever one says about Allendy always remains a supposition. He has a most peculiar way of remaining silent, suspended, of never answering directly. How far does his imagination go? I ask myself. I sometimes have the impression he does not understand me when he says that I may want to take drugs out of snobbishness, or that I must remember the material advantages of my marriage, or that I may like to go out for the mere sake of going out. There is in Allendy the slight boundary line of bourgeois convention—if he knew some of my extravagances, generosities, and unworthinesses, I would appear to him more like a Dostoevskian character than a Latin.

Today I am giving Henry the experience of security, ampleness. He is rejoicing at the new feeling of possessing money, clothes, books. He is leaving this morning for London to escape June. I am to meet him the Monday after Christmas, on his birthday night. He, too, is traveling; he was already *gone* yesterday, picturing London. He said, "Imagine me, tomorrow, in a hotel room, lying in bed and thinking of all the things I should have told you and couldn't."

But he does say them.

We kiss in front of Mother's apartment. Then I feel the terrible splintering of his leaving me. I feel his absence. Today the world is altered for me because Henry is on a train, Henry, who is a half of me.

I can stand away from myself and see myself in my "role" before Allendy. To own him, I let him believe the analysis has brought my masochistic devotion to Henry to an end. And how completely, how carefully I have elaborated the story of this end. When he first asked me in such an anxious tone and I said yes—that I had broken with Henry—I enjoyed Allendy's outburst of condemnation. Three different layers of my mind worked simultaneously. One layer composed the tableau of the break with Henry; the second layer registered the fact that Allendy had never understood Henry because he saw Henry as an enemy; the third layer was a full awareness of my perfidiousness and a realization that now Allendy, the psychologist, could be deceived by my lies. It was a scientific discovery—and one which touched me humanly. Allendy is unable now to think objectively. I am deceiving him. And all because I had not the courage to say, "I will love Henry always—and I can love other men, too. But Henry remains the center of my life. Do you accept sharing me?"

Before Allendy's expressions and sincerities I have sometimes the same feeling as I have before Hugh's face: an obscure humility and adoration for a quality of integrity I do not possess. So, out of cowardice, I begin to deceive. Allendy, the psychoanalyst, believes me simple and pure. And what would he make of my lies? The break with Henry became such a vivid conflict in me that there were moments when I felt as if it had happened, and the depths of my regrets for Henry proved to me how I could not separate myself from Henry! To report it to Allendy, I entered into a full imaginative game. When I was upset twice by June, I transferred my agitation and attributed it to scenes with Henry. Henry acting as in the dream he told me—broken, overwhelmed. And I tell Allendy as an actual fact, a statement which remains true in all aspects except in tense: I would never have the courage to abandon others because I know too well the pain of being abandoned. I have done it—but I need strength to sustain this decision.

The "strength" I get is in Allendy's pleading: "It was only your neurosis which made you love Henry, you—such an extraordinary woman—such a rare woman."

As I look back on this, its only value comes from Allendy's sincere devotion; but to me it appears ridiculous in the light of a deeper knowledge of Henry. A few years from now, I may be forced to acknowledge Allendy's wisdom and recognize again that my illusions make me utterly blind. But nothing that Henry can do now will ever surprise me—the greatest crime—*I know him*; I could forgive him anything.

I did tell Allendy yesterday that in analysis one could not give all the details which make a simple statement less true. They are all too simple, his phrases, sometimes too literal.

While I am writing, my life crashes suddenly with the full-blast revelation of Henry's weakness.

I must have known when I gave him the money for London that it would be a test of him. I knew that if June caught him she would get it from him. Or that he might spend it on a whore and drink. Why did I do it? Exactly, to know. So June does catch him the night before he leaves, and like a perfect gold digger and blackmailer frightens and terrorizes him and empties his pocketbook.

Very well, if this were intelligent charity—but Henry knows, and he said the other day he was sick of June's stupid way of throwing away money. So he knows the stupidity of his gesture, the weakness of it. June is simply *blackmailing* me, that's all.

His letter to me is so weak. Assertions of anger now, courage to face the worst. Nothing. It is all weakness—that's all. Weakness. And that is the man I love!

I had begged him to go to London—because the image of Henry, the coward, listening to June's insults about me without stopping her was intolerable.

I begged him to come to Louveciennes and waited, quite broken. He telephoned: "I'm angry, furious at myself. Of course you're hurt. I feel terrible about you. I hate June. I'm leaving tonight for London. Fred has come to my aid. I'm leaving so it won't happen again. It seemed right then—that's all I know. Forget about it. Don't worry, Anaïs."

> *In his letter:* After a bitter, nauseating conversation, I feel humiliated, deeply ashamed. You were covered with mud. It was agony, what I endured. And why I stood it I don't know, unless it is that I have a feeling of guilt. June is beyond reason. She has become a madwoman. The vilest threats and recriminations. It's only you I'm thinking of. *You* were tricked, and she had to use me to trick you. That's why I broke down and wept. She is capable of anything—I love you, that is all that matters.

I ought to understand all this—expect it. *I* am weak. I am weak in my love of Henry. It is a weakness in me to love a man like Henry. Immediately I forgive him. I wish I could join him in London.

I could have handled June. My God, I'm weak in love, but courageous in every other way. June couldn't frighten me with threats. My poor Henry, how he needs me, how he fails to protect both himself and me. Now I see he cannot cope with life, that I cannot abandon him. I know how hard Allendy would be if he knew this story. Already he feels Henry uses all kinds of unfair tactics to melt and disarm me. Allendy, who is strong, resents all this wealth of my love wasted on Henry, and I suffer from the wealth of love Henry wasted on June.

The impotence a strong person feels to help the weak one. When I left Henry last night and kissed him, after the talk we had, he should have been strong enough to overpower a dragon. Certainly June can be terrifying with her violence, her passionateness—but Henry has no guts, no fighting spirit. He can't fight—he has to run away. Now he is in London and I feel equal to fighting anybody, anything. As long as Henry, my love, is safe—away. From now on it is very simple. I have to assume leadership. I must not count on Henry. Mine is the protective love. I accept disillusion, defeat—I will never find my man whole. Henry is the nearest I can reach. He has given me so much! This is the nearest I can come to *absolute love*. To demand all, to demand perfection, *that* shows ignorance. I demand nothing more!

I will give my due of love to Allendy's strength—pay my tribute. I am willing to try to love a strong man. Willing not to wreck myself with Henry. I need them both. I need Allendy's strength. As soon as life terrorizes me, I think of him—I need him. The femaleness in me needs him. I need man. And men have been so protective to me—so good even when they were weak—that I need them forever, that I confess this need, this dependence on man, that in return I give the woman's only gift: love, love, love.

Throughout all this fevered living, it is amazing how careful and tender I can be with Hugh—how I never "overlook" him, how aware I am of his little victories, little self-masteries, his awakenings, his every feeling and thought. He lives with the sensation of being loved, appreciated. *Il y a assez pour tout le monde.* Care. Care. Awareness. Gifts. I forget nothing, whether I am happy or unhappy. The passing from one role to another sometimes maddens me. I wanted to go and see Henry off tonight, but I must wait for Hugh, who is coming home early because he is tired. I wear the costume he loves, fearing and knowing he has been desiring me these last days and that I cannot elude him anymore. And I get Allendy a copy of Spengler and write him letters about his own books.

Oh, God, I cannot make myself happy. As if to compensate always for my eternal cravings, I think of extraordinary details to embellish the lives of others. Hell! Why do I mention these things? At this moment, when I am unutterably spoiled with love! Simply because I feel it is unjust to me that Henry, my Henry, should be a weak man! Well, well. And then what? The fundamental pattern of life is based on ironic injustices. Or perhaps on justice. I might also say that everything is conspiring to reward Hugh's love—the greatest—and to keep me for him by depriving me of the discovery of my true husband!

I asked Henry if he is uneasy about my journal. He answered, "No—because usually it is I who make characters of other people, and I enjoy being made a character. Of course, it may be because up to now it has been mostly flattering!"

I have been absolutely truthful with Henry (letting him read the red journal, and most of the next black ones, and most of this one). What a sensation of giving myself. I risk so much! While he reads, I suffer torture. I perspire and shiver. It is a harrowing ordeal. My journal is my one mystery.

What would Allendy do if he knew the truth? He always says that one can feel lies. Yet he cannot feel that I am still Henry's mistress. He cannot tell that I love Henry. Or else he takes me for a more superficial person than I am. Or he hopes I will love him better. I have no scruples, because so far I am Allendy's adventure. He is in no mortal danger. I am drama, exoticism, the island he never saw. I am the unknown. It is what you might call a high-class adventure. But it is an adventure. We do not really know each other. The superficial quality of my attraction for him is not so very different from his for me! Now, when I talk to him, he almost interrupts me to kiss me. He isn't listening! *Voilà*. I asked for that; I got it. And then I get furious because I feel that he doesn't know how deep I am!

Of course, when I talk about the quality of Allendy's love, I may be neurotically undervaluing a love because it has no flamboyance, no depression. He is controlled. But I know enough now. I am sure enough to believe. As soon as I am sure of others, I begin to get unsure of myself. Do I love Allendy as much as he loves me? Humorous reversal. Healthy.

Why is it that I cannot picture his life, or that if I do, I do not like it—just as I would not picture John's life, which was distasteful to me? And my life is equally strange to him.

Why this obsession in me to interpenetrate with people? Why can I not live more on the surface, accept Allendy without that minute struggle to understand all? Everything Henry does is comprehensible to me. Comprehension and love are inextricably interwoven for me. For me, understanding is love. That is why I doubt I will ever have an *expérience de passage*, a one-night stand.

June, in the end, is not very clever. She is leaving a parting impression which is certainly not beautiful! Revealing an ugliness which will brand Henry's sentimental naiveté. Her selfishness. Money. The desire to exploit me—all this has revolted Henry. Her callousness. (You only imagine that of which you yourself are capable.)

One can't pity June, because she is well able to take care of herself, so aggressive and demanding. She now *demands* that I should give her the money to return to America!

DECEMBER 18, 1932

FRED GAVE HENRY THE MONEY TO LEAVE FOR LONdon because, soon after June left, Henry realized he was not rid of her, that this scene would repeat itself and end in violence. That night they wanted to kill each other. June was clever enough to frighten him about me—threatened to throw vitriol in my face, to shoot me, crush me, walk on my face, blackmail me.

Saturday morning I rushed to Clichy, and it was a relief to know Henry was gone, safe. It seemed to me that now life could not frighten me. I can face June. I am waiting for her move. I took away all my letters from Clichy after receiving a telephone message from a man to be careful of all incriminating documents. And to lock my doors. *Très bien*. Fred and I had breakfast together. I liked his packing Henry off to London. Now June cannot hurt me if she cannot hurt Henry. I think constantly of Henry, expecting his letter, selling things to get money to send him.

On the surface of all this, the utmost frivolity: the casino, Cabaret Montmartre, dinners, movies, the Café Colisée—chicness—aristocracy—talks with Louise—scenes with the dressmaker. Unreal to me. June, in her black cape, looking perhaps for the ultimate sensation of revenge for all the humiliations of her race and of her life, unable to understand, to transcend the meaning and cause of her defeat. And I lanced occasionally—not by a sense of guilt—no—because I am too aware of having saved Henry, and he was the one worth saving—but by *pity*. Yes, it is incredible, I can still pity June, who wants to destroy me! And I know she is evil and a criminal; I know also she is not *all* evil—I wish I could hate her. I only hate her when it is a question of defending Henry. I know her pain is mostly egocentric, that it is not Henry she wants, but her victory (if she were given Henry now, she would not stay and live with him). And when I used to talk about accepting June and sharing Henry, I wanted Henry so much I was ready to endure any torture—the worst of all tortures for a woman, to be in a secondary role. I didn't know then that I would become the favorite and then the only woman—for now Henry can be only sexually unfaithful, that is all.

I have the impression of having had many children: Joaquin, Thorvald, Eduardo, Hugh, Henry—and a husband only now and then.

I'm lonely tonight. It is Allendy who is the husband for the present, the man I lean on. But I feel this, too, is an illusion, because . . . well, because he is not interested in my favorite child, Henry!

I sit in the cave and I think of how much poetry there is in Henry when his Faustian blue eyes watch me and he says, "Hands like music . . ." Where is he tonight, and what is he thinking of?

Hugh says, "I have got good seats on the train. I want this trip [to London] to be like a honeymoon. You are coming with me. It is so wonderful that I can take you away with me. I want you to be so comfortable."

He will not hear of economy. And I think how I would like to have this money for Henry.

I am determined to earn money, to be able to give always and to protect Henry always.

How spoiled I am—how spoiled. How I am being compensated for the emptiness of my past life. Rich in love, rich in friends, rich in my home and beautiful things, rich . . . so full in myself, so full of plans, books, ideas. When I look at my typewriter, I am aware that I cannot catch up with my writing.

DECEMBER 21, 1932

*H*ENRY, MY LOVE, HAS JUST LEFT ME. INCANdescent. He was stopped at the English frontier for carrying too little money! Questioned. Grilled. Deported. He was wearing his shabbiest clothes.

I rush home Monday when I hear he is in Louveciennes. I coax him to stay the night to calm my anxiety. And then the usual thing happens: we flow into each other, we get knitted together. I have to act superbly to calm Hugh's jealousy in the evening. We three read Rank together—Rank's book *Art and Artist*, the book I wanted to write! Although Hugh is at his very best—lucid, alert, comprehensive—there are so many currents between Henry's mind and mine. What we are reading, Henry has been saying to me or writing. Sometimes I have been saying and writing it!

The next day, Henry's good-morning is a gesture of his hand into my satin royal negligee, and we come together standing in the hall while Emilia is setting the table for breakfast.

Another day of talk, talk, and reading with Hugh. Hugh says,

"When is that fellow Henry going to leave?" He scolds me, nags. But I'm divinely happy. When it is for Henry, even cooking is blissful. I lift up the satin train and pin it to my waist to make coffee and sandwiches at midnight. The weight of our talks is fermenting in my head. If I could pour into the journal the reading and the things Henry says, it would be a symposium of modern metaphysics, psychology, art, science, biology. Gigantic.

The morning brings good news. I don't have to go to London. Hugh is going alone. Henry will stay in Louveciennes. We will work together.

Henry and I have a strange, cold talk about Hugh. Hugh at his best appears to Henry as a man with limitations. From the outside, to other eyes, it appears that I am like a part of Hugh's worldly, earthly possessions—that essentially he is the man of power, that the *sun* (success) is his ruling planet. I am an acquisition. I am an instrument to his *rise*. He has selected an artist, and a woman who can charm. He uses me (social life in too great a proportion, always invading my work hours). In return he protects me, loves me, spoils me. But he also imprisons me. I am an artist, but I am not living as an artist. I am wife, social woman; I have a thousand duties. The very, very few friends I have *selected* for myself (June and Henry, my only stimulants), I have had to fight to see.

This, to Henry, explains my rebellions (I am always ranting against society life), the experience of my journal as an outgrowth of frustration (oh, the years of frustration), and it also explains my cold decision to take trips, to take the liberty I need, because I must live as an artist and I have humanly served Hugh, compensated him as fairly as I really could. He is proud of me, he is on the road to success, to power. I don't want power, only art, art and passion. Proof of this is that if I had wanted power and social life, luxury, I would have married a wealthy Cuban, whereas I married Hugh thinking I married a poet, an intellectual, an artist. Thinking the bank submerged the artist, I tried to detach Hugh from the bank. And this was wrong. Hugh is interested in art, devoted to it, but he is not an artist. I am his ideal justification for his love of power. I am the object, the ideal receiver of this tribute. But he expresses himself through power. Occasionally

I have had this feeling when he says to me, "You're a great investment. You're a great help to me in my work. I like everyone to know you. Then they think more of me. I'm so terribly proud of you."

But any attractive woman could accomplish this. But Henry says no, that Hugh, who has a sense of value, chose a valuable woman, a woman stamped with genius, an *article de luxe*. Of course, none of these things were planned. They became so. Instincts lead us. All kinds of self-interested instincts. It is also quite possible that an instinct told me that any one of my Cuban suitors might not have been as loyal a protector for me because they did not have the more subtle appreciation of the artist.

One does things which appear innocent and yet reveal a hidden self-protection. Henry seems to think I have been caught in a life unsuitable to my development as an artist—an ordinary life. Caught, tricked! He worries about my pages lying there while I am running around shopping for Hugh's family, entertaining Hugh's clients, while Hugh and Allendy are discussing how to prevent me from mixing again with the Montparnasse crowd. Allendy confuses Henry with Montparnasse bohemians! Hugh at least rises in defense of Henry's intellect. And I rise, inwardly, against Allendy's limited world. The artist rebels. And Henry saves me. Henry nurtures me, strengthens the artist with beautiful thoughtfulness. He is concerned over me, so thoughtful of my work. Incredible, his faith in me. "Nobody else is doing anything like this. Ecstatic. Wonderful. What Jolas and the others wish they were writing. Your only defect, Anaïs, is that you waste too much time aiding others. And often uncritically. The very fact that you could think Hugh was a great intellect, a writer . . ."

"No different than your expectations about June!" I tease.

Très bien. But as soon as Hugh comes home, the curtain falls on my lucidity, and I find much injustice in my objective judgment— and I feel guilty, exactly as Henry feels guilty about June, because we are both overtender, oversoft dreamers. And the more likeness I find between Henry and myself, the deeper our understanding of each other, the greater my old fear that Henry should be taken away from me. There are moments when he looks so careworn, so profound, so thoughtful, so good that I could weep. And at these moments I adore him—and at others he looks so sexual, all flesh, winetinted, expanded, moist that he stirs me to frenzy. The scholar, the philosopher, the sensualist—at every point I meet him, love him, fit into him.

He is amazed to discover a new side of me. A mocking, tricky, rascally side. Hugh discovered that the radiators were too hot—there was serious talk about Emilia's stupidity. Hugh went down to the cellar to see, very, very earnest. I stood before Henry and mocked, "Henry, the radiators are too hot. That's serious, very, very serious." I bent myself like a gnome, laughing, making faces, all mockery. Henry responded immediately with his own devilry. He laughed and ran his hands between my legs.

I dedicate myself entirely to sending Hugh away beautifully comfortable. I have spent hours thinking, planning, working for the gifts which will make him popular with the people in the bank. I take care of a thousand details—all practical—with the utmost thoroughness. No loose ends, no letters unanswered. And all this I can do because Henry and I are going to spend ten days together, ten days, ten days!

Henry, books, our work, our work, our talks, and the big, soft Oriental bed. Everything is right.

Yet I am sad, because everything is right only relatively—Hugh, for example. Hugh, after a week of hard work, must leave me to be with his family, where he is not happy. Hugh, who wants to stay with me. So I atone, three times, in utter contrition, with little gifts, care, acting. *Mon Dieu!* I will wear the satin gown he loves—I will be so loving, so loving, in atonement for tomorrow. Henry telephones every day—fearing our plans may change. And with amusing proprietariness, he is taking possession of Louveciennes and of me. He will tell Emilia how he likes his steak!

Much that I am reading in Rank will illuminate intimations I had about the artist. What efforts I am making to understand! There are moments during Henry's talk when I feel truly tired, truly like a woman who is reaching for the most difficult knowledge. I tremble because I wonder when my mind will fail, prove inadequate. Yet, like Louise, I have the feeling that I can be made to understand everything—that at Rank's age I may be able to write a book like Rank's—but I am a woman, I know, and woman's mind is imperfect—or I could say rather that it is insufficient. I should not be so ambitious. My ambition tires me. I want Rank, Henry, and Allendy to do the big tasks. I will do my woman's task. I will learn enough, understand enough so that Henry can talk to me.

The *pendant* to June's remark about my odorlessness: Emilia goes to clean the bathroom after I have taken a bath and says, "It is so wonderful to go into the bathroom after the *señora* has been there; it smells good—fragrant—and before, the other two ladies I worked for—after their baths, I hated to go in, it was so smelly."

Emilia's adoration of me is based on my "goodness," on my "strangeness," and on my "beauty." She loves to touch my hair because it is silky, she admires my elegance, my ideas, my tallness. She collects all the photos of me which I throw away, and has them in her bedroom. She loves Henry and our enjoyment of each other. She lies for me, serves me, protects me, will do anything for me, would work for nothing.

Christmas night. Just a note. Change of atmosphere, of life. Henry is sitting at my desk, sorting numerous notes so that I may have them bound. My desk is covered with his manuscripts. His books of reference are lined up before him. He is in his shirtsleeves. Those notes which made such an overwhelming impression on me when I first read them, on the back of his letters from Dijon. Those notes on his adventures, his bohemianism, his *Bubu* life, which he lived with a fullness rarely experienced by one man.

I lie on the couch, with the surrealist number of *This Quarter* magazine.

It is the first time I write in my journal in front of Henry. I am self-conscious and awkward. At the same time, I want to write just as a drunk wants to drink. Everything is twinkling inside of me, as if someone were pressing his fingers on my closed eyelids. Twinkling. Four or five images superimposed: Hugh in London with his family. Allendy at the Sorbonne. Mother alone, sad over the great changes in her daughter. There are no more duties. No more Christmases. Only Henry and I, working together in the stillness of Louveciennes. The church bells tolling. The serenity of knowing what is supremely and divinely right. The world is at last focused. This is the center. And strange—the center can only be a fulfilled circle, of course, which I never knew before because I was only a crescent moon, a curved half circle, curved in gaping, dolorous craving, bowed around emptiness, arms surrounding to meet nothing, a line unfinished, a life unrounded, a curve unfilled, suspended over the world, pale with unfullness, and now shining round, rounded, complete in geometric splendor, in totality, in full magnificence. On Christmas night the moon shone full, and that alone is holy; for that alone the bells should toll, and music should rise, and mouse-stepped people climb cathedral steps; for the miracle of great rounded fullness between man and woman, for the miracle of totality.

Henry says occasionally, when in a nonsensical mood, "Don't put this down in your diary!"

Henry and I settle down to work. I write three pages of dream stuff. He works on his brochure. It rains. I index my journal. I dream. I dream. I cannot familiarize myself with completeness. I swim in it, exploring it. I look round eyed at exuberance—he makes cabrioles in my room, naked. We talk ourselves dizzy. I get fantastic doses of ideas. Ideas on a soft bed of flesh. I marvel. I sink into my pleasures with an oriental softness.

DECEMBER 26, 1932

WHERE MY THOUGHTS RAN PARALLEL WITH RANK'S: "Greek homosexuality—the master—whether philosopher or sculptor, or, in other words, artist in living or in shaping—was not content to teach his pupil or protégé his doctrines or his knowledge. *He had the true artistic impulse to transform him into his own image, to create.*"

See what I wrote about Ana Maria: "I realize how far I have moved from true lesbianism and how it is only the artist in me, the dominating energy, which expands in order to fecundate beautiful women on a plane which it is difficult to apprehend and which bears no relation whatsoever to ordinary sexual activity. Who will believe the breadth and height of my ambitions when I perfume Ana Maria's beauty with my knowledge, my experience, when I dominate and court her to enrich her, to create her?"

Henry is typewriting madly. He stops to dazzle me with words. Hours and hours of talk, of work. Henry is so wise about me and my work—*he is good to the artist*—concerned because he thinks I am too womanly, that I give too much time to the house, to him, to others, that I evade the final big task of my art, that I circumvent it with the journal—that he doesn't believe in forcing the end of the journal, but that one problem is simply displaced by another and that the art should overshadow the journal. The journal is an escape from my art problem, it supplies what I lack in communication with others, companionship, but now I myself have experienced the need of making it more artistic, or a notebook for my creation.

However, when I have a free half hour, I give it to the journal. But it is a circuitous route to the book. The page in the journal is my *starting point*. Henry wants to see me *swing out* free and produce more *art* and less *journal*. I believe I have been tending that way.

Just now I am in bliss as a woman—running the house, subordinating everything to Henry's work. He is writing extraordinarily well—amply—deeply. It is a joy to see the heavily loaded desk. It is so right that he should be given for the first time the security and all he needs to work—no anxieties, not even interruptions.

I don't believe the artist in me is in danger because, certainly, what I give Henry he returns a thousandfold.

Of course, I have not worked. I have been swimming in my contentment as a woman. Danger, danger, I suppose. But Henry is watching out. And after all, *as a woman*, purely a woman, I have been so rarely happy with this fullness.

"We are leading a rich life," Henry says as he talks to me about Jung, Ulysses, Rank. He makes me read Spengler to him while he rests his eyes from his work. I am kept always on the alert. I have been ejected from my miniature woman's universe, always revolving around *persons*—Joaquin, Hugo, Eduardo, June, Henry, Allendy, Ana Maria—and I am swimming into extraordinary new worlds.

JANUARY 1, 1933

I LEFT HENRY ALONE WITH MY JOURNAL IN THE cave and prepared for bed because I wanted to be rested for Hugh. Henry drank a bottle of Anjou and wrote the following:

New Year's Day, putting the finishing touches to my notebook of Paris, record of the first three years—in the quiet of Louveciennes. Anaïs pasting her eyes, her hair comb on my loose-leaf pages and envelopes from the Tyrol and fragments of [Howell] Cresswell's room in the Hotel Odessa. All this reviving in me the kaleidoscopic memory-picture adventures in Paris, so that as I finish pasting the fragments together my temptation is to sit down and write a book on them immediately. Coming out to Louveciennes on the train, the picture of the countryside so indelibly engraved in my mind—I know every foot of ground along the route, and with each billboard, each sign, each crazy house or road or movie, even a chicken run or a cemetery or a vacant lot, there is a welter of associations. And so when Anaïs remarks that I have never made any notes, strangely, of my experiences here in Louveciennes, it is only, I think, because everything is still so alive and meaningful, everything still so unconsciously exploited. When I collect my notes for my first Paris book there is the tender, sentimental, regretful feeling of putting between covers what was once a rich, throbbing life which literature will never reproduce, as indeed it should not. But as I was putting together these random notes, what a joy when I found there were little souvenirs of Louveciennes which could be inserted into that chaotic mass of facts, events, incidents, phenomena—quiet strains of collected living, as it were—even a trifle like the handbill from the Louveciennes *cinéma*, which will always remind me of my walks to the village *tabac*, or to the *épicerie* for a *"good* bottle of wine"—Châteauneuf, Barsac, Meursault, etc. No, if I have not written of Louveciennes it is only because I am not writing history, I am making it. I am so aware of the fateful, destined character of this Louveciennes.

That is why, for instance, I listen to Anaïs so eagerly when, as we pass the Coty estate at night, she explains the story of Madame du Barry, the lover's head thrown over the garden wall, her dainty figure, the Watteau shepherds and shepherdesses. In Louveciennes some tremendous, significant unity and purpose has been forged. I have matured here. Even if it is only a dirty picture out of *Frou-Frou* that we discuss, for a moment it leads to greater things.

Here, in the big billiard room, where the rats once scurried, sit Anaïs and I—or I pace up and down, gesticulating, while I explain to her the bankruptcy of science, or the meta-anthropological crisis. Here, at her desk, littered with shattering materials for the future, I hammer out my impetuous thoughts and images. Here all the images that grip and invade us are given free rein and new cosmological frontiers established.

My notes—it is when I think of them tonight, being embalmed, as it were, that I realize the inadequacy of human expression. No artist can ever catch up with his life. Here a thousand thoughts burst in my head over a simple utterance. Nothing can ever be brought to a finish. The important thing, I was thinking tonight, is that Louveciennes becomes *fixed* historically in the biographical record of my life, for from Louveciennes dates the most important epoch of my life. And I was thinking in the train how strange it was that just recently I should have become so concerned about the record of my life.

Spengler's philosophy of Care, which the Chinese had and the Egyptians—all the historical peoples! Here in Louveciennes everything is "categorized," "labeled," "filed," "annotated," "bound." Here is the soul of a historical romantic's "I," conscious of its great destiny, attracting kindred spirits, aye, attracting even her future recorders and biographers—as tho' her voluminous diary were not sufficient. Here one has only to turn the photograph around and the husband sees himself, the lover sees himself, the friend sees himself. Here you are permitted the luxury of always seeing yourself while all the while a thousand eyes are seeing you, studying you, recording you. Here the eye regards the eye that regards the eye . . . *ad libitum, ad infinitum*. Here all the great cosmological processes are unraveled, skeined, knotted, loosened. Here all things, the great cosmological processes, are disheveled artistically—a chaos to be ordered again the next morning.

"Did you sleep well last night?" "No, I was disturbed by the prelunar character of my dreams." "What did you say Rank said about tattooing?" And so, at breakfast, it commences—from tattoo to taboo, thru all the vagaries of the incest prohibition, thru all the layers of the geological "I," to be dissolved in the end in ink—pp. 50–99 of the journal of my life. And yet this spiderish activity, this du Barry geometry of the *novecentisti*, is the breath of life to all thirsty artists. While one meditates, words dance out from the walls, plots are nailed down, perfumes distilled on beautiful scented paper—and perhaps Madame de Staël herself may be nailing down a torn carpet or putting a new toilet seat in the privy house. And when Madame de Staël returns she is perhaps filled with those great primordial images which Salvador Dalí would have us revive: excrement, masturbation, love. The goldfish, which used to race at ninety kilometers an hour in the cement pond outside, are replaced by glass monsters swimming in an electric bowl—psychologic fish that have no problems, except of Time and Space. Fish of the late city-man that were never baited, hooked, or scaled. Fish who swim motionlessly—as a substitute for living. Glass, translucent lives, lit up from below by shining quartz and rock crystal.

Louveciennes, then, looms up on the horizon of my mind like some laboratory of the soul. It is by no accident that the problems discussed here are such as they are. The most important thing here is the soul—everything else takes second place. And so it is that here life expands to its richest, that a few days take on the magnitude of time, that the slightest event acquires significance.

For a moment I am interrupted—Anaïs reads over my shoulder these lines I have written, and she has a momentary fear that if she leaves me alone I may turn back the pages and glance at her secret thoughts. But it has never occurred to me to do this! And yet, if I stop a moment to reflect, I realize that perhaps on the page preceding these words of mine may lie embedded a catastrophe. Is it that I do not care? I cannot say that. But in a sense it is true—in a sense I do not care too much what is done outside those bonds we have established together. To care too much would mean disaster. This world is not built merely of love and faith and hope, etc. This world reflects an eternal duality, in thought and action. The basest things are sometimes inspired by the good. It is futile to try to control lives, thoughts, events. Liberty—that is the utmost one can demand. And whoever has a great desire to be free will respect that desire in others. And what about the great human emotional dramas? No denying them. They will occur again and again. But they occur in the measure that one surrenders to his biological self. Even though tomorrow all this rich world of Louveciennes, which I crave with my entire being to have perpetuated, should explode about my ears, I refrain from worry. I think, if I have learned anything from my manifold experiences, it is that the greatest victory of man is his conquest of fear. What a powerful, all-dominating force is fear, few of us ever stop to realize. It is fear that lends so much drama to our lives—and principally fear of self. To this kind of fear, or to fear, nameless, indescribable, uncategorized, I owe the terrible picture of my life with June. Fear of losing her, fear of being alone, fear of combating the world—fear of everything. And on the day when I realized that she could no longer terrorize me, I became a free man, an individual in my own right—though it happened that at that moment, in the eyes of the world, I was the sorriest specimen of a man imaginable. But who could tell the strength I felt in my bones? Who could tell that beneath my shabby, unkempt exterior, there resided now a kingly soul? Was it because I realized so keenly that no chains could enslave me that I wreaked such havoc about me? People often said that I was a dangerous individual. I emanated danger (bad English). People sensed a shattering, destructive quality in me, though I did little talking—or perhaps that is a lie. Perhaps it was *me* they were listening to, when I thought all along that I was listening to others. Perhaps when I was talking to myself I had my biggest audiences. Perhaps here, in this period, when certainly I knew the meaning of what is called "salvation," I was doing what Jung warns of—establishing contact with the "collective psyche." And what is my greatest wish now? That when at last I confront an eminent psychoanalyst I may thrash out once and for all this question of false values, of "inflation," as it is called. "To see life steady and to see it whole"—this phrase immediately leaps to my mind. And with it another curious, fleeting thought—will there ever be a psychologist sturdy enough, patient enough, deep and knowing enough, to listen to me when I break the barriers of communication? Will there be enough pens ready to take down what I have to say? Because who knows better than I the paltry, meaningless compromise that art is for me? Why my perpetual wail about "catching up"? Because I am too keenly aware of what living means, of the worlds I traverse in a few minutes, the volumes that pour out of me in one ecstatic mood. And to me it is as though all the rest of life were but grist and preparation for these moments, had no other worth or significance. These inspired moments are eternal and immeasurable. They cannot be weighed, judged, or viewed and interpreted psychologically. It is in these moments that things are born which re-create the world, which shake and unmake psychologies. Just as Spengler described so marvelously the evolution, or appearance, of the science of physics as "an incident" in the diluvian era of the history of the earth's crust, so I see psychology, as we know it today, as a transitory, immanent phenomenon among the other sciences which the artist can shatter with a single breath if he but blows hard enough.

Because the great question is forever one of personality—power, individual value, force. The rest is schematizing, explanation, system, cause and effect, interpretation. In some there is the sense of destiny, and these, who are one with destiny, have no need of psychology—or of any -isms, cults, theories, etc. There are those who *make* the world.

Oh, God, how the reel runs loose: I see a broken glass on the floor, with a big stain of Anjou, Anjou on my black satin dress, and my opening white legs. Henry sitting like a sage on an armchair before the fire and covering my face with moth kisses. I am sewing a button on his pants. He is lying in my stately bed, copying out passages from Spengler—his color is Chinese blue. He is romantic about women, yet he rises in the morning and writes his friend Emil Schnellock that what occupies him most of the time is "taking his pants down." He observes my face one evening and swears that at that moment I look Egyptian, dark, invulnerable, unyielding—with glazed eyes. Another time, at dinner, he says he has never known anything as wonderful with a woman as this life of ours. He takes Banco out for a walk. I defend psychoanalysis and furnish him with new resistances, new ideas to combat; and sometimes he plagiarizes, as I plagiarize him. He wants to become an analyst to earn his living.

One evening Fred came, and Henry and I had been living so intensely together we didn't know how to talk to Fred. The evening dragged. We had lost contact with the whole world, having been so absorbed in each other and in our ideas and our work. Fred urged us to get married. He wants us both in Clichy. This talk about our marriage was incredible to me. At this point my imagination stops. I do not want to face the problem. Henry thought it was only a financial problem—was telling Fred how we had to wait until his books were published. But then I said that was only half the problem—I have my *human* problem, an insolvable one which Henry understands. He would never have abandoned June, and he knows I cannot abandon Hugh—that, like him, I wait for the other to do something, I wait for something to happen. I could never deal that deathblow to Hugh, however much is at stake; and now I know my whole life is at stake, for I desire a life with Henry at the cost of whatever suffering or precariousness, instability. These well-rounded days have been a revelation for me. It is the wealth of Henry both as an artist and a man, as a mind and as a sensualist, that I have been so hungry for, so hungry that I see my past twenty or thirty years of life (since I was born!) as the years of famine! Abnormal appetite? Perhaps!

And now the ten days close. I lie in bed preparing myself for tomorrow. Hugh has been delayed a day, so I have a night and a day to prepare myself for my new role. Other times the transition has been too violent. Tonight I have the feeling of being a traveler. I am journeying, I am journeying, on land and sea, away from Henry, toward Hugh. I close doors upon Henry. He is to recede. He is in Clichy. And as my writing creates this distance, this black night in between miles of earth and miles of water, my *déchirement* is more and more terrible, as if Henry were the very sap in me ebbing away—I think of a forest of trees slit open and the sap running down into cups. Bring a thousand cups! Pages—the pages culling my yearning for Henry! My memories. I have *no vision of the future*. I look on the hostile face of tomorrow. Hugh! The stranger, the stranger I married when I was so young, the brother. And because I am one of those "historical romantics" conscious of destiny, of the past, the past is more *potent*, and I cannot move, I cannot destroy, even if it means destroying one human being for the sake of two artists! Tonight I'm terrified of my own *inexorable goodness. I do not live for myself*. I am paralyzed and sacrificial—I stand on the threshold always—always—and it is only the *ideal* which stifles me.

What frightens me is that Henry needs a home, a wife, a woman always there. Henry, deep down, is also in need of a private, intimate, secret, two-beinged world from which to draw strength for creation and living. Tonight I am a great Mother—womb, house, and bed; glow, warmth, light, and fire; courage and passion; and food—I am all these. And what I cannot bear is to let Henry return alone to Clichy.

I work, and every moment I imagine a life with Henry as repudiation of all things but art and passion—class, society life, comfort, refinement, hell, hell, hell. It is all empty—*all* but these ten days, a desk, books, a typewriter, a bed, ordinary food. I hate lies, double lives, continuous insincerity, shifting, transition, deceits. I want wholeness, wholeness with Henry! I need absolutism. I hate this wise intellectual floating over life, this balancing, this keeping up of many lives and loves, this living on three or four levels.

JANUARY 5, 1933

HUGH AND [HIS SISTER] ETHEL ARRIVE. I AM plunged into a new life—*dépaysée* at first. Scene with Hugh of love as in a play. Renewed contact, or rather, new contact with Ethel interesting. But I have outgrown entirely my first interest in her. When I saw her I realized how much I have lived through in a year—centuries. I feel old.

Evening at the Millners', admirers of my book. Showers of compliments. They are Russian. Think I look Russian, with deep, sad Russian eyes. That I look like George Sand. He is writing three volumes on Spinoza. Dinner at the Majestic, Boule Blanche, La Coupole. When I come home I vomit—the compliments I have received I rejected because I didn't want to shine before Ethel—I wanted to efface myself and let her triumph. Sense of guilt!

I'm also ashamed to see Allendy. Don't know what to say to him or what to do. Life with Henry has been a dream. I feel splintered, blurred—floating. I want again to reintegrate myself by work. I suffer from this feeling that I travel too much, that people change too quickly before my eyes like shifting panoramas from a fast express train—that I am rushing along surfaces, that I am thirsty for depths. I am not a very successful extrovert. I am *dépaysée* in extrovert life—I lose my soul, my dreams. I would like to lie at the bottom of the sea, live there *au fond des choses, toujours au fond.*

Last night I missed June. June is the only woman I will ever love in the manner I loved June, fantastically, erotically, literarily, imaginatively—the only woman who has deeply stirred me as an artist, who makes all others pale and lifeless. I miss her. I miss her.

J A N U A R Y 6 , 1 9 3 3

*H*ENRY, HENRY. I MISS HIM. WHEN HE TELEPHONES me I dissolve in yearning. He has been sick. I can only see him on Sunday for a few hours. He says, "Can't you stay for the evening? It has been a long time"—six days. It is the first time Henry *asks*, demands. Immediately I know I would take all risks to *answer* his demand.

Ethel and I can talk frankly—about the past—John, June, but no more. At Henry I stop. I talk a great deal to her, because she needs to understand herself. She is unconsciously trying to charm me. But I'm not interested in Ethel. And it is the new me who demands too much now in people—who gives herself less uncritically! I owe this to Allendy.

When I impulsively lie close to Hugh and tell him I love him, it is because I am moved by regret and an obscure sense of guilt—pity. I would like to find faults in him, to be able to hate him, but he has no faults. He holds me by my sense of guilt, of responsibility, my incapacity to inflict pain. Why has Allendy not realized that he should have assented, condoned my separation from Hugh? Why has he not realized Henry is my husband? Allendy has been blinded by his personal interest.

I saw Henry one night, and he received me by immediately throwing me on his bed. I had the impression of sadness at my *visiting him*, feeling cheated of the great joys of fusion, distressed by the ephemeral contact. Then Henry left for a few days' trip with Fred, and I went to see Allendy.

Allendy had been thinking that he had not enough to give me—that a woman like me needed absolutes—that he was imprisoned in his own life and not free to give me enough. But meanwhile, I, with my usual lack of confidence, was beginning to think he didn't love me enough! This lack of faith Allendy is fighting desperately. He feels that he has failed as an analyst by giving way to his attraction for me before the end of the analysis (before he had weaned me from him).

At this moment I realized that I had wickedly enjoyed this very victory, defeating the analyst and disturbing the man—that I had wanted this, my gentle revenge on a man on whom I depend too greatly for my happiness! However, I never make a cruel use of my victory. I am so touched by Allendy's vulnerability.

For a moment I fear this new life of triumphs over men in which I am beginning to discard, to abandon, to betray, to hurt. I began by abandoning Hugh, Eduardo, now Allendy. My God, I can't bear this. Allendy the noble, the heroic. Too civilized a man. Why didn't he take me in his arms when I was under his spell and let wisdom go to hell, have me, know me, even if it all leads to tragedy?

Henry returns, and we have such a scene of passion in the kitchen, he is so aroused. And I am so drunk still, so full of the devil that Henry observes a difference and says, "You are more natural."

I feel that if I can give up Allendy I will give up the last of the idealists, the heroes that I have loved; that from now on I am an unfettered being—that this may be either my salvation or my death!

Henry and I both have this terrifying faculty of immersing ourselves in an atmosphere to the extent of forgetting ourselves and our love. I in the Tyrol, where Henry became unreal to me, and while Henry was in Luxembourg I became "unreal," incredible, he could not believe he knew a woman called Anaïs. He looked at me last night when I arrived as I looked at him after I spent an hour with Allendy—estranged. Is this the ultimate fickleness, the susceptibility to the moment which is called weakness?

JANUARY 17, 1933

*L*AST NIGHT I BEGAN TO TALK FEVERISHLY ABOUT wanting children—a *human* creation. I have been dreaming of carrying Henry's *head in my womb*. Louise's eldest daughter (five years old) threw her arms around my neck impulsively. This aroused a chaos of feeling in me. The strongly *protective* maternal instinct in me is frustrated. I broke into sobs. Hugh was flabbergasted.

When Henry telephones me, wants to see me, the world begins to sing again, the chaos crystallizes into one desire—all the heavings, fermentations, constellations are soldered by the rich sound of his voice.

I run upstairs in my kimono and add five pages to the dream book. I obey only instinct, senses, and they are subjugated by Henry. I am afloat again. Children. What are children? Abdication before life. Here, little one, I transmit a life to you of which I have made a superb failure. No. No. What a female I am! Even children. I must have been tired last night. *Allons donc.* Pull yourself together, you fake artist, you.

Even when I possess *all*—love, devotion, a match, Henry, Hugh, Allendy—I still feel myself possessed by a great demon of restlessness driving me on and on. I am rushing on, I am going to cause suffering, nobody can enchain me, I am a force, and all day I feel pushed, pushed. I cover pages and pages with my fever, with this superabundance of ecstasy, and it is not enough. I pace up and down the cave. I have Henry, and I am still hungry, still searching, still moving—I cannot stop moving. Allendy will be a lucky man to escape real pain from me. His wisdom has saved him *from a woman he does not know*—the woman with sudden destructive impulses—sudden outbreaks. He knows the beautiful me, not the dangerous me. Only Henry senses the monster, because he too is possessed. I too will leave a scar upon the world.

Analysis has only awakened me, awakened a monster full of unreliable dangerous power. I am only beginning—I am like a wheel just beginning to turn. My own strength kills me! Chokes me!

> *Note to Henry:*   Answer to the riddle! Hugh is hostile or anxious because he is not *sure* of me—so he is suspicious of my writing. He would destroy this *joy* whose source he suspects. As you would destroy June's joys because you suspect their origin. You and I, though no less jealous, are more *sure* of each other—more aware of our possession of each other. Being aware, we can afford to be very generous, very tolerant, very lenient! We are sure of the core. When one fights, one fights one's fears and one attacks windmills, as you attacked June's apparently harmless stories, as Hugh suspects my writing, my stories . . .

Talking about why Hugh throws cold water on my writing. Henry threw cold water on June's stories of her daily exploits. Why do Henry and I never do that to each other—never fight? I joked about his name, *Henry*. Said he ought to be called Otto. Told him about aristocrats calling each other by diminutives—silly ones, Lulu, Pompon, Lolo, *affecting* informality and simplicity.

Hugh last night, when I read to him from my dream book, was intent on discovering whether or not I had slept with June, rather than affected by the tone or lyrism of my *work*.

The other day, Hugh took me to a hotel room to fuck me—playing at an adventure. "You whore, you, you whore." He loved the strangeness of it, and for a moment as I touched his body it seemed like a stranger's body—but it was a joyless game for me. I'm physically obsessed by Henry. I'm afraid I'm a faithful female, all in all!

I'm becoming bad! I tell Hugh cajolingly, "Do Henry's horoscope, to see how it doesn't harmonize with mine!" And I am still wet from

Henry's caresses. I laugh. I laugh, too, when Henry says, "It is Hugh's tenacity which makes his grip on things boring. He has a good mind, but it is not flexible enough, not sensitive, changeable—Hugh takes up a subject and it loses its fluidity, its livingness." That is true. In Henry and me there is a shiftiness—a quick movement, awareness of the feelings of others. Often I am aware of Hugh's tenacity in company and aware of their dying interest—it is then I interrupt him. *"J'ai été mechante souvent; je ne m'en repens pas."* I believe that from now on my journal will become more interesting. I feel that Henry gives me the necessary latitude.

I suspect that I am most of the time in a *dream state*. That what I see in life, during the day, are the composite personages Freud mentions. The man who has a voice like John's and the Russian painter who has heavy-lidded eyes like John's, they cease for me to be themselves, and I am launched into a hypnotic state in which I seek to experience again the emotions I felt when I heard John's voice or saw his eyes on me. I do not treat the resemblance as a mere resemblance, but I submit to the composite personage who stirs me in my dream life. Yet John himself, in reality, has completely ceased to exist for me. So, obviously, I am continuing a series of sensations as one does in dreams, irrelevantly, fantastically, incongruously—carrying still regions of profound susceptibility to impressions and emotions I have long ago outgrown—with the peculiar sensitivity of the regions of the body which bear a scar. Exactly as when Henry caresses my buttocks I experience vividly my first impressions of sexual pleasure: I was nine years old, and with four or five children, little neighbors in Uccle, I was shut up in a dark porch and we decided to show each other our behinds. The little boy's hand on mine—the first quiver of sensual mystery.

André de Vilmorin says over the telephone, rigidly, like a marquis, *"Je vous présente mes hommages, madame."* And immediately I regret Clichy, the kitchen, Henry in his shirtsleeves . . . and I realize that I stand before each new person, each new world, hesitant, unsure, hating the passing from one person to another, hating the very adventure I bellow for on restless nights—and it is all because of a lack of courage.

Fear, lack of confidence, has narrowed down my world, limited the people I have known intimately—the difficulty of communication. Who is he? What is he? Politeness is like a shield. Culture is a shield. We love our love because it is *our* love, because it is ours.

Daydream of renewing the process of psychoanalysis again—with Rank, perhaps—to see if I can complete my half-born confidence. Sublimation just now is impossible for me. I am in full movement, voracious, desperate, whole, and I cannot sublimate. I cannot receive from Allendy any more analytical direction. I only want kisses from him. I have thought about him all day, have wanted to telephone him, write him. Was awake last night—formulating letters, planning scenes, lies!

Dream: my hair turns white.

JANUARY 19, 1933

GAIETY LAST NIGHT AT THE POISSON D'OR—IRrepressible, ebullient. Gaiety; high, high mood. Drunk with the unusual effect I create. The chief of the gypsies singles me out and asks me to dance.

Hugh awoke me in the middle of the night with his sobs. He was dreaming. I kissed him, awaking him tenderly: "I was dreaming that the gypsy had taken you away!"

I wish I could get rid of my preoccupation with my triumphs— my childish pleasures! It is too much for me; it turns my head after so much sorrow and so much solitude!

Saturday evening. Last night Hugh discovers that astrologically he and I are only bound by mystical, Neptunian ties, and that I am bound to Henry by the strongest sign that can exist between husband and wife! I laugh at the discovery, but I am overwhelmed. I knew my destiny.

What will Allendy feel tonight when he discovers I am astrologically bound to Henry by the strongest ties—my moon in his seventh house?

The riddle of destiny. Allendy once said, "You seek weak men." He was going to heal me so that I could love strength. It is written now in heaven that I am Henry's wife. I remember the desolate nights of brooding on Henry's weaknesses, of rebellion against his weakness. *Ce soir j'ai peur—je me sens faible—j'ai besoin de protection*. If Allendy could hold me very tight and help me fight my destiny—conquer it, escape it. My fate.

Tonight I see a troubled life, danger, pain with Henry. I feel the earth quaking—everything toppling. I called out for adventure! *La voici*.

Henry strong—ah, then what a life that would be—what splendor! What a conflagration!

Allendy says I'm the most marvelous woman he has ever known. He used superlatives! He explained his horoscope with his arm around my waist, his hand on my knees, under my dress. And we kissed as we talked, while I marveled at the fears in human beings—their mysterious weaknesses. Allendy never happy with a woman. Confessing that whenever he saw me he was upset, unbalanced, he could not talk as he wanted to. He had not the courage to surrender me, and yet as an analyst he was aware of the insufficiencies, deficiencies in his nature which would hurt me. "It is a malady in me, perhaps, but I have never been a passionate man, never knew anything but tenderness for women."

Well, it is almost humorous. Eduardo and Hugh going to Allendy to cure themselves of passivity. Didn't I suspect Allendy several times? The feeling between Eduardo and Allendy?

However, I am going to piece my Osiris out of fragments whenever I find them. I want Allendy now no longer as a trophy but as a man for whom I experience, blindly, a powerful attraction—the type of man who has haunted me all my life, whom my masculine side courts:

half men. And I feel a strange faith in Allendy. I believe in his sensuality (but, oh, didn't I believe also in John's sensuality?).

He didn't want me to base all my hopes on him. He thought I was relying on him for my whole life's happiness. No. I have learned that I am two distinct persons—one of them in love with mystical men and one with earthy, fiery, martial men. And so tonight I again accept the split, the sundering, and I let the double currents flow. In Allendy, I love Eduardo and Hugh fraternally—in Henry, the lover, the insatiable lover and fecundator.

I accept division within myself because nobody will be cheated—I have enough love for all!

Allendy says I am *not* connected with Henry astrologically.

Last night I concealed Henry in the guest room. When Hugh came home at midnight he found me writing in my journal. This morning Henry is sleeping, and I am thinking of Allendy. These men whose femininity makes them passive and elusive arouse me to distraction. I am reconciled to playing the stronger role. Allendy wants me to telephone him, to write him, to be active, exactly as Hugo, Eduardo, and Henry like me to be. Henry is distressed when I don't take the lead. Very well. I accept this role which my femininity hates. What is timorous and delicate and yielding in them arouses my strength—tantalizes me. I am fated to be the *lover*—I—what a tragic fate.

Allendy talked about the veil between himself and reality—and pleasure. Never could enjoy life—all blurred—until a few years ago, when he began to see colors.

Henry is sitting at the black Chinese table, working, revising his novel. I see so clearly now the aim, mood, temper of his work that I am able to help him alter it, cut it, change the order of chapters, and we are constantly creating together.

Henry thinks of nothing but work and me. No more whores, no more vagabondage. He says the fact that I let him free, that I never infringe on his liberty, never oppose the little whores, never tyrannize or even ask questions, makes him absolutely faithful, aware of a deep responsibility, glad that he has a ballast in our love—too easy for him to run wild—and now he enjoys his deepest life. The first half of his novel is all incident (before our love). The second is all exaltation, ecstasy, penetration, significance.

I can never say enough about the influence we have had on each other—I on the artistry of Henry's work, he on the matter, substance, vitality of mine. He has given me the impetus, and I gave him the depths. And how obstinate I am—merciless on his childish rantings.

I live in terror that my journal should be discovered. Henry is still here (Hugh went out the night before and last night—by the time he comes home, Henry is locked in the guest room—and we have had two days together).

At night when Hugh came home, I was already asleep when he tried to awaken me with his desire. In a state of semiconsciousness, I repulsed him violently. And in the morning he was hurt—he asked for explanations (Henry! Henry! My love, my passion, Henry!). I invented a nightmare! I said I had been dreaming that he was sticking a knife between my legs—that the pain in the dream made me fight him off—that I wished he had awakened me—that I was suffering.

The painful effect of this scene I have been trying ever since to erase—yet when he approached me last night I became hysterical— laughing—and I wounded him again. There is a limit to my pretenses—a moment when my nerves betray me! Oh, God, what is going to become of him? Henry is constantly thinking of the day his book begins to sell so that we can get married.

It doesn't frighten me that Henry's sensuality will inevitably make him faithless. That is only an excursion, an incident, a phase. I have no fear, even though I may suffer from jealousy, because I know he belongs to me, and do I not also deceive him? Don't I see that my feeling for Allendy is only *un petit détour*? That I belong to Henry as I have never belonged to anyone, by vital, fiery, and creative and intellectual ties?

It is Henry who has poured blood, muscles, organs, glands into the legendary me, who has fucked the idol into a human being. In other journals, I am a *linotte*, a ghost, a faun, a princess, a spirit, a creator, but until Henry's blood flowed generously through me I was not human. Hugh used to dissertate on humanness, beg me to sprout roots—but the miracle was only accomplished by blood and joy.

I received from Allendy a deeply needed religious absolution for my past. I feel now that I stand at the point where I dare to live my own life (faithfulness to Henry) in spite of all his wisdom, warnings, pleadings, teachings, and personal power over me. I will not believe that my passion for Henry is merely physical passion and desire. Yet I tremble and I feel that the proximity of Henry's hatred and warring spirit has aroused echoes in me and that I am suddenly flooded by a great hatred of idealists, a great desire to destroy idealism, to wound the world which has wounded both of us—to ally myself with Henry, to unleash the instinctive, passionate forces of the world—against the mystic who has distilled and controlled these forces, not so much because of his idealism, but because of his composition of being, which fitted him for sublimation. I do not feel suited to this total mysticism. I am between two worlds, always between two worlds.

Enough, enough egoistic maledictions! "Only when one is liberated from one's ego does one begin to love," I wrote Allendy. Enough egoistical pains!

I realize fully, and with cruel lucidity, that my analysis is not finished, that I am trying to get well by a great effort of *will* and a kind of love for Allendy which makes me want desperately that he should be victorious as an analyst and as a man, for I realize that if he fails with me, his emotional life will be destroyed by fear and his doctor's pride hurt by his own weakness. For his weakness before me, as a woman, I love him—I don't want him to have to repent his élan, his forgetting of himself. I want to give *him* confidence and a happiness he has not had. But, oh, there are moments when I feel the precariousness of my equilibrium, the fragility of it—when my hypersensitivity seems unbearable, when I oscillate between the desires to become a bloody anarchist or a saint—when I know that very little happiness in love will be granted me. Those terrible letters of Eduardo, and my fight against my overardent nature, in 1921! The cruel hesitations of Hugo: "I feel that I do not love you enough yet"—the night of our first kiss! Henry's old doubts: "This vivacious feeling you expect, I could never give to a woman!" Yet they love me, for years, jealously, tenaciously. And I, who rail, rave, and commit various forms of suicide for each circumstance, I deceive them all! At once. In the end I am coming to believe that within their capacities they have all loved me sincerely. When Eduardo thought I was weeping over him and he was in one of his devoted moods, I was already in love with Hugo. While Hugo wrote me belated but ardent letters from Europe, I was already galvanized by Ramiro Collazo. John, well, John I tried to replace by Eduardo, and when Eduardo's love reached its climax, I was Henry's worshipful mistress. By the time Henry is absolutely sure he cannot live without me, I am seducing Allendy, whose whole love I want, although I am deceiving him with Henry. Is it that they have all been just a little slow and that I want to punish them a little for it?

Too much thinking. At bottom I'm greatly confused and lost by the diversity and multiplicity of my feelings.

I'm amused by the fact that the only way I can get rid of my neurotic broodings on my loves is by beginning to ask myself how *well* (or faithfully!) I love, and by dwelling on my trickeries! Then I can laugh a little and get rid of my suicidal fits!

The most magnificent of all moments is the march toward the catastrophe—the slow accumulation of details and events and people who swell the procession, the progression, in a livid, lurid light, the march of an imperious, inexorable fatalism. I see my whole life always moving in that direction—only a small incident prevents a conflagration. If I had not truly, deeply loved Henry, if he had been nothing but an adventure, if Allendy had succeeded in estranging us, and if I had turned the whole force of my love, hopes, dreams, aspirations toward Allendy—with that terrifying impact my élans have, those strong impulses which break and shatter me—what a catastrophe again! The danger of wholeness! I see that I have learned caution! That despicable measure! I refuse to die again as I died over John, so I am more wary of absolutism. I always leave a loophole, a way of escaping tragedy.

I hate to feel that my incapacity to face the greatest pains of love is making me afraid of absolutism. It is true I had no fear of my absolute love for Henry, yet even then I was counting on Allendy's *paternal* care of me, and I turned toward him the day June returned, during my panic.

My God, what a morbid vulnerability. Trickiness and deception are my defense against a treacherous life too tragic and too destructive and too terrifying for me.

And the ironic thing is that I owe Allendy this knowledge of how to blunt dangers, elude suicide, escape tragedy.

The effect of Allendy's sexual timidity is more intense on me than the effect of my happiness with Henry is, because it is related back again to the first and ineffaceable pain of my Father's abandonment—of which I am not yet free. I still feel the roots of this pain stirring when any event takes place that can distantly remind me of it. However farfetched is the connection between Allendy's remark "I cannot express myself freely with the woman I love ideally" and the departure of my Father that day, in spite of my hysteria—for me there is a connection in feeling—*la détresse est la même*. However, what I know now is that all those doubts of my Father's love and of all other loves are erroneously based on my distorted, morbid, neurotic fear. That is why I am again stuck—suffering from fixation with the past.

I thought the poet in me masked a ferocious realist. The realism is sexual in particular. I feel this taste of earth more desperately tonight, as a revenge upon the high spheres Allendy is dragging me into—I don't understand myself. I think men like Eduardo, Hugo, John, and Allendy drive normally sexed women to suicide. When I think of the plenitude of my life with Henry, I wonder what deters me from following him anywhere.

Added to my hatred of destroying Mother's security, Hugo's happiness, and Joaquin's love, now there is a fear of hurting Allendy. Oh, God, I'm talking like a fool: What does Henry deserve? Allendy has made a Christian of me again! *C'est impardonnable!*

I rush to my passion, Henry, last night, and we indulge in such an orgiastic fucking that I do not wish to awaken from it. And we laugh together—he says obscene words which I repeat. Afterward, lying in bed, we talk gravely about Dandieu's book on Proust.

Then today, here in Louveciennes: astrology, Huysmans's *À Rebours*, "*Le Théâtre de la cruauté d'Artaud*" (magazine article given to me by Allendy), and kisses, kisses. Henry sits on the chair and I sit on his knees, and it is I who am fucking savagely, and he is in bliss. He carries me up while we are still soldered together, and I'm in a frenzy.

We awake after a short rest and I am not tired. I am blazing with energy. I must be a sexual superwoman who, as Rank has written, is stimulated rather than exhausted by sexual life. My mind is blazing. When Hugo comes home I talk brilliantly, profusely. I write four pages in my book. Everything is clear to me—philosophy, history, metaphysics, psychology, Rank, Dandieu, Proust. It is clear to me now that I am playing tricks not on men but on life, which does not answer what I have demanded of it, and so I accept this juggling and my treacherous handling of life—it is life I bear a grudge against, for its absence of perfection, of completeness, of absolution. I will live my lies bravely and ironically, and dually, triply. In that way alone can I exhaust the love I contain.

I am laughing sadly at the tricks I have had to play on life, the deceits, the lies—to find all its treasures and hold them after so many, so many years of famine. What hunger, oh, my God, what voraciousness! I was cheated once of my Father's love, and I do not want to be cheated again. I had always so much to give! Nobody would want all I have exclusively for himself because it is too much to answer. I have a desire to travel all through the world fulfilling people's dreams— magically, carefully, giving to them the minute and tenderly passionate attentiveness I give to my loves in daily life.

Dream: Thorvald and I are watching a play. The stage is an aquarium, a gigantic reproduction of mine—the actresses slide into the water. Dorothy in a white dress, very lovely, sliding in. In the aquarium they look fragile, like Kay, translucent and transparent, fluid. Thorvald and I (or it may be Joaquin) want to buy liquor. And liquor glasses. I look them over. I want to be given a liquor glass for nothing, but Thorvald is made to pay 180 francs for two big, coarse glasses. I am shocked and furious.

I dream essentially of water and glass—I feel either like a fish swimming in water with very pleasurable sensations, or like I am collecting beautiful glass bottles.

To hell, to hell with balance! I break glasses; I want to *burn,* even if I break myself. I live only for ecstasy. Nothing else affects me. Small doses, moderate loves, all the *demi-teintes*—all these leave me cold. I like extravagance, heat . . . sexuality which bursts the thermometer! I'm neurotic, perverted, destructive, fiery, dangerous—lava, inflammable, unrestrained. I feel like a jungle animal who is escaping captivity. I am also fully aware that this feeling is close to June's *délire de persécution.*

Allendy tells me about the research work I can do for him at the Bibliothèque Nationale.

Coming home in the car I lie back on Hugo's delighted chest with my hat tumbled over one ear, and I talk like a drunkard. Observe the changes in the sky since I was a girl: the progress of electrical advertising—the stars are red, radio-station lights twinkling; and the copper stars, the authentic ones, are being used as automobile headlights. What are we coming to, my God, what times are we living in!

FEBRUARY 4, 1933

*I*T IS THE FIRST TIME IN MY LIFE THAT MY monthly illness cannot affect my mood, drag me down—depress me. It is as if I have at last conquered my body. But my happiness last night was frightening. When Hugo and I came down to bed I lay on the quilt raving like a delirious person—fantasy making—telling him tales, how I would set out in the world uniquely to fulfill everybody's dreams—I felt possessed by magic powers, by magical puissance.

I went to Allendy perched on the pinnacle of my elation. And I realized I don't love him at all—that he is another big, inert, unecstatic load to bear up—color gray—livingness feeble—adventurousness timorous. My élan died completely. I wondered why I was sitting there on his knees, why I was preparing to help him with his books—and he sought out caresses which I yielded quietly.

A passive man's way of possessing a woman is to keep her away from life. Eduardo's jealousy was enormous; he would have liked to kill every man around me. Hugo also holds me in. Allendy would destroy Henry, because Henry is the only man who can win me away from him.

The neurotic is the one who interprets all facts *against* himself. For example, June thought Henry and I had concealed our relations from her to make a laughingstock of her, instead of understanding it was out of feeling for her. Allendy himself thinks I chose Henry (his antithesis) as a reproach to Allendy's sublimated life. Henry is more than jealous of Allendy, because Allendy's achievements hurt his pride (he is obsessed with comparisons of their output, number of books, etc.).

Today I have finally understood these mental, patient, controlled, Saturnine, cold men I have loved so passionately and consistently. I understand their way of loving. I can achieve with them an affectionate, fraternal relationship, and with the others a passionate one. *Tout va bien.* I have come to terms with life, the relativity of love.

When things get dark, I will take whiskey! But I'm happy.

I am late for Allendy. I leap up like a gay little whore while Henry is lying down, and I ask him what black magic he has practiced on me (he is so jealous of Allendy's magic!). As I walk out it is soft, it is spring, like the first time I walked out of the Hôtel Cronstad to buy bread and wine around the corner. I live so fast now that the seasons surprise me. Spring is on me—unexpected, intoxicating. I used to sit and wait for it, and now it rapes me; it catches me with my dress unbuttoned, my hair wild, running for a taxi, late for my engagements! In the taxi I am in such a disorder that I imagine myself still in Henry's arms and imagine so ardently that I experience a second orgasm and lie back panting while the taxi drives into spring.

When I came home I gave Hugo a kiss which elated him—a kiss of gratefulness.

How clearly I see the darkening, stifling influence of Saturn (on Hugo, Eduardo, a little on Henry—not on me), and I defeat Saturn by my tremendous luminosity and joy. This is the *book of joy*, of a *luminosity* I am eager to shed uncalculatingly—the titles I wrote, the subtitles of "Schizoidie" and "Paranoia" refer to my feeling that life has played tricks on me (a metaphysically incorrect statement, because I believe in the *fatalité intérieure*) and to my quadruplicities in love. To talk about life playing tricks is to be like the wife who enumerates her husband's shortcomings to justify her lovers, since I feel I am playing tricks on life and men!

I don't believe I was *born* melancholic, but that I became so by an accident, that for the moment at least I am fruitful, abundant, a joyous Venus.

I awake with the word War on my lips. War. I feel that Henry's Mars has fired mine, that the ignition will cause explosions, fires, earthquakes.

In order not to destroy, I decide to leave my home and Hugo for a week. I am pretending to be leaving for Holland with Natasha, and a week from today I will be with Henry.

Unconsciously I am—or rather, my unconscious is—in great rebellion. That is the meaning of my glass breaking. Last night, while Hugo was doing astrology I got drunk on whiskey, which I took because I am racked by neuralgia. I fell from the couch to the floor, as June did; I raved, I asked Hugo to get me my *heart back*, I laughed and cried, sobbed. Deep down I was aware of my drunkenness. I had no control over my gestures, my equilibrium, or my utterances, yet I knew I was *being* June. I made wild gestures—I knew the sob and laughter were like June's. Hugo let me lie on the black rug in front of the fire. He was angry; he is terribly afraid of what he calls my exaltation. I lay there feeling that I was still falling, but I wanted to fall, to roll in defamation, degradation—I wanted desperately to drown, to insult, to spit, to vomit the idealism which kills me. I wanted to destroy the soul which haunts me at night, the damned soul which makes me love these soulful men with feeble sex!

It is good that with Allendy's own help I could at last turn my back on that type. But I remain haunted by a gigantic dissatisfaction. Because I am aware that the others will always disturb me, distress me, as if I had hurt or turned my back on my own soul, a half of me.

This imperfection, this enigma, this oscillation in life, is what moves me to great bitterness, stupendous rebellion, dark anger. Anger against myself that I should be so attracted, so held, so spellbound by the men who have no physical power over me, no physical power to conquer me.

FEBRUARY 14, 1933

ALLENDY'S FINAL AND STUPENDOUS VICTORY, THE analyst's triumph. With all my *will*, my mind, I wanted to understand—but I did not until today. It is all so very simple. A phrase of his unleashed the illumination: *"Pour moi les* gestes *ne comptent pas."* A simple phrase: Gestures.

Gestures don't count.

The sexual gesture I demanded from Eduardo as a proof of his love. My need of gestures. My glorying in June's ardent demonstrativeness. My storm of rebellion when Allendy, in *spite* of his love, would not make the final gesture. My resentment against John. My need, my need of gestures. Situation aggravated by the fact that I am an unusually expressive, demonstrative being, that I exteriorize constantly, that every feeling I have has instantaneously a form, an expression—so that by comparison Eduardo, Hugo, and Allendy seemed inert. But the need of gestures came from absence of confidence.

If I could have realized in time that Eduardo loved me, Hugo loved me, and Allendy, too—in fact, all of them more deeply than Henry ever has loved—I could not have been offended by the absence of gestures. Henry blessed me with gestures . . . yet I always knew that Henry's love was less deep. Allendy, knowing that this is *exactly what I would not accept*—that to satisfy myself I had to possess the man body and soul—that I would not listen to any reason, compromise, deficiency, neurosis which made fusion impossible—that my *possessiveness* was tremendous in proportion to my fear of abandon— struggled to impose this realization in me so that I could at last rid myself of *pain*.

It became clear to me how desperately I had sought to *possess* Allendy *wholly,* as a trophy, whereas what I want is a father, a friend. How he sensed all this, fought it, effaced himself to cure me. Today the power of his will and the keenness of his intuition amazed me— because I did seduce him, enchant him; he did tremble in my presence, waver in his talks to me—and he triumphed superbly.

It was when I left him that I realized everything, walking the streets, lost, talking to myself. Gestures! Certainly I had gained in confidence, yes, but I still wanted gestures, trophies, victories.

Now I run over the entire course of my life, choosing the salient points and discovering events I had never realized: The day my Father was about to beat me, after beating my two brothers, and because of the look on my face, the hysterical, unbearable, humiliated grief, he left me alone, almost tenderly—actually moved; the day he brought me a compass when I was ill and came to work in his room. His letters from France, when I was in New York: *"Ma jolie!"* As against this I have no more terror of his coldness, his sadism, his unspeakable cruelties, his cynicism.

Eduardo's lifelong devotion, timid, rare, difficult—his letters.

Allendy's words: "I want to give you more than Eduardo, more than Hugo. Eduardo has those cold narcissistic crises. Hugo—well, Hugo I don't know. Hugo has been helped by you and by me to come out of his chaos and vagueness—but I can see he is not sufficient."

When Allendy mentions the word *guilt*, I laugh because the scene which flashes through my mind is of the night before. Hugo brought home to dinner two "magnates." I coughed severely and hysterically for three days and used that as a pretext not to go out with them. They had barely driven away when I opened the door to Henry. He presented me with his gift, and I forgot my cough and I served him some of the squab left from dinner, some of the finest wine, dancing around him, making fun of the magnates, giving him one of the expensive cigars—enjoying, enjoying his eating, his smoking, as if I were doing it. Take, take everything! A feast of joy.

Then I install Henry in the guest room at midnight and while I am waiting for Hugo I lie in Henry's bed, and he is scandalized by my recklessness. When I hear Hugo opening the gate I leave, but not before kissing Henry good-night, which again frightens him so much that he dreams that Hugo catches us and begins to choke me and beat me and that although Henry rushes to my rescue he is aware that Hugo is only doing a morally *just* thing! My temerity reawakens in Henry the honest Protestant moral German that June used to complain about! When he told me this dream in the morning I laughed.

Just as jealousy obsessed Proust, I have been obsessed by the *potentialities*, the mysteries of unflowered lives, of the secret obscurities and heavy, inert weight of Saturn! And just as the eternally recurrent pain of jealousy aroused Proust to paroxysms of illumination, analysis, research, this pain of recurrent difficulty of bringing my half-alive men out of their caverns has aroused in me paroxysms of fury, despair, and tenacity. The desire to illumine chaos; to create out of chaos; to lift masses; to tackle mysteries, elusiveness, inertia; to arouse and conquer *passivity*—all this has caused me my greatest pain and my greatest joys. It has killed me and yet fascinated my intelligence and my imagination. The potentialities in John! In Eduardo! In Henry, too, who is so much my creation. Love, passion, and creation gush from me simultaneously. I must perfume the mouth I kiss; I must be dazzled by the man I worship; I am Pygmalion always awaiting miracles! The mysterious, narcissistic disappearances of Eduardo; the mysterious silences of Hugo; the mysterious evasion of depths in John; and the promises of sensuality, the covered and attenuated sensuality, in Allendy. I walk like a lamp-lighter; I push ships into the open sea, I unearth precious objects; I rub the patina off dark paintings; I tune, attune, bring forth, mold, bring out, ignite, support, sustain, inspire; I plant seeds; I search caverns; I decipher hieroglyphs; I read the eyes of people—alone—alone in my activity. Mars in blood-red gown and steel bracelet and necklace.

FEBRUARY 18, 1933

SUMPTUOUS DINNER AT THE ALLENDYS'—MRS. Allendy heavy, earth-formed, active, intelli-gent, martial, dominant. Allendy with a secret, pearly laughter like Eduardo's—stooping—head in his shoulders like a bull. *I cannot bear to look into his eyes.* I am dazzled. I am afraid everybody will see how much I love him. He has remembered that I smoke Sultane cigarettes. He has the eyes of a child who is being told fairy tales. He does not talk very much. He is nervous. Mrs. Allendy talks well, and so does Mr. Bernard Steele the editor. Hugo looks as of old, inert, crushed—a regression to his former state. No ecstasy. No ecstasy. None in Allendy either. No nerves, no bristling, no floating, no madness.

To my surprise, I am witty, malicious, piquant. But I cannot talk to Allendy, because I have such a mad impulse to kiss his long-lashed eyes and his woman's mouth.

It is as if I were still sitting beside my brothers, telling them stories. I take him away from his organized, railroad-tracked life. He is afraid of my eyes. His hand trembles when he lights my cigarette, and he gives me an ashtray as if I were an imperious and impatient queen. I am so afraid of my love for him that I turn toward Mrs. Allendy and charm her by understanding her great contribution to the ascension of Allendy, her secret contribution without glow or form or beauty (the tyranny of a household mechanism!), without a face, without illusion—the mere nourishment—this nourishment which I would love to be for Henry.

I wrote to Eduardo my first truly forgiving letter: "*Mon petit frère chéri . . .*"

I feel inexhaustible! Tonight I will love my Henry. I would like to be his wife, to have a home with him, to make him supremely happy; we would forgive each other our little infatuations for others; we would work and read together, have informal, bohemian but exquisite banquets, be surrounded by Eugène Jolas, Otto Rank, little whores. Work, work with that ecstasy in both of us which is great enough to shatter the world.

I see in my red-faced Mother and in naughty Louise caricatures of my strength, and I forget that mine is concealed behind delicacy and tact, and wrapped in softness so much that the effect of it is the opposite of the effect of Mother's combativeness and Louise's tyranny—instead of antagonizing, I charm; instead of angering, I melt others. This fear of my force has always prevented me from shining, from bursts of brilliancy, except at rare moments. Last night I was also uneasy. I was afraid I might eclipse Mrs. A. I was so glad to feel her the more dominant. I was afraid Hugo would feel inferior (and, unfortunately, he did; he was treated as the "financier"). I was afraid to talk to Steele about books Allendy did not know.

Hugo generously analyzed me this morning and said my spiritedness and impudence were unexpected, like those of a child, charming, amusing.

We are lying softly together and I am telling Henry what I wrote about wanting to be for him what Mrs. Allendy has been for René. Henry says, "When you talk like that you make me weep, Anaïs." And he is tremendously upset. Later he says, "You are a wonderful, wonderful woman."

He says: "I feel jubilant tonight!"

As I rode in the taxi on my way to meet Hugo, I was in ecstasy.

I found Hugo studying astrology and disappointed in his exploration of the Moulin Rouge apache museum and dance hall.

Allendy was very contented with the evening—jealous of Mrs. Allendy's admiration of me. He loves the aquarium I brought him and will place it by his bed—to be the last thing he will see before falling asleep. I have seen his bed—a sober Empire-style divan placed in an alcove—and I like to imagine his eyes on that beautiful, twinkling, multicolored crystal Atlantis.

It is easy to oscillate between Henry and René—to remain receptive and merely responsive, passive, letting the rhythm of tides move me. Not desiring Allendy—men, objects—but receiving: patient, female, unquestioning, undriven, and no longer unsettled by neurotic fixations, the strained hold upon life, the duel with difficulties, the forcing of destiny, impotent rages, sterile, masochistic pursuits.

Calm. Joy. Contentment by understanding. *Je ne veux plus rien.* And I smile a little, like a weary mother on whom her multiple children have played so many pranks. I feel the all-mother—womb and earth with enormous protective wings! Passion and motherhood fused—the mother as night, covering the world, blanketing it, lulling its pains. And as the night, I am lonely again—active, independent, restless. Hugo sleeps on his security, Henry works in the hammock of my passion; Allendy sleeps on the down of dream marriages; Eduardo sleeps on the warmth of my letter. *Je suis suprêmement heureuse.* I am the night who watches them through curtained windows with very wide-open eyes.

In the morning I awake singing because I know they have all slept profoundly, lulled by the lies I have told them, beautiful lies always, necessary, creative, the fairy tales!

Lies: To explain to Henry why I could not spend this week with him. Inventions. Color. Drama. To explain to Allendy why I still go out one evening a week. Lies to Fred to attenuate effect of Henry's furious cruelties because Fred steals a kiss now and then. "I love you like a brother," which is not true. Fred's sensitivity is like a barometer, but it has the depth of a feather.

Lies to conceal from the world my struggles against bad health. As I am often too tired to last through a day, I invent activities while I run home to take a sunbath. Lies about the source of the income I give Henry out of extreme sacrifices, because a job is more attractive than the pinching I have to do. And I couldn't keep a job because I haven't the strength. Lies to Hugo to preserve his security. Lies to Emilia. Lies to Joaquin to calm his jealousy. The lies of night nurses, doctors, and Utopians.

The only person I do not lie to is my journal. Yet out of affection even for my journal I sometimes lie by omissions. There are still so many omissions!

What often concerns me are my small but multiple infidelities! Dorothy, softened by Allendy and so expectant of caresses, stirs me, and I am moved by the kiss she gives me. The homosexuals, the pretty young men at Smith's Tea Room, arrest my attention. A face I see in the street I follow for several blocks. Men follow me and it amuses me. Zadkine the sculptor says, "Let us get together some evening. I want to see more of you." I ought to be working, and instead I am thinking of love, like a young girl who is beginning to live.

Because I am beginning to live! With what youthful impatience I await tomorrow and my visit to Allendy. When I think of him, my blood turns.

When I was seventeen and writing so much, sitting near a window and watching the snow fall, why didn't Nietzsche, Henry, June, Allendy, Rank, Spengler—all the Titans—come to me? I was doing so much then to deserve them!

FEBRUARY 21, 1933

MY THIRTIETH BIRTHDAY BEGAN WITH A GIFT FROM Henry, a riotously humorous page on which he has been writing memos to himself like "Steal good books from American Library. Be a Taurus. On cold days paint walls of bedroom *con furia*. Get Anaïs *À Rebours*. Invite Zadkine to dinner." And then he telephones me.

I spend a sweet hour with Allendy.

These last two days I have been sober, a little burdened by the tasks I set myself. *A little aged by my love of agedness.* I myself was old at thirteen, when I first felt the horrors of life and began mothering my brothers. That Allendy has completely given his life to others is a point of resemblance between us. Fundamentally, I am not yet living for myself. What I really want is to abandon Hugo, Mother, Joaquin, Allendy, and Eduardo for Henry and for adventure. And that I will never do. I will not do to others what was done to me, ever!

There is a great continuity in my relations with people—in my devotions, rather. I fight hasty, casual, careless contacts. In this there is no trace of Mars, no love of interruption, war, action—just a patient, subterranean, delicate effort to destroy the solitude of human beings, a concern with details, with completeness. I give to this creation a care I give to no other. It is no wonder my loves and friendship occupy such an inalterable importance in my life.

All this that I recount, *all* the places, people, incidents, become like an adventure, a voyage, when I am lying in Henry's bed with his head on my breast. He is asleep, heavily, peacefully, holding my hand, and I am lying there marveling at my contentment, at my sensation of landing, of reaching the end and object of my activities. It seems to me that I am at home here, and I get frightened. Perhaps Henry does not feel this *finality,* this marriage. Perhaps this is only a phase of his life. But he awakens, and I realize how much he clings to me. Yet life frightens me. I understand Allendy's fears. I still love too much, cling too much. Even by dispersion, my love does not lose its intensity.

Another, and the last, pinnacle of my life: when I discover how much my Father has suffered from my abandon! He loves me then. Gustavo Duran tells me about him: "He is very sensitive, very effeminate, and extremely selfish, of course. Needs to be loved and pampered. He came one day and talked for several hours about the sorrow of having lost his children—said he sometimes rereads your letters—which he adores—cannot understand why you abandoned him—has suffered very much from this."

I say, "Write to him that I will see him when he comes to Paris."

When I came home I looked at the fire and hallucinated. The feeling of an *unbearable* joy came over me, the feeling that I had reached the *end* of life, that by the excess of my pain, the excess of my imaginative expectations, I had made human happiness such a climax that I could not survive it. Twenty-one years of famine, dreaming, renunciations, detachment made realization a dangerous and overwhelming consummation. *All my wishes are being realized.* My joy is so great when I contemplate all I have been given that *I feel prepared for death*. I told Hugo I was like a woman on a deathbed, with all my loved ones around me. Closeness to all. The love of my Father, my Mother, Allendy, Eduardo, Henry, Hugo, Joaquin. Too much, too much for a human being to bear! I am too accustomed to want—I am not accustomed to fulfillment. It kills me. Joy kills me!

Gustavo Duran—physically brother of Eduardo in age, blondness. Only, Gustavo is determined, active, passionate, voluptuous, earthy. He was the pampered, fêted, popular young man whose attractiveness I once commented on. I was attracted to his ruddy, dynamic youthfulness. He to that strange phenomenon: a woman pleasing to look at who can *think*. Joaquin lent him my early journal—and Gustavo was ignited! He can recite pages of it. The other evening, we invited him for Dorothy, but he only paid attention to me. He asked to see me alone. I visited him today. He read to me from his journal—restlessness, dissatisfaction, swings between mysticism and sexuality. Reading Bergson. Gustavo's worldliness used to frighten me. Now I see the hunger, the melancholy. We talked well through a boring banquet at the Godoys'. He is a superb talker, brilliant, egotistical, magnetic. Says that in my early journal I always bordered on sentimentality but was never really guilty of it. The flair of the artist.

The other night I was reading about the sign Scorpio and I said, "It is too bad we don't know anyone born under that sign—it's a fascinating one." As soon as Hugo observed Gustavo's admiration of me he "horoscoped" him. He was born under the sign of Scorpio!

I have seen Nestor de la Torre's paintings. The first modern painter who has excited and stirred me deeply.

I must always make myself believe I am making a sacrifice for somebody. I got cured to make Allendy happy. I don't die when I want to because I won't hurt Hugo. I don't abandon Hugo for the same reason. Human reasons alone restrain me. I do not even believe the things I want are wrong (devoting myself to Henry)—I know they are not wrong. But I guide myself by the pain I may cause others.

At the same time, I see so well by what an infinite amount of trickery I get relatively all I want without hurting anyone. As I wanted to see Gustavo alone and because he also wanted it, I used trickery, lies. At one moment my lie was in danger of being found out—so I invented a better one. And it all works well. I use veritable ingenuity, cleverness. I have recourse to the half lie, which is the best of all because it diverts suspicion. I appear expansive and confiding—never reserved. The conviction that none of my lies are in any way malefic gives me a feeling of security and innocence which glows in my face.

FEBRUARY 25, 1933

SOFTLY I CLOSE THE DOOR UPON THE WORLD. I draw a long mystical bolt. I pull in rustless shutters. Silence. I have imprisoned within myself the admiration of luminous, willful Eduardo; the blood-rhythmed music of Stravinsky; Joaquin's chaste face at the piano; a new understanding of Thorvald, my long-lost brother; thoughts of a "feminine" Father!

How strangely innocent I feel as I wash myself before Henry, dress quickly, powder again, run out and get into the taxi to go to Mother's, to meet Hugo there. I bring my joy like a bouquet to all!

The taxis are my wings. I cannot *wait* for anything. Wonderful to step out of the train at 3:25, to run down the stairs, to ride dreaming through the city, to arrive at Allendy's at 3:35, just when he is about to pull the black curtain. To run to the café and find Henry there. *No art can equal life.* When I slander life it is because I am afraid of my passion for it, its frailty.

Evening. Enchanted hours with Henry. Work. Talk. A long sensual bout. He is dreaming of following me to New York when I go with Hugo. Wants to see his old "cronies," especially Emil Schnellock. As soon as he *wants* something I feel I want to devote my whole life to giving it to him. Often it is something I don't want—for New York means perhaps June and scenes with June. But how I love to see Henry enthusiastic, smiling up to his ears, homesick, eager. That is of supreme importance to me.

Meeting Eduardo yesterday, who went away to escape pain—the pain of his negative life; who can lead an extrovert life away from me and who recaptures his pain as soon as he sees me again—his bondage to pain.

It is I who, having well learned my lesson, point out to him the two ways of interpreting the fact that Allendy did not answer his letter. The neurotic's—that Allendy is neglecting him. This I prove to be untrue. The second, the normal one—that Allendy, feeling he has failed to cure Eduardo, unconsciously is hurt and wants to punish Eduardo a little. This second explanation, the *human* one, is the one Eduardo can accept intellectually. But emotionally he is offended and feels overlooked. My intuition is proved right by the joy Allendy expresses at the sight of Eduardo—a joy which hurts me a little, even.

Eduardo amazed by my unknowing *knowingness* of astrology.

Recurrence last night of my love for Hugo, because he looks a bit battered by life, very *human*, very humanly passionate with me (as Allendy is) . . . and at this moment I love him—the lines on his face, the perspiration on his brow, the burned look in his eyes, his live jealousy of Eduardo, his throbbing sexuality.

I see in Eduardo the green demon of pain slumbering within his English, vegetative, superficial life; this green demon is aroused by my presence, and I become conscious of the war, the upheavals, the pain I bring *together with the life* I bring.

Henry remains at the center of my life and being—fixed—the passion of my life. I am *afraid of the wholeness* of my love for him—afraid to hamper him with it. And thus I spread myself into smaller loves—definitely smaller, like constellations. The axis is Henry, Henry always. Tonight I tried to make literature out of pages I've written about him, and I couldn't—they were too-*alive*, too-human things. I couldn't bear to handle them. It moved me deeply to even think about him, to remember that March 8 is the anniversary of my first visit to his room—*incredible year*. My passion for Henry is like a sun which throws *rays* on the others: Allendy, Hugo, Eduardo, Joaquin, Father.

Phone call from Henry: interview with Otto Rank 100 percent successful. Rank has made a *friend of him*. I sit back in utter contentment. Henry's ascension.

Eduardo said what I called the de Vilmorins applies to me: I'm a *lusty decadent!* I have not a single *earth* sign in my horoscope! Mostly water.

Henry spent an evening with Walter Lowenfels the poet. Talking about Lawrence, Lowenfels said, "Only book on Lawrence worth reading is by a woman with a strange name, Anaïs. It's fragmentary, but most illuminating."

I stand dazed in the middle of the studio, thinking of Henry and Rank—feeling like a visionary, feeling how keenly, fanatically I have desired Henry's ascension. Hearing him say, "You are too quick, Anaïs," on the day I talked exultantly ("This man Rank will appreciate you. You must see him"). Henry a little uneasy at my "exaltation," but *trusting*—trusting me, too, when I made him meet his agent and his publisher. I love him for his *faith:* He knows *where* and *when* to yield. And then he rises up gloriously, magnificently in his work. My God, how happy I am to have found Henry, a genius to serve, to worship. Someone big enough to *use* my strength, to subject it to his complements. God, God, *marriage*-marriage, a *fecund* marriage. There is no fecundity in my marriage with Hugo. We *create* nothing. I should have had children, but I am an artist, not a mother.

Hugo says jokingly I have a harem. To each one I say, "You are the favorite." The real king is Henry. My harem gives me a lot to do—to keep them all happy. I'm happy, happy, happy. It is spring. I don't walk on earth—I fly, fly through the house with love of my harem, adoration of my harem. Today Allendy, Eduardo, Henry—I love to see them all in one day. It makes me feel rich. I'm overfull!

Evening. My stupendous human happiness today over Henry's happiness. He had written me a letter last night about his meeting with Rank, which I read in the café in front of him with tears:

If this contains anything of revelation, of wisdom, of real vision, take it as a gift which only you have made it possible for me to offer. *You* have been the teacher . . . not Rank, nor even Nietzsche, nor Spengler. All these, unfortunately, receive the acknowledgment, but in them lies the dead skeleton of the idea. In you was the vivification, the living example, the guide who conducted me through the labyrinth of self to unravel the riddle of myself, to come to the mysteries. And that is the meaning of the wandering through the labyrinth, of the so-called exploration of self. Not self, but the fringe of mystery, the not-self by which it is permitted to know, if it is a knowing, that I know. The best is a mere divination, the ecstatic glimpse into the far and high places, the flash in the dark that sustains the illusion in us. Often when you deplored your inability to act as analyst, I had glimpses of what I now perceive clearly. Over a short route and for a vulgar cure you may be a failure, but that is because the prize is too ignoble. If one goes the whole way with you, if one *can* go the whole way, indeed one is rewarded by a different product entirely, something quite unpragmatic, something, and I am glad to say it, *unreal*. One is privileged in the end to drink of wisdom. I say this very,

very romantically! It is sheer romanticism in this day to speak of the value of wisdom, for it is a value that is no longer wanted. It has no efficacy in this world of reality which has been created, because this world of reality is a world of death. It is the bitter unreality, the world that lies outside of the psychologist's pen, the world to which we *should* never become wholly adapted, that you have led me.*

MARCH 9, 1933

ASTROLOGICAL PREDICTIONS FOR MARCH: TEMPO-rary depression. Boredom.

The month began with a paralyzing neuralgia.

Financial debacle of the world. Great worries. Scenes with Hugo like those during the Crash. To keep him from drowning I remain hard, firm. Only the artists are rich today. Hugo, until last night, was poor, so poor of true values. Tears, arguments, anger. I struck his face, struck at his Scotch dourness and obstinacy, which make him disregard my intuitional guidance. Now I must stand by him, stand by his *eternal depression*, his *eternal darkness* of being, the *weight* of him, the heavy anchored being, who when he loses money feels he is losing his power and the reason for his existence! How I fought to liberate him from *fear*. It is strange how I, who am obsessed imaginatively with a million fears, gather myself together at the moment of crisis and become fearless. My poor love. Tonight we are at peace. He is happy because I delivered him of humiliation, of his sense of failure. And now let the worst come—we are philosophical!

What a mess the world is in. I keep my face turned away as much as possible. It *stinks*. I never read the papers. I refuse to worry about politicians. When war comes to my door, very well, then I will act. I

---

* For a complete account of Henry Miller's visit to Dr. Otto Rank see Henry Miller: *Letters to Anaïs Nin,* pp. 80–86.

am only interested in what I can help, heal, act for, love, serve directly. My beloved ones! My adored ones!

Hugo is saved from debacle. All is well. I leap like a squirrel about Paris, laughing at astrological predictions. The machine in me which functions wholly, the great well-knitted elements constantly directed, this willful hand of mine on the rudder, draws the vacillating ones: Gustavo, in quest of himself; Louise, in fear of madness. All those whose lives are frittered away, ungalvanized by a supreme, all-conquering vision, gather around me—the *catalyseur*—and thus I sublimate my woman's vanity, which is great, reducing the inordinate joy which fills me when love surrounds me.

The extraordinary people gathering around me—as I see them, they all are *très grands*—need to realize, in one way or another, their aggrandizement in the magnifying glass of my idealism, my livingness.

Eduardo, who is so pleased with my dream book, thinks I have found my style, that my erotic, crapulous, decadent writing is the contrary of my Rimbaudian terrific innocence (see how many believe in my innocence—would this journal deceive them?), that I am leaping *out*, imaginatively, *out* and beyond my horoscope.

I write Henry to be very severe with me—that I'm afraid of the adulation I am getting. It was better for me when I was alone.

It is a strange fact that I am born under no earth signs!

MARCH 12, 1933

AT THE ALLENDYS': ARTAUD—THE FACE OF MY hallucinations. The hallucinated eyes. The sharpness, the pain-carved features. The man-dreamer, diabolical and innocent, frail, nervous, potent. As soon as our eyes meet I am plunged into my imaginary world. He is veritably haunted and haunting.

I was afraid to meet him, because a few days before, I had read some of his writing and there was an extraordinary twinship. Henry said I might have written these pages. I knew I was going to meet my brother in imaginings and styles. I did not expect that face. *"Je suis le plus malade de tous les surrealistes."* He read us the outline of his play. He is a broken, quivering decadent, another "lusty decadent"—opium, perhaps. How his eyes transcend what he looks at. The burned-up face, the malice, the passion, the violence. I was hypnotized, afraid to talk to him. Yet he was gentle, and he, too, was spellbound. He said, "You look like a priestess of the Incas." His eyes following all my gestures. I forgot everyone else in my absorption. Our eyes were constantly converging.

Today I immersed myself in Artaud's few pages and tried to write him.

All during the last week I realized I did not miss Allendy, that the impulse which drew me to him was ephemeral, that by his wisdom he had dissolved my impetuosity. How can I tell him *now*, when he has begun to suffer with jealousy, has begun to demand? Last night, how anxious he was.

I also finished in a sense with Gustavo. I don't like him. He is dogmatic, tyrannical, over*sane*, overbalanced, too simple, too mental, and too lucid. One talk sufficed. He is literal, too, although intelligent, overrealistic. He likes patterns, perfections, meticulousness—as I used to before I met Henry. Now I feel more easygoing, more bohemian—more artist and less lady—less *logical*, less orderly. I have broken through the shell of form which stifled my Father—the elegance and form of crystallization which produces aridity.

I am *against* nothing, because I have my own way of using everything, of turning all things into nourishment. Even our nights with bank vice-presidents have produced pages of imaginative writing!

These days I write pages on Louise, on "eyes," watches. Chaos has enriched me and nourished me—that is all I know.

I would like to gather all my experiences together and give them to Henry. *He would understand everything*. But I love him too much to make him uneasy. He would doubt the *solidity* of my love for him, and yet it is the core of my life. The humor in this is that he is equally impressionable, equally faithless, at times—he happens to be marvelously true now because he is in quest of ideas, not experience, whereas I am having experience now: Artaud (the dramatic personage of Artaud the actor, the creator of a surrealist theater), Nellie, Allendy. It is the counterpart of Henry's active, ebullient, many-sided life with June, the counterpart of his full days, full life which I once marveled at.

The visitors have left. I'm sitting alone in the studio. A stifling, choking timidity ruined my evening, because the occasion meant too much to me, because the expectation was too intense. There is no progress, no progress. To have René and Artaud here! Parts of it were like a dream, where I let my house speak for me, the garden, the crystals. Artaud was strongly moved: "The house is magic; the garden is magic. It is all a fairy tale."

But I am sad and lonely—disconnected again, choked in my mood. Oh, the effort, the effort at connection! The heartrending effort.

Artaud talks ardently about legends, myths, cabal, magic. He resents René's psychoanalytical explanations! We did pillory Marie Bonaparte. Artaud's eyes now weary, malicious, his gaunt face so keen.

Suddenly I have a great feeling of being *only the victim of a mood,* that they have left me contented carrying images—that perhaps they, too, lost their confidence because they felt themselves in exotic surroundings. When René first came in, he said, "I feel here as in a very distant country."

All alone, I begin to laugh, because I remember the good things.

The *unfaithfulness* of artists! As I predicted, Henry is getting stimulated by Walter Lowenfels while I am being stimulated by Artaud, and it is *only* because I, too, am living multilaterally that I can understand Henry's new idolatry! His extravagant pages on Lowenfels are the counterpart of my extravagant pages on Artaud.

And so tonight I am prepared not only to participate in his enthusiasm (instead of arresting it or marring it by my jealousy) but to assimilate Lowenfels as well, to learn, to make room for him, to expand, *letting* Henry expand at the same time. If you live you can *let live!*

When Lowenfels writes extremely eccentric English, Henry accepts it, but if I did it he would call it bad English (because there is a difference between "the deformity of drawing of one who does not know how to draw, and the willful deformity of the artist who knows"?). It is necessary that the world should not know I was not born into English! I'm laughing as I write this.

I described Lowenfels's poetry as the glance of a cross-eyed man. Not that I dislike it. It is original but unfocused. And it is precisely this lack of focus in Lowenfels in which Henry finds nourishing chaos, exactly as I found sustenance in Henry's chaos.

Home. I am in paradise again. Henry at my desk, wrestling with Lawrence, delving into hills of notes, sighing, smoking, cursing, type-writing, drinking.

So sweet to come home to his tenderness—his hands always ready to caress, even while he is talking about the meaning of art, the rise of schizophrenia, the universe of death, the Hamlet–Faust cycle, Destiny, the Soul, the macro/microcosm, megalopolitan civilization, surrender to biology.

He uses everything, even what I told him about Eduardo's jealousy, which he correlates with Proust's.

MARCH 16, 1933

AWOKE THIS MORNING TO RECEIVE A BOOK FROM Artaud, *L'Art et la mort.* Also a pitiable note from Eduardo. He will never understand the disinterested "tyranny" of the creator. He is myopic. His vision is feminine and myopic.

When Henry and I live together there blows constantly a potent wind of creativity. In the excitement last night, we both pursued a final interpretation of Lawrence's painting and then fell into each other's arms with joy at the ideas attained. Henry says with typical overestimation, "You're writing this book." But these are only the sparks of friction, of equal effort. He creates the gigantic fresco, the cosmic fresco. I bring crumbs like an indefatigable ant, and he uses, drinks, fecundates, eats with the same abandon with which he gives his ideas and his knowledge!

Eduardo's way of enraging me is to talk about "class" and the incongruity of my alliance with Henry. Then I flare in utter disgust because I do not believe in *class* but in sensitivity and talent, and I believe that Henry is more sensitive and more talented than Eduardo, that Henry's boorish exterior conceals a softer and tenderer and more delicate being than Eduardo himself.

Henry is worried by Artaud. But he will not oppose Artaud or say mean things about him. We accept each other's enthusiasms. Henry *wanders*, as I do, loses himself, explores, dissolves, forgets me, superficially, in a great imperative movement which I understand. Each one of us possesses his own soul, respects the other's ego; though we may suffer tortures, humanly.

Great sadness when I left Allendy yesterday. An Allendy tortured by jealousy and, so, passionate. I was overwhelmed and I could not talk. He is amazingly intuitive, and my lies are useless.

As I advance into greater and greater complications ("Everybody loved you the other night," said René) it is the other's jealousy which now concerns me, because I know the horrors of it. And it is getting more and more difficult to make four men happy.

Leaving René to meet Henry at the station to come *home* with him—the quiver of joy and tenderness as we meet. Yet I feel wistful and think of René, of how much I want him, too, and of how unwise my impulse is because René is almost Eduardo, another arrester of motion, another dead man.

MARCH 18, 1933

END OF FOUR DAYS' LIFE WITH HENRY. HE, TOO, has known *for the first time* with me utter *satisfaction*, utter *contentment* (my feeling lying in his bed in Clichy!). He, lying in my bed, experiences the end of restlessness.

Tristesse inouïe—after rare days of work and talk. And the unbearable sweetness of completion, of fulfillment, for two beings so restless, so unsatisfied.

When Hugo's telegram arrives [from London] Henry looks stony. In the morning our sentimentality is shelled in.

I rush to my research work only half-awake mentally, lying in that biological substratum, instinctive, the blood still fermenting. I steal the book on the Black Death from the American Library for Henry because he stole the Élie Faure. Because I feel Rabelais's phrase—"*Fay ce que vouldras*." Because I feel unfettered. Uncritical. Amoral. Because Henry's life—although *all* of it is not necessary to me, necessary to live—*is* life, *because* it merely sweeps and flows—*sans accrochage*. Because, as Rank said so wisely, there is a difference between deprivation and renunciation!

But my beautiful wisdom shook a bit when I discovered that Rank's book, which I gave Henry before I myself had time to read it, he loaned to Lowenfels!

Henry and I cannot marry because of Hugo, and because we would starve together. Against this blank fact I stare sometimes with infantile despair, because to be wise is to accept relative happiness. But the absolute, the absolute haunts me.

And tonight I take refuge in beauty. I lie in bed waiting for Hugo and I look stupidly at the beauty of the room, cataloguing both details and ambience—the legendary aspect of it. The small sandals at the side of the bed. The sienna-colored satin nightgown, breasts showing through the black lace. The Arabian bottle next to the bed. The open lacquer box from which spill out steel necklaces, steel bracelets, and coral. I think of nothing. But I hear Henry's voice, the rumblings and animal furriness of it, the soft huskiness, and I see his spare, athletic-shouldered body, muscled, vigorous, but frail looking at moments. The bell rings. Hugo is at the gate.

Oh, God, there are moments when my sincerity and my wholeness kill me—I cannot *act* anymore! I don't want to act anymore!

MARCH 20, 1933

*T*HE END OF ALLENDY. REVOLT AGAINST HIS LACK of imagination, his practicality, his arrestive and stifling jealousy, the way he translates my poetical facts into *facts,* the way he scientifies, medicalizes. No more desire to give him any-thing—only a self-protective flight from that which perpetually deludes me, for I am a visionary who wants to make a poet out of a physician, a live man out of a dead one, *always tempted by the unattainable and the difficult.* And I get hurt in the process of *human creation:* whenever I attempt to create human beings, I get humanly hurt. When I create in art I never get hurt. I have been hurt by the nonbirth of Eduardo, the inertness and weight of Hugo, who does not know ecstasy. Henry alone was fully born. Hugo is born to the extent of satisfying himself but not me.

Enough, enough masochism and superhuman tasks. I felt so clearly today Allendy fighting to dominate me by using his power of "judge" always *against* Henry—and this to enjoy me in a nonhuman way, like

Eduardo. His talk about "purity" gave me nausea. I have gone beyond him. I am out of his reach. I am ensorcelled by the imagination of Artaud and the livingness of Henry. I don't like Allendy's language (I never did), the bareness of it, the *vacuum* it leaves.

I want to use this human energy which drives me to unsatisfactory human relations for art, which is all-satisfying. In art I find the absolute—in all that *I create myself*.

And so, after wasting much time, much time, I begin to work again.

Always because life has *hurt* me.

Fugues. *All human relations* are relative and insecure and undependable. All I can say is that Henry and I have more courage than Eduardo, who balks at life, and even than Allendy, who has chosen sublimation and death. Eduardo's flight to London—Allendy's flight into analysis and objectivity—mine into art—more or less extensive voyages among human beings, according to one's endurance and courage.

Fears. When Hugo returned from Holland and saw the house dark (I was asleep) he imagined I had left him and that he would find a note on the door.

*I write to Artaud:** In the few lines I read before, I had divined the tone, and now in *L'Art et la mort* I have discovered the expansion and plenitude of your writing. I have never read anything so faradic, so fluid, so arrowed. It seems to me that you have covered all the experiences of fiction, that you have visited the regions we could only suspect the existence of, like those planets unknown to our eyes. I have an almost painful impression of the exhaustiveness of your expression—like the ultimate statements, an absolutism of vision. I am unable to say very simply, "I love your book," because the multiplicity of intention and perception in each one of your words gives vertigo (which is what you want); fear, too, as one has of myths.

---

* Letters to and from Artaud as quoted in the diary are in French in the original.

One sees too much. A vision relentless and almost intolerably acute. . . .

For the moment I cannot do more than this: to abdicate as a writer and return to you your own phrases, to remind you that what you wrote about drugs applies to the effect of your work, describes the effect of it; that when I emerge from this splendor I may say more.

P.S. I gave you "Alraune" because I talk through writing, but I forgot to tell you that it is not finished, that the three women who are projections of the one emerge from death through man and liberation from the self. A trilogy of narcissism.

March 25, 1933

HENRY CAME AND LAUGHED AWAY MY BLACK MOOD. said he felt so *innocent* of any disloyalty. I said, "You are only true to the impulse of the moment. I cheat and play tricks, but you remain at the *center*—immovable." He was tender and truly irresponsible. Laughed because he said I understood the big liberties and tripped over the small obstacles (his lending my Rank book to Lowenfels). I realized he was right about his *innocence!* He sent me a copy of his letter to Lowenfels, but I didn't send Henry a copy of my letter to Artaud! But that is out of a desire not to hurt Henry by my flights and fancies. I am *aware,* and Henry is unaware. You might call it thoughtlessness, but how contrite he was, how soft. It is impossible to remain hurt. He heals me so deeply. He said, "I can't be disloyal to you, because I live *in you*—I'm obsessed with you! I never forget you. The rest is literature. I'm sucking Lowenfels. I'm nearly through with him. I'm fully aware his poetry didn't justify what I wrote."

"Incidentally," I said (the writer gaining the upper hand), "it was damned good, what you wrote."

We laugh. We lie together, fucking softly, gently, swimming in it, and for the first time the orgasm comes to me unsought, peacefully almost, like a slow dawn, a slow flowering out of relaxation and yieldingness and nonbeing. No reaching out for it. Falling like rain, flowering, drowning the mind.

Dream: I enter a luxurious *grande maison de couture*. I find that the saleslady is Comtesse de Vogüé. I feel I do not know how to treat her, not wanting her to realize I am embarrassed for her that she should be working. I try hard to seem at ease. The mannequins are very ugly. At the same time the showroom is the salon of Nellie, and there are visitors. I have a feeling in the dream that Nellie is very dissipated and decadent. She shows her knees and breasts brazenly. A big window in the room, like the window of Mélisande, giving on sea, space. Suddenly Nellie accuses me of having stolen some rare gold pieces. I am very angry. I say, "It isn't that I mind being called a thief; I believe in stealing. I stole a book from the American Library. But gold—why should you think I would steal gold?" An old man admits the theft with a debonair gesture. Out of the window I see several men in a field of heather and bushes preparing to frighten a woman with a big fake snake which they hold up like a pole. Woman is very courageous and starts beating the snake with a stick but falls into the hands of the men, who bite her. Atmosphere of catastrophe—sulfurous color. I am anxious. I feel sorry for the woman. I empty my small black purse into her hands. I am aware I won't have any money to go home with, but I don't care. I walk. Come upon Nellie and her family in a kind of open-air massage parlor—small rooms, bunks, etc. Nellie's father is preparing to show a movie. Nellie sits in a bunk like in a theater box. He says, "You must look at this movie before I sell it." Just before this, Nellie and I were standing by the window and we saw silhouetted against the sky an enormous, gigantic hand pointing to the left of us—threatening. But I am aware that it is made of cardboard and handled by strings, like the shadow figures in Balinese theater. Now the hand travels on the horizon, unevenly behind mountain edges, etc., and I see that it does not move suavely, like the sun, but like a Guignol doll, in jerks. I am not impressed, but Nellie is. I feel as if I were in a theater.

Just when I awake, the hand pointing stays in my mind, super-stitiously, like the hand of God or something like it. Hugh thinks I feel the downfall of the aristocrats and personally laugh at fatalism, the catastrophic aspects of our epoch.

I enjoy telling Henry a fantastic story of Hugo's preparations to leave for South America to manage a precious-wood ranch (an idea Hugo has played with on days of depression because a rich Cuban has offered him the managership). Realistic details: Hugo has given notice to owner of our house—lease expires in October (what Hugo really did was to write asking for reduced rent). I liked to see Henry's panic and hear him say in a low voice, "You can't go—why, I can't live without you. When I stay in Louveciennes I realize that it is only with you that I live fully . . . Everything is right when we are together. You will have to tell Hugo the truth—and let things bust up. I want them to."

At the same time I notice he loves to make me repeat (How often he asks me the same question!) that I cannot live without him, that if I were forced into such a decision I would follow *him*. He relishes my words, too, my assurances! Human, human; and as far as I can see, oh, God, a world *ruled* by *jealousy*—jealousy, the dominating theme of pain in all of us. To follow Henry would mean exposure to the *greatest pain* and my greatest *fear!* Every time I think of this I shake with terror, in the most abject cowardice.

I know my greatest fault is *hypersensitivity—incurable.*

Henry believes he is passing through a great transition from the romantic interest in life to *interest in ideas.* He has become sage, phi-losopher, metaphysician. His mind functions continuously. We sit in a café and he drinks but continues to talk about Spengler. I am proud, yet I feel cheated of my *adventure!* Of the underworld of gaudy trib-ulations! Of pleasure. Of lesser but romantic values!

That is why, Saturday afternoon at Zadkine's, I accept the atten-tions and invitation of an English painter—to see, to hear, to explore.

Deep down, I am happy, happy to have found a relative absolute! I wish I could test myself in a life with Henry—see if I am big enough, courageous enough.

Henry. Henry. *I only live fully when I am with you.* This is frustration, a half life, as you say. How long can I bear it?

When Hugo came I was silent, withdrawn, my whole being clamoring with my worship of Henry. Henry. An immense resounding of my being, deafening me to the world. I wanted to run after Henry when he left me, *to stay with him.* I don't care a damn about the pain!

I make crafty plans so that if the war breaks he should be able to escape safely. I awake out of my dreamworld only to *act*, with hensureness. Then I forget reality again and sink back into *my* world. Henry needs my courage, my practicalness, my decisiveness. He leans on them. His helplessness in reality arouses me to fierce warring for *him*. The idea of "war" unnerves him. He has been living within his book only. Whereas big fears always arouse my courage, my shrewdness. Henry is tired of struggle and insecurity, of wars, and of pain.

I am still a child, and life baffles me. It seems to me I was born wise and have become a romantic. That I am at the lyrical, passionate pinnacle of my life—that nothing but the absolute (Henry) can appease me, that I refuse fragments, games, amusements, morsels. I don't know. Allendy has said; "I want to teach you to play with love, to amuse yourself." And that is just what I can't learn. I can't change my fundamental self.

Why is it Henry can write crudities which would revolt Allendy and yet make me feel illusion, while Allendy, with all his finesse, gives me a feeling of literalness?

I'm trying to rationalize my *no!* I hate to say no.

I feel I do not understand ordinary life—that there is a deformity in my vision which no intelligence can cure.

I could *"faire l'amour"* at a high moment. I cannot do it wisely, lightly, properly dosed. Henry is the only man who plucked the fruit at the right moment; he *knows* fever, and he knows abandon, and he knows ecstasy. I am not made to mate with wise men.

Day of self-criticism for my lies, for my love of testing my *puissance*, ashamed of Allendy's sincerity. Guilty of playing a game. From the moment I knew I didn't love Allendy, I should not have played the game.

This chaos I must live.

Henry finds now that my *obedience* to his sexual desire—I never take the lead, and only tempt him with coquetry when I feel he *wants to* be tempted—is the woman's rightful attitude. In that sense he is lord and master. I always wait. And now he feels *free*, free of the woman's love—demand, *will*, appetite. He blossoms as a *man*, a man who is lord and master in sex, as it should be. But at the same time, this obedience is only possible to the woman whom the lord and master *satisfies*. I *know* I do not have to wait very long; I can *count* on the ever-restless, ever-fiery penis!

A night! What a night! The schoolroom hall of the Sorbonne. Artaud and Allendy at the podium. Allendy cryptic, direct, factual. Artaud the essential poet: tense, contracted, dramatic. The crowd half-antagonistic, half-amused, mocking, not understanding.

I was surrounded by Henry, Hugo, Boussie, Davidson, Lalou, Madame Lalou. All but Hugo and Henry are jeering. There are protestations, insults. People walk out boldly, ostentatiously.

Artaud, when all is over, walks almost straight up to me and kisses my hand. He asks me to go to a café with him.

Hugo could not go because he was entertaining Davidson, who did not speak French. So I stayed with Artaud until he was left alone.

We are walking, walking, through the dark streets. He is hurt, wounded, baffled by the public. We talk. We sit in the Coupole and talk. He forgets the conference. He rereads my letter to him, I translating it. He likes what I wrote him. He tells me he was an opium addict for fifteen years. Describes his sensations, his fears, his struggles to achieve work. He recites poetry. Says I have green and sometimes violet eyes. We talk about form, the dream, his work, the theater. My extreme timidity makes me utterly calm, calm, listening. We understand each other, and we walk and talk for hours.

Today, Henry. To Henry I confess the great shock it gave me last night to see a sensitive artist confronting a hostile public—what *brutality* in the public, what ugliness in the public because they cannot tell when they face a sincere artist and respect his sincerity.

Henry admires Artaud—was moved by what I told him. Henry is the *least petty man I know*. I was moved by his generosity, because this attitude comes with another feeling he confessed to me: The moment Artaud entered the hall Henry recognized a poet, and he visualized in a flash and understood that I might love Artaud. And as Henry said this, how mellow he was, how moving.

We had an emotional afternoon, anyway! Father's letter came to me in the middle of it—a beautiful, tender letter—which made me weep. I made Henry promise that he would write to his daughter someday. I translated the letter to Henry. I was overwhelmed by the beauty of it.

Then Henry and I talked about jealousy, how grateful he is that I do not use jealousy to tyrannize him. I do so much to preserve his security because in this security he works, expands, finds equilibrium and himself. That was important. He has found himself because I have not made a slave of him. I have respected his entity—he feels I have never encroached on his liberty. And out of this his strength was born. And with this strength he loves me, wholly, without war or hatred or reserve. It is strange how to Henry I have been able to make the greatest gift: that of *not holding*, of keeping our two souls independent yet fused. The greatest miracle of *wise* love. And it is this he gives me, too.

It is this Allendy failed to give me. Last night, out of jealousy, he was petty and tyrannical. I had taken pains to telephone him to say, "In spite of the people who will be with me tonight, remember I will be thinking only of you." Yet he watched Henry light my cigarette and approached me severely, like a policeman, to tell me it was forbidden to smoke. I blushed like a child. I did not like the pettiness of his jealousy.

Henry says; "You see, I would not bear what Lawrence had to bear—I came out of it—because I have you. I refused to be destroyed by woman!"

I refused to play the tormenting role of the woman, to torment Henry, and I have liberated him. I have been the creative woman. I didn't need his jealousy to satisfy or prove my *puissance*. I believe in his love, his great egoistical love, as he says! My great egoist suits me.

For the first time, in the middle of our talk, we kissed chastely, sadly! Later we relaxed, lay together, he and I, the strangely vigorous decadents! Henry and I, alone in our modern world, possess a deformed imagination, hypersensitivity, neurosis, all the stigmas of the age, and *yet health*—health by our sexual vitality—a strange contrast to the others. A healthy, sound being and a suitably sick mind!

Father's letter, Father's coming visit, they lie like a flower in the pages of a book. In the center of my book, my journal, my life. My first idol.

My life, the great tumultuous flow, eddies around . . .

What makes me sad is that Allendy has given me life and that I have not been able to repay him. I have been given more than I could give. I hate to abandon him to his narrow, tight, pain-stifled world. I would have liked him to know joy.

Last night his magic wavered, flickered, pale, somber. Jealousy, jealousy, his only expression, darkened him, estranged him.

Adventure is dead.

Il reste l'amitié.

Artaud's eyes. Before the eyelids come down, the pupils of the eyes swim upward, and I see only the whites. The lids fall in the whiteness, a slow flesh gesture, and one wonders where his eyes are. He, the man who has invented new dimensions of feelings, thoughts, language.

Eyes blue with languor, black with pain, rebellion. Gentle last night, at the end, humming as we walked. A knot of nerves, tangled.

I'm fascinated by the mystery of human beings. I had to solve the enigma of Allendy. I was enthusiastic to discover him. And now I have clearly the impression of rushing on . . .

Henry and I are so *aware* of the movements of life, of fatalism, of the necessity of treachery; so sadly, wisely aware, healing each other's wounds by the great miracle of our fundamental *unity*.

I laugh when I detect in Father's letter the true emotions, two lies, and one theatrical phrase. My beloved Father! What a *sursaut* of joy when I read, *"Anaïs, ma fille! Ma chérie . . ."*

What I find difficult to bear is my solitude, again. I had let Allendy guide my life, judge it, balance it. The period of subjection was sweet.

But when he became human he used his power pettily and erroneously. His jealousy became a dark tyranny.

Tonight over the telephone his voice is cold, furious.

So now Allendy, my god, acts like Eduardo, and I am disappointed. I should be *humanly* pleased, flattered; but no, I am sorry to have lost a leader.

I cannot place *this* faith in Henry because I know him to be as passionate, as imaginative, as naive a being as I am myself. Allendy was wisdom. I regret his transformation into *man*.

It saddens me to have become again an independent being. It was a deep joy to depend on his insight, his divine guidance.

Hélas!

What a demon there is in me!

Today Bernard Steele, Artaud's young publisher, came.

The night at the Allendys' I was so ironic. Today I can't bear his eyes on me. They are open, open, drinking, alive; and I feel three times a kind of tremor—a sensual terror.

I don't know anymore whether it is my power over him which disturbs me! I seem to be floating from one ecstasy to another. Steele for me is Eduardo *alive*, a young John, young, handsome, full, heavy featured.

Our war of ideas ceases. We sit alone for a moment in the garden and find accord upon the word *livingness*.

I am furious with myself.

The woman, the damned *woman* in me! Her head turns. Only the artist is valuable. The artist must save me. Depths. Values. I keep them both in the foreground, fighting my sensuality, my susceptibility.

Steele playing the guitar delicately. Steele's intelligence. Steele's admiration of Rank, as well as of Allendy. Steele's race. A man with multiple elements in him, contradictions. A musician. A man of conflicts—emotions—Taurus and Leo. Aristocracy.

And I laugh.

It hasn't happened to me yet, the gift of myself to a man I do not love. I have been faithful to love.

But the coquetry, the immense coquetry. And yet never the *game.* And because Allendy carved down my infatuation to wise proportions, ordained a human *diapason,* a French *liaison,* measure, I turn my back on him.

I disregard the proportions, the measures, the tempo of the ordinary world. I refuse to live in the ordinary world as an ordinary woman. To enter ordinary relationships.

I want ecstasy.

I'm a neurotic—in the sense that I live in *my* world.

I will not adjust myself to *the* world. I am adjusted to myself.

Henry said the other day; "At that conference, I looked at Allendy, at other men of my age, and I felt so young, so alive. I felt so young. They seemed dead to me!" Henry is young.

APRIL 11, 1933

A DEMON. A DEMON IN ME.
Allendy refuses to die. He is roused to fury and to passion by his jealousy. He reproaches me for coquetry; he reproaches me for not noticing him at the conference. He saw me going away with Artaud. He saw Henry sitting next to me. He reproaches me for playing with him. For ceasing to want him as soon as he became my slave. He begins to bite me, to caress me wildly. He sweeps me off my feet. We lie on the floor. And he is nervous, nervous,

frightened. And I am gentle and understanding, and I make him laugh, and I put him at ease. I am so at ease! I'm really laughing. There is no feeling in me. He misunderstands me completely. Every word he says is wrong. All the better. Pleasure. No understanding. Anger. Jealousy. Collision. Everything devoid of poetry. Just a big, handsome, vital man roused to passion. Coquetry in me, that is all. Everything in miniature. I feel cynical, and I realize I'm facing reality, that Allendy has stripped all things of their illusion. For him I am the most charming and seductive of women, *petite fille littéraire*. I'm exploring a new world, playing with it. Cold. I am not giving myself. I am divesting sexuality of its overimportance. The core of me is untouched.

I meet Henry and I give myself to him. Adoration. Henry marvels that he and I should find ourselves in a hotel room. He wants to *live* with me, *live* with me. He says his feeling for me makes animality pale, that for the first time he has given himself to a woman other than sexually. If I am a narcissist, Henry is an egoist.

We talk, talk about June. The feeling of the sacredness of their bodies narcissists have. June, Louise, I.

Then they throw themselves away on nobody. Why?

Because, because they know themselves, they are afraid of giving themselves, they throw their bodies to someone with tremendous pride—as a delusion. In an effort to come out, but unconsciously doing the very gesture which preserves the core—as June did.

June *wanted* to give Henry the core. Henry wanted to give June all. And neither wanted it. He fought her efforts to possess him wholly; she fought his sexual love, which *disregarded* her core. She would have given her life to obtain from Henry what I obtained. I would have given my life to obtain the whore-love. But not now. Now I realize the preciousness of what is given me. It is what I want.

I said once I was very hungry, so hungry I wanted *all* the loves. It isn't true.

I'm going to Allendy simply because I haven't the courage to say, "My illusion is cracked. Dead. Behind the god in you there is a Frenchman incapable of the ridiculous, the exalted, the mad, the fantastic, the immense, the dangerous, the ravaging, the consuming, the flames, the fever, the ecstasy."

Métro Cadet. I take Allendy's arm. He says; "Beware, we might be seen." I laugh. We talk together. I have been drinking a little to fortify myself. Rue de la Boule Rouge. Allendy says; "I have telephoned for a room. Monsieur 'Heden.' This is a quiet place; we won't be disturbed. There is no one about—no one looking. Let us go in." Darkness. A sulky day outside. Darkness. *Rez-de-chaussée*. A room in red. Bed in alcove. Oh, I like it, I like it. Curtained, tapestried, shutters closed. French. French. French. Allendy kisses me passionately. "I'll help you undress." Experience. Adventure. Curiosity. The unknown. Fear. The dreams scurrying right and left, dispersed, alarmed. Naked bodies. Allendy looks like the man in one of Lawrence's paintings. So much flesh. Soft, white. No nerves. His nerves. They are tight, alarmed by experience. Discovery of bodies. Kisses which fuse nowhere. Flesh without sparks. Sparkles of expertness in me. The gestures, necessary; the knowledge. I relax his nervousness and arouse him. His is a soft-fleshed, lulling sexuality. Is that all? Is that all? This fatness and flab-biness—like a child's—the comedy, the comedy. I play the comedy of crispations and delight. To meet life, the challenge of life. Allendy is satisfied. It is over. All that interests me is his satisfaction. We are laughing and talking. He says, "Always after making love, I feel pro-phetic. Next time . . . but there will be no next time—you said—we said: Once. Only once."

The jealousy. "You have been with Henry. I feel it. When did you sleep with Henry last? I will tell you. I know it. It was Tuesday (exactly!). You are a liar—always a liar. I love your lies. They are so delicate. But I know. I sense Henry around you."

Which I deny.

One moment he says, "You have the loveliest body—I haven't seen it clearly enough. It is always thus. Things happen to me, and I see them as through a glass door—indistinct. Afterward I remem-ber . . . I enjoy it."

At this I melt. I don't know why. The distress of the dying and the dead, the timorous, the distant. A phrase from the man that touches me. I become sincere. I am sincere as we walk out and I see his eyes dim. The day has become beautiful, drenched in light. Allendy's joy is rising. "Oh, I feel good, I feel good. It was sweet and I have wanted it from the first day I saw you." Then in the taxi we hold hands, and he is so gentle and so sentimental.

As I leave him, my sincerity grows, expands. While I sit in a café with Hugo, I experience the memory of his body's contact and feel tenderness. That is all. A kind of pity. I remember his stories: The woman who was so angry because he couldn't fuck her immediately—would never see him again. How differently I sense man's ordeal and diffidence. Laugh it off, conquer it. And make the man happy. And that is all. A gift. I make a gift in return for the tribute of his love. And I feel free of debts. And I walk joyously away, debtless, independent, uncaptured. A little ironic. Will I write all I thought? Oh, I was diabolical. He, the more cautious, the more realistic, the more reckless; I, the more ironic. Then my irony falls like a burst balloon because Allendy is anxious, and I forgive him, the world, reality, the delusions of sexual inadequacies. Armed with irony, disarmed by understanding, because I see behind Allendy's inadequacies a great inexpertness with women, reality, a terror of it, and insecurity, a distress. I hear all his questions: "Are you satisfied? Was I more than Eduardo? Was I as much as Henry?"

He wanted to beat me; that was how he excited himself with another woman. He began to slap my buttocks, slap, slap, and I laughing. But suddenly he was *touched*. And he stopped, overwhelmed with feelings, because he saw the marks of his hands on my "satiny, satiny skin."

"You won't write this in your journal?"

"No. No. Besides, I've disguised you as the astrologer (in the 'Alraune' book). And I wouldn't say that I had slept with the astrologer. It doesn't seem right."

When he saw my breasts he reminded me that he had seen them before. We laughed at my coquetry.

Allendy *enjoys* through jealousy. The salient point for him yesterday was the jealousy—more important than possession. He sees Artaud, Steele, Henry, Lalou hovering about me, and is roused.

I will only achieve my own salvation sexually when I can go sexually to the men from whom I will not get tenderness. After all, I am attracted by softness because I am afraid of the brute, and then I am disappointed by softness, oversensitiveness, sentimentality, devotion, worship!

The other day, Henry came with William A. Bradley the literary agent and friend of many writers.

Immediate sympathy.

Bradley was enthusiastic about me, quite mad. He was enchanted. Was sure I wrote interestingly!

Today he telephones me. Has read my childhood journal. Says it is remarkable. His wife and he have laughed and wept over the journal. Tragedy. That is it. He says it has a tragic tone—deep tones, so rare in a child.

I see Millner again, the Russian who is writing on Spinoza. Millner is the man who admired my book on Lawrence before he met me, mentioned it to Hugo, only to discover I was Hugo's wife. I should have written the final synthesis of Lawrence, he says. Instead I illuminated the path for others. Thinks I lack confidence, egotism. Wants me to parade my *moi* for a while. Wants to guide me, teach me, form me. Says I have all the elements and do not know my own value.

His wife says, "He always demands soul and brains in a woman."

When he glances over my childhood journal he says, "It's Russian. Absolutely Russian. That *tristesse,* that precocity. I feel I've known you for centuries. I feel I know all about you. I may be wrong."

I don't know. I look at this intensely restless, psychic, intellectual man and wonder. His admiration embarrassed me from the very first. Last night I felt the intuition, the enormous appreciation. I'm uneasy and strange in my new role of *receiver*. I'm dazed. An overabundance of appreciation. I must write here to keep lucid, to keep sane!

I have the impression that I am overestimated.

APRIL 19, 1933

*H*ENRY COMES AND WORKS ON MY "ALRAUNE"
story with the *thoroughness* I do not possess,
praises me, gets hysterical over my last pages, which are a frenzied
sensual orgy, gets passionate over them; and we plunge into a world
which only exists between Henry and me. So sweet to walk into his
room to awake him and to be pulled into his bed—to lie at his side
for a siesta and feel his hands lighting another fire a few hours later.
Work *in between!*

He notices Hugo's strange dead regions, how he responds for a
moment, sheds a halo of learning, takes an obstinate, tenacious grip
on life, and then dies out into vagueness, into nothingness, so that
Henry's ardor is deflated, too, and enthusiasm expires. I am glad simply
that I find I am not unjust to Hugo, that my feelings are true. That
the strong fraternal love which keeps me bound to him goes to his
immense kindness, passive understanding, disciple's loyalty, qualities
of feeling and sincerity, nobility; but that, oh, God, I *need* Henry.
Henry is food to me. Henry is life to me.

He says no woman has ever written as I am writing. He gets fevers
and chills from my pages on lesbianism.

And as I finish this book of one hundred tight, compressed, quintessential pages, I do not feel exhausted—I feel fuller than ever, haunted
with ideas. Already writing new pages.

I can only *move* into reality when pushed by great exaltation. Otherwise I cannot move. In cool moments I am again caught in the net of my
sensibilities, timidities, as if I were moving in a foreign atmosphere.

I *admit* my abnormality.

Today I receive from Henry amazing pages in which he has re-
written my "Alraune" preface, added to it, enhanced it, said all I

intended, penetrated not only my meaning but my furthest intent, a veritable intermarriage and creation, as much a creation of *our* blood and *our* flesh as a child would be. I'm flabbergasted.

Strange. As I analyze myself I feel an untying of nerves, a breaking of diamonds. The feeling that gestures are sacred dissolves. Gestures are sacred? I want to divest them of their sacredness. I, who am such a transcendentalist, I am defeated by gestures. I give importance to gestures. Gestures are my ultimate duel with life. On the plane of imagination, I reign. On the plane of experience, *I fear*.

A terrible sacredness. The moment in the red room when I *hated* to be naked and to see Allendy naked washing his beard. Reality is like a violation to me. Throughout my struggle to espouse reality, I have done violence to some essence of me that I do not understand. Henry alone . . . Yet I remember certain difficult moments, certain paralyses.

The effort to live!

If only Allendy could understand me!

I want to face life.

My greatest fault is criticalness. Criticalness. Or am I finding excuses for not being able to amuse myself sexually, freely? What if Allendy is literal? What if Steele does not think as I do?! Sex—I want to bathe in sex as Henry has done, uncritically. As I write the word down I think of Steele, vividly. Another nibbling?

What a devil I am. What contradictions and puerilities!

What woman never tells to the man is the quality of his sexual vigor. The ultimate lie. A great deal of my vagaries about Allendy are to conceal from myself mainly what a flabby lover I have won for myself. Who would sleep with magicians? Prophets are sexless. Lawrence. Jesus. And women adore them. Women are masochists. The truth!

What am I? Is not a great portion of my sensuality diffused into the ecstasies of writing, of beauty, of sensations without culmination? Is not most of my life spent either in suspense over the world or on the margin? Am I not perhaps another Rimbaud, who could only be either innocent or obscene, but nothing humanly nuanced?

Henry on "Alraune":   It's hard for me to state the subtleties which make your writing so enigmatic. I have come to a strange conclusion about your writing. I think that, instead of being so Pisces as you imagine, you are on the contrary quite bound up, knotted, restricted. Now and then you break it and you rush on with convincing power and eloquence. But it is as if you first had to break diamonds inside you, powder them to dust, and then liquefy them, a terrific piece of alchemy. I think again that one of the reasons why you have lodged so firmly in the diary is because of a fear to test your tangible self with the world; surely, if what you had written were offered to the world, you would have already altered your style. You have gotten ingrown, more and more protected, more and more sensitive—and this produces poisons and gems, the clotted, spangled phantasmagoria of neuroses.

Observe Henry's acuity and intuition. I have never talked to him about my neurosis. How much insight he has.

Tonight I realize that the diary is a struggle to seize on the most unseizable person on earth. I elude my own detection. I do not tell all my lies—it would take too much time. I cannot write myself out. I think in a hundred directions. Last night, three hours of talk with Henry. And I realize that my love for him is the most *fearless* of all my loves and acts in life, because all of Henry is made to hurt: his fugues, enthusiasms, impressionability, uncritical fancies, sexualities, contradictions, martialness, brutality of language, frankness. Yet I understand and accept everything. For him I want to conquer my sensitiveness.

Every day I must say, "Courage, *audace,* maturity, *face* life, *face* the public as woman, as artist. Harden. Toughen. Toughen."

When Allendy was dressing and his scene of jealousy of Henry had exploded, it occurred to him to lie to me. I saw the lie being invented. Knowing me capable of jealousy, he said, "I have a mistress who would be very angry if she knew."

Now there had never been, in all Allendy's confidence, any question

of a mistress. He had told me his life was empty, that his last experience
with a neurotic woman had frightened him. I *felt* and *sensed* him free,
since his relation to his wife is fraternal. I knew, too, how wholly taken
he was by me!

I was putting my stockings on. I stopped to make some gay remark.
I was chuckling to myself about it.

Later his lie came back to me as a useful instrument.

As a matter of fact, when Allendy invented a "legitimate mistress,"
although I knew it was a lie even this invented woman annoyed me
and I wanted to supplant her, annihilate her. That is, although I did
not want Allendy I could imagine and even feel a jealousy of any other
woman possessing him. The mechanism of jealousy functioned as usual
as a phenomenon distinct and separate from love.

When I began to invent the scheme by which I was going to free
myself from meeting Allendy on Thursday, I was making a mental
plan, but by the time I told Allendy all this I began so vividly to
imagine how I would feel if I loved Allendy and discovered he was
dividing his love between me and another woman that I became deeply
emotional and thoroughly sincere.

And then I saw that Allendy understood beautifully this neurosis
which did not exist—how when I learned there was another woman
I wanted to withdraw because I did not want to expose myself to pain,
nor—and this is a marvelous touch—did I want to hurt Allendy by
a sudden neurotic action on my part, because, I said, "You know how
I have always acted: winning the man, as I won Eduardo, and then
punishing him sadistically, as I did that day in the hotel room. And I
don't want ever to act this toward you. I want to save you from my
own neurosis, which is dangerous for you. I warn you in time. I want
to preserve our friendship."

I saw how Allendy understood, how beautiful his eyes became,
how soft, when he said, "I understand you too well. You need absolutism, purity, wholeness. You are sensitive." Then I was moved by a
great admiration of his goodness, of his tenderness, selflessness, mag-
nanimity.

"I knew all this before," he said. "I knew you were not a woman
who could play with love—but then I lost my insight, lost my head,

became quite crazy. *That* you can't hold against me. I'll do whatever you say. I'll be your friend for life. I will give up the pleasure I took with you. I love you. I understand you."

I became aware that I had moved Allendy with a most unauthentic attitude, which I was beginning to believe in. At this moment it is increasingly difficult for me to remember that Allendy has no mistress, because I am moved by my own story and Allendy's sublime interpretation of it!

Moved by his wisdom and gentleness, I let him kiss me; and he kissed me passionately, begging for Thursday as a good-bye meeting, promising me a *big scene,* a drama, promising to be violent, since I like drama! His *humor* was magnificent. He became again the superb, joyous Allendy of the analysis (because I consented to meet him Thursday). He was radiant and a tease, and his eyes were strange and *inquiétants* when he said: "I'll *beat* you up. You deserve it. You will enjoy it. I'll beat you hard, you coquette, you."

Now the theme of "beating" recurs so frequently in Allendy's talk (from our first kisses almost, I remember his asking, "Did Henry ever beat you?") that when he mentioned it today again with eyes flashing, I was impressed. Could it be that Allendy reached stronger sexual expression by inflicting pain and thus annihilating his too-great tenderness for woman? My curiosity was keenly aroused. He talked about supreme voluptuousness—he talked as if he *knew.* Now I also remembered he had mentioned a woman who loved to be beaten, and whom he loved to beat. He was standing up, another Allendy, vital, laughing, demoniac. I was stirred. We kissed violently and I felt his desire.

On the way home I was laughing. Thursday promises to be interesting!

I am aware that in my unconscious there is a fund of cruelty and fear which makes me want to punish and abandon man.

Henry walked up and down the studio criticizing the "Alraune" story and making suggestions. He was immensely excited about the few pages on the astrologer—thought I had not fully developed the idea. Began to talk inspiringly about the legend of Alraune: How I ought to work out the astrologer like the alchemist who produced Alraune from combination of whore and semen of a criminal—*a creation*—as I had been the spiritual creation of Allendy. Alchemist falls in love with his creation—Alraune tries to destroy him. Idea that when you tamper with nature you get punished. Allendy tampered with me. Created and produced a force—for evil or good. And as I am awakened he falls in love with me, not as he should, as a father, but *carnally;* and then I realize this is not the tie of true marriage— and I turn to the earth, to the man, to Henry.

Now, as Henry elaborated this story, the legend, my book, without knowing the real conflict between Allendy and me (how true that he created me, then loved me, then desired me, and that I only wanted to win my Father and destroy him, assert my power), my face showed clearly how perturbed I was. I talked excitedly. "It is all so true." Henry suddenly had an intuition. He was hysterical. He raved about the literary interest of this scene, showed great pain and immediately a tremendous exaggeration, believing me suddenly capable of *all* things, jumping at once to the most fantastic and the most realistic facts, and somehow missing both by the excesses of his imagination and realism. I mean by realism that I have slept with Allendy and it has meant *absolutely nothing to me*. By imagination—well, the truth is simply that I succumbed to a psychological automatism—a transfer with all that is mechanical *but* that I invested with a sum of feeling—because I give feeling to everything. *Neither love nor betrayal.*

We came to the question of lies. It seemed to me that I knew then why June and I lied:

1—because, lacking confidence, we fear that what we reveal may not be admirable. Being narcissists, we also hate to show what we believe to be a failing or a weakness.

2—because of the fear of hurting.

Now, June could not get beyond this impasse.

I will, because the *truth* does not hurt Henry as much as his imaginings. Truth has not got that monstrous, terrifying aspect.

As to the confidence—that I certainly lack. Henry and I are sure now that my literature is as much a tissue of disguises as June's multitude of lies are. Her duplicities and my enigmatic, symbolic, hieroglyphic words. Her inventions and my mad fantasies through which nobody can trace the fact.

The effect of my denials, explanations, on Henry was terrific. *I am his slave*. I not only regretted the past terribly, but I hated Allendy violently and myself more. Not to cause Henry pain seemed the most sacred of laws from now on. At the same time, the literary value of our scene, the discoveries, the drama and the revelations, all this fascinated us, as if I were reliving for Henry each step of June's complexities in order for us to unravel them together—I with my experience and Henry with his intellectual passion for problems—for June remains the psychological puzzle for both of us.

How am I to do this without humanly hurting Henry, how am I to bring him truth and absolute fidelity?

The halfhearted way in which I go into experiences proves the extent of my devotion to Henry, yet I am tempted by curiosities, weaknesses, pities.

Tonight all I wanted was our security again. It even seemed to me that "infidelities" were only caused by the extreme preciousness of our love. I have thought to myself, I ought to become tougher, more experienced, for Henry. I ought to deceive him so as to be able to bear his deceptions and thus leave him free. It all reverts to and issues from Henry. Would he understand this?

Tonight I sit here melted, sorrowful. He has gone to his whores (only twice!) and I can't go anywhere, because I can't play with whores and the consequences of my excursions are always more serious.

So many lies I would wish to efface. Our only saving grace, the humor and the ironies of *literature,* the interest removed from the too-human.

What touched me most was when we were discussing our plans for the month of June (Hugo may go to New York), Henry didn't want to travel or roam—wanted Louveciennes and me and work and books. Perfectly contented. Dreaming of it. And so we agree if there is any traveling to be done he will go alone because I want him to be free—free of me, free to run loose. I want to give him everything and set him free. For him I have all the courage and all the wisdom. Yesterday he repeated, "You may think June got the most from me—but it is you who have—you have got things from me June always wanted and never got." And I know it is true.

He laughs at himself now, at his timidity before Louveciennes. When he felt a boor and wanted to kick things around because they frightened him. Now Louveciennes is his property, his love. He has conquered a fear—a world. Aristocracy. Beauty. All that he deeply craves and appeared to loathe.

Artaud is one of the personages in my literary life like June, Louise. He has dramatic, theatrical qualities.

We acknowledge a difference. "I disdain reality and I am content to sleep and dream. I love my nightmare."

"Yes," says Artaud, "I noticed you were satisfied in your world. That is rare."

Suddenly I realized it wasn't my dreamworld which satisfied me, but Henry—Henry *in* my dreamworld and Henry the reality. I was almost ashamed of my joy before Artaud.

He leaves to have his regular Wednesday-night dinner with the Allendys.

Now when I think of Allendy I have lost the image of a dressed, imposing, enigmatic analyst, and I see a body—a body I don't want. What I want ardently is that month with Henry.

Métro Cadet. I'm late and Allendy thought I was not coming. Experience, curiosity, comedy. But I would like some whiskey. Allendy doesn't like my wanting whiskey. He says he never takes anything to drink in the afternoon and so he won't now, it would upset his habits. When he says this I drink more fiercely. It's humorous. *Allons donc.* The French room, in blue now. Shutters closed. Lugubrious. Lanterns and velvet. The alcove. As in eighteenth-century engravings! The beard and the French and all! The alcove.

Allendy doesn't kiss me. He sits on the edge of the bed and says, "Now you will pay for everything, for enslaving me and then abandoning me. *Petite garce!*"

And he takes out of his pocket a whip!

Now, I had not counted on the whip. I didn't know how to regard it. I was enjoying Allendy's fierceness—the fanatic eyes, his anger, the will in him.

He ordered that I should undress. I undressed slowly.

"You are going to play with men—torture them. Very well. You have won me, and then I can only possess you once or twice. Believe me, you will remember it, then. No other men will do to you what I will do—they haven't dared. Henry hasn't beaten you, has he? I'm going to possess you as you never have been possessed. You devil."

As I write all this I recognize the dime-novel quality of it. If I had read more cheap novels I might have recognized it immediately, but I only know them by hearsay.

Experience. Curiosity. Coldness. I don't know yet how to treat that whip. When Allendy tries a few preliminary lashes I'm simply angry and feel like hitting back. I don't yet see any "voluptuous" quality in it. In fact, I'm laughing. My pride is gravely offended. It seems to me this is like my Father beating me. I feel I ought to be cute and charming so he will be disarmed.

I had been fighting off Allendy's blows and decided to take my chemise off to affect him. At the same time, I provoked his fury by saying, "No, I don't want it. You can't do that."

"I'll reduce you to a rag," said Allendy. "You will crawl and do everything I bid you. I want you to abdicate—forget your pride—forget everything."

"I won't."

"You can't help it. You can scream. Nobody pays any attention to screams in this house."

"I don't want it because the marks will show. I don't want Hugo to see them, nor Henry either!"

At this Allendy laid me on the bed and whipped my buttocks, hard.

But I noticed this: His penis, after all this excitement on his part —lashes, struggles, caresses of fury, kisses on the breasts—was still soft. Henry would have been already blazing. Allendy pushed my head toward it, as the first time, and then, with all the halo of excitement, threats, he fucked no better than before. His penis was short and nerveless. Voluptuary! He found it. I played a comedy. Allendy said he had reached the height of joy. He lay panting and satisfied.

I was thinking; I'm going to write the absolute truth in my journal because reality deserves to be described in the vilest terms.

Faute de mieux, my body was warmed and burning from the whip. I had been given one sensation in place of another.

What amused me was to be able to deceive Allendy so deeply—psychologist! intuition! astrologer! The man who said before our meeting this terrible phrase: "My work is becoming monotonous. It is sad to see how human beings are all alike—react the same way at the same moment. Always the same pattern."

He sees only the resemblances—he misses the marvelous variations. Poor Allendy! That is death. Knowledge in place of faith. I have faith!

He kept saying, "I feel good. I feel wonderful. I knew you would like it. It brings the savage out in me."

What a savage—*un sauvage à faire rire.* And it is because he was not really, deeply savage that I'm savage tonight in my descriptions! Woman the whore. Yes, man is the one who did evolve! The sexless sage who must whip the savage back into life. After all, I liked that whip. That whip was virile, savage, hurtful, vital! It still stings!

I wonder if Allendy knows how uncapturable I have been. What a comedy it is for me to have been kissed, fucked, when I was not there at all. How intact I feel tonight here with my journal and a letter from Henry. Reality has no hold on me when it is stupid, or ridiculous, or ugly, or feeble.

How well I acted, so that in the taxi he had recurrences of "passion" (I talk relatively) and he was joyous.

He is enjoying the illusion of "mystery." He says when we are both celebrated no one will ever imagine such a scene possible. Nobody. I'm laughing. No, nobody could imagine!

"Not Artaud, for instance," said Allendy, with vengefulness, because he is jealous of Artaud.

"Not even I myself could have imagined it!"

Allendy has not understood that what I crave are the flagellations of passion alone and the enslaving by an authentic savage.

Each man's work is a *justification* of an insufficiency, a compensation. Allendy's wisdom, evolution, mystical annihilation into the whole, desire for death are all understandable.

He said, "This way you reach a kind of vertigo."

I reach vertigo when Henry opens his mouth to kiss me.

If one saves oneself from the terrors of life by knowing, from the dangers by wisdom, from the catastrophes by objectivity, to find at the same time that all living becomes unreal and a comedy—then I say for God's sake it is better to die, to suffer. What I hated today was, with Allendy, seeing through life as a drama which can be handled, dominated, tampered with—to feel that to know the springs of life is to destroy the essence of life, which is faith, terror, mystery. Today I saw the horror of wisdom. The mortal price one pays for it!

The question is: Have men died today because they have tampered with the sources of life, or did they tamper with the sources of life because they were dead and obtained an illusion of livingness from the handling of life?

Tonight I'm terrified.

I have walked through the universe of death. I was fucked by death!

MAY 1, 1933

HUGO IN LONDON FOR TWO DAYS. HENRY COMES immediately. Terrific talks and terrific passion.

I'm so right about Henry. He is so healthy, sensually. So vital that he is simple, unconcerned with vice, perversion, artificial stimulation. Lusty—as I am. Fundamentally healthy, taking pleasure in sheer vitality. Only the imagination deformed, gigantic.

Yet he does say, "The first day I saw you, I felt and believed you perverse, decadent. And apart from *our* personal experience, which is neither perverse nor decadent, I still feel in you an immense yielding, so that one feels there is no *limit* to you, to what you might be or do—that is decadence—an absence of boundary—a perverse yielding, limitless in experience."

Strange how Allendy has become split for me: The man of the whip is a ghost, disconcerting. In calm moments the ghost is the sage, idealistic, compassionate analyst, haunting that alcove, that Grand Guignol–French-novel scene without grandeur and without sincerity. I see the sage floating disembodied, eyes of the firmament. My dream! I see the body, the sexless body, expressing with a whip the rage of its own frustration!

All this in a crepuscular light.

If I do not tell Henry the schema of my neurosis, it is because I feel like a criminal who wants to be given a chance in a new country, with new people. It is a way of defeating the past. We do talk sometimes, in an effort to explain June, about the origin of June's and my eccentricities in clothes. June's bitchiness in sex (like Frieda in Lawrence's life).

We talk all day! Henry pours out all he knows, reads, thinks. He talks to find himself, his ideas. Lawrence—sex—his boyhood—a million subjects, explorations, discoveries. If there were no sex between us there would still be worlds and worlds of passionate common interests, interdevelopment.

Tonight, of all nights, is the one I chose to say my last word on Hugo—now that there is no more in me of that feeling of reproach or resentment. *It was all due to a need of justifying my passion for Henry.* And I regret the faults I attributed to Hugo. *He has none.* He is the most perfect of beings. I had great needs; I made unjust demands of him. I had inhuman expectations. Hugo has given me a divine and unmerited worship. He has lost himself in me. He has served and understood me and saved me. I owe him ten years of gifts such as few men have made a woman. I feel tonight a kind of flawless devotion. My railings, accusations were monstrous, unjust, and revealed a lack of understanding, because understanding means acceptance. I have tortured, tormented, nagged Hugo. He has given me his maximum. Just as I have tortured Eduardo with unjust demands—*demands for the impossible*.

I have never loved Hugo in a fraternal way as deeply and as

steadfastly as tonight. It may seem a sacrilege. It is because my contentment, at last, makes me only now truly wise, and truly human. I can say that I have understood only tonight Hugo's particular great value, independently from my needs.

Evening: The war against fragility. If I write too much, a whole day, my eyes are worn and dim and useless. I cannot read at night after I write.

I cannot do without sleep. I must calculate and economize my energy. I know my energy revolts against my driving will—revolts ferociously. I am trying to live without antagonizing it. I yield to the tide of fatigue. I accept that the day is too long for my endurance. I take siestas so as to be fresh until ten or eleven P.M. Yet I had to send Henry home after two days—to conceal my fatigue from him. It is true I exaggerate my shortcomings. But to fight a fragility and not a real mortal disease humiliates me. I cannot drink. One night of excess leaves a mark for a week.

At least I can count on my will in crises.

Often I am terribly sad. I tell myself that even if there were no Hugo I couldn't follow Henry because I would be a burden.

I am physically unfit for a big life—I have to split it in doses: space my orgies, my ecstasies, seek strength in the garden, condemned to an ease and rest I do not want (I loathe my siestas!). My mental, imaginative, emotional activity devours me and is in disproportion to my physical vitality.

I must drive myself. I laugh to think I must say to myself, "Tomorrow Artaud is coming. I cannot go to bed late tonight, then. I must accumulate energy!" Pathetic and ridiculous. Infuriating to me. If I had been given a normal energy I would be a great woman today.

The flagellation has left streaks of mauve.

Boussie doesn't like "Alraune." At first it hurt me, and then my *confidence* told me I am right and Boussie is aging. She will not come all the way with me. She turns French: asks for logic, sequence, the possible, translates pages but with an unconscious revolt. When one's friends begin to drop off it means one is doing something, getting somewhere. Opposition is good. I have to learn to face it.

Hugo returns and I begin to make him divinely happy. No more expectations, even that he should remember to mail letters and bring bread home!

MAY 5, 1933

I HAVE FOUND MY FATHER, THE GOD, ONLY TO DIS-cover that I do not need him. When he comes to me, he who has marked my childhood so deeply, I am already woman, and I am liberated of the need of Father and god. I am so absolutely woman that I *understand* my Father the *human being*—he is again the man who is also child.

Henry broke the chains. I faced my mature love. When my Father and I truly meet, after twenty years, it is not a meeting but a realization of the impossibility of meeting on earth except as man and woman, in the completeness of sex. The Father I imagined, strong, cruel, hero, tormentor, is soft, feminine, vulnerable. With him, God, too, becomes human, vulnerable, imperfect. I lose my terrors, my pain, the sacrilegious passion. I find a Father who is sacred. I find sacredness. I may, as Henry says, "reconciliate" myself with God, too, because I am free.

The love of Henry was the supreme test of my *womanhood*. In that test I was strong. I meet my Father and I am strong. I possess my own soul, my own integrity, my wholeness.

My Father comes when I have lived out the blind, cruel instinct to punish; he comes when I have gone beyond him; he is given to me when I don't need him, when I am free of him. My Father comes to me when he is no longer the intellectual leader I craved (Henry now), the guide I wept for (Allendy), the protector which the child in me leaned on (Hugo). He created a child and failed to inspire in her anything but the terror and pain of life, as God does, and I have outgrown the terror and the pain. Today I am preparing to liberate my Father of the pain and terror of life.

My life has been one long *strain*, one herculean effort and struggle to rise, to surpass in everything, to make myself a great character, to create, to perfect, to develop—a desperate and anxious ascension to efface and destroy a haunting insecurity about my own value. Always aiming higher, accumulating loves to compensate for the initial shock and terror of my first loss. Loves, books, creations, ascensions! Frenzied. Always attempting greater and deeper achievements, setting up ideals, images, shedding yesterday's woman to pursue a new vision. When I met June I absorbed and became all I admire. I became June. Now I feel again the beginning of a new ambition. I forget to enjoy all I have—incredible treasures! I forget that Monday, Bradley comes; Tuesday, Artaud, who is awed by me; Wednesday, Father; Thursday, Allendy; Friday, Henry; Saturday, Steele. There aren't enough days in the week! I have a waiting list: Millner, Gustavo, Nestor, André de Vilmorin. And my enjoyment is nullified by the image of Louise's mother, who had countless lovers and is a drug addict. Immediately my incommensurable ambition is roused. I am set traveling again, pursuing new difficulties, seeking new heights. Restless while there is land to discover, lives unlived. What madness! It is a *poison, a curse*. I want to enjoy; I want to stop and enjoy. People have been aware of the strain, the inexorable direction, and the purpose in me. It is over. It must be over, or it will kill me. It is always: I want! *I want!* Never: I have, *I have*. Insatiable. But today I arrest myself, and *this will be the journal of my enjoyment.*

Evening. I think of Allendy's pulpous flesh, and the feminine way he stands when he utters the word *pure,* with a certain yielding, oblique grace. I think of Allendy the furtive bourgeois waiting at the metro station, Saturnine, secretive, the woman's mouth and lacquered teeth glowing in the dark beard, feminine, and the strange dark feeling of flagellation. *I hate him.* He is repulsive to me, but repulsive as reality is, as a glaucous newspaper story, a Grand Guignol scene, repulsive like scenes of *Voyage au bout de la nuit* which impel one's attention. Some literary and morbid curiosity in me is watchful. I think of June flagellating the masochist who killed himself. I experience Allendy's voluptuous joy at whipping my own frailness, the terrible delusion of that vertigo which leads to an almost lesbian coition, a penis like a woman's finger or mouth—frustration—and I loathe Allendy with all the loathing one can have for senility and impotence become perverse by deviation, substitution. The very trick played on my senses by the substitution of the whip for the phallus enrages me and hypnotizes me.

I am not going to meet Allendy! I am not going to meet Allendy! I am certain now.

I am fascinated by the mere contemplation of an act of cruelty. I laugh to think of Allendy arriving at Métro Cadet with his whip in his pocket and I not there.

At the same time I cannot help remembering that he exposed himself, his secrets, his flesh, his doubts, his fears, to me, and I cannot hurt him. I see his head bowed as he said, "That first abandon marked me for life." I hear him saying, "All the women I have known until I met you *étaient des garces*. Bitches." I have a great desire to hurt him, and at the same time, humanly, I cannot. I melt and harden at the same moment. "Your only defect," said Henry, "is your incapacity for cruelty."

Bradley cannot imagine me "sociable," nothing but solitary and sheltered, unknown. His illusion! When I say I have an eventful life he is disappointed. Imagined me all alone (perhaps, too, rejoicing over his discovery of me).

What distresses me is that I seem to play on the feelings of people. They always melt. Something arouses their pity, and sometimes I feel like Henry. Beware of the man you give pity to: Henry, who also melts everybody. And June, the actress, reproaching him for playing the *rôle du martyr*. I have often wondered whether June was not the least effective liar of the three of us, because so easily discovered!

This straining after sincerity always leads me askew, into insincerity!

I expected the man of the photographs, a face less furrowed, less carved, more transparent. I found it so heavily engraved, stony, and at the same moment I liked the new face, the depths of the lines, the power of the jaws, the femininity of the smile all the more in relief against the tan, almost parchment-toned skin, a smile with a forceful dimple! The neatness of the figure, compact grace, the vital gestures, ease, youthfulness. A gust of imponderable charm, false charm. A supreme frank egoism. Webs of lies, of defenses against unuttered accusations; preoccupation with opinions of others, fear of criticism; susceptibility; continuous, inevitable distortions; wit and linguistic facility; violence of images; childishness; disarming charm. Always charm. The predominance of charm. The undercurrents of falseness, puerility, unreality. A man who has pampered himself, cottoned himself against the true, deep pains, deep living, yet occupied with my own essential problem—expansion, explosivity, fear of destructiveness. A passion for creation, and at certain moments a deep, inevitable cruelty. No psychology: "It is Nin," he says, the sudden darts of cruelty, the sudden explosions.

Source of feeling dried up by overacting, by self-consciousness, by egoism. My Double! My evil Double! He incarnates my fears, my self-doubts, my faults! He caricatures my tendencies. Something human and warm in me fights, fights against his coldness. I seek the *differences*. I see that he cares for money, that he is self-interested. I breathe with relief. I am clear of that. Also I see through myself. That is my sincerity. I know my insincerities. I am finished with any ideal image of myself. Father still carries this image. He must appear to himself kind, charitable, generous, altruistic. He is not, and why does he dread to admit it, recognize it?

I look at my Double, and I see in a mirror: My punctuality—a stressed, marked characteristic. A demand for punctuality. A need of order, like a carapace around the possibility of disorder, destruction, self-destruction.

The fragments of my life which did not fit my desired image, how I discarded them.

The necessity to act, to pretend.

His power. His power to give an illusion of sincerity by the fact that he deludes himself. The desperate need of giving illusion to others, out of an insecurity about the true value of the self. When I look at him I am sick of my lies and wonder if they are as transparent as his.

The long explanation of how and why he got sick and had to go down south for four months. The uneasy feeling which forces him to this display of explanations before the other person has even appeared to doubt the need of this trip, to ask for a justification of it. The need to demonstrate that he works enormously at something absolutely necessary, because he is not very certain that his work, or he, is necessary, vital, valuable.

Pride. Immense pride in conflict with the need of others, the need of love.

When he walks up to me talking and laughing I am unsettled, he does not seem to be my Father, but a man, a youthful man of infinite charm and fascinating falseness, labyrinthian, fluid, uncapturable as water.

We are gay, playful. We flirt like lovers. I remind him that I have left traces of rouge on his cheeks that Maria Luisa will see. I am seductive, and he says, "You have never looked so definitely Spanish as you do now."

He has yielded to his overcritical nature. He forgets to feel, to enjoy. His sensibilities are sudden, self-centered, puerile; or violent and cruel, vindictive.

He frightens me only at the moment that I remember that when I was a child he seemed always severe, displeased, discontented, and that his criticalness, hardness terrified me.

Now I escape from this terror by turning criticism against him. While he talks I am busy detecting the flaws, the revelations in his lies, the vanities, the poses of a man always in dread of being found out, condemned. He is always creating a defense before any attack.

My Double, from whom I have always run away in great terror, *wanting to be different*.

I ask Hugo plaintively, "Am I selfish?"

I have lived not to be my Father. His existence is a caricature, a ghost of my self-doubts, self-criticism, of my malady.

My malady returned yesterday. *The loss of myself*. The torture of tangential reflections, resemblances. "You garden, but with gloves, of course! As I did." Then if we both garden with gloves, we are perhaps also squeamish about poverty. We dread squalor, we are affected by it as by mire, we strive desperately out of it, we seek security, protection.

Cowards! Yet I have been bravely poor, unflinchingly poor, with perhaps a secret joy at defeating my Father's fear. I have made great sacrifices. I married a poor man. I have never calculated I would live with Henry any time. In actual fact, I have been fearless, capable of immense devotions. Yet the scrupulousness with which I have set out to destroy in myself any overattachment to luxury, to beauty, the endless qualms of conscience, doubts, the need of ultimate sacrifices as if to expiate a possible and still-inexistent fault—is a malady, a malady. I live in opposition to my Double. I live with a caricature of my faults in order to be disgusted by them.

At night I dreamed that my Father caressed me like a lover, and I experienced an immense joy. I awoke to find it was Hugo. I also thought at night of the many resemblances between my Father and Henry. But Henry has broken the chains of my servitude and devotion to my Father by being greater than my Father within his own realm.

MAY 10, 1933

ARTAUD'S VISIT HAS LOST ITS VIVIDNESS, YET AT the moment it engrossed me powerfully. We talked with passion about our habits of condensation, of rigorous sifting, our quest of the essential, our love of quintessence all through life and literature, untiring. We discussed analysis, at first aggressively. He is bitter about the pragmatic employment of it, says it serves only to liberate people sexually, whereas it should be used only as a metaphysical discipline, to reach the Whole. We discovered he was not, in a sense, ever as much in need of it as I was, because he has never entirely lost his equilibrium as I did. He remains lucid about his self, objective. I am either more naive or more emotional, I don't know which. He enjoyed discovering I was born mostly under water signs. Said it suited me exactly and talked of me as having a substance, but a slippery one, like that of a fish that is difficult to catch although you can feel it! Is that the true meaning of my first story's title, "The Woman No Man Could Hold"? Henry alone has got a grip on me!

I am beginning, like Henry, to enjoy seeing things go wrong, to seek harmony less intensely, to let catastrophes and misunderstandings accumulate, explode.

Yet I can't bring myself to let Allendy wait at Métro Cadet. His voice is very cold when I tell him I am coming to Passy to see him instead of to Métro Cadet. The farce and game of flagellation becomes more and more nauseating to me as I come upon *real* and deeper conflicts and torments.

Evening. Allendy puts order into my chaos by saying that as I still have a great sense of guilt because of the nature of my feelings for my Father, I displace the realm of the punishment and I punish myself and express my feeling of guilt only in regard to my lies, smaller actions, and other faults, all but *the* one, as if to elude the true crime or sin by a long enumeration of smaller, extraneous crimes and sins! *Très bien*. But then, I have resolved to use this sense of guilt to free myself of relations with Allendy. I overemphasize, accentuate it, I invent a scene with Father at which he begs me not to have lovers, and I tell Allendy I have sworn not to have them because I love my Father and his tyranny. I let Allendy believe me a masochist of the most obstinate, obdurate sexuality.

Does he believe me?

How uneasy he is with my lies, my truths, my convincing distress. He kisses my arms and neck and puts his hands on my legs. I see that I tantalize him, that he is again beside himself. And I'm sad. All because I can't say brutally, "I don't want you for a lover."

He is rejoicing because he thinks my Father is at least dislodging Henry. It makes him feel almost friendly toward my Father. He says, "I almost like that Spaniard preaching morality to his daughter."

When I see how intensely vulnerable Allendy is, when I hear the anxious tone of his occasional doubts, I feel less and less capable of telling any human being the truth. Nobody can bear defeat; everybody, even an objective analyst, is mortally offended, injured.

I was still warm from two hours spent at a café with Henry, who, to stay with me, had walked with me almost to Allendy's door. While we walked, we planned Henry's coming to Louveciennes Friday night, an hour after Hugo leaves for Switzerland, and my Father for Spain.

Allendy certifies my intuition that Artaud is homosexual, and immediately I realize why he was attracted to Hugo, an attraction which at first puzzled me. And I chuckle to myself: Always a homosexual in the background!

I sit waiting for my Father and fully aware of his superficiality.

The bondage to my Father is broken. Allendy may have helped me again. But the one who truly broke the chains is Henry, by what he is. The deep, deep wells of feeling in Henry, the gravity, the weight of his fervors, all so deep and rich.

I am dreaming. This is not living. My Father arriving with arms loaded with flowers and a delicate Lalique vase. In a sincere mood because no longer uneasy. Confiding and gentle. And we sit for hours, discovering our sameness. I had divined everything, and so had he. Maria is Hugo. We adore their goodness, this perfection. We create harmony, security, a shelter, a home, and then we chafe. Like tigers, says Father. Restless, vital, fearing to hurt, to destroy, but avid for life, renewal, evolutions. Cowards before the goodness, loyalty of Hugo and Maria. Our disciples and worshipers! These two who have power over us. The world may think we are the tyrants. Father and I know how enslaved we can be by tenderness, pity, the goodness of the others, enchained. Wishing Maria and Hugo would be cruel to us so that we could be, too!

We say, "We don't need to lie to each other!" Yet we do, of course. I must lie to him about Henry coming tonight, because my Father does not want me to see him. And he lies, too, but not about essentials.

He tells me, "You have become beautiful. Lovely, that black hair, green eyes, red mouth. And one sees that you have suffered, yet the face is placid. It is made beautiful by suffering."

I am standing against the mantelpiece. He is looking at my hands. I jerk backward suddenly and push the crystal bowl against the wall. The bowl breaks and the water splashes all over the floor. The meaning of this I don't know.

He had been saying, "In June, when Hugo goes away, you must come to the Riviera with me. They will take you for my mistress, that's sure. It will be delightful."

He talks about the Nin illnesses as proudly, almost, as about a Nin possession. The Nin liver, the Nin rheumatism, the Nin pallor. He injects pride into our humiliations, even. Pride. Pride. And I realize suddenly the enormousness of my selfsame pride. Only I choose to express it by humility. I am humble, but the more humble, the prouder the core, the hard Nin core, which disdains the world which hurts it. How profoundly I suffer from poverty, humiliations, so profoundly that only a great pride can explain the wounds, the depths of the wounds. If I were not proud I would not be so mortally offended. I forgive offenses, but in that, too, there is a contempt for the world. I forgive and I feel superior. I humble myself because I know my pride. I am too proud to give myself, to confide, to reveal myself; I choose esoteric writing, a secret journal, a single passion. Too proud to yield to ordinary liaisons. Noble. Everything must be large, noble.

When I see my Father I feel this pride awakening fiercely, like a serpent. I feel the tigress now! Under the goodness, under the sacrifices, under the pity, a burning pride. I am immensely proud of my Father!

I understand in him, as in Henry, the artist's egoistical quest of protection by women (which is, as I said once, like the childbearing woman's quest for a male supporter, protector). I see the sincerity beneath the apparently calculating gesture. I understand in him, as I do in Henry, the need for independence, for stimulants, for whores. It seems to me that I felt how I should interpret Henry and divined all of Henry's needs from my blood-knowledge of a Father about whom I knew nothing consciously, all that I knew being only distortions, for it is clear that nobody has understood my Father—nobody except Maria, who worships him.

Henry and I fell asleep peacefully, joyously, in the Arabian bed. My first thought this morning was to telephone Father: *"Bonjour, mon très, très vieux chêne."*

"Farceuse, va," says Father gaily.

He believes Mother is staying with me while Hugo is away. One liar against another liar. It is Henry who comes down to breakfast while I am telephoning my Father.

When I broke the crystal bowl and the water gushed out, was I shattering an artificial, unreal, contained life and letting life break through and flow? Catastrophe and flow.

Father said, "I wasn't worrying about being old—I know I'm not old. But I was anxious lest you should come too late—when I would be old. Anxious that you might not see me vivid and laughing and able to make you laugh . . ."

And suddenly I felt a surge of admiration for my Double! I regretted the years I did not know him, learn from him. I was proud, and I suffered from not being up to his ideal when I came from New York. I felt unprepared. I feared disappointing him. Together with forgiveness, there was much of the need to give Father the best in me. When I felt strong, I felt the time had come. But if I had been humble I might have learned from him.

Now I have become what I am alone, and only then do I make the gift of myself. Yet I have much to learn yet from Father. As I had much to learn from Henry.

Henry. Henry is painting watercolors of me. Talking and fucking. Enjoying peace with me. But sometimes we are on the brink of a tiff. Henry, in his warring mood, attacks my aristocratic impermeability, feels like breaking down this ultimate superiority. Henry has always been a bit disconcerted by my bearing. He says the first night he came with June I sat royally aloof, impressive. The more timid, the more royal I get.

We teased and joked. I said, "You can break down everything except that. I will always be kind to people, but never familiar . . ."

I sit by the fire on orange pillows. Henry is painting. There are watercolors on the floor, books open on the table and on the desk, notes, manuscripts. I am in paradise always, with Henry.

From one of Henry's letters: Now I see I can really complete something. Previously, everything was aborted by this or that—by myself, I suppose. Now not even an earthquake could keep me from carrying out my plans. . . . It's not Lawrence, it's myself I'm making a place for. . . . I will put Lawrence high and dry above the sniveling corpse diggers who are writing about him. If I have buried him, I have at least buried him alive.

M A Y 1 4 , 1 9 3 3

*H*ENRY AND I WERE SOUNDLY ASLEEP EARLY THIS morning when we heard the doorbell. It was Henry who was anxious, immediately alert, by a strange intuition. I was going to say to him, as I have said other times, "Don't worry. It's the baker or the milkman." But suddenly I heard Hugo's voice talking to Emilia. He was coming in quickly. Henry leaped out of bed and picked up his clothes. I rushed out to meet Hugo on the stairs, to stop him, to give Henry time to go to the guest room. The turning of the stairs saved us. Halfway down I met Hugo and kissed him, trying to gain time. Two more steps up, and he could have seen Henry passing.

Then we came up. But Hugo had seen Henry's coat and hat in the hall. A profoundly suspicious and angry look came over his face. I have never seen such a look on Hugo's face, of *absolute knowingness*. He said, "Who is here—Henry?" I answered, "Henry came to see me yesterday, and as it was Emilia's night out I was afraid, and he stayed because I was afraid."

And then I went back to bed, trembling, and I began to talk, to talk. I had the intuition to talk about my Father, raving about his charm, our resemblance, until Hugo, who had been jealous of Father, began to get anxious over him. I ended with, "When Father came

Saturday he offered to stay and keep me company. Would you have preferred that? Henry seemed a less dangerous prospect."

But he said, "I imagined I heard Henry rushing out of your room."

"What an imagination you have! Do you think that if I were to deceive you I would do it as blatantly as that!"

He needed to believe, poor Hugo. He wanted consolation, support, protection, security, because he has been tired and worried about money matters. I gave him enormous tenderness. I calmed his fears, doubts, jealousies. He went to work almost gaily. I waved to him from the window. Then I went to Henry's room.

Henry and I took up our work, our reading. Then Father telephoned: "I must come to see you, even if only for an hour." I had to rush to give Henry lunch.

I hated to let Henry feel I was sending him away. I kissed him, excusing myself because I had to go and change my dress. "It's like a theater, your life," said Henry. "Now for the next act. How quickly you must change . . ."

While I am taking a ten-minute rest, he comes into my room. He has been sitting by the fire meditating over his liqueur. He comes in and walks restlessly about, saying: "Listen, Anaïs, if things go smash, let them go smash. Don't try to patch them up. Don't worry about me. Then you can come to Clichy and we'll manage somehow. Don't be anxious or terrorized. I'll be glad if things go smash. It's right."

This assertion of fearlessness of consequences in Henry, who has for the first time enjoyed a security which makes his work possible, was a great offering. An unselfish offer. I was touched by it. I reassured him. Nothing terrified me, I promised him. But I liked hearing him say this. He came up to the bed and we kissed. He had seemed so supremely man and responsible.

He felt sorry for me. My last words were, "I'm not anxious about anything."

Only tired.

And Father comes, resplendent, and we understand each other, so it is miraculous. I see the equilibrium that is the basis of our natures.

Is Father going to keep me from breaking loose? It seems to me that when we are together we are both *stronger*, as when Henry and I are together.

Father, too, is jealous of the journal. "My only rival," he says.

Henry notices again that nothing in my house, however beautiful, is useless. Henry has seen me hammer, repair the typewriter, set up a lamp, make him comfortable. "What a head you have," he says. Suddenly, yesterday, I said to Henry how I would not mind at all now being uncreative in art, that I would be contented to put my talent for living at his service, to be of use to his work. I have no immense personal ambition for a "work"—only to live and to submit this life to my love, the creator, Henry.

Hugh's confidence will never be the same. In his unconscious there is a doubt now. I cannot forget his face that morning. I have lost all sense of security. He *knows*. He had the same look as Henry Hunt the night Louise met her lover in the cabaret—a green, angry, hate-filled look. It terrifies me. I write to Henry, "There was no crash, but there will be no more trustingness. I don't want to be a burden to you, ever. I am determined you will have your security and your independence always. My life is subjected to your needs. It revolves around your needs."

I write Artaud, sending him a little money.

I realized that the *pleasures* of love are nothing to me without everything else around it. There is no pleasure for me in the "five-to-seven." Which definitely disposes of Allendy and all other games. That's settled. In my dream I humiliated Allendy for thinking of life as a game.

Pleasure elsewhere. Pleasure in giving Artaud relief from servitude to material needs and, above all, relief from his feeling that the world is against him.

I remember Allendy's jest, "Don't play with Artaud. He is an underdog, he is too miserable."

He is always so brutal and so direct, believing that my Father wants to sleep with me, jumping always to the conclusion and missing all the *étapes*, as Henry missed all the constellations of lesbianism. The sleeping together is the least important and the most obvious, the most unsatisfactory and stupid way to continually picture life.

I say to myself that I am treating Hugh cruelly, shabbily. I think of his loyalty and I feel mean. I think of his life and feel I am sacrificing it to my expansion. I prepare myself to love him. All afternoon I muse on his qualities. I see him studying astrology, so much like a saint. I hear the car, his step, his voice. I meet him smiling. He is young, peaceful. But desirous, too eager, too clinging. I submit to his caresses. My body is so indifferent. But before his desire, then, I am in revolt. I hate his mouth on mine. And the pain, the big, clumsy ravages, always like a violation. My face is twisted with pain. I must conceal my face; and the sighs and shouts of pain I pretend to be sighs and shouts of joy. Fortunately, he is swift, like a heavy-clawed bird, and I am all bristling with hostility, distaste. I hate him at this moment. All my desire to be loving is annihilated. I would like to hurt him. I have to repeat to myself, "He doesn't know, he doesn't know what torture it is." But I hate him. And if a few moments later he loses something, or asks me for a favor, then I feel an immense irritation at all his small faults, a fury that he should be absentminded, dim, careless, forgetful. All the little faults seem unbearable because I don't love him. I feel like spitting fire. I wash myself quickly, angrily. I feel bitter. I'm tired of driving and controlling myself into love. Tired of pretending. Doesn't he feel my body cold to his, against his? Why does he desire me so stubbornly, blindly? He senses nothing. It is ridiculous, and disarming, too.

Our life together is a tomb. When I hear music I imagine myself breaking out violently. Just breaking out. Weeping, shouting, hurling truths, going mad.

Hugh sits calmly under the lamplight, drawing horoscopes. Innocent. Blameless. Blind. Void. Here and there a few live islands in him, vibrant regions. But great spaces of void indifferences, lethargies. A partial blindness and deafness. Maybe I chose this as an antidote to my hyperawareness. But now I've outgrown this need of cotton, passive peace, loyalty, everything. I mustn't let my sexual sacrifice and hatred drive me into injustice. But it is no wonder I desire a war, an earthquake which would tear us asunder.

MAY 16, 1933

*T*ALK WITH JOAQUIN, WALKING BLINDLY AND wildly around the lake. Words. Seeing nothing, all absorbed in pain. Begging Joaquin not to judge his Father, because then he judges and condemns me. Joaquin furious, saying there are no resemblances in the essentials—only in details. Father lives in a nonhuman world. But so do I! But suddenly I remember Henry and I melt. And Joaquin says, "You see, you see, you are human!"

Joaquin talked about Father's bad conscience (Father is still trying to justify to everybody his abandonment of Mother). How far back does the crime date? What was the crime? I know that when I blame myself with morbid scruples about my conduct toward Hugh it is not because of one act or another, but because of a fundamental sense of guilt at the root of all our uneasiness and overscrupulousness. Truly a morbid self-criticism. As, for example, when I tell Henry about our financial difficulties and then purchase, for nineteen francs, the little glass castle of *"Les Ruines."** I am so conscience-stricken that when he looks at it I say that someone gave it to me. I am aware of the violence with which I desired this object, this trinket, the fact that when I got it I was only thinking of my desire, that my imagination was ensorcelled, and that when I became sober, I was not happy to have indulged myself.

Yet on other days I have carried heavy bags full of books to be sold to get Henry the books he needs for his work. I wear worn sandals, and I have only two nightgowns, but I send Artaud two hundred francs and incur Hugh's anger by doing so. I believe the story of the

---

* *"Les Ruines"* was the name of the house in Arcachon, France, where Anaïs Nin had last seen her father when the family broke up.

nineteen-franc trinket explains many of Father's lies. He is afraid to be judged, not because of the details of his life, but because of some deep and secret sense of guilt which colors and permeates his whole life.

Hugh says, "You can't go to the Riviera with your Father. You belong to me." Outside of sex, as soon as the sexual possessiveness is over, I can be tender again. I begin to think of expenses, and I am ready to give up the trip.

I believe that instead of being honest criminals, Father and I have been too cowardly to live our lives bravely and unflinchingly. That is, indifferent to others' feelings. There is in us, as in Henry, a treacherous, nonhuman core. But we don't dare expose it, live by it. We are always compromising with human life. Father endured Mother for eleven years. Henry was forced by June to abandon his wife and child, and more or less by me to abandon June.

MAY 18, 1933

*T*HE MORNING AFTER MY TALK WITH JOAQUIN, I awoke vomiting, and for a day I was racked by fever, stupor, chills, a feeling of being poisoned; so weak that I wept when Hugh kissed me. Henry offered to come, but I didn't want to see him. Henry is for my brave days only. Henry loves me selfishly, as I love Hugh, not for myself but for what I give him. When I'm sick I feel I cannot face Henry—that he would be impatient with my frailties. Because together with illness I experience a crisis of hypersensitiveness: I doubt the whole world, I fear the whole world, except Hugh. Joaquin telephones me, having thought a great deal about me. Mother *does* things for me, knits and runs errands because she feels remorseful and an unconscious desire to compensate for the lack of understanding. I am always indebted to her, for *things* only. But I am no longer a slave to my debts.

Allendy has done nothing for my hypersensitivity. I was lying here listening to music, and broken down by everything, horribly *exposed*, weeping with gratitude just to have Hugh, a house, a bed, to be able to lie somewhere protected. In my fever I imagined myself walking the streets, Hugh having thrown me out because of Henry, all of them against me. Allendy furious and unforgiving. Henry occupied with a whore. All of them cruel. Eduardo cold and fishlike; Mother vituperous, viperish, unforgiving, moralistic; Father critical, fearing that I should make a mess of my life. Hugh and Maria the infinitely superior ones because *they alone have loved.*

M AY 2 1 , 1 9 3 3

SLOW RECOVERY AND REAWAKENING TO JOY AND livingness, after reaching the depths of weakness and inner delirium. The sun! Warmth! Long hours of somnolence. Henry's southern voice over the telephone. Euphoria. Bath. The joys of water, of freshness. Body sane and light. Immediately I think Henry must need money. Henry. And I write my Father a letter. The divan lullingness of a summer day. My Father, my Father. Powder, perfume, the Italian dress (a recombined black velvet with Florentine puffed top of blue-green velvet dotted with gold). Who is there? Open the doors! The house is festive, singing, with odor of mock orange. *Olé, Anaïs!* Gustavo, radiant; and Nestor, with a beautifully bestial, Negroid face, prominent jet black eyes, the great painter of water and earth.

The joy they bring! Gustavo says, "Your Father, who was a man who had never given himself, is no longer the same man. You are truly the first *aventure sentimentale* of your Father. He was swept off his feet by you, Anaïs."

I sit absolutely still, inundated by joy, quivering in it, gloating, almost dying of it. I can give at last! All I have in me is wanted! And nobody knows yet all I have! The more I love Henry, the more full I am! Inexhaustible. And I can love my Father. He needs me; he does not *face himself*. I have wisdom to give him, joys, a new experience, a stimulant. Life! I have gifts for my Father, and he craves them. "Nobody, nobody," he said in front of everybody, "not even Maria, has given me the feelings Anaïs has given me." Poor Father. In one moment I understood so much, so much, that I was overwhelmed. I wanted him to return immediately. I talked rather wildly to Nestor and Gustavo about *faith,* faith creating miracles. Miracles. I believe in magic, miracles! Everything is strangely beautiful, breathtaking. Life takes my breath away.

Joaquin came and surprised us. He investigated my desk, read Father's letters, looked at Father's photograph, and I remembered Gustavo's words, "These two would not harmonize. Any attempt at *rapprochement* would end in tragedy. It is you he loves. With Joaquin it is a question of a composer who has a son who is also a composer. Joaquin will never love his father."

And he is afraid of my Father's influence on me, of losing me to my Father.

*To Father:** All the discoveries I have made about your life and about you correspond to what I so deeply wanted them and you to be. I realize that I searched dimly for them in others, but you, only you, fill a great void that I found in the world. Do you know what the shattered crystal meant? All of that represented the unreal world I lived in. The boat, the sea. I always wanted to go away, to leave the world behind. When you came back, reality became beautiful, completely satisfying. I broke the imitation, the dream—the artificial, congealed, dead world. As you yourself also wrote, "Resurrected!"

---

* In French in the original.

Thinking constantly of my Father. I am not going to restrain myself any longer. No more breaks! I realized that I opened his letter with the same intensity as I had opened Henry's:*

> Above all, tell me about Hugh's plans, for I dream of our escape toward the sun and of having you completely to myself for a few days. We both deserve that heavenly joy. Our hearts, scorched at every flame, will burst joyfully into flower. The good seed will send forth strong, healthy shoots under the ardent warmth of our resuscitated souls. Fugitives from a painful past, we come to each other to reforge our broken unity. . . . But that extraordinary communion will require hours and hours of uninterrupted outpouring, in solitude, between heaven and earth. The gods will never have known greater happiness. Bless you, Anaïs, always.

Tonight I am sad. The torturing ironies of life. I *gave Henry all that my Father wants*. Dislocations. I cannot give Father now the same wholeness in passion. I am divided. Yet it is true I loved in Henry resemblances to my Father.

The answer, the response, comes when I have spent myself desiring.

But now I am still fuller than most beings. Full enough to return Father's love, if not to surpass it!

I dream of making him live, feel, forget himself, know joy, élan, a whole giving, for I know all the joys of giving oneself.

My gratitude overflows. Gently, gently I detach Allendy from me. He said he was afraid of his mind giving way, that it was getting vertiginous, dark! I gave him back his security, serenity, so precious to him. But I did give him moments of vertigo. A "delicious mistress," he said, begging me not to abandon him completely. I realized women must not demand sensuality from Christs and creators. Allendy's gentleness was beautiful, a sexless softness, all charity. He presents me with a stray cat he loves but cannot keep. Allendy is a woman.

---

* In French in the original.

To cheer me up while I was ill, Henry sent me a copy of a letter to Emil in which he described full-length his exuberance, his well-being, his joy, his bicycle rides.

I hid my breakdown from him. I sent for him when I was *well*.

When I talked to him he was unfeeling, callous—like a man who was not interested in anything but his own life, his work. I saw his face and I stopped. I said, "You are in one of your cold moods." He was so empty, so self-engrossed. I stopped talking. I withdrew into myself. I tried to forget it all. Something had died in me. Oh, so utterly, utterly selfish. He hung his head. He was sorry, but in such a dull, merely conscious way. He didn't care. Suddenly all the accumulated egoisms overwhelmed me. All of them I realized in one minute, as a drowning man realizes his entire life. The love of the supreme egoist for the woman whom he can use.

I began to tremble and shake. I had to run into the house. He stayed in the garden, dull, blind. I asked him to leave me. He said, "You have seen the ugly side of me."

I was crushed by what I had seen.

I wrote him a letter, accusing him. A terrible revolt, all the more terrible because I constantly excused his selfishness: The artist! The artist! The monster!

I don't know what happened to me. Something broke down, my faith, my blindness. I am tired, tired to death of pain. I want the love that I deserve. Nothing less. I'm weary to death of giving, emptying myself. Constant devotion to Henry. His well-being a perpetual fixed aim for me.

He was at a creative period of his life, and he took the woman who demanded little—one day a week of humanness!

How cold physical warmth can be, deep down: All Henry's caresses, nothing. Ashes. All June's words come back to me: "I gave myself wholly, and he hurt me, betrayed me. That is why I took refuge in Jean."

Everything crushes around me. His letters to his friends after days spent in Louveciennes—never a word about *me*, only what he *got*, what he *gained*, what he learned or discovered. Louveciennes is a food. I am a food. My love is a food. I'm sick of it, sick to death!

When there is tenderness or pity or thoughtfulness, it is *of the moment*. Naturally, in my *presence* those things flower, and I believe in them. I believed in his phrases. It was enough that he said, "I want to give you things."

But he is honest about all this. He knows it. He knows he *retains* nothing. That the center is always *him*. That is why he hates American women—because they are selfish, cold, bold, self-defensive. You can't enslave them. I have been a slave.

Today I'm rebellious. Of course, I may forgive him. I always *forgive*. But I want the farce ended—the farce of love. I have seen too starkly the ugly in Henry, the limitation. I have got to free myself, save myself. My God, I want to love, I want love!

Hugh is in London. I saw Steele. I accepted an invitation to his house. I was weak enough to go to Henry to say, "I'm through—I'm through." He wasn't home. He telephoned me. But he telephoned at about three, after sleeping soundly, probably.

He telephoned again: "I don't understand all this! I don't know what it is all about. You sent me away yesterday like your gardener. Your voice sounds cold and imperious. You frighten me!"

Obtuseness. Innocence. That is always his response: "I didn't know—I didn't mean—I never thought." He who is so touchy, feels so easily humiliated, is *insensitive* to others' feelings. There are in him large insensitive areas regarding others. *He always fails to understand others*.

M A Y   2 7 ,   1 9 3 3

*H*ENRY CAME. I SAT ON THE COUCH AND IN A LOW voice I made a long accusation, reproaches. Not angrily, very sadly. Whenever I said, "You don't love me," he wanted to laugh almost.

But after a while he sat crushed. He bowed his head: "I didn't know I was as bad as that." This said in a grave tone, and his head bowed, with the veins swollen under the delicate skin. I couldn't bear it. I walked over to him and knelt. I hid my head between his knees and I sobbed. Henry kissed my neck. And then he said, "Anaïs, about the selfishness I don't know what to say. I didn't know I was as bad as that. But about loving you, you've just got to *believe*, that's all." We stood up and he kissed me so fervently, so fervently, that I believed again, I believed.

And he laid me on the couch and simply took me, with such a mixture of hunger and tenderness, stopping to say, "My God, Anaïs, don't you know how I love you?"

I knew. I also knew that the doubts and accusations in me were exaggerated. He had been callous for a day, but deep down he did care, as a man can care. It was natural that he should be the preoccupation of my life, but that the preoccupation of his life should be his work and himself, himself as bound up with his work. I had simply been too much woman. I had needed a proof of the closeness, because most of the time we live out such an independent, courageous, mature relation.

Poor Henry! He was overwhelmed by our scene. He had been made to suffer. And I had irritated him Tuesday. He had been jealous of my Father and of Joaquin, of my breakdown. He had made himself hard. Had refused to feel.

He defended his attitude in a letter, wisely. "You were quick, you know. Ordinarily you wouldn't be hurt by my selfish enjoyment of life. You would relish it."

He suspected I concealed from him the real cause of my breakdown and that it was something else.

He was jealous of the diary! Fearful of it:

I know that there must be shadows around all those images of light you read to me. There must be cruel things in the diary, things much more cruel than I could ever bring myself to admit. I am deeply, deeply regretful that I failed you yesterday. I tell you still, it is all confusing and mysterious to me. I came in high spirits, with the intention of putting my arms around you immediately and loving you to death. And then, as always happens—it isn't a new thing—I enter the house

and I am conscious of being a guest, even though a very privileged one. It is not my house and you are not my wife. You
stand there in the open door and I always see a princess who
for some secret whim has condescended to offer me her love.
I feel like nobody. I feel that I might be X. Everything is a
gift. And a crazy delicacy comes over me and I stand there
and shake your hand and talk about intermediate things and
I say to myself it's so wonderful here and none of this is real
it's all a dream. I say it because though I know I deserve a
little of life, I do not merit all that you give me. And even
when I talk so much about myself, which must be terribly
boring to you, it's probably because I'm trying to talk myself
into the reality of all this which you bring to me when you
just stand by the open door and greet me. You don't know
what a great moment that always is for me. Then I become
so human that I grow delicate. And so it was yesterday. My
callousness was delicacy. I was hungry for you. I could have
pulled your clothes off when you brought me back to the
hammock; I could have devoured you. But I sat there opposite
you and I talked. I made a detour and got lost so that I might
be with you five minutes sooner. But you looked awfully frail
yesterday; you looked as if you had been ill. And I felt that
my devouring hunger might seem truly indelicate. I wanted
you to have the best part of me. And so we talked, and what
really hurt you was that I did not put my arms around you.
Well, it was a strange kind of callousness that prevented me.
Not your imagined callousness. I thought that my "healthiness"
would dissipate all the fumes of illness. I thought—and I guess
that's romanticism—that I could just sit there and be with you
and make you feel wonderful inside. What I really wanted
was to lay you down in the grass and go with you. I'm still
naïf and clumsy. I left you in a dazed way, a little pleased at
you sending me off that way—because I like it, too, when you
play the grand Spanish lady with me! (The writer Henry
watching the grand scene! Amusing, this: he in bicycling suit
and I in lace, with a cape, ordering him to leave me!)

On the way down the hill I felt very happy, because I

imagined you going upstairs and writing some more "Alraune" pages. And if driving me away like that would help you to write some more, Anaïs, then I am always at your service. You can always make a human doormat of me—for *your art*. That ought to please you a little, Anaïs. Because I think you're a great artist. And as for that personality of yours . . . you have a great personality. Even if you had kept no diary . . . there are days, like yesterday, when you don't know what you are, artist, human being, personality, or self-portrait . . . and then you make others miserable. But that is all right. I approve of it. You *should* make others miserable once in a while. You have your bad moments, like all of us . . . and when I wrote that exultant letter to Emil about being filled with the Holy Ghost, I thought to myself how queer it is that we palm it off on the Holy Ghost. You are the Holy Ghost inside me. You make my spring.

His good nature, simplicity, humor melt me. We laughed about my scene afterward. He quoted Lawrence, " 'We shouldn't pamper each other. We should stand alone.' "

I appeared unexpectedly at Henry's door at midnight, Saturday, after Steele's dinner, abandoning both Artaud and Steele, and waited sitting on the doormat. Henry arrived and he had a cold. And though he pretended to be tough, he slowly *melted* entirely into me, became soft and tender, *wanting* love, wanting to be pampered, exaggerating his cold! And we laughed and fucked and teased each other. And Saturday was magical. I had an errand to do, and Henry began his trick of following me until Hugh's return. We wandered through the city like two southerners, like convalescents, he said, very close, very soft, very sentimental. We ate when we got hungry, in the rue de l'Abbé Groult, in a little bistro—ham and salad and cheese—and I got drunk on one glass of white wine. I could see the radium sunlight lighting up the archway of the trees' foliage, shimmering, when in reality the day was gray. I felt and saw light and constant warmth. I wanted to make Henry a gift because of his cold, and he confessed he craved a phonograph. We went shopping together. We brought the phonograph back in a taxi. It was raining and we sat lulled in the warm taxi, so contented, so soft, so close. Arm in arm. We went to bed and slept soundly in the warm of this magical womb containing both of us, lulling us. A womb of warmth, like a tropical sorcery. The salad, the ham, the wine, the streets, the phonograph, the taxi rides, the bed, all bursting with a magical content—our double enjoyment, heightening everything. Henry expands, roseate, flowing, handsome with glowingness, and I feel his joy, his appetite, his enjoyment. I become hungry and roseate. He gives me the savor of the present. Nowhere else do I find this magic, this beautiful, complete present. Together the moment becomes infinite.

Henry says, "I never feel this when I am with Fred. He spends all his money and we do not enjoy ourselves. He bores me." So I add to Henry's enjoyment by mine. I spread, I sprawl, I feel the bench of the bistro, and I have never seen such a golden mayonnaise. Never felt everything to be so good. The people who talk like Céline's *Voyage au bout de la nuit*. Henry's voice and mouth. Drunkenness. This moment of utter and absolute tasting of food, of color, of absolute human breathing, of wholeness. For I am all gathered there in the bistro at Henry's side. It is the end of all restlessness. There is not, as there is every other moment and place, a fragment of me detached, errant, disconnected, tragically rebellious, like a piece of a puzzle that does not fit into the pattern. For a day I stand with Henry: a whole image, without regrets, without past, and without future. No dark spaces around me, no horizons, no shadows. Life encompassed in a day, and the only thought in my mind is the day, the hour, Henry, the taxi, the meal, and I would want to be *nowhere* else, with *no one else* but Henry. I would want not a cent more than what we have because that is sufficient for the needs of the day—and those are the only needs we have. How simple the fulfillment of one's lifelong desire and strain. Yesterday was the realization of all these dark hungers—that simple yesterday, rounding off into our heavy sleep to get warm while it rained so heavily outside. Henry's extreme and simple lovingness— stripped of all ornament and literature—when only a few days before he had been roused to the old automatic fury and hatred because someone wrote that June had talked bitterly about him and he wrote a melodramatic letter which, twenty-four hours later, nauseated him because *he did not mean it,* and he realized he had experienced the last *sursauts* of a hatred which is a "stronger bond than love," but which calls forth phrases and literature and aftermaths of nauseas.

Such an immense pity I have for Artaud because he is always suffering. I realize how *extremely rare are the moments of physical well-being I have known, and equally rare the moments of absolute joy,* and I want to create those moments for others. I know Artaud's nerves and sensitivity are assuaged here—I remember what Henry was when I met him, and now he is an exultant, joyous, creative being. It is the darkness, the bitterness in Artaud I want to heal. Physically, I wouldn't touch him. But the flame in him, and the pain, these I love.

MAY 29, 1933

*T*HESE DAYS I FEEL CONTINUOUSLY AND DEEPLY sincere. More serious than ever, more contented, more human. I don't write. My imagination is lulled. I am always tormented, yes, by ghosts, but relatively in control. Moods. My moods are growing stronger, more tyrannical. I am more gripped by them. They come to the surface; they explode. Less control. But a wonderful flow. In short, both the normal and the abnormal are strong. I feel life and I feel the dream, both of them, absolutely.

Cycles of neuroticism; but awareness keeps me afloat. What a struggle to keep afloat, gay. Henry gives me a letter, and my fingers tremble when he hands it to me because I fear it should contain one of these phrases which suffocate me—a trivial wound, a little hurt, immense for me. I fear this magnifying vision. I am so happy when the afternoon is over and he has not hurt me. Then I wonder if I have hurt him. He is hurt that I am going away with my Father. One word can darken the universe. It is no wonder I am so tender with Artaud's mood, self-depreciation.

MAY 31, 1933

*I*SPEND THE DAY SHOPPING—IT TAKES TIME because I have no money, and so I search and walk for hours! But every day I have to go and see Henry. I have to. I am closer to him than to my past. I enjoy getting him records better than I enjoy getting myself much-needed gloves, stockings. It moves me down to my toes to see that gray room in Clichy, the few clothes he has, the shabby bed. Henry's cold and cough I feel in my own chest. I cannot enjoy my flight to the Riviera. I think less of the trip, that colorful new adventure, than I do of Henry's face when he said the coffee was doubly good because I had made it. The human roots in me move like seaweed. I have such a love of his body, even when it is sick; and God knows I hate sickness. Such a feeling of his moods, feeling his unconscious moods—his humiliation, his hypersensitivity, his morbidities. I see in him the same tortured being as Lawrence, only a being to whom I give peace, the minimum pain. I am glad of the continuous torture I feel because it makes me so aware, so acutely aware. I believe if I have genius it is a genius for loving. This journal could be a manual of love, passionate love, fleshly love, understanding love, pitying, maternal, intellectual, artistic, creative, nonhuman, like my love of Henry's writing.

Lawrence was right when he wrote, "Only an unsatisfied woman needs luxuries. A satisfied woman can sleep on the floor."

We joke about this. When Henry buys me delicate rolls because I prefer them, I object, "Don't pamper me, because *I am satisfied.*" And it is true, I have been very happy in my worn-out shoes.

Tonight, as on so many other nights, I am full of Henry and I am smiling to think that I began by adoring Lawrence and I end by worshiping a man so much like Lawrence, like Mellors, like Somers, really a little and powerful man, intense, honest, bitter, martial, in-stinctive, profoundly human. Only, Henry is a greater *man.*

VISIT FROM BRADLEY, WHO UNDERSTANDS A GREAT deal, who said many interesting things. He knows that an artist must be an egoist, nonhuman. Says Lawrence was weak; Lawrence was killed by Frieda because he was weak—too human. He should have extricated himself, saved himself. Henry, too, stayed too long with June. I was too human with my Mother and too human with Hugo.

As Bradley talked to me, I remembered vividly how often I have returned to the old problem: the journal, the art, what to include, what to tell, how to tell it. Bradley says, "Leave the journal aside. Just write as you talk to me."

It is true he makes me talk! His questions are endless. His interest in me and in my work is intense, and I am touched. I would like to preserve everything. I feel proud, secretive, as before a public. It hurts me deep down to be giving myself away, my journals. I feel naked in a crowd. It is torture. When I talk, I feel that I lie imperceptibly in order to cover myself. I put on costumes. I hate to expose myself truly. Lies seem like a costume, small lies, deviations mostly, because I am afraid not to be understood, and I am afraid of the pain. And then what I do not tell, I pour into the journal. I chafe because people don't understand, and it is my fault. The truth is I only face human beings in fragments. Henry, who has the largest portion, Hugh, Allendy, Joaquin, Father. I always find the *mensonge vital* necessary—the one lie which separates me from each person. Will Father alone have the whole, as the journal has? What will I have to conceal from Father? Always a secret, and this secret creates the journal. And then William Aspenwall Bradley comes and bids me, in the world's name, to relinquish all my secrets.

Before he arrived I began to open the iron boxes in which I keep my journals. Two of the boxes I could not open. One key broke and the other turned uselessly inside without functioning. Symbols!

A NORMAL BEING ATTAINS HAPPINESS AND *BELIEVES* in it, holds it until it is actually shattered, but an abnormal being attains only a relative happiness which is constantly fluctuating.

I begin a day in a golden mood which I carry like an egg. Only, instead of sitting on it I carry it against my breast, exposed. I rush to Henry to awaken him, to present him with my egg, to tell him it is a tropical day, to bring him out into the sun. I offer my mood like another gift. But Henry is depressed by his cold and because someone has knocked persistently at the door. He would not open because I was there, and whenever someone knocks at the door Henry thinks they have come to get him, to pursue him, to catch him. He fears. All his life he has been pursued by the knocking at the door—the feeling of being persecuted. It darkens his day. It makes him furtive, upset, dissolved. He could not gather himself together.

We sit in the sun and Henry begins to wander in his talk. He asks me to go on *our* vacation without my journal. He would slay the journal. Yes, because the journal is a *personage*. Out of jealousy (it is lying on the café table) he won't read it. What I pour into it is like a confidence I have given to another, like an unfaithfulness! And I am thinking to myself how often I have said I will live without the journal, step out of the refuge. But I don't do it. Because it is true, as I say to Henry, that I have confided in him; but it is also true that I only tell him what he *wants* to hear, and there is a great deal which he does not want to hear, and *who* wants to hear it?

So Henry says, "Come away with me without the journal," and the journal lies on the café table like a person—an ultimate rival. I am baffled, because I am quite willing to confide entirely in human beings, except that at some moment or another human beings get preoccupied, moody, busy, inattentive, and there comes an end to the interest, and this never happens in the journal!

Henry himself said today, "When we go away, we will never get bored—that I know. If it rains we will go into the hotel room and I will amuse you. I feel I haven't done that enough. I have been so preoccupied always. We have never relaxed together, enjoyed ourselves. I sometimes regret that."

At the same time, after a long afternoon, I ask Henry, "What time is it?" and immediately Henry thinks I have been bored by what he was saying—just because I have to leave him! And he walks with me to the metro with that same feeling of distress I have when I think I have disappointed someone and I would like to right things before I leave because I know the dissonance will resound in me, for days, perhaps.

Dream last night: I enter a house where I have become a servant. The woman is unfamiliar. She is at first very brusque with me, says her only objection to me is that I look like a *poule* and begs me to make up less so as not to attract her husband's attention. I am very good-natured and I tell her I will powder and rouge very imperceptibly. She teaches me how to make a dessert out of an orange. First she cuts the inner white skin of the orange into an algae shape and places it in an aquarium bowl, where it begins to sway like a sea anemone, to swell and sigh and drop and rock. The seeds, too, are thrown in, and they move like jewels. She continues to prepare the orange and teaches me how to cook the outer rind. I learn so quickly and I am so pleased that we become friends. She sends me marketing, and I enjoy my walking so much that I forget to buy oranges. I stop at a bar where I see oranges in a basket, but the barman won't sell them. I attract the attention of two men who look like the two Spaniards in the café yesterday who were interested in me while Henry went down to the lavatory. I snub them, but as I walk away an apache comes up and gives me 250 francs, asking me to follow him to a hotel room. He looks very much like Carco.

I look at the money and observe it doesn't look right and I explain

this by saying, "It's probably the new money they have been making."
I say to him, surprised, "You give me all of that?"

"More if you come along," says the apache. But I begin to think that if he gives me so much money it must be because he is diseased, syphilitic, and I refuse.

JUNE 3, 1933

ARTAUD AND I WERE SITTING IN THE GARDEN. HE put his hand on my knee. I was surprised by the warmth of it. We looked at each other openly and heavily. We both felt unsettled.

Later in the evening, while we leaned over a book, Artaud put his hand on my shoulder. And I liked it. He seems much more human than I had suspected.

I understand in myself now this warm spontaneity which I also showed Henry. The first day Henry came to our house, I said, showing him the imaginary studio on top of the garage, "We could fix up this place and you could come and work here." And my telegram when he wrote me that his job in Dijon was intolerable: "Come home to Louveciennes."

In both cases, these two men who have lived and are cynical on the surface were affected by my simplicity and directness. Surprised by my hospitality. If their cynicism and experience prompted them to interpret my invitation as sexual, at the same time my tone imposed on them a certain more romantic and more profound interpretation. What prompted me to seek them out is a swift sense of their timidity and a curiously accurate intuition in me. Those are the impulses I trust.

When Henry has recorded his dreams in which he possesses either imaginary women, whores, or June, I have been jealous. But what would Henry feel, then, if he knew that in my dreams I sleep with everybody? After Artaud's visit, it was Artaud. In my dreams I reveal the amorous whore that I really am. Henry and I, having each other, rarely dream of each other, or only of each other's cruelty. There are moments in life when I feel this loss of will and loss of moral inhibition. Both Henry and I feel this when we follow only the current of our sensations, our impressionability. The other day I said to him that he and I ought to be able to capture the atmosphere of dreams better than anyone because we often live in them, and by that I mean that absolute willingness—that subjection to a desire which only we experience.

It is easy for us to yield. Deep down I would enjoy being possessed by Artaud, Steele, and Nestor, as my dreams reveal. That is my true unconscious female amorality; the great inexorable will which prevents me from doing it is false.

What would have become of this evening in Henry's hands? Hugh and I went to a cheap, obscene little theater. It was not very full. While we waited for the show we sat at the bar. The checkroom girl smiled at me—a beautiful smile. I smiled back. She came near and said, "Be very careful when you get up not to catch your dress on the nail—that chair has a nail, and your dress is so pretty." I thanked her. We began to talk. She told me her life story. We compared the prices of our dresses. The barman gave me a rose. The girl came when we were sitting in the theater and touched my wrist: "Come, I'll seat you in the third row."

I asked Hugo to give her ten francs. He did so very seriously. I said, "You should have smiled. Now give her another ten, but smile."

"Must I smile?" said Hugh. "I only did it because it makes you happy."

Henry is beginning not to want to know. A wiser love? About June he was relentless. Yet with me he trusts. At first I was disconcerted. When Father began to show an intense curiosity, a great desire to *know everything,* I began to wish Henry would have this curiosity, although a deeper feeling tells me Henry is shying off pain. He is weary of pain, of tortures, of holding, of grasping. He accepts life now; he is more resigned. He is older. He has in a deeper sense exhausted the noisy romantic love. And I am not quite ready to do without it. I seek that. A wise Anaïs attracts wise love. And a neurotic, distrustful me craves unwise love.

I ask Henry about all this. He says it is a kind of trustingness, that he believes in our essential connection—he didn't believe in June (nor did June believe in Henry's fundamental love). And if you believe, the rest can go hang. Not quite, says Henry, who has been listening with a strange carapace on to my talk about Artaud—the carapace I put on when he talks about other women, when I am trying not to mind.

I feel that my excursions are a defense. The only time I feel a relief from my too-human love of Henry, the only time I am the kind of independent and valiant woman he needs, is when I am engaged in smaller loves. Otherwise I yield to sentimentalism; I want to envelop Henry, and he needs to be left alone—all men want to be left alone. Keep busy, lead a full, wide, rich life. It is better for Henry! Absolution! I give it to myself. Yet if it had been possible I would have preferred to live only for Henry, to be all, his wife, mistress, servant, partner; and then Henry would have tired of a woman lost in him, lost to herself. I cannot reconcile myself, resign myself to life as it is. I'm always rebelling and spitting fire—why is Allendy, the Taurus, the Will I wanted, a sexual weakling; why is Artaud a drug addict?

JUNE 8, 1933

*H*UGH RUSHES TO LONDON. HENRY COMES TO Louveciennes. I leave Henry to see Artaud, who meets me with a tormented face: "I'm clairvoyant. I see you did not mean anything you said the other day. Right after our talk in the garden you became cold and distant—your face impenetrable. You eluded my touch. You took flight. Oh, you're dangerous and I always knew it . . ."

"But there was no question of a human love."

"But we are human beings! It's monstrous, what you expect of a man!"

Artaud, I knew, was a sick, tormented madman, and I was interested in him, but not humanly; and he, being so morbid and so hypersensitive, also wanted the trophy which he knew Allendy, Henry, and Eduardo claimed, and he wanted it all . . . I don't know why. Sitting in the Coupole, we kissed, and I tried to prove to Artaud that I was sincere, that I was a divided being, that this was not a game but a tragedy—because I could not love imaginatively and humanly at the same time. And slowly the story of my own "madness," so much like his, touched him . . . For human beings appear to him as spectral, and he doubts and fears life. He said he loved my glidingness, my alertness, my vibrancy . . . that I was the plumed serpent . . . snake and bird . . .

I was stirred only like a leaf in the wind, that is all; and the more Artaud pleaded, telling me that he knew I had many lovers, the more strangely deceptive I became; and the more he hunted down this deception, the more I acted; and I sat at his side, so warm, and so mad, and so unlike other women, and so tragic . . . and the kisses were of no pleasure to me . . . only like more spiderwebs thrown around Artaud, empty of feeling and impelled by some demoniac force to tantalize, to act, to give an illusion of closeness.

I know now I am driven to this impasse over and over again, and faced with the same outcome, the physical possession; and that I am interested not in the physical possession but in the game, as Don Juan was, *the game of seduction, of maddening, of possessing men not only physically but their souls, too*—I demand more than the whores.
Already today I was satanically pleased when Artaud said, "I have divined that Allendy loves you. Do you still love him?" I refused to answer his question. Quite definitely, today I felt classified, categorized as a species of seductress not often encountered. I play not only with sex but with souls, imaginations. A whore is an honest whore. I seduce men's bodies and souls, and I play with serious, sacred things. As Henry said once, I love sacrilege. I am a new kind of enchantress. The men of serious, deep lives who are not captured by the whore, the men

185

who are least subjected to the will of woman—these are the men I possess. I am a poison which does not work into the flesh alone, but into deeper sources. I saw Artaud imprisoned by the Inca priestess, by the plumed serpent, by the plumage and the fluidity, the trickery and the gentleness. "So soft and so frail," he said. And he looked at me with absolutely mad eyes. Absolutely mad. "People think I am crazy," he said. I knew at that moment by his eyes that he was, and that I loved this madness. As I looked at his mouth, whose edges were blackened by laudanum, a mouth I did not want to kiss, by a curious trick of superimposition I remembered the absolute freshness of Allendy's mouth and body, the rosiness of Henry's mouth, healthy, fruit-like, and I knew I was drawn toward death again, always drawn to death, to the end, to culminations, to insanities. To be kissed by Artaud was to be poisoned, and I knew those shivers of a spectral life, and it surprised me that Artaud considered me warm and incarnate, and that he should seek immediately to give a form, a definite form, to our relationship. I was disappointed that he should be so concrete. I had wanted a love like Eduardo's, which makes no demands on the body. I asked Artaud to make no demands on me. He said, "I had not expected to find in you my madness." He talked like a poet, and I was laughing to myself to think of my great hunger for poetry. Was I sitting there with Artaud because he poured out poetry; because he believed in magic; because he identified himself with Heliogabalus, the crazy Roman emperor; because his theater, his writing, and his being were interwoven; because he talked in the taxi like a Hamlet and pushed back his hair from a terrifyingly wet and ravaged face? He has imprisoned my imagination. He rules in it; he walks, talks, reads, evokes mummies, Roman decadence, drugs, insanity, death. And I was trying again to enter an experience, to swim through it without the gift of myself, and it was getting more and more difficult. I entered Allendy's life; I bit a morsel of it; I tasted it, barely touched it. I brushed against him and I passed on. And, oh, the bitterness of the man so tricked by my unseizableness. And now I step warily into Artaud's fantastic regions, and he, too, lays heavy hands on me, on my body, and like the mandragora at the touch of human hands, I *shriek.*

I come home and marvel at my deep love of Henry's flesh, at my love of his mouth, his fingers, his veins, his neck, his white stomach, his penis, every part of his body. There is no moment of coldness or retraction, never. I melt inside of myself. Everything else is a dream, a fantasy, a game, including the pattern, the rigid fatalistic pattern which impels me to take my revenge upon all men except Henry and Hugh, like the whore who loves only one man and extracts money from the other men, coldly, unscrupulously.

Yet I told Artaud there was no calculation in me, and that is true. All this that I write today is an explanation of attitudes, actions, speeches which at the time I made wholeheartedly. My talk with Artaud in the garden was real. Do I conceal my motives from my own eyes? Did I choose to play with Artaud, or is it not true that I am ensorcelled imaginatively and not physically?

I looked at myself in the mirror when I came home, and I saw the tigress. I saw the green-eyed and mocking tigress. Cold, too. Cold. Artaud said, "a face of stone."

When I looked at my face and I saw the tigress there, I ceased to disbelieve in it. I accepted it. I looked at my face and I smiled at the tigress, invitingly, tolerantly.

"Why, why did you offer to dance for Steele?" asked Artaud.

"Because he said he loved dancing."

"No, because you know he loves you and you want to please him—and then hurt him."

The face in the mirror with that cold clarity of features, the transparent eyes, said, "Yes." I want to acquiesce to a truth. I don't want to disguise the tigress. *"Bonjour!* You're hunting today, soft pawed, eh? Gliding." At night I come out and drink in the river. A jungle secrecy.

I have no feelings. Artaud torments and Allendy stirs me. Yet Artaud said, "You know, the least thing hurts me immensely. The tone of your note, its coldness, that cuts me deeply. I get dejected so easily."

It was a big day for Henry and me. At breakfast in the garden, we planned to install a printing press in the space over the garage and to print his books. Henry formulated the idea, which had been latent in me and which we had sometimes vaguely considered. But he has been so pitiably blocked by editors—so humiliated, so discouraged—that I am determined it will be done. We are making plans.

Henry is working on his *Self-Portrait*. He is sunburned. He wants to come and live near me and near the printing press. He is absorbed in work. He works and he pampers me, too, and I sit here making plans, dreaming. He needs independence, freedom of expression to be able to expand. I, too, am making plans for greater independence. Henry and I will take long trips together. We want to go to India. Henry urges me to do all I want—what I could be if I could expand without limits! Urges me to run away from Hugh and from him, to run loose. He talks impersonally, exalting himself about my potentialities. But I smile. I could never run away from my feelings, my feelings that life is not liberty but love, and that love is bondage, and that no expansion could mean anything if three or four human beings had to be sacrificed. It is I who create the bonds, the walls, the loves, the devotions which encircle me. It is I who direct my life into channels of subjections to Hugh, to Henry, to Joaquin, to smaller loves.

A woman who had not seen Henry since he lived with June five years ago found him looking ten years younger.

When I met him he was at the lowest ebb of health and pessimism and bitterness, frail for a man usually in superb health, lost, broken. We were recalling this period. The room I went to the first time—the misery, poverty, starvation, the great wearing anxieties. He said he had had his bellyful of misery, war, poverty. He was tired of wandering, of homelessness. He wanted to create. He wanted serenity, time, security. And he got all that, and a great love too.

And I got all I needed—I, too, was starved.

Evening with Henry in the studio ended in an infernal talk. Henry read Hugh's letter to me—and analyzed it ferociously, the unvital, conventional, dull tone of it: "My darling . . . I have been thinking how wonderful you are," etc. I have always excused the inadequacy of expression. But Henry relentlessly attacked Hugh's emptiness; his spectral aspect; his assents, which I take for understanding; his imitative, docile, dull, automatic phrases; the unfocused awareness; the absentness. And no matter the nature of Hugh's inadequateness, Henry emphasized the truth—I am caged in. Hugh does not give me the liberty, the tolerance I need. He clutches me humanly. He does not do what he should do if it were true his whole life is lived for me. Unreal, everything unreal, young, misty. Only when I give Hugh great pain does he coalesce into livingness, anger, passion (the John incident on board ship, and his unexpected arrival the other day—the unforgettable expression on his face).

All that Henry said shocked me. I doubted it. Yet I know Henry was fair, because for his own interest it would be better that I continue bound to Hugh.

At that moment I was cold, inhuman. I did see what my life could be without Hugh: a splendor. I had an infernal vision of my freedom: a flexible connection with Henry. I realized how blocked I was by human considerations. I said to Henry, "Listen, when you get your book published and can stand on your own two feet, then I will escape; by that time Joaquin will be able to take care of Mother."

When I came down to bed I knew all this was useless, that I was incapable of it, merely because Hugh might awake in the middle of the night, as he often does, in a morbid mood, and not find me there to talk to him, caress him into serenity and sleep.

The next day Henry said something like, "All literature does not make up to one for the tragedies of life, the struggles. It makes literature pale." At this moment literature appeared to both of us remote, inadequate, and human life unbearably vivid.

Only one goal was attained by last night's talk. I am going to travel with Henry for months at a time. We discussed the wonder of our intimacy, the preciousness of what happens to us when we live together, and we want that. We want that and our liberty. If I could marry Henry today I wouldn't do it. I want him free; he needs that, and intimacy, too. I was born to understand the needs of the artist—probably because I have them!

Even the irony of the artist always working on the story of his old love when stimulated by the new! Henry upset because our love stimulated him to write about June and Bertha. And later, when living with other women, he will recall me.

He is always profoundly shocked when I say, "If I lived with you would you bring your whore to the house?"

"My God, Anaïs."

"But you did that, you did that to your first wife."

"But I couldn't do that to *you*."

He is amazed at his faithfulness to me.

JUNE 12, 1933

SO MUCH IRREVOCABLY CHANGED IN MYSELF SINCE our talk about Hugo, although that talk in itself was a deformity—an untruth. But it provoked a "white criminal fervor" in me. My sails are again set against a yielding pity which balks the course of my life. Feelings may again upset me, delay me, but they will have no power over me, ultimately. I saw all things clearly, coolly, with a stark wisdom, a total absence of sentimentality. The necessity to expand and to flow as far and as deeply as I am capable.

Henry and I looked at our life with naked eyes, and what I saw was again an ultimate isolation.

He has written twenty-five superb pages. He has read ten pages of my journal, discussed them for an hour, wanting to be interested, and was deeply interested for a while, but ultimately more interested in painting watercolors, in reading aloud the *Satyricon* for himself. And it is all very right. It doesn't mean he does not love me. I feel my presence in his body, in his mind—permeating his life. We talked about our trips together and I told him all I knew about the artist's need to wander off, to devour new experiences—how I understood it all because I felt it. And then yesterday, after a week spent in Louveciennes, I divined his restlessness, and I urged him to go to Paris, and I was right. He wanted just to move, to walk, to be free, to wander;

and it was right. I didn't mind it. I knew how many times I had wanted to leave Louveciennes just to go off.

So I sent Henry off last night and I don't care where he went. I stayed alone contentedly, planning my work, full of ideas, full of the certainty that I have written great pages in my journal, and that I will write greater ones the day I can stop covering all my emotions with veils of ideal hypocrisies, consciously wanting things to be noble when they are diabolical. More truth! This wanderer, Henry, is the man I love, and what would he be if domesticated?

Ironically, it so happens that today I see Artaud. Who knows but that Henry wandered off last night with the same fear of intimacy and its consequence (pain) that I experienced? He left me after reading my journal about my Father and after I said he could not help me copy my journal because there were things in it which would hurt him.

JUNE 13, 1933

MADNESS. WHEN I ARRIVE BEFORE ARTAUD HE stands nobly, proudly, with eyes mad with joy . . . I have come in black, red, and steel, as Mars, at war, warring not to be touched by Artaud. I feel his taut desire, oppressive, obsessive. I look at his room: like a cell, gray, bare. I look at the photographs of his amazing face, an actor's face, bitter, dark, changeful . . . We talk, and I repeat what I said before, that I don't want anything but the connection between our minds, the exchange between our minds, and he talks darkly against me. I don't remember our talk. Everything was whirling around and within me. He knelt. He knelt before me and he talked violently, holding me with his eyes, and I forget his words. All I remember is that he drew me out of myself, out of my resistance. I sat there magnetized and my blood obeyed him. He kissed me devouringly, fiercely, and I yielded. He bit my mouth, my breasts, my throat, my legs.

But he was impotent. There was a dead, heavy pause. His face twisted, then set, stony: "Go away," he said, "go away." Hard, cold, brutal.

I looked at him and I said, "No. Why should I? I won't go away." And I wiped his wet face with my handkerchief and stood up.

"Go away now or later, it does not matter. You'll despise me anyway. I'm lost in your eyes. I take too much opium."

"I don't despise you. All this has no importance, no importance whatsoever."

"It has a terrific importance for all women."

"Not for me." I spoke subduedly. As if I knew the scene by heart. The second between Artaud's command that I should leave him and his "You'll despise me anyway"—in that moment flowered all my wisdom of love, born of the greatest pain. I never felt Artaud's impotence as a lack of love. I knew that I must save him immediately from his humiliation. As I lay there so quiet after the futile outpour of honey, I almost smiled. Artaud said, "You don't have the same reactions as other women." His humiliation was appeased. He stood up and made a gesture of despair.

"I'm absolutely satisfied, Artaud. I didn't want the human connection. I'm wary of it. I've suffered too much. Let us forget this moment. It means nothing. Gestures mean nothing."

JUNE 18, 1933

*I*CAME HOME TO HENRY. I DESCRIBED ARTAUD'S dramatic gestures, qualities. I invented a great deal, that Artaud had tried to make me take drugs. I entertained and excited Henry. I was feverish and he was jealous. He said, "Your eyes have a subdued brilliance, as if you had made love."

I could not sleep. I was haunted by Artaud; I had to see him again.

I sent Henry away the night of Hugo's arrival, and I met Artaud at the Viking, at the same table where Henry and I first looked at each other with love. I was trembling. And then began a night of ecstasy. We left the café because the Quatz Art Ball students were riotous and it hurt our exaltation (the last time I saw them, Henry and I were in a hotel room and I wanted to join them!). We walked in a dream, in a frenzy, Artaud torturing himself and me with doubts, with mad talk about eternity, God, wanting me to feel him physically, and I transported, melting, carried away, so much that we stopped on the quays and kissed violently, an ecstasy like that with June, different, rising upward, in frenzied ascension.

"I'm living through the greatest moment of my life. This is too much, too much!" Artaud walked, stumbling almost with joy. "What a divine joy to crucify a being like you—you who are so evanescent, so elusive. What ecstasy to hold you entire, you who never give yourself! *Mon amour, mon grand amour!*"

We sat in a café and he lulled me with endless tender phrases, and I was frightened by his fervor. He said, *"Entre nous il pourrait y avoir un meurtre."*

Letter to Artaud (sent from Valescure–St. Raphael): Nanaqui, I wish I could relive a thousand times that moment on the quays and every hour of that evening. I want to feel again your violence and your sweetness, your threats, your despotic spiritual power . . . all the fear you inspire in me, and the piercing joys. Fear because you expect so much of me . . . eternity, the eternal, God . . . those words . . . all the questions you asked me.

I would answer your questions gently. If I seemed evasive it was only because there was too much to say. I feel life always as a cycle, a long series of events, a circle, and I can't detach a fragment because it seems to me a fragment has no meaning. But everything seems to work out, to melt in an embrace, in trusting one's instinct, in the warmth and fusion of the bodies. I believe completely in what we feel when we arc together. I

* In French in the original.

believe in that moment when we lose all idea of reality, of the separation and separateness of our beings. When the books fell, I felt relief. After that everything became simple . . . simple and great and sweet. The *you* which almost gives pain, so tightly does it bind . . . the *you* and all that you said to me . . . I forget the words; I hear the tenderness and I remember that you were happy. All the rest is only the torture of our minds, phantoms that we create . . . because for us, love has immense repercussions. It must create; it has deep meaning; it contains and directs everything. For us it has the importance of being mixed and joined with all our impulses and our inspirations. . . . It is too important to us! We get it mixed up with religion, with magic.

Why, before we sat down in the café, did you think I was distancing myself from you—simply because I was lighthearted for a moment, joyful, smiling? Will you never accept those movements, those underwater currents? Nanaqui, you must believe in the axis of my life; my self's expansion is immense, deceptive, but that is only in its shape. I wish that you might read my childhood diary so that you could see how faithful I have been to certain values. I think I always recognize real values . . . for example, when I singled you out as a royal being in a realm that has haunted my whole life.

Nanaqui, this evening I don't want to stir up ideas . . . I only want your presence. Does the same thing happen to you, choosing a precious moment (our embrace on the quays) and clinging to it? I close my eyes and relive it intently, as in a trance, when I no longer feel my present life, nothing, nothing but that moment. And after that, the night, the procession of your gestures, and your words, the fever, the restlessness, the need to see you again, a great impatience . . .

*Second letter:** Can you accept my spirituality, so different from your own, because it manages the ascent even though it is heavy-laden with life and joy? You won't torment yourself

---

* In French in the original.

because of my human roots? I don't know happiness in the ordinary way, but a day of sunshine, of warmth, such as the day when you waited for me at the railway station, gives me great joy, and that day you spoke as though you were struggling against the light because it threatened you with dissolution. You said, "I have only painful sensations." All those joys change nothing of the center of my life, and the center is *the tragic feeling of life* which unites us.

I read nothing but your book. You speak of the harm I do. It seems to me that I am cruel unintentionally, by a great fatality. I do harm without meaning to, and only to those who have disappointed me deeply. No, perhaps that's not true. I would like always to tell you the truth, Nanaqui, and not try to justify myself.

Anyhow, all of this is unimportant, because we never live two identical experiences, you know that. Each new contact creates a new experience. You will never know me through my past, only through what I am to you and with you. And that is so because you and what you are call forth the best of me; you exorcise and bring forth a *me* that others have not known. And by that I don't mean that I will cease to be what I am, because I have much to give you. Our "opposites attract," our complementary quality, is good. I feel that I will bring you the marvelous savor of material things, a coalescence born of warmth and the facility I have for moving like a river. I feel that with me, you will feel alienated less often. You will unite with life because I will offer it to you saturated with spirit, and that is an embrace that also works great miracles. There will be less fog, fewer halts, less anguish—the union between you and me will be prolonged in a symbolic coalescence of all the elements. Water is movement, and in water one creates! I love you.

JUNE 19, 1933

I AM HERE IN NICE BY MYSELF. I RAN AWAY FROM Hugo's mother, from Artaud, from Henry, to conceal the breakdown of my body. I write love letters to Henry, to Father, to Hugo. Not to Allendy, because he is acting spitefully, like a woman. Not taking his defeat like a sage. And Artaud asked me, "What have you done to Allendy? You have done him harm." And, "Why do you give that terrible impression—of evil—of cruelty—of seductiveness, trickery, superficiality? Is it an appearance? I hated you at first as one hates an all-powerful temptress. I hated you as one hates evil."

I feel supremely innocent, yet I have done evil. I have committed all the sacrileges. And I must be all evil now, because I am even free of remorse. I feel no remorse toward Hugo or Artaud or Henry. And I am becoming aware that I am wreaking a kind of revenge upon men, that I am impelled by a satanic force to win and abandon them. I do not know the truth. Did I abandon Allendy because I only wanted the pleasure of winning him, or because he disappointed me? He did disappoint and disillusion me. Life, or my own ingenuity, provides me with beautiful justifications. How exonerated for betraying Hugh I would be by anyone who knew the sexual tortures I endured from the beginning. Even my Mother knows of my despairing visits to the doctors when I thought there was something wrong with me.

Solitude. I seek to be divided—I seek this tension and multilateral flow. It is the true expression of myself. As I walk for hours alone, I accept myself, I accept what I am. I no longer censure myself, nor will I let others censure me. Obedience to the mystery, which the journal seeks only to describe, no longer to explain.

Henry sleeps in me like my own blood and flesh, sleeps and stirs.

Artaud haunts my imagination and arouses fever, arouses the supernatural efflorescence straining in space, aspiring upward.

Henry has noticed that when I live a few days with him I become heavier, slumberous, oriental—thicker—my body expands, exaltation downward, in heavy, perfect circles and tides and flow.

Here, alone, I walk with a heavy body and a light conscience.

I knew that something was hardening in the core of me, that I was determined to bring life as well as pain to others, that you only bring life when you also bring pain. Henry writes me, "You were dancing around me that day like the wind. I miss so much that fire and light you shed. Things seem to have gone dead since I left Louveciennes."

Life and pain. Water, earth, fire, evil.

The course is traced for me. I cannot stop myself. I recall vividly now the legend of Alraune. Alraune, created, impelled to destruction like one possessed. Oh, God!

Immediately I remembered several little scenes: Hugo returning from London after ten days' absence, and I feeling as if Joaquin were returning. And still carrying in me the fever of Artaud's words. Hugo and I in our bedroom—his body, which is beautiful, naked—and I so cold, so cold, so cold I find a pretext to quarrel, to delay the embrace. And Hugo is opening a small package wistfully while I launch a quarrel, pretending not to notice his gesture. He is appalled because, he says, I have never received him like this—something has come between us. Suddenly I feel a surge of pity. I excuse myself, pretend I am jealous of his mother's visit, angered about it; and I submit to his embrace, I accept his little gift.

And today I said, "There must be suffering." Suffering is life, too. But it tortures me a thousand times to torture others. Tonight I am insane with pity.

Henry, too, is sitting in a café and weeping because I am gone for two weeks.

All my joy killed. I sit down and I write Hugo letters, letters which remind me of Henry's words about June's letters: "A letter like this wipes off everything."

I HURT ALLENDY BY WRITING HIM IMPERSONALLY.
I hurt Eduardo by writing him about Artaud.

*I write to Artaud:** Nanaqui, my love, I love you so much
that I don't want to hurt you. I have come to tell you the truth,
as far as I know it myself. I have come to ask you to forget
me, to forget me, to erase me from your life, because the
appearance you spoke to me about is true. I do harm, I cause
a lot of pain, and all I know is that it is I who suffer most,
more than those I hurt. It's a mystery to me, a terrible, frightening mystery, which Allendy hasn't been able to explain.

Listen to me. I have given life, light, and warmth to those
I have loved, but I have given them pain as well. Allendy, in
whom I confided, thought I was a saint, I swear it, and yet I
hurt him, too. Do you understand now why I have written so
much about the legend of Alraune—the woman created by
an alchemist? Natural forces are poisoned by scientific formulas—and Alraune is created to destroy. The two forces clash
within me. Allendy thinks that I am avenging myself for the
terrible suffering that I endured.

Listen, Nanaqui. As a child I adored my Father, body and
soul (always together, the body obedient to the soul). When I
was ten years old my Father left us, abandoned my Mother
and made her suffer. But for me—it was I he had abandoned.
I was already strange, not really a child at all, and I had a
foreboding that he was leaving us. At the moment of his departure I clung to him. My Mother didn't understand my
despair.

---

* In French in the original.

I didn't see him again until a month ago. Twenty years! I became very serious, and for years I wept. I completely distrusted life. I withdrew into myself and began a secret life in my diary. I turned away from real life.

We were terribly poor in America. I sat as a model for painters. When I was sixteen, Eduardo, a poet and actor, fell in love with me. As I told you, until a year ago my physical, sensual life was a long martyrdom because my soul was not involved. My body's impulses obey those of my spirit. However, Eduardo was a homosexual and his love was incomplete. At that time I wanted it all, an absolute love.

At nineteen I fell in love with Hugo—above all with his kind, honorable character. I can't explain why, but our marriage was and is a physical martyrdom for me; yet for seven years I was faithful. A year ago, an explosion of distress and passion threw me off balance, first into the arms of a woman, then into the arms of the man I told you about. I gave up the sterile struggle in favor of the ideal.

It was at that time that I went to see Allendy. And I began to do wrong—to commit every sacrilege. Allendy told me, "Learn to disassociate." He discouraged me from pursuing the absolute, because my hunger for the absolute always led me straight to catastrophe. I felt a deep disappointment. All those compromises, those adaptations to normal life, nauseated me. I feel I am worse than people think I am, and also I have greater powers of sublimation than they realize.

I have given you the plain, simple facts. When I tell you I think that few women have been as severe with themselves as I, I believe that is the truth, particularly because I have always been so strongly tempted, so sought after, so flattered. It is true as well that I have asked too much of life and have been cruelly disappointed. I have moments of great bitterness. It is true that that first painful shock which obsessed me for twenty years caused me to withdraw, to become elusive, hypersensitive, narcissistic. For every contact, every human experience, seems to me heavy with sadness. I am only happy in my imagination. Or in a life such as I have led this past year, an elemental life of sun, earth, fire, a life not of the mind— or very little of the mind.

When I first met you I told you that I didn't want us to be together physically. I really have divided my life; I have voluntarily torn it in two. I am weary of suffering, of being so terribly complete myself. I am afraid—no, terrified—of disappointing you, Nanaqui, of hurting you, and the saddest part is that I am a woman in my weaknesses and yet am capable of great devotion—I am a mixture of everything, am capable of everything. But you, whom I sense as sorrowful and painfully sensitive, I don't want to hurt you.

I tremble . . . today . . . too many people are unhappy today because of me. It's terrible, Nanaqui . . . I have made Hugo suffer. The worst, the worst you thought of me that first day is true. You were right to hate me, to flee from me. Do hate me. Do think that I am only a flirt, a frivolous, cruel woman. Run away. You said you could forget, could efface an image. . . . Believe, then, that I lied to you, that I am lying now. That I gave myself so completely when I was a child that I am still bruised. That since then life has seemed full of terror and cruelty, and all the love offered to me now cannot rebuild, re-create, or give me back my confidence.

And yet I have used all that so well; I have sublimated so much and used my experiences to understand others. I like to use what I have learned through my own suffering to give to others and protect them. I love compassion, Nanaqui, because when I am not possessed by my own demon, I feel a limitless compassion, a pity so great that it makes me a coward. I could have done you the greatest good, because for someone like you, gentleness and kindness also need to be impregnated with intelligence. One must know how to love with understanding. The greatest good and the greatest harm. If only you were not so much like me, if only you didn't expect everything of me—the all, the absolute! I recognize in you my own lack of compromise. Oh, Artaud, those who bring life and light also bring harm. . . . Tell me that you understand. Forget me. I give you proof of an extraordinary love!

J U N E   2 1 ,   1 9 3 3

*I*MAIL MY LETTER TO ARTAUD, FULL OF REMORSE
for having entered his life. Then my Father
telephones me as soon as he arrives in Paris from Spain.

Then Henry writes me: Am waiting anxiously for a letter.
What shall I do? I'm wretched. I would have boarded a train
and gone south today to be somewhere near you. I hate telling
you that I'm miserable, but it's the truth. Maybe all I want is
to hear from you. It seems so long ago since I left Louveciennes.
Write to me at once. Everything looks rotten to me. I *hate*
Paris. Hate the whole world. Jesus. I don't know what's come
over me. I love you—terribly. I wouldn't be able to do a
damned thing without you. I've just realized that you're the
whole world to me. And when I talked so glibly about my
self-sufficiency I was just a braggart and a liar. I'm completely
disoriented . . .

Strange days. Weather bad, so I created my own weather. I ignored
the place, the hotel. I lived within myself, writing letters, dreaming,
contented.

When I arrived here I found a telegram from Father. Today,
knowing him ill, I telephoned him. All extravagances which we have
not the money to pay for. It is these things I often deny myself, violently,
furiously, with utmost severity.

JUNE 22, 1933

*T*ODAY I AWOKE AND FELT INNOCENT—FELT THAT my letter to Artaud was born of an overscrupulousness. That I exaggerate the evil I do. That I'm not really courageous enough to do evil . . . I'm in a deep confusion!

To Artaud:[*] I believe you must have sensed an excess of scruples in my last letter. I am very hard on myself, Nanaqui, and I feel all the severity of your soul weighing me down. Your first hatred of me, you who are so intuitive, upset me and hurt me very much. For your sake I have tried to look at myself straight on. If one has a soul, it shows itself in strange ways, not through deeds. What do you see now? I believe in your insights.

My own concern is for your happiness. That is the only purpose of all I write to you. I am waiting for absolution. Do you know what it means to seek forgiveness? Allendy forgave me completely. But you? Your doubts have wakened new and terrible worries in me.

Do you remember Dostoevsky's novel *The Possessed*, which says, "I get as much joy from doing evil as from doing good"? I don't feel that way myself. I feel great joy only when I create. The greatest joy I felt the evening we spent together was when you spoke of your happiness!

Yes. No joy the day Eduardo rang the bell at Louveciennes while Henry and I lay in bed. No joy when I said to Allendy, "I loved you" (in the past), and he corrected me. No joy the day I left Eduardo in the hotel room. No joy when I hurt Hugo. The devil which possesses

---

[*] In French in the original.

me and makes me exert my power, impels me to win men, does not give me joy in destruction. Is that a proof of anything?

With the power I have, what evil I could do, merely by telling Eduardo the truth about himself, Henry, Hugo, and Artaud, and this evil I do in my journal. My evil will be posthumous—the ruthless truths!

Yes, the evil I do not act out, I write out.

Donc, I am both a force of creation and destruction.

Assez. I am weary of my disquietudes.

I do not think of Artaud as a body. Of his body I know only his eyes. I like his leanness, his gestures. He looks like his thoughts. When I saw him at the Sorbonne conference, from afar, he looked like a poet—which is not corporeal description. I do not want to be near his body. Why does he want this nearness? I lie to him about it. I have no desire for him. I'm in love with his mind, with the most subtle of all intelligences, of all supernatural manifestations. I would like just to write to him, not to be with him. He is the genie of abstractions. He rules over the abstract. There he holds me spellbound. "My only target is the clockwork of the soul. I transcribe only the pain of an abortive adjustment. *Je suis un abîme complet.*"

I have thrown myself into that abyss of abstractions.

Henry cannot bear his solitude, and he goes off on his bicycle to come nearer to me.

I think of Henry on the road, eating in a cheap restaurant with gusto, making friends with waiters and workmen.

Too much convolution of thoughts . . . brooding. I await my Father with deep joy and impatience. My Double. What shortcuts I would have found with him. Yet it is a joy, too, to confront each other already created, already old. Though he and I are never to be crystallized. Always in movement.

Tomorrow, tomorrow begins another romance!

[J U N E 2 3 , 1 9 3 3]

*F*IRST DAY OF FATHER STORY.* KING FATHER AR-
rives after conquering a paralyzing lumbago.
Pale. Suffering. Impatient to come. He appears cold and formal,
but I will learn later that he is distressed that he and I should meet
at the station—formally. He conceals his feelings. His face is
a mask.

We set out immediately for a walk. He talks about the "system"
we have constructed and live by. Our own. But we have found nobody
to live it with. It works for ourselves. It is a world. We are alone in
it. We have a peculiar way of looking at things. By current standards
we are amoral. We have not been true to human beings but to ourselves.
To an inner development. We are barbaric and subliminal. We have
lived like civilized barbarians. The most barbaric and the most sublimated.

We are not talking. We are merely certifying each other's theories.
Our phrases interlock. There is not a tangential word. Focused . . .
on the same attitude. He says, "Exactly. I have always wanted to be
complete—that is, civilized, but barbaric also, strong but sensitive."
This aim he has realized as no other man in this world has. His whole
life is a masterpiece of equilibrium, where the greatest elements for
unbalance gather. An equilibrium of extraordinary finesse, over the
deepest abyss. I recognize in him the king—the leader of the mental
world I created alone, and in which Henry triumphed by his force,
livingness, Allendy by his abstractions. But the similitudes, the final

---

* This section in the original text is preceded by the notation: "Chamonix, July 8, 1933.
Hôtel du Fin Bec. *Chambre* 208." It follows several pages of short notes which, apparently,
served as the basis for this coherent recollection of A. N.'s meeting with her father at
Valescure.

complete synthesis, is in Father. I see in Father the whole—the finished, the created whole. I am dazzled.

We had soared for an hour. At lunch he was sober, and the "doctor." Again cold in appearance. I realized how this mask had terrorized me. The tense will, the criticalness, the severity. How as a child I had the obscure terror that this man could never be satisfied. I wonder what this sense of my Father's exactingness contributed to my haunting pursuit of perfection. I wonder what obscure awareness of his demands, expectations of life, moved me to the great efforts I made.

He did not let me help him unpack. He was humiliated by his stiffness. He treated me as his fiancée. (He had told Maria, "I must go and join my fiancée." He used to call me his betrothed after I sent him a photograph of myself at sixteen.) I saw his pride, his vanity, too, his hatred of showing himself weak, sick, at a disadvantage. And at the same moment that I saw these traits in Father, I saw them starkly in myself. The coquetry. The fear of intimacy. The inordinate respect of illusion. Yet in all the days of his illness there was not a moment of disillusion. He bore it with such grace and such dignity. Though it hurt him deeply to move, he took his bath, he shaved; his hair was perfumed, his nails immaculate.

I did not insist. I knew he would yield slowly to intimacy, to my care, to my tenderness.

He rested a while. He met me looking fresh, immaculate, dressed with an ultimate, subtle elegance. Walking stiffly, but head high, joking about his infirmity. The people of the hotel, all at his service, adoring him, catering to his whims.

He took me out in his beautiful car. And I saw the car was for him, as for me, a toy which gives a sense of power. He was proud of it. We attended first to those things he could not live without: certain biscuits, Quaker Oats for breakfast, syrup, etc. Here his world was inexorably ordained. Order. Order in details. The need to have things at all costs. All logical, part of a vast web. The biscuits a necessity of health. An arranged universe in which the struggle against bad health is constant. The sole tragic flaw in both of us. The health which fails to obey the tyranny of our aspirations.

I could see in him a more rigid pattern. At certain moments I can yield, do without everything. His life is more molded than mine. I love certain things like breakfast in bed, Sultane cigarettes, taxis, perfume, but at any moment I can surrender them.

In the car, then, Father organized the details of his life. And then he sped out along the sea, reveling in the lights, the colors. We sat on a rock, facing the sea.

This moment he had imagined, visualized, and he had set about realizing it. And there he talked about his love affairs as I do, mixing pleasure with creativity, interested in the creation of a human being through love. Playing with souls. And I watched him, I watched his face. And I knew he was telling me the truth, that he was talking to me as I talk to my journal. That he was giving me himself. This self was generous, imaginative, creative. And at certain moments, inevitably untrue. He abandoned the woman when she ceased to have a meaning for him, because he did not love her, as I did not love Allendy or Artaud.

Evening. In his room. He tells me about his life with Mother. It is a revelation, and I know it is all true because I recognize the traits in Mother which made such a life possible. I am profoundly shocked. First because it is strange to discover the sexual life of one's parents —one's mother. Secondly because Mother had seemed a Puritan to me . . . always. So reserved, so unsympathetic, so secretive about sex. Religion. Morality. Bourgeoisie.

And now I discovered a war, a sexual war, like the one between Lawrence and Frieda, June and Henry. Father trying to ascend as an artist; Mother the spider, voracious, bestial, not voluptuous, naturalistic, unromantic. Destroyer of illusion. Unkempt, dirty, without coquetry or taste. She could take off her wig before Father, lie about in kimonos. Terrible list of crude details. Smell of perspiration, strong smell of unwashed sex. These things tortured my Father, the aristocrat, cursed besides with an excessive sense of smell—a passion for perfumes and refinements. The period bandages left in the night table, the underclothing not changed every day. Voracious then, sexually aroused to exasperation by Father's ardors (and that night I discovered his ardor, which I had sensed), for he was capable of taking Mother several times a day, and every day, and after the hardest work, and after a visit to a mistress—to calm her suspicion. Mother *understood nothing,* could not be reasoned with, was primitive in her jealousies, irritable, tyrannical. Terrible quarrels burst between them. Violent scenes in which Father wore out the energy he needed for other purposes. Finally, for the sake of peace, he would yield. He read at meals to evade quarrels (this was a detail which I had interpreted as indifference to us).

What prevented him from abandoning Mother was the children. Father has a strong Spanish clannishness, a sense of paternity, sacredness of family.

I cannot note down the entire story of Father's life as he told it to me. What I want is to seize him, the king, the solitary and obstinate visionary, visionary of balance, fairness, logic, transcendentalism.

The pity that this marriage aroused in me was replaced suddenly by a spark of ironic amusement. We were talking about our diabolicalness. I told Father about my liking to go with both Henry and Eduardo to the same hotel room (not at the same time!)—and why, I asked him? This simple statement revealed a world to him. He smiled: "I have done that, too." I could see the statement creating repercussions in him—revealing secrets. A secret, ironic pact of similarity between us.

When I left him I kissed him filially, without the feelings of a daughter. He suddenly bowed his head and kissed my neck.

As I walked down the hall to my room, he stood watching me, but I did not know it. Before entering, I turned back, expecting to see him. He was in too dark a recess, and I did not see him. But he had seen me turn around.

The next morning he could not move from his bed. He was in despair. I enveloped him in gaiety and tenderness. I finally unpacked his bags while he talked to me. And he continued the story of his life. Meals were brought to the room. I wore my satin negligee. The hours passed swiftly. I talked too—I told him the story of the flagellation. When I described how I stood off and observed the commonness of the scene, Father was amazed. This fact seemed again to touch some secret spring of his own nature. He appeared for a moment not to listen, to be absorbed in the dream of his discovery—as I get with people. But then he said, "You are the synthesis of all the women I have loved."

He was watching me constantly. He said, "When you were a child you were beautifully made, formed. You had such a *dos cambré*. I loved taking photographs of you."

I sat all day at the foot of his bed. He caressed my foot.

Then he asked, "Do you believe in dreams?"

"Yes."

"I had a dream of you which frightened me. I dreamed that you masturbated me with jeweled fingers and that I kissed you like a lover. For the first time in my life I was terrified. It was after my visit to Louveciennes."

"I also had a dream of you."

"I don't feel toward you as if you were my daughter."

"I don't feel as if you were my Father."

"What a tragedy. What are we going to do about it? I have met *the* woman of my life, the ideal, and it is my daughter! I cannot even kiss you as I would like to. I'm in love with my own daughter!"

"Everything you feel, I feel."

After each one of these phrases there was a long silence. A heavy silence. A great simplicity of phrases. We did not even move. We looked at each other as in a dream, and I answered him with strange candor, directness.

"When I saw you in Louveciennes I was terribly upset by you. Did you feel it?" he said.

"I was disturbed by you."

"Bring Freud here, and all the psychologists. What could they say about this?"

Another suspense.

"I have been greatly afraid, too," I said.

"We must not let this fear make us unnatural toward each other. And I was all the more afraid, Anaïs, when I realized you are a liberated woman, an *affranchie*."

"I have already felt myself putting on the brakes."

"I have been desperately jealous of Hugo."

Father asked me to move nearer. He was lying on his back and could not move.

"Let me kiss your mouth." He put his arms around me. I hesitated. I was tortured by a complexity of feelings, wanting his mouth, yet afraid, feeling I was to kiss a brother, yet tempted—terrified and desirous. I was taut. He smiled and opened his mouth. We kissed, and that kiss unleashed a wave of desire. I was lying across his body and with my breast I felt his desire, hard, palpitating. Another kiss. More terror than joy. The joy of something unnameable, obscure. He so beautiful—godlike and womanly, seductive and chiseled, hard and soft. A hard passion.

"We must avoid possession," he said, "but, oh, let me kiss you." He caressed my breasts and the tips hardened. I was resisting, saying no, but my nipples hardened. And when his hand caressed me—oh, the knowingness of those caresses—I melted. But all the while some part of me was hard and terrified. My body yielded to the penetration of his hand, but I resisted, I resisted enjoyment. I resisted showing my body. I only uncovered my breasts. I was timid and unwilling, yet passionately moved. "I want you to enjoy, to enjoy," he said. "Enjoy." And his caresses were so acute, so subtle; but I couldn't, and to escape from him I pretended to. Again I lay over him and felt the hardness of his penis. He uncovered himself. I caressed him with my hand. I saw him quiver with desire.

With a strange violence, I lifted my negligee and I lay over him. *"Toi, Anaïs! Je n'ai plus de Dieu!"*

Ecstatic, his face, and I now frenzied with the desire to unite with him . . . undulating, caressing him, clinging to him. His spasm was tremendous, of his whole being. He emptied all of himself in me . . . and my yielding was immense, with my whole being, with only that core of fear which arrested the supreme spasm in me.

Then I wanted to leave him. Still, in some remote region of my being, a revulsion. And he feared the reaction in me. I wanted to run away. I wanted to leave him. But I saw him so vulnerable. And there was something terrible about his lying on his back, crucified, while yet so potent—something compelling. And I remembered how in all my loves there has been a reaction away—that I had always been so afraid. And this flight, I would not hurt him with. No, not after the years of pain my last rejection had caused him. But at this moment, after the passion, I had at least to go to my room, to be alone. I was poisoned by this union. I was not free to enjoy the splendor of it, the magnificence of it. Some sense of guilt weighed down on my joy and continued to weigh down on me, but I could not reveal this to him. He was free—he was passionately free—he was older and more courageous. I would learn from him. I would at last be humble and learn something from my Father!

I went to my room, poisoned. The mistral was blowing, blowing, dry and hot. It had blown for days, from the moment I arrived. It racked my nerves. I thought of nothing. I was divided, and dying because of the division—the struggle to seize joy, and joy unattainable. The oppressive unreality. Life again receding, eluding me. I had the man I loved with my mind; I had him in my arms, in my body. I had the essence of his blood in my body. The man I sought throughout the world, who branded my childhood and haunted me. I had loved fragments of him in other men: the brilliance of John, the compassion of Allendy, the abstractions of Artaud, the creative force and dynamism of Henry—and the *whole* was there, body and face so beautiful, so ardent, with a greater force, all unified, synthesized, more brilliancy, more abstractions, and more force and more sensuality!

This man's love, because of the similitudes between us, because of the blood relation, atrophied my joy. And so life played on me its old trick of dissolving, of losing its palpableness, its normalcy. The mistral wind blew and the shape and savors were destroyed. The sperm was a poison, a love that was a poison . . .

When I told him in the morning that I wanted to run away, that I felt brakes on, hesitancies, he said simply, "You cannot do that. You must be stronger than that. You must have courage. We are living out something tremendous, fantastic, unique . . ."

"And if I resist you?"

"I will seduce you," he said, smiling.

"Do you regret nothing?"

"Nothing! Last night was the San Juan feast. A beautiful night for our union. We burned away all the prejudices. We flamed up with a new passion. I have never, never felt anything so absolute. How I gave myself to you! All the other moments of love, I realize now, were

*Anaïs Nin, costumed
as a Spanish dancer,
about 1930*

*The house at
Louveciennes, on
the outskirts of
Paris, where Anaïs
Nin's family lived
in the early 1930s*

*Henry Miller at
Louveciennes*

June Miller

Henry Miller's portrait of Anaïs Nin in a fur hat

Hugh (Hugo) Guiler, Anaïs Nin's husband

Dr. Otto Rank

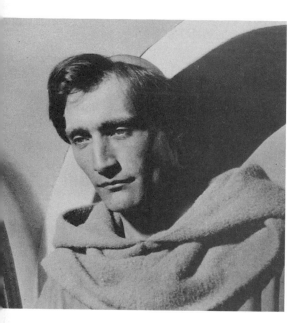

*Antonin Artaud
as he appeared
in the 1928 film
"The Passion of
Joan of Arc"*

Dr. René Allendy

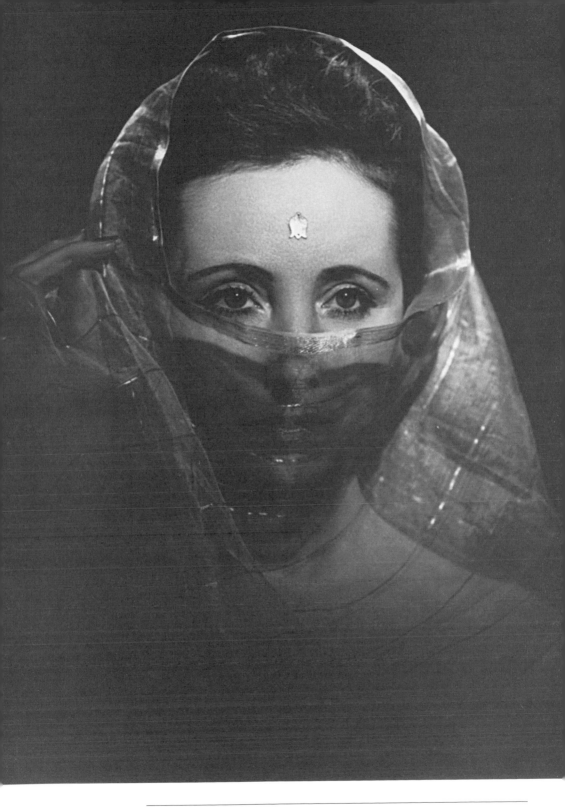

Anaïs Nin with the shawl mentioned in the diary. She presumably sent this 1934 photo to Dr. Rank while he was in New York.

*Joaquin Nin, Anaïs Nin's father,
approximately 1908—a few
years before he left his wife,
Anaïs, and his two young sons*

*Joaquin Nin, in the late
1920s or early 1930s*

Eduardo Sánchez, Anaïs Nin's cousin, in Paris in early 1930s. This snapshot was found in one of Anaïs Nin's original diaries.

Mon Journal

and Note Book # ~~#~~ 42

Anaïs Nin Guiler

From June 13, 1933 to Aug. 1933

Father
Henry.

Antonin Artaud

Incest

2 bis Rue Monbuisson, Louveciennes
Grand Hotel Coirier, Valescure' St Raphaël B.45.
Avignon - Chambery --
Hotel Fin Bec - Chamonix - Hotel Bellevue
Hotel Eden-Palmyre, Annecy.
Hotel Helder, Aix-les-Bains.

Nanagui

(X)

incomplete—a game. Last night I realized what love is. I poured my whole being into you."

It all seemed too wonderful to destroy.

We spent another day in his room. He moved with great difficulty and pain, yet he shaved and bathed. He sat in an armchair and read me his manuscript on musical opinions and sketches. In between, there were autobiographical sketches and poems—romantic poems. The whole book was romantic, idealistic, not as muscular or as dynamic as his own life. It is his own life which is a masterpiece.

At night—caresses. He begs me to undress and lie at his side. His caressing suppleness and mine, the feelings which run from head to toes—vibrations of all the senses, a thousand new vibrations . . . a new union, a unison of delicacies, subtleties, exaltations, keener awareness and perception and tentacles. A joy which spreads in vast circles, a joy for me without climax because of that deeper, inner holding back. Yet missing only the climax and revealing by this very absence what intensity he and I could bring to the envelopment, to the radius and rainbows of a climax.

We sat up until two or three, talking. "What a tragedy that I find you and cannot marry you." It was he who was preoccupied with enchanting me. It was he who talked, who was anxious, who displayed all his seductions. It was I who was being courted, magnificently. And he said, "How good it is that I should be courting you. Women have always sought me out, courted me. I have only been gallant with them."

Endless stories about women. Exploits. Teaching me at the same time the last expertness in love—the games, the subtleties, new caresses. I had at moments the feeling that here was Don Juan indeed, Don Juan who had possessed more than a thousand women, and I was lying there learning from him, and he was telling me how much talent I had, how amazing an amorous sensibility, how beautifully tuned and responsive I was. Amazed at the richness of my honey. "You walk like a courtesan from Greece. You seem to offer your sex when you walk."

When I walked down the dark hall to my room—with a handkerchief between my legs because his sperm is overabundant—the mistral was blowing, and I felt a veil between life and me, between joy and me. All this unfolded itself as it should, gloriously—but without the ultimate spark of joy, because at certain moments he was the unknown lover, the glamorous Spaniard expert in seductions, lover in love with his mind and his spirit and soul, and at other times too intimate, too like myself, with the same contractions of fear and lack of confidence, the same *survoltage*, the same exacerbated sensibilities. And what caused me anxiety were certain remarks: "I would like to replace your other lovers. I know I could have if I were forty instead of fifty-four. In a few years, perhaps, there will not be any more *riquette,* and then you will abandon me." Unbearable to me, his insecurity, he the lion, the jungle king, the most virile man I have known. For it amazes me to find a greater sensual force than Henry—to see him all day in a state of erection, and his *riquette*, his penis, so hard, so agile, so heavy.

The next night, when he was a little freer in his movements and he lay over me, it was an orgy, and he penetrated me three and four times without pausing and without withdrawing—his new strength, new desire, and new spurt coming like waves following each other. I sank into the dim, veiled, unclimaxed joy, into the mist of caresses, languors, into continuous excitation, experiencing at last, profoundly, a passion for this man, a passion founded on awe, admiration. It ceased to concern me, the attainment of my own joy. I plunged into the completion of his. I told him these had been the most beautiful nights of my life, and when I said this I saw he had wanted keenly to know if this were so. I poured out love, worship, awareness. And the fourth night was again different. He did not believe in excess, in exhaustion. He wanted the high exaltation preserved. I told him about the painting of Lot and his daughters. He said, "You are still a child." But I remembered he had said the first night, *"Je n'ai plus de Dieu!*—I have lost God."

The mistral quieted down. We laughed together about the consumption of handkerchiefs. We laughed about obscene words I taught him in English. He went into a long fantastic tale, full of puns, about a speech he would make to Mother: *"Tu m'a pris souvent, mais tu ne savais pas comment me prendre. Anaïs sait. Je voudrais l'epouser."** We laughed at the faces certain people would make if they knew.

With his will he was growing better. The first day he could go downstairs for lunch, he dressed to perfection, and with his alabaster skin, his clothes, his neat figure (he has small feet and hands), his soft hat, he looked so grandiose, so aristocratic, so unreal: a Spanish grandee, a king; walking slowly under a tropical sun, teaching me about the life of insects, the names of birds, and the distinctions between their cries, so that the world became peopled with new sounds, and everywhere I go now I cannot hear the cries of the swallows without remembering him and his walk and his face in the sun. *Le Roi Soleil.*

Once we sat in the blazing sun, alone in the garden. He had taken a chair in front of me. He observed that a stocking was wrinkled. I tightened my garter. The spectacle stirred him. He showed me his penis, tense. He asked me to lift my dress. I did so and began to undulate, moving as if in expectancy of a lancing. When we both could not bear the excitement any longer, we went to his room and he threw me on the bed and took me from behind.

"Qué picara," he said. *"¡Tan picara como su padre!* Who do you take after, you little devil? Not me!"

One night we walked along the terrace in the moonlight. He looked twenty-five years old—like Joaquin. He said, "Even your height is what I dreamed. I always wanted a woman with eyes on a level with my own. And there you are. Tall, royal. A sun. You are a sun. You not only match and meet and equal my thoughts, you sometimes precede me! A match! I have found my match.

"Such a tenuous balance," he said. "We could easily be unbalanced. Our balance hangs on the most tenuous thread. All the more wonderful if we can maintain it. Look for the *light,* for clarity. Be more and more Latin!"

---

* "You have taken me often, but you did not know how to take me. Anaïs knows. I would like to marry her."

When the servant presented the mail and Father saw letters for me, he said, "Am I going to be jealous of your letters, too?"

Our last night. He did not want to go to the room. We stayed and talked to people. When we were in bed, naked, close, he began to sob. I was touched and so amazed. Nothing ever took me more by surprise. *He, he*, weeping because we were separating. He saying, "Now you see me weak like a woman."

Another man. The sensitive, the sentimental man. And I enshrouded in unreality, so that I realized acutely that in love there is always the one who gives and the one who receives. And how uneasy and strange I feel when I receive. Awkward. Yes, it was he who gave, who gave himself. I could not sleep. I felt ungenerous. It was he who had wept. I awoke early. I rushed to his room. I felt keen pangs of regret. I was amazed at my own self, that it was I who was leaving —yet he alone would have understood why. Fear of disillusion, fear that I should break physically, be less beautiful, less than all he expected. A flight from the most precious experience at a certain moment, always. *Trop pleine*. Like him, wanting all ecstasies to remain suspended— never satiation in love. Fear of satiation. Feeling our ecstasy had been timed perfectly, that since he was so much me, he too would want the pause.

To achieve this flight, which also meant keeping my word to Henry, I had to lie endlessly to everyone. A web of lies. Father had to believe I was returning to Paris. Hugo would understand that I should not return for reasons of health. But then if I returned to Paris I had to visit Father's wife. Thus I must pretend to go to London with Hugo's family. Hugo must think I was going to the mountains. But Henry expected me in Avignon. I had never hated my lies so. I was imprisoned in all my deceptions at once. I did not want Father to know I could go to Henry after nine days with him. I did not want Henry to know I did not want to join him.

After I saw Father vanishing at the station, a great misery and coldness overcame me. I sat inert, remembering obsessively. A suffocation. A leaden mood. Tumult, nervousness, chaos. I am leaving a man I feared to love—an unnatural love. From that moment, reality sank into the sea. I was living a dream. I was going to meet a man I had loved humanly, a natural love. I wanted clarity and wholeness and definiteness, and they eluded me. For five hours I thought of my *padre-amour* . . . unfocused . . . bewildered.

[J U L Y   2,   1 9 3 3]

WHEN I MET HENRY AT THE STATION I LIKED HIS thick, soft mouth. But his embrace in the hotel room did not move me. I was terrified. We were strangers. He unchanged, but paler. I was obsessed with my other love. Too late. Now I was with Henry. And for the first time I looked at him without illusion. I saw that our unison had been achieved by my adaptability. I had tuned myself to Henry. I had closed many regions of my mind. I had entered his world. I had loved passionately. But suddenly it seemed to me that his thinking was terribly different. That thinking, so imprecise, so unfocused, so undisciplined, so awkward, I had accepted, understood, loved.

I was broken by this discovery. I tried to forget it. I thought Father had ensorcelled me, that I would awake some morning and find Henry the *all,* the *whole.*

We wandered through Avignon. I appear gay, tender. He has so many needs; he is pitiable. We buy him clothes. He is in his element, wandering, living in the streets.

All the while I am obsessed, dark, appalled. My passion for Henry dying, dying. Physically, sensually, too, he has diminished. Is the change all in me? Is it my Father who thus obsesses me, obscures and eclipses all the others?

And now the effort to delude Henry. It kills me.

While I am with him I must write Father letters which must be mailed from London by a friend. I hide my journal and my letters inside the springs of our bed, whose linen cover I have slashed open with a razor blade.

I want to give Henry his joyous trip. I hide away my feelings.

Two days in Avignon. In Chambery I fall ill. Bilious attack. And I did not want Henry to see me ill! To be disillusioned, annoyed, disappointed. I send him out. I am sick alone, secretly. Whenever he returns I am dressed, powdered, perfumed. Grenoble. Chamonix. Vertigo. Starvation. The effort of will to poetize illness for him. And I succeed. He has been free; he has not been depressed, cramped. He has been out. When he returned I was always gay, dressed up.

And the ordeal of being sick and helpless before Henry was passed gloriously. He was amazed by it all. Had never seen a woman sick like that. He was tender, very tender, very concerned. I was repeating my Father's "illness" before me. I had always borne illness like that —always the powder box and the mirror and the bath, in spite of vertigo.

Then I wanted to get well to go to the movies with him. I went to the movies with a fever. Then I bicycled with him, walked with him, and on our last night I even drank with him. For his joy. And his joy gave me great joy. It was like a child's. A modest room seemed luxurious to him, our bath palatial, Chamonix a paradise. I loaded him with gifts, enveloped him in tenderness—and my mood, my despair poisoning me, undetectable.

Henry!

I won't question myself. I won't dissect myself. Let things happen.

Henry carried in his pocket, while we bicycled, frenzied love letters from Hugo. He himself mailed my love letters to my Father.

I had wanted the journal to die with the confession of a love I could not make. I had wanted at least my incestuous love to remain unwritten. I had promised Father utter secrecy.

But one night here in the hotel, when I realized there was *no one* I could tell about my Father, I felt suffocated. I began to write again while Henry read at my side. It was inevitable. I could not kill my journal off when I reached the climax of my life, at the very moment when I needed it most to cling to, to preserve, however great the crime of my frankness.

It all stifles me. I need air, I need liberation. I must achieve liberation again, and this time alone. No one can teach me to enjoy my tragic incest-love, to shed the last chains of guilt. And my journal keeps me from insanity. I need this order. I am more ill than ever, more neurotic, and I must keep my balance.

Henry gone—it seemed to me that I was losing life, joy, reality, simplicity. He gives me what my Father cannot give me, because my Father is me, and Henry is the *other*—the only other I have connected with. Was it illusion?

Henry's physical pace too strong for me. So today I am in bed to recuperate. What a tar, a fragility like mine. And I'm sad. It does me good to write. It is a kind of order. Now comes Hugo to be made supremely happy—in atonement. He has been so tense and desperate for three weeks, living with his mother. So tortured. And he writes me passionately. I am his only joy. And I hunt all over for a room that would please him. I am preparing for him. He and Maruca— Father called them our "garages," joking. But we both know we owe our lives to their protection. What ironies. Hugo protects me, and because of him I can play the role of mother to Henry and Artaud. I would be nothing without Hugo. "Little princess, I will serve you and love you and cherish you till my last breath."

Henry, because he is helpless, because he is irresponsible like a child, drains me. He says ingenuously, "Whenever I want something you get it for me. Yet I saw you looking at perfumes, and even if I could I wouldn't get them for you. I used to say no to June. Couldn't understand her wants."

He is irresponsible, paralyzed. Occasionally he thinks and feels unselfishly, but he cannot act by it. He returns from his bicycle ride: "I was thinking I should have stayed with you and read to you."

But I know him too well. I laugh and throw him out of the room.

He is absolutely helpless, cannot do anything for himself. He can only write and fuck.

I lie here and make protective plans for him. But I don't desire him. I think of the time I came out of my bath and he said I looked like Botticelli's Venus—or like a Greek. And suddenly I looked at him and his ugliness hurt me—this bearish ugliness hurt me—this bearish ugliness I have loved. I had a great craving for my Father's beauty, my Father the Greek.

Always the eternal displacement: the lover become child—and the new love king—*le Roi Soleil.*

Le Roi Soleil, who said I angered him when I was a child because I lied like an Arab—because one felt I always had other secret thoughts in my head which I could not or would not express. And I was an *enfant terrible,* tyrannical, high tempered!

"For us," he said, "the discovery of each other brings a kind of peace, because it brings the certitude that we are right. We are stronger together. We will have fewer doubts."

This seemed deeply true. Intellectually I was at rest. I saw in him what the route we chose would lead to. I saw also how misunderstood he was, as I was. How this control, this direction, could be attacked as overconscious. Yet it was instinctive, since in me it worked *against* environment and upbringing. It is true that there is in us, as he said, a genius for orientation. I found my way alone out of Catholicism, the bourgeoisie of my mother, the idiotic surroundings of American life in Richmond Hill. I found D. H. Lawrence alone. I situated him critically alone. I found Henry. I found my decorations, my costuming, my manner of living.

Father even said (as Gide said) that we read in confirmation of our thoughts.

Our great tragedy was to find worshipers but no matches. We have a feeling that we are always running ahead. My Father did things twenty years ago which only today are generally practiced. I also foretold fashions, style; and I know there is in "Alraune" a quality that will only be understood much later. Even in love we are understood much later. I know Henry will wake up some day with excruciating regrets, for he has loved me to the best of his ability, but that is not enough. He perceives obscurely that I am the flame of his life, but he does not know all I could have nourished him with, if he had been ready for more. He has reached his highest mental peaks—but they're too rarefied. He cannot stay there. There are innumerable blind spots in Henry, and the greatest of all is his lack of understanding. He made his noblest efforts with Lawrence and with me. When I first arrived in Avignon, incandescent, talking feverishly, he did as Hugo has done: he snuffed me out. But I understood it because it was jealousy. "I must seem dull to you after your Father." This touched me, and I immediately lowered my diapason, but it hurt me that Henry should make no effort to understand, that he should impose on me an interest in the café, the Benedictine, the cheap music, the passersby, puerilities, faces, externals, food—when there was all that fecund stuff lying in me. He snuffed me out. The extrovert. Cafés everywhere. Drink. Food. Passersby. Always. And I had enjoyed that when it was new to me. Streets. Whores. Movies. Foolish talk. Yes, about foolish people. Imbecilic Fred, yet Henry can bear Fred. All inclusive, undiscerning. Foolish, uncritical. All this was attenuated when Henry began to work. No more cafés. I didn't mind anything. I had never played enough, never been foolish. It did me good. Henry's clownishness and dense moods. His mindlessness. In Avignon it palled on me. I had great needs and he fell so short.

After several days of this I began my journal again.

What use to tell Henry all this? I have learned not to struggle against people's limitations, to let them be. Not to torture them. I said to myself, "That is Henry." And I accepted him. I tried to recapture the joy I felt when we first sat at cafés together—joy, joy over nothingness—and I was bored. I was bored. Henry's interests in the green vest of a guide, in the pink color of a house, in a man's red shirt, in a child's walk, in nothingness, finally bored me. He, the man who offered no resistance to life, who sought only enjoyment, enjoyment. Suddenly I knew I had come to the bottom of this enjoyment, that it left me hungry. That it was in my flights with my Father that I had found joy, a more austere joy, a more creative joy. Reality, streets, people, and all that composed Henry's world could not nourish me.

The journal has always filled the insufficiencies of human beings.

Henry was surprised when I began to write. He looked at me, baffled. Baffled blue eyes. I had boasted laughingly about the death of my journal. He did not connect its rebirth with his own incapacity to receive my confidences (the scene in the garden in Louveciennes when I sent him away, *that* was the beginning of his incomprehension). When I have moods—so few and far between—he asks me if I am ill.

It is I who am changing again, not Henry. He said himself, "Your only defect is that you are too easily satisfied." When Henry gave me what I believed to be the maximum fusion human beings could attain, I did not ever expect to find a greater union—or a human being to whom I could talk as I do to my journal.

The greater unison brings to relief the inadequacies of the other. I created Henry as I needed him. I also *invented* Henry! I loved the Henry that might have been with greater *springs,* greater force, greater will.

Did he know why, yesterday when the train took him away, I looked at him with tremendous sadness . . .

What makes it so touchingly forgivable is always Henry's humility. There is no reproach to be made—only sadness. It is I who made all the efforts to understand.

JULY 11, 1933

*L*AST NIGHT MY HEART GAVE ME TROUBLE, AND I felt great anxiety. I thought I would die in this hotel room alone, and I was anxious about the journal, wondering if I should not get up and burn it. Whether I would have time before my death to burn all the volumes . . . I was surprised to find myself alive this morning.

I want to go to Rank and get absolution for my passion for my Father.

When I told Henry *all* the truth (when I gave him my journals to read) he failed to understand *all. Understanding,* then, exists only in *blood* relations. "You won't fail to understand me, as you failed to understand June, because I know how to explain myself." So I trained Henry's understanding.

Today I dwell on the failures. It is unjust. Probably to justify the change in me.

Understanding *means* love. The more I understand in Henry, the more I encompass and love. They are interdependent. Henry loves—but he loves defectively. His love of the world, his artist's passion for the world, is equally deformed by unawareness.

Yet, sitting together at a café in Avignon, I also told him, "You give me things nobody else has given me." He had taken me through Avignon's whorehouse street—a unique, fantastic sight, like in [the film] *Maya,* terrorizing, abject, dramatic, incredible, smoky, dense, coarse, colorful.

Even his humility is inaccurate. He apologizes when he should not. He is really the genius of imprecision. Blood-choked mind. I needed him. He enriched me. He did not understand me, but he nourished me.

Why the past tense?

Henry has not died. He is on the road, with the pants I mended, the hairbrush I washed, the bicycle handle I observed he needed, because I love him humanly and I want him happy—and thus enveloped, his slightest needs fulfilled, divined, human and nonhuman needs, he does not imagine that tonight I regret having to write in my journal because I could not talk to him. And that I am thinking of my *Roi Soleil,* who has borne his solitude for fifty-four years. What a task before me, to explore all the life of my king, all the twists of his mind. A terror chills me. Is this life or death? Is this love of my Double that self-love again? Is it lack of resistance to the difficulties and pains of life with the Other—the Thou—*le Toi?* Is it always the *moi*—my Father, the male half of me?

July 16, 1933

ANNECY. A HUGO SO PASSIONATE—AND I TOUCHED by his worship. I give myself to his needs entirely. And I suddenly realize he treats me protectively. For him I am timorous, little, delicate. And I protect him more spiritually. I have *entretien,* gaiety, inventiveness, brightness. He is heavy and somber. When I lie in his arms I feel secure. He is big, he is all mine, I know all his thoughts, and there is only me. He lives for me. It is all so extremely simple.

I watch our life in amazement, and it is all care, care and harmony. Tenderness, gifts, protection. Hugo brings me gifts, showers me with gifts. And he treats me like a mistress. He is living a romance. He spoils me. And he has to be unburdened of his sadness. I smooth him out. I make him happy. His immense worship touches me. I find love to give to his mouth (still the most beautiful mouth I have known), and I love to sleep in his arms. And his own fragility matches mine. He has pains—troubles. The altitude keeps him awake. It affected my heart. We moved. Here in Annecy the dampness gave him facial neuralgia, earache, and toothache. It gave me neuritis. We leave for Aix-les-Bains. But I'm not happy. I'm never happy. Henry's health tires me, and Hugo's depression weighs on me. I crave hearing Henry's laugh. I feel well with him, yet when I was ill, I was lonely because Henry doesn't know illness. And whatever he doesn't know he can't sympathize with—he tries to, but he cannot.

My life seems arrested. Again, I am never where I want to be at the moment I want. I did not live my days with my Father thoroughly, and I have regrets. They were veiled. My days with Henry were veiled. I am restless. I want to move. Yet I want to rest somewhere. And I'm neurotic, I know—fearfully so. I expected death on the trip over. I wept when the autocar went too near the edges of the precipices. My heart failed me. I dream endlessly. I have lost my joy. I have forgotten Artaud and Allendy—on the way.

Aix-les-Bains. Slowly, Henry began to fill my being again, like something soft, human, and the *Roi Soleil* receded to more rarefied regions—unreal—perfect. The veil lifted the day we arrived in Aix-les-Bains, and I was able to cast off my mood. For an unknown reason, things began to go right. Hugo's depression dissolved. From our hotel window we saw the solarium. I don't know why I immediately had a vision of health. I believed in it—in this steel airplanelike machine regulating sunbaths for neuralgia. Although I was tired out, I was able to walk up a tremendous hill to see the doctor there. I was keen to get there this morning. The sun! My faith in the sun! Boundless faith. Lying in the sun, I thought of Henry—I felt Henry. I do not feel my Father as well—I *think* him. He rules me mentally. In feeling I am blind. Perhaps I am afraid to feel him. I don't know. I don't want to know. I remembered Jung's idea of wisdom: to let things happen.

So I let things happen. I give myself to the sun. I am happy. I write Henry. I sleep soundly. And we go to the casino after dinner, and with 80 francs, I win 525 francs. I leave immediately. Hugo and I are gay, amused. He finds the crowd vulgar, but I'm happy. I hate snobs more.

When I see a letter from Father at the post office, I am stirred—stirred in a nonhuman way. I read it and I ask myself, Is it possible that my Father should love me more than I love him? Is there always to be an inequality of some kind? Our love—Father's and mine—is unnatural. Or am I afraid of it?

JULY 21, 1933

I WISH I HAD COPIED HERE MY FIRST LETTER TO my *Roi,* written in the little Avignon hotel, in the shabby café terrace, while Henry went to buy himself a shirt and shoes—written out of a tremendous impulse, all in one breath, four pages telling him what he meant to me, passionate pages which made him supremely happy.

And each letter we exchange is a straining after the superlative, the extreme—his sentimental, romantic; mine exalted.

At the same time, I get one from Henry, like Lawrence in his irritable, petulant moods—so contradictory. And always so self-centered. And I feel tired of all I do to augment his joys—tired of inventing his trips, suggesting, giving, divining, realizing all his wishes. And for the first time I venture what I call "being hard": "Henry, there was nothing wrong with Touraine or Carcassone. It was your mood. Don't regret the places you have not seen." (He went to the movies and saw other places and lamented, "I just grazed the right places.") "They, too, would have seemed wrong."

In his first letter, he had said, "The high peak of the trip—you —your indulgences—the peace in Chamonix." Perhaps his discontent and bad humor are due to my absence. But he is always wanting me because I made him happy, wanting me because of what I give—not what I am. My indulgence! Morbidity.

I cannot help comparing the two letters. My *Roi Soleil* writes, "*Hay momentos en que siento una nostalgia de ti, toda, tan intensa que hace daño.*"*

But then, today, I get two books from Henry. And now? I need love!

Flow. Evolution. Movement. I'm hungry, I'm hungry.

---

* "At times I long for you so intensely that it hurts."

Developed a passion for gambling. Every evening I dressed up. Hugo gave me 50 francs and I made 530 in the first few shots. The second night, with 30, I made 300. I get feverish and stirred by the antics of the ball in the round cup. I had awakened Hugo during the night to tell him: "Tomorrow I will play on number four." And I did, and I won, first shot!

The sun. Body to the sun, in a dazzling trance of silver-and-gold light, dissolved in heat. A luxuriant siesta. The post office. The wandering on bicycles. The Lake of Bourget, which inspired Lamartine. Coffee at the gay modernistic café. And the *boule*.

Dreams. Dreams of Henry abandoning me and me running sobbing through the woods. Dreams of sucking Artaud's penis—it is open at the tip like a bag of candy, and there are only a few drops of sperm, and they are salty. Daydreams: September with my Father.

I finally did reproach Henry for snuffing me out in Avignon because he was hurt when I took up my journal. Before Henry's petulant letter, I had written him so tenderly that I missed him. September with my Father, but not alone. August, printing Henry's book, feeding Henry, igniting him. Loving him, but without the great faith, the supreme satisfaction. Disagreeable confrontation with Allendy. What lies now, to disguise and attenuate my indifference? What lies to Artaud?

People plunging into the lake. Brown bodies. Radios.

Hugo's letter to Father:* Anaïs is back from Valescure, radiant because she has found her father again—a new, very young father who exists for her for the first time in her life. A newborn father, if you will, but at the same time the father of her dreams. She has always dreamed of a father she could be proud of, one who would respond immediately to the thousand and one questions she asks every day—questions that only someone like you, someone who has lived widely and has a real genius for living, could answer. I feel as though I have

---

* In French in the original.

also acquired a father and a brother at the same time, and I am happy . . .

Lui. Le Roi Soleil.

In the moments of love, with his glasses off and his long hair disheveled—it frightened me to see a woman. A Grecian woman. The shortsighted eyes unfocused, as a woman's are when she nearly faints with feeling. This strange impression haunted me. I closed my eyes.

Henry writes: We are placed in the world to be of it, part of it, to be nourished and to nourish. . . . It is the Lawrentian desire to alter men which causes more havoc than good. It is blindly egotistical and neurotic. I notice that the desire to re-form man moves man away from his neighbor and not toward him. It leads to isolation. To concern for the self. When one has grown utterly weary of trying to aid man, one returns to the flock and then one really aids—just by his presence, because then the sum of experiences, of suffering, of self-analysis, and of soul-struggle have mellowed the individual and he can aid because he speaks and moves out of ripe, conscious wisdom— not through precepts, ideas, formulas. I'm thinking that per- haps the root of all dissension between "friends" (a subject so engrossing to Lawrence and Duhamel) is the quality of idealism contained in it.

I liked all this, applauded it.

Henry adds: It is again a too-sacred, too-private, too- isolated thing. Pure love, pure friendship—these are ideals. These may exist now and then, and they are beautiful things to behold. But they are not goals. They are phenomenal and accidental. . . . When [these] two men [in Duhamel's *Salavin*] form an eternal pact they are alienating themselves from the rest of mankind, which is a sin. . . . Man and wife do the same thing when they love each other to death. They suck each other dry. They find themselves face to face, like hollow shells, after a while.

Hugo and I made the mistake of idealists. We felt we had found something ideal and we isolated ourselves. Against the world. All alone, the two of us, for years. And it was bad for us. I, being the greedy one, I began to demand, to demand more, to devour Hugo. Since I leave him alone, and am with more people, we are all happier.

As soon as I found order in my feeling again, I was at peace. Henry was situated as the human love—and *le Roi Soleil* as the ideal, the nonhuman, the rarefied. I saw Henry again at his highest, tenderest moments—all that warmth which compensates for subtlety, all that human mellowness which substitutes for understanding.

I began to live again. Even losing at the casino could not hurt me. And that feeling, that divine feeling of liberation from the one love, on which I can never count, the feeling of *security in multiplicity*.

One night [Father and I] talked about our lives—how he knew I would continue to have lovers because I was young and ardent and he could not marry me—how he would understand, and it would not affect our love; and I was upset because I knew it was true. And I gave him the same liberty. I have accepted from the first the idea of his Don Juan-esque career—separating myself from other women, realizing my unique situation. He said, "What a wonderful end to my amorous career, if I could just devote myself to you. If I had married a woman like you who had everything, I would have been faithful."

I realize I don't believe anymore in the ideal of faithfulness. It is immature. I expect him to continue his life, as I have continued mine.

All this incestuous love is still veiled and a dream. I want to realize it, and it eludes me.

Sense of guilt, Allendy would say. I need Rank; I need a stronger mind than Allendy's. I want to talk with Rank. About art, creation, incest. I want to be free of guilt. I want to confront a big mind and thresh out the subject. Plumb it.

Amazing discovery. Astrology. Astrology reveals that [Father's] moon is in my sun, the strongest attraction between man and woman.

When Hugo showed me this, fatalism choked the last vestiges of sense of guilt. And I felt awe. The immense blind fear was replaced by awe. Less blinding. I am beginning to look daringly upon the face of my incestuous love.

It was all ordained. I only obeyed my destiny. That destiny planned a great ironic marriage, a marriage impossible on earth. I did not realize the full portent of Father's words "This is a tragedy." What a tremendous marriage. *Beau à faire peur*. I am dazzled. I have been dazzled all through. To return to Henry was the human, the familiar, after a rarefied atmosphere—the dream—unbreathable air.

Cloud-sifting moods. Pity. Love. Rebellion in me against Henry's love of dirt. Remembering how often I have opened my legs wondering if he was bringing me syphilis. Resentment against his irrationalities. I desire to fight him. Then remorse for my love of Father—and devotion.

He says himself he is a coward. He needed June's courage to experience, to live. He needed me to think. And because of his dependence, he will always be a humiliated man, revenging himself through literature, just as I revenge myself for my sacrifices, my heroic lies, my charities, my compassions, my indulgences, in this most cruel of all documents.

I would hate a war with Henry. It would kill me. But as my passion diminishes, the antagonism awakens. I used to believe I could find life, sensuality, only in crapulousness, in the underworld, in danger, in dirt. I accepted Henry's world because of Henry's aliveness. And now I discover I was mistaken. That there are sensual men who don't risk syphilis—that there are clean sensualists! My Father! And I resented all that I accepted for the sake of Henry's lustiness—all that I embraced, my naive belief that I had to embrace syphilis, dirt, with sensuality because the world seemed divided into the pure men: Allendy, Eduardo, Artaud, or Henry. And Henry was the only live one.

I paid tribute to human life. I embraced all life, and the whores, and the danger, because I loved. I loved lustily, humanly. I was not repulsed by anything.

In nine days I changed.

Why did I hope to change Henry's life, which is a miserable one? Have I done nothing for him? Will he be the same when I leave him as when I met him? He still preaches death, destruction, fire, leprosy, and syphilis. He is still twisted up with anger, distorted with resentments, bloodshot with humiliations; and he has received all that a man could humanly wish for from a woman. Faith, passion, encouragement, appreciation, understanding, worship, peace, security, harmony—nothing can heal him.

My monstrous enemy melancholia. After the casino, the café, in the soft night I returned and slipped out of my frothy dress. And I knew I had returned also to my broodings—escaping from them only for a few hours. I must get Henry's book published. I must do that for him. I must enthrone him securely before I abandon him. Give him strength.

*To Father:** You see from your horoscope how right I was to crown you a king! Sometimes I go back to phrases or words that you uttered and I explore them, I think about them. A sentence of yours has vast repercussions for me; it is full of meaning.

Meanwhile I have given Hugo great closeness, and two or three "theoretical" talks—so deep—where I tell him all except the sexual connections, and where we discuss where each man failed to satisfy me! All so cool and mental and wise. Hugo believes I have been mothering Henry spiritually. His jealousy, however, is blind. He is not jealous of Father (his greatest rival); he believes Henry is dying (oh, this is close to the truth; Henry is dying for me, dying, dying). He fears Artaud. Yes, I throw smoke about, as Henry says. The result is, Hugo is serene and happy with his portion of love—truly inalterable, a love running in this groove of his with something like, for me, a miraculous faithfulness.

But it is true, as I told Hugo, that in the end Hugo's love is the

---

* This letter, and all of Anaïs Nin's subsequent letters to her father as quoted here, are in French in the original. His letters to Anaïs Nin are also in French in the original.

only one I believe in, rest upon. Father's still frightens me. It demands courage. Thus the secret of my marriage: trust—trustingness. When I loved John I submitted to pain—I died. Now I am learning to fend it off. Henry made me suffer enough. I'm weary of suffering.

Last day in Aix-les-Bains. Collected health, minor and multiple victories: an Adonis in Chamonix, Prince Nicolas of Romania, a gigolo, the doctor at the solarium, the assistant, waitresses everywhere, *garçons* at cafés. Showered with gifts from Hugo to make up for past inexpressiveness.

Astrological predictions for these months: traveling, work, and love successes. And the whole of 1933 good, and 1934 better.

Hugo's health is at its best, which relieves me of a constant anxiety.

Foxiness. Hugo left me in Munich without a cent because he had bought my train ticket, tipped the baggage man, and sent a telegram to Natasha to meet me at the station—and as soon as his back was turned I asked the concierge for the telegram to rectify an error on it and rewrote it, but for Henry.

Looking around, when left alone in Henry's kitchen, as if I were looking at everything for the last time. Looking attentively at the humorous painting by Fred of a couple making love on a bench in front of the *urinoir,* posted with *Maladies des voies urinaires* and *Chocolat Meunier*. Looking at the made-up menu hung on a nail: *bouchées à la reine, pâté de foie gras truffé, dinde aux champignons*. Looking at bohemian life, at the Quatz Art Ball, at the basket surrounded by a corset, at the pamphlet on "Instinctivism"—as if I were parting from them. Looking at Henry's coat hugging the chair, seeing the form of his shoulders and ribs, and feeling his body, without the tightening and clutching pain of suffocating jealousy. Parting not from Henry but from the immense, incommensurable pain of jealousy. Taking only the joys he gives me. Sifting away the whole cleaving, the dark dependence, the passion which caused torture, so that he might mention June or his whores without bleeding me.

I want to enjoy Henry.

I parted not from the past but from past pain. Only the humor of the sketches on the wall and the deep flowing groove of a mellow, undemanding, illusionless love, the groove I slid into as soon as I saw Henry on the station platform, forgetting the demands, the critical exaltations which strike death over one's joys.

Henry is happy. "Now I click again. I'm like a huge wheel that cannot turn until you come with your very tiny, very neat apparatus. A slight, slight touch and I am set off by you. I must admit that, like Lawrence, I can do nothing without a woman behind me."

And the irony of it all is that he has been miraculously faithful.

To enjoy, to enjoy, and to love, one must not be critical. Close one's eyes on all the blessed human imperfections.

To Father: I almost wept on opening your letter received in Aix-les-Bains as I was packing. That thought, of writing me for my departure, was so delicate, so incredibly subtle. It's something I have done for others and that I dreamed of for myself, but others love in such a different way. One must know how to love, how to be thoughtful in love, as you well know. I am more touched than I can tell you by what your gesture represents, by such a significant detail. In that moment when your letter came, it seemed to me that suddenly I was rewarded for all the art and the ingenuity that I have put into loving all my life long. It is sweet to receive, sweet to receive something that comes with so much subtlety, so much tenderness, with a thoughtfulness that enfolds one so skillfully, a quality uniquely yours. I kiss you today with gratitude that you exist, thanking not the god but you, yourself, for your own great creative effort.

Evening. To walk into the house is to walk into dawn, into the dawn colors, into the sunset tones, into music, into perfume, into the quintessence of exoticism, into a honeyed womb, into a palaquin of cotton, into fur, silk, into harmony.

I stood on the threshold and experienced the miracle. I forgot that I had made the house. I was ensorcelled, as by the work of another. A caress of color and textures, a hammock.

My joy and energy blazed. I began to ordain the kingdom, to organize, to administer, to draw around me the close web of activity. I was prodigal with my strength. I swam through a Sargasso Sea of papers. The telephone vibrated. Multiple threads. Expansion. Body so strong, phosphorescence of mind and body.

Papers. Work. Engagements. Letters. I love it all. I love living, moving. Intoxication. I'm intoxicated. Tomorrow, the copyist and Allendy. Thursday, Artaud. Friday, Henry. Benign lies to all. To Henry to attenuate his jealousy of my Father. To each I give the illusion of being the chosen one. If all my letters were put together they would reveal startling contradictions. I even tell Henry, "I talk a great deal about my Father, but he does not mean as much to me as you do." Because I imagine people need these lies, *mensonges vitaux!* Truth is coarse and unfructifying. I tell Allendy, "I have just arrived. When can I see you?" As if he were the first I called, and I have already slept with Henry.

Humor. When Father tells me benign lies like "This is the first time I have wanted a lot of money" (to join me, to make me gifts), I detect the insincerity. Father has wished for money a thousand times, as I have. Other times he may even have written so to other women. And I smile. Exudative. All the incense I give others blown back now under my nose. All my own tricks and lies offered me—as if I couldn't detect them. While he is writing me, Delia or some other woman is probably standing or lying two feet away. Her perfume could reach me. Treachery, oh, the treachery of illusion. Creating illusion and delusion. Who is going to wring the truth from others? Must we also lie to each other? I don't want this. I will tell the truth first. All of it. My trip, my lies, Henry. Then he will smile and offer his story. Father, spare me those lies that we have to tell to others weaker than we, that deformation of our nature to create an illusion for the others. Let's be brave—you yourself were the first to ask that of me. Let's keep jealousy out of our love!

This diary proves a tremendous, all-engulfing craving for truth, since to write it I risk destroying all the edifices of my illusions, all the gifts I made, all that I created, Hugo's life, Henry's life; everyone whom I saved from truth, I here destroy!

AUGUST 2, 1933

*T*HE WORK HAS BEGUN. MISS GREEN IS COPYING THE manuscript on June, or otherwise I would be like a dog trying to catch his tail. I work on the narrative.

I will make notes here of themes to pick up, to repeat. Like theme of Chinese theater and seeing backstage illusion. Compare with process of psychoanalysis. Going backstage behind illusion. And its effect on me.

Bring to relief resemblances between my lovers and my Father. Continuity of Father's image in spite of apparent blurs.

Moral of journal? What does world need—the illusion I gave in life or the truth I gave in writing?

When I went about dreaming of satisfying people's dreams—satisfying the illusion-hunger—didn't I know that was the most painful and the most insatiable hunger? What impels me to offer now veracity in place of illusion?

Scene with Artaud: "Before you say anything I must tell you I sensed from your letter that you had ceased loving me—or rather, had never loved me at all—that some other love took hold of you. Yes, I know. I guess it is your father. So all my doubts of you were right. Your feelings are unstable, changeable. And this love of yours, I must tell you, is an abomination."

A venomous, bitter Artaud, mouth ugly, tight, all fury and rancor. Repulsive. I had received him with sadness. He said he had observed this sadness, but it didn't touch him. And a few moments later he made me angry and pitiless. I got blamed for cruelty when I really was sincere. My pity vanished completely. I looked at him coldly and watched him. My God, this is the man I kissed, this is the man who expected exclusive love from me. Hurling bitterness. "You give everyone the illusion of maximum love. Furthermore, I don't believe I am the only one you have deceived. I sense that you not only love your father with a revolting passion, but that just now there are one or two other men in your life. I feel there is something with Allendy, and with yet another man—and believe me, I haven't heard any gossip either . . ."

All this was so intuitive, so clairvoyant, that I denied nothing, but at his word *abomination* I said angrily, "No, the purest love. And if you don't believe in my purity then you don't know me."

"No, I don't. I believe in your absolute impurity."

A terrible verdict went on in me as he talked. I disliked his pettiness and his rigidness. I thought of how differently Henry would have taken all this. Hugo too. I thought of how beautifully mellow Allendy had been—I disliked Artaud's medieval sentences, his lack of imagination. Like a Savonarola, with his gods, eternities, and impurities. I was glad he could not move me. The real cruelty was only beginning in the scorn I felt. He tried to injure me, to retaliate, but in such a petty way. Like a woman. Child too. What a disillusionment. I could not pity him—yes—he was sincere and he expected everything—I had made him fall from such great heights. But I could not help feeling he was acting like a vulgar, noisy mistress with a revolver. There was nothing beautiful about his pain.

Allendy knew also. And I denied nothing. I seemed to take pleasure in confessing my love, but only Allendy knew its physical realization, because I needed a confessor. My old dependence returned. He was so compassionate, so noble and large. I trusted him. He is loyal and secretive.

What amazed me was the definiteness with which I refused Allendy another rendezvous and the definiteness with which I acted toward Artaud, where before I could never bring myself to say no. As if my love for my Father had given me the courage to live myself out fearlessly. Nobody else will have to suffer for what Artaud describes as my "tenebrous oscillations." Anyway, no more excuses, no more justifications. If I am perverse, monstrous in certain eyes, *tant pis*. All I care about is my own judgment. I am what I am.

Artaud—what happened with Artaud is that he appeared lamentable, puny. I am very weary of men who inspire pity. My Father does not inspire pity. He defends himself so well; he is courageous, noble.

Now that Artaud has pronounced his anathema (fury of a castrated monk) and pronounced me a dangerous, malefic being—now what?

He accused me of "literary" living, of living romantically. Why not live literarily—why not, when it is an improvement on the reality?

When one becomes stronger, one becomes more evil. It is the weak one who suffers. I am afraid I experienced a certain pleasure at torturing Artaud. I was ironic and I snapped back. I would not be accused.

A U G U S T   5 ,   1 9 3 3

*T*ALK WITH HENRY ON MY LYING. AND I MAKE THIS speech, which has been boiling in my head for days: "I am not going to lie anymore. Nobody has been grateful for my lies. Now they will know the truth. And do you think Hugo will like what I have written about him better than what I said to him or implied by my evasions? Do you think Eduardo prefers to know what I think of him, rather than what I told him? I never could say 'I do not love you' to anybody. The mistake I made was to encompass too much. I could not feed five fires. I had to let some of the men down—and they hate me for it. I overestimated my strength. When I told a lie it was a *mensonge vital,* a lie which gave life."

At this moment Henry and I again faced each other as of old, in wonderful completeness. The whole day had been one of reunion. First, I had expected him with enthusiasm, and I walked to the station to meet him. And he said, "I had a premonition you would do this." And he took my arm and we walked in the sun. And then, in the house, we were immediately desirous and we were happy and close on the couch. Henry so eager, so passionate. In the garden he said, "I have been in such a good mood. Ever since you came back. As soon as you are back everything goes right."

"With me, too." I was so happy to have recaptured our harmony, our stimulating interplay.

Father and Henry now beautifully balanced, like the very eternal duality of my own being. One, the ideal absolute, nonhuman; the other, the human.

And it is equally true that Henry's faith in me, Henry's love, has given me life and inspiration, all the strength and all the joys, when I had nothing except the tender security of my marriage.

Tonight my love for Henry is so deeply rooted there is no need of displacement—only of expansion. There is such a well in me—inexhaustible—ample for ideal and human loves, *un foyer immense*. It seems to me that when I loved Artaud for a few days I loved him better—I mean with more talent—than other women can achieve in a lifetime. I gave him a high moment, even if it was a mirage. And Allendy for a few months, a perception, a thoughtfulness, and a warmth which is not current. They both have known something they will never again experience. I condense my gifts, in place of duration!

One cowardly trait. I feel scorn for myself when I try to justify my changes of feelings by bringing to relief the defects or shortcomings of others, to excuse myself. Coward. Coward.

Henry said something so very wise today: "Instead of accentuating the idealism and need of illusion in others, why don't you help them by not deluding them but by teaching them to expect less?"

AUGUST 7, 1933

EVERYTHING WITH HENRY AS BEFORE. NO ALTERA-tion in our passion or in our talks. He comes to help me—or with the intention of helping me. Then he admits he would prefer not to—and we laugh together at his frank egoism. He prefers to sit and copy out a passage from my Father's letter on Lawrence because that is related to his work. It interests him. I laugh because when a man is so honest one can only laugh.

Such accord and joy between us that Henry's thoughts revert again to our inseparableness. And he questioned me—again. Would I, if I could, would I live with him? He likes to hear me answer yes. He laughs with hysterical joy.

Letter to Father: I would like your advice, your opinion on the subject of my journal. I need your judgment, but to get it I would have to show you some recent pages. These days I feel like giving up as a writer. It suddenly seems shocking to me to expose the feelings one has had, even if those feelings are very distant, even if they are dead. Sacrilege. I long to become a simple woman whose life is secret even to herself.

It's curious—my entire life has been lived under a great influence—yours. Now it's as though I want to start over. I began with a new frankness—perhaps because I see more clearly the direction I want to go. Yes, it's strange—you spoke to me of building, as though you were perfectly aware of the construction I was about to undertake. We didn't talk about the future, only the past—yet that caused a renewal in me.

What is happening is that the work I do, apart from the journal, lacks the journal's genuineness. A page in the journal is more moving than my pages of artistic creation. So from time to time I feel like releasing it—anonymously—just as it is, terribly human, simple and direct, as a superhuman effort to balance the lies in the fairy stories that I thought I should give the world. It was wrong to bring us up on fairy stories. I have tried to make them come true for others, and that's dangerous. One loses one's own soul.

August 8, 1933

*B*RADLEY IS A KEEN CRITIC, A VERY HONEST, fearless, loyal thinker. He has really "pitched in to" my work—to help, to ignite, to impel, to demand. He stimulates and interests me. He sees clearly and pragmatically. We talk and forget time. He helps me to clarify, and I like to confide in him. Talking to him helped me to realize this: I have come to the end of a cycle. My life, which began with my passion for Father, ends with the same passion. And *ends*. The cycle of living has come to a close. Now I enter upon peace and work (just like Henry).

Since I returned I have been obsessed with my work. Have spent myself. My head feels immense.

Something is artistically closed—at least my life's theme, my life's novel. The rest is rounding and polishing and enameling.

I was honest with Bradley and he understood wonderfully what I told him about my lies.

Now, he said, the expanded circle of my life invention, my life, meets the circle of my work, and they are to be fused in one. Now I will live as I write in the journal, and write as I live. I have finished with certain illusions, certain lies. I am an artist now, as I tell Henry, bent on work because I am at peace. In peace one writes. My big theme has come to a close, or the close of a cycle.

While I write Henry a letter to compensate for the vacillations of his publisher, he telephones me to say nothing. Just to telephone me. Thinking of me. When am I coming? Yes, he is working.

While I dress I remember something I have never written on: the theme of jealousy. When Henry says, "Monday night I went to Lowenfels and some people came," my heart stands still for a second. I wait. I imagine he is going to say, "Among them was a woman—a gorgeous woman. She looked a bit like June." The moment of suspense is acute, breathtaking. When he ends his phrase, "I talked with e. e. cummings," it is like a knot untied from around my neck. When I find him reading Lowenfels's poem it hurts me—in spite of myself. When I hear him quoting Lowenfels's opinion of his work, so inadequate—yet Henry is happy.

Because of this I watch other people's faces for signs of this jealousy. On Allendy's face—a quiver of the voice—the slightest sign of disturbance—and I get wary. I make a detour. This awareness causes havoc with my honesty. Allendy tells me, "I am free Thursday. Let us go out together—just for tea, at least, since you don't want anything else." And Artaud was coming Thursday. I know what feeling that would give Allendy—and so I lie. And one lie creates another.

Today I carried my mood of honesty to Allendy. And I told him what I had done to Artaud and why. How it began with pity. How there was no question of love. He is too noble to be tormented by suspicions of Artaud. I would not have him deceived. So I tell him. I want things clear and solid. Does it hurt less? I watch him. Before, I gave elusiveness, indirectness; now I reveal myself. What happens? Allendy is disturbed, yet also relieved. He has something to tackle. He reveals to me Artaud's Montparnassian mind, how he showed my first letter to Allendy, boastfully, and talked cynically about the warm tone of it. It was Allendy, Allendy who is not a poet, who said, "You interpret things too crudely." Artaud and his abstract, subtle world! In life a Puritan, a provincial, a Montparnassian. *Une vielle fille.* And so the scene with Artaud becomes clearer. He so literal, even that day in the garden, and interpreting my sympathy as love. I so idealistic. Ridiculous!

That is where my faith went astray. And it frightens me, because I do not yet play lucidly. But I thought I would always know. In believing in Artaud I still believed in *literature.* I still believe the mind which traces down certain phrases cannot think differently in life.

I am, in that respect, amazingly sincere.

To Father (in answer to his letter asking me to join him in Evaux): What do I want? To see you as soon as possible—to be with you again. Last night I wondered how I could wait until October. And while I could write to you now, in secret, I am saving everything for the living moments. We need life, not letters. I no longer think. I feel. I feel you coming closer, human and alive. I am waiting to relive the moments of Valescure, to feel again your sweetness and your strength, the fears and the keen joys, waiting to resolve everything, to let everything melt away in your embrace, in the trust, the warmth, the living fusion.

The other evening, I had dinner with Henry in Clichy. Wine, music, books. Henry said, "I have so many things in this room—I could just live here."

I said, "That is what a home is for—to hold all the precious things we need—nothing else."

"It was never that for me. You know, Anaïs, I have been in many homes—and I have never seen any like yours. None gave me the same feeling. You understand a home."

When I told Henry I might leave for a week, he was hurt. "This is too much, too much," he said. "You should ask me if I will let you."

"Henry, hold on to me, hold on to me. Yes. Ask me to stay."

I felt his love, the gentleness of it. I was hurt by it.

But I wrote Father I would come.

I do not torture myself with questions. I yield to the eternally double flow.

I say to Hugo I have a strange feeling that some of Father's love is like the artist's narcissistic love of outliving himself. He has put his genius in his life and has only failed to leave an expression of his life, and it is I, the penman, who will make him survive.

"I have that feeling, too," said Hugo, "that I will live through you."

It seems to me that so much escapes me that is worthy of the love I give in writing. Today I remembered Father standing at the station when I was riding away from Valescure. He was standing in the sun, at first loose, with his white shirt open at the neck, his legs apart, his arms floating, swinging. Dreamy. Distant. In another world. Away from life, as I do when life is overacute, drawing in, breathing in, secretly, mysteriously, what will only effloresce later, like a Japanese paper flower in water, opening slowly, alone, later.

I wonder whether my anxiety for preserving is not due to a doubt of my memory. I move on. I forget.

Like Proust's annotations, a proof of bad memory.

No. I remember minutely certain things which torment me until I have set them down. When I have written a thing I no longer fear the loss of it. It is an insane love of life, of human life.

It hurts me to remember, in the middle of a day, that warm afternoon in my room when Henry lay on the couch while I dressed and perfumed myself for a dinner. The texture of that day, the colors, the temperature. I have them all in the journal. But very often I have asked myself with a pang, Have I got it? Will it vanish? Will it fall into shreds, grow dim? Will I look for it in the journal and find only pale words—meaningless words? And it is all an acute pain. The essence, the human essence, always evaporating. I cannot bear the passing of hours.

Henry saying, "All that Lawrence wrote about marriage, we have; between us there is that fine balance . . ." Yes. Air. Space. Movement. Born of wisdom. We are old, he after June and I after Hugo. June and Henry wanting to devour, imprison each other. Hugo and I inseparable. Hugo saying last night, "I would like to eat you, to be sure of you." That is the only way to be sure of me.

August 18, 1933

I'M FUNCTIONING LIKE AN ORCHESTRA—ALL INstruments at once. The drums are telegrams from Father. Father ill again and begging me to come immediately, so I have to turn my whole life upside down and rush to him. Father.

Father. The pounding on my heart and on my blood. Hugo protesting feebly, wistfully. I leave Ana Maria's beauty, Henry in a luminous, inspired mood, dazed by reality, so enwrapped in his visions. Allendy, amorous and professional, repeating mechanically all the psychoanalytical clichés, droning: sense of guilt, hatred of your mother. I almost go to sleep. Formulas and analysis have lost their reality. I am living too swiftly; the fruits are falling, they are too heavy for the trees. I look at the sky, driving home with Hugo, a sky all in horizontally piled clouds, and I look through it at the infinite liberation of my feelings and my expansion.

I have a whimsical talk with Eduardo during which I promise to keep my Mars subdued, to sit in a rocking chair fanning myself like a Creole, waiting for him to act, to write, to live. And before my new honesty he admits he is tired of his own honesty and wants to embark on a career of lies. He seems to love my honesty. A strong, fearless wind blowing. I say proudly, "My Father and I are lovers . . ."

I am overflowing. I talk too much. I love too much. I want to work. I like the confusion in my head because a whirlpool of feelings confuses my mind and destroys its control. I want to live by my feelings. Artistically and humanly, they are of better quality than my analysis.

Do not comment. Analysis is death.

As I copied my journal for Bradley, I became aware that my *feelings* were the most intelligent. While I flow I am wisest. When I brood, analyze, I am not as good as Gide or Proust. As Fraenkel said, "All of us can think. But it is the uniqueness of the ideas which count. You, Henry, have no unique, no individual way of thinking—of feeling."

My eyes are closed. The eyes of my willful, cool, mental head.

To feel and to flow, without destroying the dewiness of events by dissection. The dew. The night. The moisture of things and of human beings.

And I think of Henry's unconsciousness. How often I have wistfully wished that he would be conscious—a beautiful hour seemed to float past him, impressing his senses alone . . . and he would seem unaware. He did not hold out his hand. I often secretly expected the letter analyzing that hour, capturing it . . . I expected the second tasting, which never came. I always did my second tasting alone. Recomposed the talk, the hour, handled again the colors, and the smells, clinging.

AUGUST 25, 1933

KISS IN MY ROOM IN VALESCURE. MY FATHER PICKS up a scarab from the road so it will not be run over. He talks about failures, about music from a philosophical angle. He drops his habits during the journey. Nonchalance and tolerance. St. Canna and heat. His *wonder* at everything happening is like mine.

I love him for different reasons each night. His wit. Fantastic inventions. Sadness at Mother's unjust descriptions of him. Morbid scrupulousness about money. His preparing a bath for me in Alès.

How his reserve and criticalness frightened me. Made me ill at ease. Joyous side. Endless jokes. Asks if I have slept with Henry. My first lie. No. No, the third. Elbows on the table. Walking with head bowed. Likes to express feelings, compliments, in writing only. But I know now when he says *"C'est bien,"* it is perfect.

His judgment of Henry, made from our talks, although I never criticized Henry: "Henry is a weakling who is living off your virility."

This caused me a great shock.

Sanity, sanity, he cries. And he wants me healthy, strong, with lovers of my own stature.

My despair at leaving him. His sadness the night before. His dreamy eyes. The potency. His words about Maruca imitating our baby talk. *"Suis facée. Meddé."* (I tired. Help me.) As I used to say as a child.

Says he would not survive exposure of our physical tie. This would kill Maruca. That we are old enough to remember it all. No need to write. Yet I know this is not true. When I read back in the journal I have many surprises. Faithfulness to the nuances of continuity and progression is only obtained by the daily record. I feel it imperative. It is a kind of supreme treachery. Because Father has begged me not to write. Faithfulness to the journal seems to force me each time to write in spite of the feeble reproaches of Eduardo, the anxiety of Hugo, Henry's fears, Joaquin's pleading, and, finally, my promise to Father.

Louveciennes. Evening. I am sad, sad, sad. I can't bear leaving him. I'm obsessed with him—only him. I want nothing else, nobody else.

I haven't loved him enough. He has come upon me like a great mystery. I have been dazed . . . awed.

August 30, 1933

*H*ENRY COMES, AND THE CONTINUITY OF OUR LOVE remains mysteriously unbroken. It runs like a river, instinctively. I can break in my mind with Henry, the Henry others see. I cannot break with the Henry whose voice from the garden stirs my womb.

When Henry left I remembered Father's words—"There should be only you and me. Nobody else. Concentration. No Henrys."

"What more can you want," said Father, "than a gentlemanly husband and an ardent lover?"

Nobody knows the Henry who talks as wisely to me as he talks unevenly, blunderingly to others, as if the temperature and climate of my faith made all fine things flower in him. I look at him, and he is whole, with the voice of his work, the tone of his own assurance, of his certainties. He is pale and serene, and yet fiery, focused.

I look at him in front of Fraenkel, and he is red, flustered, he stammers, he looks dispersed, lost. He looks tottering and confused. Yes, lost. He is at his best before his work and before me. Lowenfels must say to him, "Shut up. You know you don't mean what you say."

Letter to Father: I couldn't write you last night. I think of you constantly. I awaken wrapped in dreams of you. With your picture next to me, I work with only half my mind. Everything, everything else has vanished. My work is for you. I wish it were more beautiful. My journal is for you. For you I want to make, and shall make, renewed efforts—whatever may give you joy. Sometimes I feel that the absolute you give me fills me beyond the brim, that I really overflow. That is why you shouldn't be surprised that I love you every hour of the day—not blindly, but because you are beautiful and yourself every minute, always, even in those moments that cause you embarrassment. Don't you know yet what it is to be loved for your whole self, for that mysterious *you* which appears when you think you are less beautiful, less adorable? With infinite and valiant labor you have added all those beautiful improvements to your being; but if you were stripped of them today, as of a brocade garment, there would remain the quintessential you which is the axis, the hearth that gives off so many aspirations, so many creations. Your incandescent being as I see it, my great, great love. So I can think of you at the moment when you are stretched out, when you feel the most defeated—and when you are defeated the least! I would like my letter to reach you at that moment, because what distinguishes you from other men is your eternal concern for the dreams of others. Yet you are not aware of the dreams that you yourself impart, and that is why I want to reveal them to you. You don't know that you show how to go through the most discouraging moments of life with a rare nobility and steadfastness. Another would be warped, or at least his image would be warped, by external events. Your image never is. You transform everything, be it sickness or fatigue; you give everything another color, another beauty always.

You said, "When you think of me you will remember this with regret." And tonight I think that I would give anything to be beside you at any moment of your life, because all of them are beautiful. And how wonderful it is to be able to admire the one you love! In the full light of day, with complete lucidity. As one looks at the sun. So I shall come to see you when it is morning, and from the way I look at you, you will know that I love you, that I am moved by your voice, and your eyes, your bright smile, and the sound of your footsteps. I am going to see you and I am happy, fearfully happy, because I am close to you.

I would like our love to be a great relaxation as well. Our lives have been full of effort, herculean struggles to climb, to surpass ourselves in everything, to make great souls of ourselves, to perfect, to develop, to evolve—almost painfully difficult ascensions, aiming ever higher, always in pursuit of new visions, rejecting what we were yesterday.

We forget to be joyful, to enjoy that which we have overcome. I would like to rest in you, with you. I love our serene hours and the way you make me laugh. How you can laugh! That will be our Sabbath—not a Sunday, but a seventh day of our own invention. At the dawn of the seventh day, while we eat our Quaker Oats, you will say, "It is good." And I will know that I can be happy, because it is your definitive judgment I am waiting for. And you, out of courtesy (and you are divinely courteous), you must also accept my "It is good." You mustn't be disrespectful and answer, "Oh, you don't know anything. You're in love." I say that you are great, that there is no one in the world like you. I am going to sit on your bed, and we will spread out in front of us all that we have, all we possess, instead of our eternal "I wish, I want." No more regrets and no more thinking, for example, that you haven't done enough, created enough, given enough. Those will be the days of our joy. We will feed on joy. And then, because of that wonderful seventh day, in six days you will create music so miraculously beautiful that I shall reward you with another seventh day and a way of looking at you that will be unmistakable. But for today, be content. Rest. Amuse yourself in contemplating the man I love. And I am not easy to please, since it took me twenty years to find you. We have a weakness for phantoms; no sooner have we seen a new perfection passing by than we are off, forgetful of lunch and dinner.

Let's sleep a little, joyfully, while you are in Evaux. You'll accuse me of singing lullabies. But that's because I believe that we have both gone off "in the direction of misgivings."

I kiss you softly on your eyes, whose gaze made me weep when I went away. I feel your gaze penetrate my whole life. Look: Everywhere there is only your image.

AUGUST 31, 1933

*H*UGO LEAVES FOR GENEVA, AND I DO NOT SEND FOR Henry the first night. It seems to me now that my Father will know it, feel it. All my attention is fixed on writing letters to him every day, love letters to crowd and illumine his sick, gray days, his solitude. I am obsessed with him. I would like to pour over him the love I gave Henry, yet I know it is not the same love. I seek new words and new regions and new feelings. It is so utterly different.

SEPTEMBER 4, 1933

*E*ACH DAY INCREASES THE DISTANCE GROWING BE- tween Henry and me because of his great lack of understanding. He didn't understand June; he understands me by flashes; he doesn't understand Lowenfels, nor himself. He lives constantly in a deformed world—inspirations, creations, inventions, lies, insanity.

Our evening at Lowenfels's bored me—gave me nothing, left me empty-handed and terribly disillusioned.

I looked at Lowenfels's wife and thought, If Henry loved her I would not mind. Now he thinks nothing of her, but she wants him and that means she may have him later (if I should abandon him) because of his great, great yieldingness. She was jealous of me, all bristling. I felt tired. I liked her, her type, her hard-boiledness, her domineeringness. Too tired to do anything about it except write to Henry.

I see in Father the image of my expectant years, of my lonely years, a grim image of loneliness relieved by the understanding of blood. Father, the creator, had to give birth to the woman to whom he would give his soul, and he could only give his soul to his own image, or to the reflection of it, the child born of him.

> *He answers my letter:* I won't even try to reply to this morning's beautiful and moving letter. I doubt very much that I possess all the treasures with which your love endows me. But if I am not as you see me, it is certain that all my life I have wanted to be something very similar, an approximation of it. If throughout my life, by a superhuman and continuous effort, without fear or flinching, struggling against everything and everyone, I modeled my soul, chiseled my spirit, sublimated my heart, and harmonized all the tremblings of my being, this was the obscure target I aimed at, hardly daring to admit it even to myself. But after each stage I said to myself, Why this effort, and for whom? Because the people around me strangely misread my goals, my intentions, and my wishes; all were misinterpreted or misunderstood. I suffered horribly without ever giving way or thinking for an instant of seeking another path. A secret force encouraged and guided me, and also an innate need of beauty, order, rhythm, love, and poetry. My life, painful to live because of the sustained effort it required, was beautiful for that very reason.
>
> Yet, why and for whom? And the years passed, peaceful or tragic, flashing or pale, short or agonizingly long, without an instant's deviation in my will to climb and expand: climbing, enlarging the circle around me, but each day finding myself more alone. Was I alone? No, in truth I carried with me a

world of marvels, richer, more numerous, and more diverse than all the crowds of people, and certainly truer. Then suddenly, unexpectedly, you came to me, and by means of love you guessed it all, grasped it all, understood it all to the depths of my being. My every fiber resounded at your call and exhaled its music, every fiber, even those that I thought were asleep forever. A miracle? No. It had to happen like that. The "why" and "for whom" were finished. Someone understood the most beautiful part of my musical score, the one that had never been composed nor written down: my symphony, the symphony of my whole soul, the symphony of my whole life! And suddenly all the sufferings, all the uglinesses, all the disappointments vanished, transformed into generous and living beauty. Everything is corrected, everything rewarded, everything illuminated; and even death, at the end of the race, will be ennobled. Thank you, darling Anaïs.

In spite of Father's playful tone I feel chilled. I look at him with fear. I dread to see an old face, but no, no, he looks younger than Henry. Henry, after our orgies, looked ravaged and puffed under the eyes. Father, no. Wrinkles only, a wrinkle of anxiety between the eyes. A few wrinkles across the forehead, but his body is beautiful, so beautiful, with a skin like a woman's, and the powerful muscles secret, showing only when he wants them to, and the indomitable radiancy. No, no, he cannot grow old before my eyes.

When I arrived in Valescure he met me alone, but it was impossible to detect on his face what his feelings were. Always the impenetrable mask, the coldness. Sometimes the eyes have a yearning, clinging look. And in the moment of love the face is completely transformed, exalted, feminine, joyous (although it is never distorted) with eroticism, a luminous joy, ecstasy, mouth open.

It is only later I discover he was not able to sleep the night before, nor was he able to sleep the night before we left for Evaux-les-Bains.

In the car he caresses me lightly, but we are held down by the idea of meeting Maruca soon. Maruca, so plump and beautifully made, a Tanagra, a Tanagra with a boyish face, an uptilted nose, a little girl's voice, frankness, and directness. I like her immediately, like a brother! I think of Thorvald. The quick, determined gestures, the simplicity. She is warm and I respond to her.

She takes me to my room. We are a little intimidated. She watches me take my hat off, not critically, as women do, but with an affectionate curiosity, to observe what has become of the little girl she knew in Arcachon and who slept in her bed.

I give her the perfume I have brought, hoping she will like me. The three of us sit and talk in their room.

When I return to mine to fetch a photograph, Father follows me and we stand pressed together—not daring to kiss, just body to body—and Toby, yes, Toby feels my presence and stirs. Toby, who raises his head when I talk to him. So Father has to wait until Toby's turmoil calms down.

Maruca and I have a talk while Father sleeps. Expansive, natural, feminine.

Maruca, Delia, and I are in Father's room. Maruca and I are packing his bags. He is marking the road maps. He says, "I won't be able to sleep tonight." I answer, "*Papito*, don't take after your daughter!"

Delia, who said to him when he talked about his first visit to me, "You will fall in love with your daughter. Be careful!"—Delia is looking at me. She has brilliant eyes, and the little girl in her shows through the fifty-year-old woman. That evening it seems to me that all women are youthful and innocent and that I alone am carrying a passion whose face would appear monstrous to them, and that I am illumined by it, and gliding between Maruca and Father with clear naked eyes.

I fall asleep with my legs apart, desiring Father.

Maruca says in the morning, "I will give you a blanket so that your father can take his siesta after lunch on the grass. Make him lie down, Anaïs; he must rest."

The siesta after lunch in St. Canna hotel room. Heat. Hunger and impatience. He is like glowing hot steel.

Night in Alès, while we laugh because there is a noisy fair under our windows and we hear the "*Habañera*." Intensity. Immense inner intensity.

In the morning he prepares my bath for me.

He talks in a general way. Later, he aims more directly at Henry, and for a moment I wonder if it is jealousy. But his jealousy never makes him unfair.

"Am I not enough?" he asks.

I watch his two aspects: one of severity, one of sudden tenderness. Beautiful when he sits filled with wonder at what has happened to us. Sheer wonder. Then he is young, so young. And we both dream, with clear, visionary, exalted eyes.

Pride makes him silent. He listens sometimes with an impenetrable mask. Hours later, or days later, he still remembers, "I didn't tell you at first, but it gave me shivers to learn about the flagellation episode. What dangers you have skirted."

Or after saying little about the horoscope, suddenly: "Astrology has upset my concept of destiny. It makes me believe in cosmic forces."

In Issoire, I come to his small room. In the dark. He says, like Henry, "You are always moist; I will soon be *cocu*." He tells me stories in the dark about his correspondence with Seriex, the painter. Always in a tone of fantastic humor.

In Alès, when he sat on the edge of the bed in the big, barny hotel room, taking off his socks, I discovered the beauty of his feet. Small and fine, so delicate, like a woman's.

One evening, sitting near him while he was reading, I felt the melting liberation of my sensuous feelings. It was my first going out to him since our sensual bond, because until then I had yielded. My love was yieldingness, submission, with a mixture of fear and joy. An élan held down by mysterious obstacles. Some flaw in my confidence. I was coming closer to him of my own accord. Slowly, with that tenderness which alone gives audacity to my love.

Father awed me. When I saw his feet he became a human being. When he perspired in Evaux, I was glad to wipe human perspiration from his face. Perfection has a diamond incandescence which terrorizes. Henry had that fear of me.

Closeness. In Evaux I sought closeness to this man who has never yielded himself for fear of pain and because of self-love.

I loved him for different reasons each night. His fantastic wit. His joyous raconteur moods, improvisations.

He aroused my racial consciousness. I remembered having said to Eduardo, "For love, no language stirs me as deeply as Spanish. Yet I have never heard words of love in Spanish."

When Father says, "*Ven, ven, mi alma,*" or, "*Me quieres de amor?*" the roots, the roots of my blood tremble. My blood trembles. *"Ven, ven!"*

In the center of faith, wisdom, the wisdom of his age. I laugh. I have nothing but faith. I only dread in him the cold, death-dealing criticalness. The greatest beauty of my love for Henry was, on both sides, the faith and the uncriticalness.

On our last night, soon after our union, a sadness falls over his face like a curtain. Sudden and absolute. I look at him; and I, who read him through the tentacles of my own self-knowledge, I am aware that under the surface of this man there are mysteries, there are never-ending depths, unknown regions extending infinitely. Unseizable. I look at his sadness. I know it. It is the immediate, the instant awareness of what is happening which has so often poisoned my joys.

The sensual flame. I crave a night with Henry, a whole night. I play tricks to get this night.

In Clichy, I read his last pages. Henry says, "You are using all your superlatives on these pages. What will you say about my next book?" And he does not wait for my answer. He is kissing me.

I say, "Make it last." But we rouse each other so, it is impossible.

And we fall asleep together. All night I feel his body close. We don't sleep well, but it is a joy to be there. I am not tired. I run through the city very early in the morning to arrive in Louveciennes in time for Hugo's breakfast.

"Evening with Henry and Lowenfels interesting. I slept at Natasha's. We talked until two A.M. You would have felt tired," I tell Hugo.

Hugo is quite happy because I left him a note pinned on his pillow, so loving: "I would rather stay here with you. Sorry to have promised to go tonight. Good night."

I rush to my typewriter and I write Father.

I dance.

Eduardo comes. I am not tired. We walk together. We sit on the wall of the castle moat. Like ecstatic children, pure, playing with fancies: "See those white berries? You should have eyes like that," said Eduardo.

"But look, they have flowers sprouting from the berries. If I had eyes like that, with the flowers, you would pluck them, and Hugo would say when he came home, 'Who plucked my wife's eyes?'"

Allendy, Eduardo, Henry, all observe how well and healthy I look. At dawn this morning Henry looked at me wonderingly: "You don't look like a person who hasn't slept all night."

I have never felt so much well-being. Oh, God, it is incredible. So strong. I typewrite for hours. In a week, ten volumes will have been copied. I am trying to finish the copying to lock the diaries away forever.

Peak days.

Sensual, creative. I feel my sex flame, and my mind flame, and the dream flames. A life like a furnace. Power. Thoughts beating the air, cutting it with steel wings. Desire floating with the rhythm of algae. Dreams and fantasies like pranks of the wind, and laughter.

"Eduardo, darling, we have tried everything. Let us have a homo-sexual relation now."

What lies in his mind: Only a man like her Father, whose horoscope says he is a fierce sensualist, could satisfy her.

During the *nuit blanche* I think: Henry, my love, I can love you better now that you cannot hurt me. I can love you more gaily. More loosely. I can endure space and distance and betrayals. Only the best, the best and the strongest. Henry, my love, the wanderer, the artist, the faithless one who has loved me so well. Believe me, nothing has changed in me toward you except my courage. I cannot walk with one love ever. My head is strong, my head, but to walk, to walk into love

I need miracles, the miracles of excess, and white heat, and two-ness!

Lie here, breathing into my hair, over my neck. No hurt will come from me. No criticalness, no judgment. I bear you in my womb. No mother ever judged the life stirring in her womb. You who wrote these words, "By some unfathomable accident you are outside the walls of the womb and you can never get back again, never, no matter into how small an object you squeeze yourself. You were ejected and you stay outside and your baggage is sent after you, a little bloody bag containing things of no account. You sit on the doorstep of your mother's womb."

September 9, 1933

To Henry: Just a little question stayed on my mind last night when I read that you thought June had sacrificed herself for your sake by entrusting you to my care. Henry, do you really believe I, for instance, would stop helping you and entrust you to the care of another woman while I had strength left in me to do it myself, while I loved you? And why had June ceased to take care of you before I appeared?

Father used to call me, playfully, *petite poire*. "Dupe," in argot. Yes. I sometimes tell myself: People think I am a dupe of Henry, of Henry's candor, of Henry's apparent innocence, irresponsibility. What he confesses, I exonerate. What he asks forgiveness for, I forget. I may be as duped by Henry as Henry is, still, by June. Our faiths are fire-and water-proof.

His sadness at my leaving to go to Valescure in October, instead of spending that month with him as we had planned for a year, is genuine, impossible not to attribute to love. Yet for love of me he cannot spend a little less on records when I am at wit's end to find money. His passion for music seems beautiful to me and immediately becomes right in my eyes. His notes are all being bound, whereas I cannot keep the copyist to copy my journals for Bradley. Yet all this his work glorifies, his work is more important than mine; I am absolutely certain of his genius. And the moments when we read, those pages pour their perfection over everything else. Every other consideration is attenuated; it pales. The records also nourish it, the movies, the cafés. And so everything is engulfed in the ocean of his work, which justifies the man a hundred times.

SEPTEMBER 10, 1933

DREAM: I AM IN A TRAIN. MY JOURNALS ARE IN a black valise. I am walking through the cars. Hugo comes and tells me the valise with the journals has disappeared. Terrible anxiety. I hear that a man has burned the journals. I am furious, with a sense of great injustice. I ask to have the case brought before a court; the man who has burned my journals is there. He looks like Joaquin. I expect the lawyer to defend me, the judges to see immediately that this man has committed a crime, that he had no right to burn the journals. But the lawyers don't talk. The judges are apathetic. Nobody says anything. I have a feeling that the world is against me, that I have to make my own defense. I get up and make a very eloquent, passionate speech: "In these journals you can see I was brought up in Spanish Catholicism, that my actions later on are not evil, just a struggle to react against a prison." I talk, I talk. I realize that everybody is aware of my eloquence, but they say nothing. One of the judges interrupts me to correct my language. I say, "Of course I am fully aware that I cannot talk pure legal French. I beg you to excuse the inaccuracies." But this does not deter me from continuing a passionate defense and accusation. But everybody remains inert. The extent of my despair awakens me.

Dream the same night: Henry says to me, "You know it is necessary for a writer; I went with five whores this week and one woman who was not a whore, who was rather bright, even, more like you." He is saying this with a puckish face, as he does sometimes when he confesses, "I am in debt because I have bought more records." I began to sob desperately and then I held my temples in my hands and cried, "Oh, give me drugs, please give me drugs, I can't bear this."

SEPTEMBER 14, 1933

*H*ENRY SAID IN ANSWER TO MY NOTE ON JUNE: "You were so damned right, so damned right. But I have to let myself be duped, to write my story. It's the story of a blind fool."

Hugo says I do things which go over people's heads—too involved, he teases. I give my enemies the instruments with which they can strike at me afterward, by my excess of scruples in regard to myself—like my jokes about my own jealousy, my admission to his sister where I made mistakes toward Hugh and Eduardo. Nobody else puts himself at others' mercy as I do. Nobody is more truthful than I am when I admit I am a liar. But when others use these revelations against me, they are lost forever in my eyes.

Maruca took me to Father's house. I saw there a photograph of him just after he left us, at thirty-four. I fell in love with this image of his inner self. The face before the WILL asserted itself. The face of his ecstasy, of his moment of love.

I was shocked and sad.

I placed this photograph on my desk. It is a face which I see only when he is in my arms, the *woman* who had startled me so in Valescure.

And then I realized I was falling in love with a reflection, a shadow, a face which is disappearing, and the full horror of Father's aging struck me, chilled me. His age. And I felt nostalgia for a face, a softness, which has passed, and of which I only caught a reflection in the moment of our caresses. My father was, at thirty-four, the lover of my dreams. Today, today I see the crystallization and I love it, and hate it, too; I love it as one loves wisdom. I hate its closeness to death, like Allendy's detachment, Henry's satiation with experience. I am always too young, always too young!

What makes me able to give Henry the leniency and the liberty and the indifference he needs are my own infidelities. What makes me the only one among his friends and mistresses who did not wait in despair for a fair portrait of herself is that I am making my own portrait better than Henry can! What makes me a fit companion for him is that I can laugh at him now—that I don't depend on him humanly. And thus I can match his antics and be humorous. I am beginning to want to hurt men. I am glad to have hurt Eduardo. I am glad I can, at any moment, hurt Henry.

Lowenfels is hurt by Henry's portrait of him. When he praises him, it is false. When he caricatures him, it is also false. Henry is truly insane, in a deep way.

Tonight I am going to punish him for his habit of deforming me before his friends, as he did June. He can never be truthful, never acknowledge either admiration or love when he is jealous. He is jealous of Lowenfels's admiration of me, so he pretends not to admire me. I am not going to appear in Clichy as I had promised. And I want to enjoy this; I want to begin to torture Henry. He writes to Lowenfels, "One carbon copy for my patron" (that's me). Then he explains to me, "And that hard, callous line about my 'patron,' done purposely. Otherwise I'd fall into his clutches." This means: *Otherwise Lowenfels would know I love you and he could torment me. This way I appear not to care.*

Although I understand this, I want to make Henry suffer a little.

SEPTEMBER 17, 1933

I ENJOYED IT. AT NINE LAST NIGHT I THOUGHT, Now Henry is beginning to be anxious. At ten, Now Henry will worry a little.

Today I was laughing. I am not angry anymore. I don't know where I get this inexhaustible fund of tolerance for Henry. He is a little crazy, I think. He is writing great pages. He will always do the most unaccountable, the most foolish, the most low-down, the most vulgar, the most ignoble things. He lives to deny logic, nobility, morals, humanity, humanness. And I laugh. What nonsense, my God. What a perverse, irresponsible child. It is just funny. Just erratic, contradictory. He has got to say the reverse of what he feels and means. It is plain cussedness. Not worth being angry about. Just nonsense. My poor Henry. Why can't I get angry with you for more than a day?

Henry telephones: "What has happened, Anaïs—I've been so anxious."

"Nothing. I went out with somebody else."

"I don't understand."

He never imagined I could be angry. "May I come and be punished?"

I waited for him joyfully. I knew I was not angry, that I understood Henry too well to be angry—but I liked the game. I watched Henry come into the house. As soon as he appeared at the door, I knew I would always forgive him, always.

I realized suddenly that if I ceased to believe in my Henry, he would get lost—he could not find himself again. He would not know what he was. Now he counts on my faith. If I say his callous statements are nonsense, if I am not fooled by his insincerities, he remains whole. The nonbelief of others makes him cussed.

"Did you ridicule me?" he asked again, seriously now. I was smiling. "Did you go out last night?" I wouldn't answer. We made love.

After our caresses I said, "I didn't ridicule you last night." And that was all.

Here I almost lost my desire to make Henry suffer! It is true he is always so honest. He tells me everything. But isn't that another way of hurting, too?

To torment Henry really is impossible to me. It is like allying myself with the world against my own flesh and blood. I cannot be against him because I am close to him—terribly close. I was harder today than I have ever been—for the game of it—but I get no joy. I always stand by him, *with him,* against the world. I laugh with him even if it is against me.

SEPTEMBER 19, 1933

HENRY POURS OUT IDEAS WITH A MAD EXULTA-tion—burlesque ideas, grotesque; his understandings of people are like the figures of the primitive Africans, deformities of the imagination to imitate the feeling, not the object, to attain the personal inner vision, not the real observation, as I try to reach the core of Henry always through and beyond reality.

The trick stimulation of the new. Lowenfels tells nothing new, nothing that Henry has not already read, or heard from Fraenkel or me—but it is an experience with a man. And inwardly I chuckle at Lowenfels's banalities. Whenever Henry announces, "Lowenfels said something good," I wait, and I get nothing new. But Henry does. And I pretend to, now, to indulge Henry. Lowenfels is a quack thinker. But nothing matters. Henry feeds on anything; he can be nourished by garbage-can leftovers. It is always himself, the producer, engenderer, inventor. He is really, most of the time, the loneliest man in the world.

The question is whether my love has given Henry more strength to be what he is today than irritation and war and pain. He needed what I have given him, and what June gave him. To each her karma, well filled, well played, fully realized. Let me be as fecund in my role as June was in hers.

Bradley is a literary sadist. He enjoys lampooning, testy criticisms, butchering. "Henry," he says, "doesn't come off as a character—it's overdrawn, overwritten, overintense, exaggerated, inhuman . . ."

I fight. He says, "There is no denying there is a great literary affinity between you and Miller. Your writing is the feminine counterpart of his. But you have the same qualities and the same defects. He, too, possesses wonderful elements which he hasn't found a way to present. You are absolutely on the wrong track—the romantic, the symbolists. Some of these pages belong to eighteen forty."

But now, now he comes to his real grievance. I had expected it, divined it. For a moment, during the talk, I had lost sight of it. I had even told Henry how Bradley would feel. He says, "The trouble is, of course, that I know Miller. It would have been better if I hadn't known him, for I am constantly comparing your portrait, and I do not agree with it. I think you overestimate him, that you have invented him."

Bradley's mean and petty attacks, however, arouse my fighting spirit—I can't forgive him for the effectiveness of his narrow and literal and unjust condemnations! But I go to work with a vengeful fury against the whole world! To show them, to show them if I am not a writer who has a right to write about two writers!

My attraction for Artaud—so ill and impotent.

These days, when my body has been most healthy, I have been filled with the most morbid thoughts, indulging in them, enjoying them. How I have become expert in detecting the signs of jealousy in others—the almost imperceptible quiver of the eyelid, the faint shadow in the pupil of the eye, the barely noticeable narrowing, a fleck of light—these I catch instantly, in the most inexpressive face. In a room where I don't see all that happens, I feel things, and I interpret the smallest, lightest word as revelatory of the unconscious desire.

My love of standing on a balcony which faces two streets—corner houses—feeling of duality, of two separate roads—the partition and the joy, too, as if only then I know fullness. I saw in a dream long ago such a balcony as belonged to Proust. It happens that Bradley has one—and his room, like the room in my dream, is also lined with books. A prophecy.

I am surcharged with dreams and moods. I don't want to go to Valescure. I don't understand myself.

To travel? To travel one must love the sky, countries, fall in love with cities, but detach one's self from individuals. The cure, the secret of happiness, is there: to love the universe with its changing aspects and its marvelous antitheses and its analogies more marvelous still. The exterior world thus becomes an inalterable source of joy, and all the more perfect because we are its only mirror; the shocks and wounds only come from human beings.

"It is not Olympus—it's Montparnasse, merely," said Bradley. "You tend to ennoble and embellish." And he is all wrong. We are greater than Montparnasse only by our own vision of ourselves and things and levels. If I am guilty of hoisting too much, it is also true that I feel I could go to Montparnasse and experience things nobody else could—and Henry is not Montparnasse, Henry is not [Lawrence] Drake, not Farrant, drug addicts, not [Edward] Titus, not Titus's dog, not the failures and the little artists who talk themselves into life.

I want to yield, to yield to the impetus of my dream—like flow-ingness—unthinking psychic floatingness. My mind was only for the *others*—a guarantee for them. Let it sink.

I am against my Father because he is all mind and reason.

I want to live alone in unknown hotel rooms.

Lose my identity.

My memory.

My home and husband and lovers.

SEPTEMBER 21, 1933

*B*RADLEY: "SO THAT IS ALL YOU'RE GOING TO SHOW me?"

"That's all there is to this story."

"What has Mademoiselle R. been copying for you, then, all this time? Why can't I see that?"

"That belongs to other themes. Not to June and Henry."

Curious. Curious of what—not of literature?

Clichy. Henry. On the way, in the train, I read his last pages, on China, on the tailor shop, on a bicycle ride—and they were sound, smooth, inspiring. They effaced my annoyance at Bradley's banderillas. But when I saw Henry I read him all I had written, and we laughed together, we scalped Bradley, we boiled and parboiled him. Henry put his finger on the true source of my fury: "Bradley is effeminate—he fights like a woman, with small tricks; and these, like Eduardo's sly hints and petty ridicules, have the power to make me feel like a big, apoplectic man who cannot kill off a mouse!"

Henry borrowed ten francs to rush out and buy Benedictine. I was laughing hysterically. Our two moods were again like wine and drugs—overdoses! Mood of strength, sarcasm, and humor.

There was tacked on Henry's closet door a paper with his name and address carefully printed. I asked him, "Are you afraid to forget your name—who you are?"

"You give me ideas," said Henry.

Henry did not show Bradley a violent letter he wrote him in defense of [the childhood] journals two and three because I asked him not to. He says, "You told me not to," and he obeys. But like a child who enjoys playing pranks on his mother, he enjoys slyly mocking me sometimes with Fred and Rudolf Bachman. And I laugh indulgently, because I'm so sure that he is amusing himself. And usually, when he acts insanely, destructively, I can always trace it back to jealousy.

I yield to my somnolent moods—I yield to the influx of vague dreams—yield to the relaxing of the will and reason. I melt into the world.

I am no longer interested in pity. I am no longer trying to right things. Henry Hunt's telling me yesterday about the difficulties of his life with Louise did not arouse my pity, nor any desperate resolution to take his burden on my shoulders. I was curious, interested, unmoved. I was offering understanding and help, but without feeling. I will not try to heal Louise. I enjoy the troubles they are suffering. I enjoy the dark conflicts. I feel detached and satanically amused. I have no human need to improve, harmonize, dissolve pain. Something in me is hardening with the artist's indifference, the indifference Henry is writing about. I let the spectacle be; I let drama evolve; I let the accidents happen. Ever since I have lost my self-pity because I am stronger, I feel less pity for others, proving that I was all along pitying myself in others. A new callousness. When Henry Hunt left, I was not worn-out. I went quietly on with my work.

I'm good at understanding and explaining others. I'm not good at explaining myself. I get off the track. Whatever here is revelatory is the incidental self-revelation, not the rationalization. Shut up, rationalization. Let the acts and feelings speak for themselves.

SUNDAY EVENING

*H*OW HUMOROUS IT WOULD BE IF FATHER AND I were married. He could not deceive me, nor I him! But we would both look so innocent, and I don't know what lies there would be left to invent! He would come home and say to me, as he said to Maruca once when she asked him where he had been, "Why, I come from the arms of a beautiful blonde." And Maruca laughed, not believing him, whereas I would recognize one of my merry admissions which nobody takes seriously, as when I said to Ana Maria, "Hugh hasn't invited you to go horseback riding probably because his wife was jealous and wouldn't let him!" (Which was true, but Ana Maria laughed incredulously.) But I doubt if we would laugh at them as heartily as we should. Father wouldn't like to have his own tricks played on him!

I have an idea that Father is making love to Jeanne while I am sleeping with Henry. Both of us are always wishing for an end to our amorous careers—an ideal end—a dream of fidelity! But it's only smoke.

Which one will admit the truth first?

It takes so much courage to admit such truths, because one fears retaliation!

As soon as one becomes strong one has to accept the consequences. Brave, strong ones are never pitied. People fight them. (June never got pity.) Today I'm stronger and therefore I will be less gently treated.

SEPTEMBER 25, 1933

MY REBELLION AGAINST FATHER—MY SUDDEN ASsertion of independence—is all directed against his restraining influence. (I fought Allendy for the same reason.) My Father has used the "don't" and the "nay" too much—far too much. Immediately, I balk. I am in the yea period of my life. Independence stronger than my love. The chains of love.

Henry has written down the cosmic plan of his novels—a very moving, philosophical, metaphysical pattern—inspired by astrology. He has been in a mood of order, organization. He meets me severely groomed—clean shirt, cast-off formal suit sent by his father—the one he wore for me one day in a mood of aristocracy—and the hair cut off his nose! He is sober-looking, frail, all spirit, noblesse. And tender. He has been observing that he has never in all his life written better, or written more. "Since I am with you," he says. And he implies great, soft gratitude.

"I write about violence, hatred. Yet I am the happiest man on earth. I have a constant feeling of joy."

"I'm your shock absorber," I say.

Bradley's virulence has had the effect of accentuating my awareness of the *note* quality of the journal. It is mostly notes which my enemies may say I present as literature. My life has been one long note taking—sum total: little writing. I owe him this realization.

How quickly Henry's eyes can fill with tears, pitying Lowenfels for having to work. These skin-deep sympathies I don't take seriously, no more than some of my own quick impressionabilities, forgotten the next day. Henry and I are the great vibrators, *par excellence*. Constant vibrations. Mediumistic, fluid, yielding, receptive.

The only difference between the insane man and the neurotic is that the neurotic knows he is ill. The neurotic is not necessarily weak willed. Remember that. It's the vibratory apparatus which is too sensitive.

Dream of word: *Hoder*—Spanish for *fuck!*—which Father taught me.

Evening. The grave money problem—pressure of debts washes away the plan of going to Valescure. And then I realize how it hurts me not to see Father for a whole month. I write him a desperate letter. I feel imprisoned. Hugh is not going to New York. I had wanted freedom. I would have seen Father for ten days.

Yet I was against Valescure—the Grand Hotel—with people all day, Maruca, Delia, Maruca's mother. Hotel dinners—Father formal —all so sunny and empty when it isn't alone with him. I remember tonight scenes which torture me, expressions on his face. How hurt he will be. I know how he imagines—as I do—how he expects, how he pre-enacts in his mind all the future scenes. How much is destroyed when people like us fail to materialize their plans! For we have lived in them like solid constructions. We are bound to them.

I make notes as I copy the journal, but it is like running after one's tail because I write new pages almost as fast as I can copy the old ones. I will never catch up!

While I copy volume thirty-three, I imagine what a beautiful piece of cruelty it would be to give Henry the four or five volumes which concern him and our love just before parting from him for good (say, on the eve of my leaving for India) to read that night, alone, with the knowledge that I have vanished.

When I leave Louveciennes I tack another beautiful note onto the bed for Hugh. He returned home at midnight and the note put him to sleep peacefully. I arrived the next morning for breakfast. And my manner effaces all the hurt my demand for liberty could cause him. I say gaily, "You see how good it is to let the cat out . . ."

After this night out I am contented.

Yet I have been ill—ill with morbidities, obsessions, susceptibilities. I am perpetually hurt by something or other—trifles—I cannot free myself. I feel that people mock me, overlook me, misunderstand me. I add up small grievances and forget all the admirations, compliments, triumphs. Anger at a small offense blots out all the day. If André [de Vilmorin] is ironic, I fear it is at my expense. I feel I don't talk well, that my irony only appears in my writing. If Louise forgets to offer me a cigarette, I am hurt. Lillian's hostility distresses me. I am jealous of Henry's writing so much about Lowenfels when I can predict that someday Lowenfels will crumble. I understand how the minor characters are those we write up best (I wrote of June and Louise better than Henry). I suffer from Henry's work, which is a continuous recollection of scenes with seventy-five women (and he writes, "I am omitting the women I have merely slept with"!).

All battered by small things, I come home to Hugh and I'm discouraged with myself, with my hypersensitivity. I go to work. I swear

I will never leave Louveciennes again, that I will withdraw from the world, live alone, because life is too difficult, too painful.

André de Vilmorin monologues to me on duality—on his own duality. Makes a neat exposé. "Conflict only when one half takes it upon itself to judge the actions of the other half. Solution is not to proceed from any principle of morality, but from sincerity. Sincerity to oneself . . ."

I discovered this years ago, but I have only lived it out a few months. A certain critical estimate I once made continuously—a moral estimate, or more exactly, an estimate made to satisfy my self-esteem —has died. I never pass judgment now.

SEPTEMBER 30, 1933

I HAVE LEARNED TO DEFEAT MY MOODS. I RUN AWAY from them. *Change d'air.* I felt my tragic mood stifling me when I awoke this morning. I copied fifteen pages and then telephoned Henry. I seek his laughter, his white house painter's suit, his mood. He has been writing up the Lowenfels evening in a highly nonsensical vein; the humor of esoteric words and extravagance.

To me, who saw the evening coolly because of my jealousy (My jealousy is very definite, and very definable: That Lowenfels should be the Poet in Henry's work, when I am the truer poet, still hurts. I cannot yet resign myself to the unworthiness of Lowenfels), it is miraculous and beautiful to see what Henry has made of it. I sit in the Café du Rond Point, trying to understand that Lowenfels is a puppet and Henry needs something to write around. His starting point does not matter.

A green demon in me impelled me to work on copying right under Hugh's eyes—taking risks with a beating heart, terrorized when I had to go downstairs and leave my work, yet incapable of acting otherwise.

I felt a demoniac elation: If he reads it, then let things happen. I await the catastrophe. I *desire* the catastrophe, and I dread it. I want to see things burn and crumble around me. Each time I left the room I looked at Hugh. He was sitting with all his astrological books around him. He will not move, I thought; he is too absorbed. And I went downstairs, with a voluptuous anxiety. I rushed quickly back. Hugh was still reading quietly.

The day passed. We went horseback riding in a warm, brilliant forest. We laughed. We returned hot and thirsty.

The new maid arrived. In the middle of my typewriting, she came to get me to help her. While I was in the kitchen, Hugh came downstairs: "Come upstairs. Tell the maid to delay the dinner." He was white and shaking. I followed him all the way upstairs to the studio with an unaccountable joy. He has read. What has he read? What will happen now? I want him to chase me away.

Hugh stood in the middle of the room: "I know everything. I've read that." He pointed to the open journal, where I describe meeting Henry in a hotel room for an hour. "I'll forgive you. Don't lie to me anymore." He sat down, tormented, crushed.

And when I saw his face I began to lie, to lie eloquently. "You only read the invented journal. It is all invention, to compensate for all I don't do—believe me, I'm a monster, but only imaginatively. You can read the *real* journal anytime. Ask Allendy. He knows about the invented journal. He called me '*la petite fille littéraire.*' I need to write these things. I have too much erotic imagination—and that way it spends itself. I will show you the difference between the truth and the literature. Why, don't you see, if it were *true* I couldn't talk to you so quietly, I would be desperate. But look at me; I feel innocent. I couldn't write next to you, either, if I didn't feel innocent . . ."

"Let me see the real journal."

"I will. Why, there is such foolishness in the other—such crazy things." I tell him about those pages of the sadistic journal I really invented. Ridicule them.

"Bradley—that was his criticism—that what I wrote about June sounded true—what I wrote about Henry literary. Precisely—you see—I really lived the June episode—I didn't live the Henry one."

I talk, I talk, earnestly, fantastically. I delay showing the "real" journal. My face is quiet and sad. I see Hugh's confidence returning. I ridicule the need I have of imaginary living. "Oh, for that, yes, I'm willing to confess. I need to imagine a lot of events, so much ebullience, so much activity. I've got to transmute it into writing. And then I'm satisfied. You know how some of the most erotic tales come from chaste men. Well, I live this life with you and I have *débauches* in writing. You never have time to keep up with what I do; otherwise I would have shown you all this. You remember, several times I began to explain to you . . ." I talk fervently. I want him to get his faith back. My desire for destruction is burned out—although deep down it gnaws me. Destroy this life to live another.

I wanted Hugh angry, but he had said, "I will forgive you." So even if he knew the truth he would forgive me, and I would remain here—here. Protected, loved, forgiven. It was the word *forgive* which set me off lying, playacting. His attitude—broken—sad—not resentful, not egoistical. Suffering, that's all, like an animal. And, like an animal, believing in my voice, the touch of my hand, in the voice, not the words. He was quiet, reading astrology. The blow—it was like striking an animal—he was so dazed, so inhuman, baffled. "I believe you, little pussy. I believe you. But isn't all that bad for you?" (Never a thought for himself!)

The desire to see everything burn—and to bury myself in the flames. A feeling that life wounds me, wounds me bitterly, and that I want to destroy it, twist it, burn it with myself. That I want to strike back, to strike back so hard that I cut all the heads off, that I break and crush all the perfection, all the false serenity, all the mocking beauty, all the glazed surface of life, its constant mocking music, its colors, its fabrics—its settings, all the paraphernalia which deceives us, deludes us, promising voluptuousness, rest. I hate the war, the war that life is, and I want to have one last war of horror, of such horror as to be final. Ah, final, I seek the end, I'm all full of banderillas, I am snorting fire, I am in a fury after persecution and duels, after the scenes of ironic elegance—oh, the mockery of our scenes, our wars in lace and velvet, with night because of the darkness, with music because it exposes the naked soul, with beauty because it sets the nerves vibrating so that the shock of pain may penetrate more deeply. All life a slow war, and I want it all in an hour of horror, but an hour with an end;

I want an end even if it be the crumbling of stones, the calcination of flesh, the suffocation of cries—the end, the end, the end. I am calling death!

WHAT IRONY! THIS HYSTERIA CAME WITH THE PERI-od—a purely biological phenomenon. Today I laugh at it. At the same time, I am frightened at my own intensity and at my obsession with jealousy. After I wrote that last night, I read the last page to Hugh and I began to weep. He was very tender. He leaned over this journal to kiss me—where he could have read my lie!

Eduardo came. We spent our time working on astrology. He mentioned certain dates and I found them in my journals, dates of my obsessions, neuroses, hysteria. Coinciding perfectly. On certain malefic days I escape the bad influences by hard work or sublimation. (I wrote "Tishnar" story one depressed day in Caux.)

Evening. I cover my typewriter with a sigh of satisfaction. Henry has telephoned me. I have written Father. I am out of the inferno. The sun again. I have worked like a demon. Thirty pages copied— more than the stenographer.

Hugh says, "Here is five hundred francs. It has to last you seven days." (And Henry needs three hundred francs of this!) Like the ostrich, I stick my head under my feathers. I've got to stick to my work. I've got to. I don't know how to earn money. I must try by natural means. I would like to become a *cocotte* grand style. No sacrifice idea. Just adventure. But Henry needs a winter suit, and Hugh a woolen kimono.

Allendy said I have been hating my Father because I blame him for my sense of guilt. I load others now with my guilt instead of

annihilating myself! I call that a lack of nobility. I don't punish myself.
I simply revolt against Father. But tonight my hatred has died. I was
looking at the photograph of him when he was thirty. I thought of
his stoicism—the will with which he dominated his moods, his chaos,
his melancholia. Father and I both give only the best to the world. I
was thinking of his whimsicality and gaiety when he is saddest. How
I have been breaking down this year, exteriorizing my moods, how I
do not want this plaster cast of stoicism over my body and face! I want
to cry and roll on the floor and get drunk. I want to get out of my
own shell. Out. Eduardo mentioned, while reading my horoscope, the
terrific timidity. I was thinking how at Lowenfels's, out of timidity, I
barely talked, and I envied him his drunkenness! I was thinking that
my horoscope says a touch of either genius or insanity! My insanity is
jealousy. I must beware. Live out, expand, love many, so as to evade
obsession. As soon as I get too close to Henry I become obsessed with
him and with jealousy. I must think of others, love others, spread.

I asked myself, How deeply jealous is he, Father? So enigmatic,
so secretive, but oh, deep down, what infernos inside of us. Is there as
much darkness in him as in me? How desperately he seeks out the
sun, beauty, harmony! Yes, to heal himself, to keep his balance! I run
away from my inferno. Yet see how it strangled me Sunday evening
after a gay day with Hugh, the astrology, the forest, the horseback
riding!

Now I enjoy Henry's legend of "Cronstadt"—Lowenfels. He has
been adding to it. I was wistful. I said, "Such things make me disgusted
with literature—they are so false." The personage of Cronstadt evolved
from Lowenfels is immense and striking. And every day I see the
disproportion. But Bradley thinks I have done the same with Henry!

I take refuge in intellectual amusements. This "real" journal that
I will write for Hugh—that amuses me as a tour de force. If I should
die and both should be read—*which one is me?* I am beginning tonight.

To Henry: My imagination is all aflame with that "real" journal
for Hugh. You don't know how I would love to write it all
at once. I began it tonight. Five pages. All craft. It may turn

out a marvelous piece of mystification, the two sides of an attitude, and it becomes so real to me while I write it (for example, the determination never to be possessed by you because men remember longest the women they have not had) that I believe if you read this journal I could almost persuade you that you never had me at all. To confront the two could easily drive a man insane. I would love to die and watch Hugh read them both.

OCTOBER 6, 1933

I'M HELLISHLY LONELY. WHAT I NEED IS SOMEONE who could give me what I give Henry: this constant attentiveness. I read every page he writes, I follow up his reading, I answer his letters, I listen to him, I remember all he says, I write about him, I make him gifts, I protect him, I am ready at any moment to give up anybody for him, I follow his thoughts, enter into his plans—passionate, maternal, intellectual watchfulness.

He. He cannot do this. Nobody can. Nobody knows *how*. It's an art, a gift. Hugh protects me, but he does not respond. Henry responds, but he does not find the time to read what I write. He doesn't catch all my moods, nor write about me. Father cannot enter into my work. He can only give me thoughtfulness—like a woman. I get it all in shreds, incomplete, insufficient, tantalizing. And I get lonely, and I have to turn to my journal to give myself the kind of response I need. I have to nourish myself. I get love, but love is not enough. People don't know *how* to love.

I will throw away my mood! I rush into my new-old green coat, old coat dyed new, into the autumn bitterness. I trip through cool streets, shopping for the best feather pillow for Henry! I arrive at Clichy and find what I expect—a sleep-touseled Henry. "What do you want for breakfast? Bacon and eggs. I'll go out and get you bacon and eggs." And I run out and I run back, and I make coffee. And Henry says, "That is what I need—a woman in the house. Just before you came, I was awake. I wanted to go to sleep again, but I was awake thinking. It's hellish to wake up alone. And you came!"

With breakfast we ingest his last pages on the Lowenfels–Cronstadt legend. We laugh. I ask to see *Black Spring* and I catch, impressionistically, the order of it—and find where it should begin, knowing that Henry's voice only gets firm and sure after a few pages and that his first notes are always a little shaky. I sew a pillow cover while he plays me the new records. He shows me on a map of Brooklyn the streets where he played.

He was tired from a late night. We lay in bed, softly kissing. He went to sleep. I lulled him to sleep—but when he was asleep I felt a dark, dark loneliness. I prepared to leave him. He had asked me to set the clock for dinnertime. As I powdered my face I thought I would die, I would die before I would go to sleep while Henry was there. I couldn't go to sleep.

The noise of the door, as I went away, awakened him. "Are you all right, Anaïs?"

I wanted to weep. I went toward his bed. I knelt to kiss him. Then my despair stifled me and I bowed my head: "I'm lonely, Henry."

Lonely. I'm lonely, I'm hungry—I'm so lonely nobody can ever heal me! But Henry thought I was lonely for a few moments only, because he had gone to sleep.

In the street I wept. I weep now while I write.

Henry writes me: You don't know what your words did to me, "I feel lonely!" I don't ever want to hear you say them again. Rather than you should say this we ought brave everything. I want you, and I think it's a crime that we must keep putting things off indefinitely . . . It's a crime to live apart. I don't know what to do about it. I don't want you to come to grief. I'm helpless. But if you see a way, and whenever and however you want to arrange it, just do. I love you and I want you to be happy. . . .

To Henry: Your letter was a beautiful gift to me. I was hoping you had not realized that when I said I was lonely it was not because you had gone to sleep—it was an immense loneliness which I felt at that moment unbearably. I wrote you when I came home that I was sad about writing, and that was not it. I didn't want to reveal the other. But you divined it. No, Henry, there is no way out, and what is the use of my coming to you with my lapses of courage? . . . Don't feel any anguish. I get joyous again as soon as I am with you, and it lasts me for days.

I'm coming Tuesday for breakfast and the night—to work with you—to be with you. Coming only as the south wind.

I was laughing and talking with Henry. Then there was a silence. During that silence I thought: What I am, what I say, you are not aware of now, at this moment. Your mind is on the past. But all I am, all I say, you watch blindly—and I will be, and say, for later. I will live now for that memory you will have of me. Later, when there will be distance between us, you will remember so vividly. It will hurt you then, as it hurts me, to be so aware of today, so aware of this moment, the supreme anguish of knowing and recognizing the face of every moment without the attenuating softness of distance. I understand and see too quickly. When you take me through the old streets, I am living not only in the joy but ahead, so far ahead into the future absence of it.

"You say nothing. What are you thinking?"

And why do I compose an answer, a banal answer, to protect my thought, the starkness and the bleakness of it?

Two absolutely contrary feelings: One of callousness. Shutting my ears to the economic troubles. The desire to write, to let all else go to hell. Let Hugh care for us. Determined to write the book on June. A feeling that it is crystallized in my head. Furious to read in Father's letter that he has been sacrificing his time to Maruca's mother—automobile drives and movies. Bourgeois life. Bourgeois ideals. Henry the only true egoistical artist. Amoral.

At the same time I ask Henry, "Would you like me not to write?" And I write him a letter saying I want to give up my writing for his. The other day, when I arrived, he was concerned over his economic helplessness. I consoled him, "Stick to your own karma. What you do best is writing. My own writing can wait. I'm younger, and besides, yours is more important. I will work for both of us."

I did not intend to do this. I don't know why I said it. I have no more scruples. I give Henry Hugh's money. I feel the seeds of my book sprouting. I feel I am tired of sacrifices, that I am an artist. Today I worked ten hours, stopping only for lunch. Doggedly. I will finish this book quickly. I am hurt by Bradley, by Henry, by everybody, and that makes me angry and strong. I stand alone. Not Father, not Henry, nobody can really follow me all the way, understand me completely, accompany me. My journal and I. I have been again too feminine. Today I feel hard and strong and alone. So alone it frightens me. I am in every way such a fool. A lonely fool.

Henry writes: I have finished reading the pages for Bradley in the black folder. I can understand a little better now Bradley's irritation, his faultfinding, his exasperation. He forgot that it was a journal and that it had been excised. The story interested him, as it will interest everybody in the world, from China to Mexico. A marvelous story. *But a bad diary*. That is, if you judged from these pages alone. And the diary writing mars the story, strangles it . . .

To Henry: Do you know what I think about your criticism? That it is good for a Bradley, for an outsider, for the world. That coming from you it is wrong . . . You may think I have not been treated roughly enough—that I need toughening, as you say . . . You may think we have pampered each other, but then you forget that we agreed that the world would give us plenty of beatings and that what we needed was the *support* of each other. That, you have failed to give me . . . A cold letter. Thanks. And a cold response from me. That's good.

That leaves me alone again, and as you read in the journal, I am strong when I am alone.*

OCTOBER 13, 1933

I GAVE HENRY MY LETTER TO READ. HE WAS SUR-
prised, and as usual he laughed at the end,
laughed half-sadly. He fought me. He stuck to his guns. He added
worse things: that I had marred the story with my defects, botched it!
I talked with tears in my eyes, but quietly. Then he understood the
personal emotional tempest I was going through. He understood I
thought he had lost faith in me. When I thought he had faith in me
I took very well his criticisms of my John novel and "Alraune." Slowly
my intelligence won over my femininity. Henry was firm, but gentle,
too. He said, "A woman's loyalty is always different from a man's.
You are loyal to me; I am loyal to a truth. If I agree with Bradley I
say so. And as to my new enthusiasms—they're only on the surface.
I always come back to you, and you know it. You know I believe in
you."

My poor diary, I am so angry with you! I hate you! The pleasure
of confiding has made me artistically lazy. Such an easy joy, to write
here—so easy. And today I saw how the diary does choke up my
stories, how I tell you about things so nonchalantly, carelessly, and
inartistically. Everybody has hated you. You have hampered me as an
artist, but at the same time you kept me alive as a human being. I
created you because I needed a friend. And talking to this friend, I
have wasted my life.

And yet, my poor journal, if I had not considered you as the only
one always interested in what happened to me, I would never have
written at all, because facing the world, the world who seemed to give

---

* See *A Literate Passion*, pp. 215–226, for the complete text of this lengthy exchange.

me nothing but sorrows—I could not have done it. Writing for a hostile world meant nothing to me. Writing for you gave me the warm ambience I need to flower in! So I can't hate you, but now that I have made my peace with the world, and now that I can address it as an artist, I must divorce you from my work. Not abandon you. No—I need your companionship. Even after I have worked, humanly I look around me, and who can my soul-mind talk to without fear of incomprehension? Where do I find serenity and painlessness? All else is war, and all else takes so much courage!

Yesterday I wrote the first twenty pages of the June story objectified, artistic. For the first time I have become objective.

O C T O B E R   1 6 ,   1 9 3 3

EDUARDO MUST BE ADDED TO MY COLLECTION OF strange personages, my morbid "Alraune," the universe of insanity. He buys books he never reads; he begins horoscopes he never finishes; he buys paints he never paints with; he buys workmen's suits he never wears, a Spanish cape he never wears; he makes notes for a book he never writes; he is jealous of the woman he does not want; he wants women, only to leave them, unread.

Neptune, weird Neptune, ruling June, Louise, Artaud, Eduardo, and me.

I write my Neptunian book at the same time as the human "story," and I also add fuel to the journal.

To Eduardo: I want to crown you with something today. You have become a character in my eyes. You want a definite role in life. Are you not content to *be?* Leave the becoming alone. You inspired me last night. The other day, at the café, I told you I intended to begin enjoying you. That means I have

a new kind of love of you. Nonhuman. I am preparing my
colors to make you alive as a personage, as a legend.

O CTOBER 19, 1933

*I*LEFT LOUVECIENNES AT FOUR O'CLOCK WITH A
little valise. A note for Hugh pinned on the
bed, the note he expects to find at night before falling asleep without
me. And it was like leaving for a journey, and another life, to become
Henry's wife. He begins by taking me luxuriously. He is in a clinging
mood because he has a cold. We have dinner together. He takes me.
He reads my new pages—and is satisfied with the technique. Proud
of my courage. Through dismal streets. We sleep like a pair of snakes.
Breakfast. Talk. I say I must go, but we go on talking. Henry says,
"Now you must stay for lunch." After lunch he gets in a dreamy,
fantastic mood. And together we begin to invent our astrological fairy
tale. I give him ideas. Then to bed again because it is cold. I only get
back to Hugh, Mother, Joaquin at five—dazed, joyous, full of ideas.

The next day, to work again. But what haunts me is the moment
I stood in Henry's room, thinking: I should stay here. With Henry I
could easily forget the other life. It is hard for me to remember it now.
This is real. And the other is unreal. I am at home here.

In the evening, drunk with fantasy, I begin the fairy tale.

Today, work.

I am making notes, and fully aware of it. This is my notebook. I
sweat over my story, and when I come to you I am tired out. When
I am Henry's wife, I entirely forget Hugh and my Father. When I

am with my Father, I forget Hugh and Henry. When I am with Hugh, I think of my Father and Henry.

Dissonances with Father. I write him two letters with certain news of Thorvald and of my talk with Joaquin. The interest of the news is marred for Father because our letters crossed. That was the essential point: that I, having written him without waiting for an answer, caused a disorder, which is painful to him.

This month of October proved to me definitely that I cannot live *with Henry alone*. It is too precarious a companionship. It leaves me as lonely as Hugh's incapacity to respond. I tried to make him replace my Father, my friends. It can't be done. I am glad it is over. My own spreading is beginning again: Father, Nestor, friends right and left, companionship. I have had a great yearning for absolution. It is nonsense.

O CTOBER 2 7, 1 9 3 3

*A*LL GOES WELL WHEN I AM SHARING MY LOVES AS before—all in splits and fragments. Whole love is too dangerous, too feminine. Henry is an artist, not a man. I must not expect everything from him.

Day and whole night with Henry. All doubts and fears calmed by his passion, by his tenderness. I am all impregnated with him, married to him. I want to live with him. He is lonely. He wants me. We must live together. It is becoming a torment. I am sad tonight; empty, lonely. When I am with him I have no fears. He makes me gay and mellow and courageous. All this three days before my Father returns! I am wishing they would all die, Hugh and Father, and that I might live with Henry. It is Henry I love in this criminal way—madly. For him I would commit crimes. Insanity again. This morning, lying awake at his side, watching him sleep. So contented to be there, so happy that I was able to lie there awake for three hours without getting restless! Henry is there. That is all I want.

In the movies we hold hands. All this is *out* of the book,[*] the work of art, but all the more reason for preserving it here. In the book, restraint, indirectness, trickeries! But I need a place where I can shout and weep. I have to be a Spanish savage at some time of the day. I record here the hysteria life causes in me. The overflow of an undisciplined extravagance. To hell with taste and art, with all contractions and polishings. Here I shout, I dance, I weep, I gnash my teeth, I go mad—all by myself, in bad English, in chaos. It will keep me sane for the world and for art.

Henry is amused by the things I make him say in the book. "Don't sentimentalize me."

"I won't. You'll see. If only I could get cool enough to use my irony, too. I have a fund of irony which I can't exploit because of my overseriousness." (The Spanish sense of tragedy again!)

When he heard my Father was returning, he was not happy. He was upset when I told him Father's plan to send a piano to Louveciennes and come and work here on weekends.

OCTOBER 28, 1933

So NOW I SEE THE HUMOR IN THESE CLINGING moods. Henry gets them, I get them, and not always at the same moment; but they are undeniably the same moods!

He envied the Lowenfelses' contentment. They don't need to go out, because they have each other.

———

* The "book" about H. M. and June eventually became the novella "Djuna" in the first edition of *The Winter of Artifice* (Paris, 1939), eliminated from later versions of the same title.

Hugh read a list of neurotic symptoms and found that I have them all. Began worrying. Read to me the list of causes. Which one? I deftly pointed to the one: conflict between wishes of the ideal self and the instinctive self. I wish for a bohemian life, but I do not wish to hurt him. Hugh understood that these wishes, these unfulfilled wishes, make me restless and neurotic. That the compromise (an evening out a week) only brought into relief the clash between them. The quick transitions upset my equilibrium and my nerves. He had, I said, given me a great deal already, but my own feelings, my own conscience, bother me. He offered to give me more time to myself. He was generous and clairvoyant.

"It is all self-interest. I don't want you to hate me or to wish for my death." (He does not know I have wished it!) I was amused by his chess-playing mind and his cleverness. He has foresight! He read and talked with a Buddhist wisdom. "I want you to be contented and satisfied so that when you return to me, you return wholly. Otherwise your attention is straining away upon the other desires. Your imagination is occupied with your conflict, not with me."

I have made Hugh believe my bohemian life is not sexual. He said wisely, "I can see you have sublimated your sexual attraction for Henry. When you say your writing is the wife of his work, it is very revelatory. *Everything is sex.*"

And suddenly it appeared ridiculous to me that Hugh would suffer on account of a merely physical gesture but accept the wanderings of my imagination and my fancy.

OCTOBER 30, 1933

*D*REAM: I AM GIVING A BIG FÊTE. BIG DISHES ARE served, as in the movie about Henry VIII. We are in the courtyard, miscellaneous people and I, looking up at a house with balconies. It is in the evening. I see a shutter opening and a room full of people preparing for a party. I call the attention of the people to the fact that they are awaiting someone. Right in front of the window is grouped a trio about to play. The leader is standing up, nearest the window. She is a small, old, thin woman. As she gives the signal to play, a woman comes out on the balcony and begins walking across the house from balcony to balcony, toward another window. The balconies are all connected. Another shutter opens, and there appears the man for whom the party is being given. He is old, he looks like Paderewski, and he is dressed like Christ. He walks forward somnambulistically, with his arms outstretched like a blind man, following the woman. When he comes to the window where the music is going on he passes it and walks on toward another window, where he sees something that frightens him. Suddenly there is no balcony, and he falls several stories to the courtyard. I experience no emotion. I have an idea that what frightened him is a woman with a sword. The fête in my sumptuous house continues. I am in a room with several women. One of them has been dancing, and she is flushed and perspiring. I offer to dry her body because I wish to enjoy her nakedness, but she refuses. No anxiety in the dream. Mood of bountifulness.

Associations: Jeanne, the woman Father came nearest to loving, is an orchestra leader. But she is tall. I compared the orchestra leader in the dream to Jeanne and Maruca. I thought of my Father's asceticism last night, reading [Wilhelm] Stekel—excessive hygiene and food diets are a form of asceticism. He must be the Christlike musician of the dream. I am probably jealous of the two women and wish him dead rather than at their party. My dreams are always very *stagy* in contrast to Henry's, which are more often realistic and natural. Colors and details of costume, background, etc., are outstanding. *Always unreal.* Does this reveal my sense of unreality?

Today I received a plaintive letter from Father: He dreads the return to his home, his pupils, responsibilities. He dreads facing problems—problems of money, of house organization. He dreads the invasion of people, noises, pain.

He fears life.

He regrets his solitude, the sea, the trees. He clings to them as I cling to Louveciennes . . .

This letter touched me, like the revelation of his delicate feet.

Henry telephones.

I would like to give Henry a room here, and security for life. Father, a room and piano here, and an escape from his bourgeois life. When it is for others I'm full of courage. For Henry I would kill a dragon a day.

But I would come to Hugh with my scratches. I might even ask Hugh to help me.

Comedy. We are all afraid and in great need of two-ness to face life. Love is a recognition of the Thou. A need of the Thou. Somehow or other, I always lose my guide halfway up the mountain. I don't think I am looking for a man but for a god. I am beginning to feel a void which must be the absence of God. I have deified man. One after another, I have called for a guide, a father, a leader, a sustainer. I have a husband, a protector, lovers, a father, comrades, but I still miss something. It must be God. But I hate God the abstraction. I want God in the flesh, the incarnate God with strength and two arms and a sex. And no imperfections.

Which proves I have got my human and my divine loves mixed, and that they won't mix, and that the quicker I separate God from man, the better for the men I love. I have loved genius, which comes closest to divinity.

Henry I was able to love without obstacles because he is the god of the human—he is divinely imperfect.

But my Father is nonhuman and should have been God. He is the one who has imposed perfection, who has initiated the gods, who has no love of human naturalness. But in the end he is like me, a hypocrite. The ideal self exalted. A strong instinctive self concealed.

I love Henry for his honesty. Henry says, "I am a thief. I am a liar. I am a brute. I am a sadist. I am a coward."

Father and I say, "No matter what I am, look, this is what I would like to be. Love my intention."

Our intention is perfection.

Poor divine hypocrites.

We are pretenders.

Not *we*. Every day I become more honest. I refuse to pretend. I know, for example, that I am lying to Hugh about the causes of my neurosis, lying ignominiously. But it doesn't matter. I tell him my life with him is real and all the rest a game. I know that I stay with him because I am a coward—I don't dare reveal myself to him. I should leave him and earn my living and live with whomever I please. I should tell my Father that I do not love him, that the love I give him is narcissistic, as is the one he gives me. Love of the one who *can understand*, answer you, diminish the solitude. Whatever is truly *his* and not mine (his science, his order, his reason, his logic), I don't love. Not as I love in Henry all kinds of motley traits which belong to him and with which I have no relation.

I will yield to my Father when he comes, out of loneliness, with a love of coming close to his own loneliness, a love of these secret qualities in him which I love because they are like my secret qualities. I love him with the thousand divinatory eyes I want to be loved with. It is the *disease* of love, not the fruit. It is when one's self has become so masked to the world, one's language so unintelligible, one's loneliness so consuming, that only one's Double can penetrate one.

When I think of this letter of Father's with its fragile wistfulness, I know I will not tell him about Henry. I know I will lie to him and that I will be sick with my lies.

Henry is the most courageous one—and yet he lived in terror of June; he is always expecting me to punish him; he is timorous in the streets; and his greatest obsessive fear is fear of *poverty*. I have no fear of poverty, only of being deprived of love. And a fear of sickness.

As Father comes nearer (he leaves Valescure tomorrow) I begin to attune myself to him. I listen to a piano playing on the radio, and I begin to imagine his sunburned Grecian body, the cold brilliance of him, the impossible masklike face mobile only in passion. What an effort to appear strong willed!

My feminine Father.

And my feminine body, inhabited by a male spirit, is tormented by a conflict again.

But through the torment I am beginning to laugh at myself. The little tyrannical monster carefully hidden in its niche of suave seductions and smiles. After all, all I ask of my dragon killers is love, and in that they are overgifted!

I must someday investigate the Miralles story. How my imagination was so ensorcelled by Miralles's career as a dancer—stories of dancers, trips to Russia, ballets at the big operas, music halls all over the world, the pungent atmosphere of the dressing rooms, the odor of the dancers, the new experience for me of sitting at cafés, Miralles's shabby hotel, his gaudy costumes—that I let him kiss me and contemplated one day going to his room. I could see myself dancing with poor Miralles here and there, sharing his vagrant life, living in his shabby rooms with Spanish costumes and postcard photographs of Lola, Alma Viva, l'Argentinita. In bedroom slippers and flowered kimonos, opening the door to . . .

To what? To a Hugh who had found me. And I like an amnesia patient who had forgotten my name and home and husband.

Poor old Miralles, who could charm my dull life with his gaudy adventures. Taking the bus to the rue de Clichy gave me a tremor.

My Father would be pained: "*Who* are you? Do you forget your class, your race, your name?"

Hugh: "You forget your nonhuman, your mystical origin."

Henry would have said, "And your mind—how can that life mean anything to you?"

Illusion. Miralles had asthma. He saved his money to retire in Valencia. He was good, homely. He used to say to me, "You know, I have no vices like the others have. I would be good to you." While I listened to his stories he glowed. He went at his dancing with renewed vigor. He rejuvenated. He bought himself a new suit. He adored me.

When I awoke from my amnesia, he was snuffed out. He had turned gray and ashen.

He died last year of asthma, in his hotel room.

OCTOBER 31, 1933

*P*LAY WITH THIS IDEA OF AMNESIA, WHICH IS ONLY the atrophy of the "ideal" self, the critical self—the assassination of it in order to live liberated from scruples. I know when I let myself be hypnotized (with Allendy, Artaud). When I awake to my life with Hugh or to my relation to Henry, I awake as from a dream. I do not blame myself. I refuse to take any responsibility (and therefore guilt). It is only a little comedy I play with my conscience. And I find that I ask fewer and fewer questions, that the ideal self is slowly becoming a ridiculous figure. I laugh at it. I live on, with qualms attacking me only when I face a human pain (Hugh's sorrow, Henry's pain the day he thought he had divined I had been Allendy's mistress). Then I do awake to acute, unbearable regrets. But most of the time I feel that I have forgotten Artaud and Allendy, as Henry forgets his whores. I have the power to forget. Stekel would say, to repress?

NOVEMBER 1, 1933

*C*ARICATURE OF HUGH: HE STICKS HIS FINGERS IN his nose. He loses the pen he has been using. He loses the book he has been reading. He forgets, at the bank, a letter he wants to show me. He forgets, at home, the key of his desk. He loses his *briquet* and cigarette holder. When we go out with friends he forgets cigarettes. When he buys something he forgets it in the car. He is always late. When he eats his breakfast it is already cold. When he shaves, the water is already cold. Disorder. In his papers, effects, accounts. He does not observe, retain what he hears. He is finicky and whimsical about his food. He has no buoyancy.

All this is nothing. Henry has a thousand more faults. But when there is no longer love or enthusiasm . . .

I want to get my book published and be free. Cowardice keeps me here. When I look at Hugh I think I could never tell him. And his protectiveness touches me. Cowardice. Cowardice.

Decision: As soon as Henry's first book is published, and my first book, I go to live with Henry. With our two books out we should not be left to starve, and I can always find work.

I will make Father give Joaquinito pupils so that he can support Mother.

I will try to find Hugh a woman who can make him happy.

I will break with all social ties, with all my aristocratic friends.

NOVEMBER 3, 1933

FATHER IS SO TIMID WHEN HE ARRIVES THAT HE walks from the gate to the door reading, and then launches into discourses like June's—covering, covering his timidities, his uneasiness.

A torrent of words.

Slowly and gradually I make him feel at ease by my calm. He becomes natural. And gently he begins to make love to me.

I feel mildly amorous. I yield only for his pleasure. Gaily. Indifferently. He is a very expert and delightful lover. It is all very light and swift.

I am far more interested in his mood—trying to define it, to flare it out, to attune myself to it. I recognize that today he had no sense of reality, that he was dazed by his return, the shock of realities, uneasy and alarmed.

I urged him not to treat me as an ordinary woman, to continue his life as before, to enjoy other women, that love must be big and enlarge his life rather than narrow it. He answered, "No—I could never do all that again. I want this love to be the apotheosis of my life. It is too great a thing to spoil with other affairs. It must remain clean, single."

And when he questioned me, I had to answer in the same idealistic way.

Since I can only judge my Double from myself, I believe he wants to make our love the ideal finish to his Don Juan career; but I don't believe he can do so. He will get involved, as I get involved. He will lie to me, for the same reasons I lie to him. I only ask myself: Does Father's age make a difference in our case? Is he tired of his loneliness and his loveless affairs? Does he want understanding in place of sexual diversions? Therefore, can there be some truth in his statement? And if so, how can I be the first to destroy his ideal?

Another difference. Father's narcissism is far more ingrained than mine—therefore his self-love, which he can express with me, is stronger than mine—because I love the *Thou*, Henry, more than myself.

I also love myself in Father. His moods of distance, which I understand so well, his difficulty in entering life, reality completely, his nervousness and timidities. It arouses my compassion deeply.

When we were standing in the hallway, while Hugh took the car out, I made the little cry I often uttered when he was caressing me too effectively: *"Ay, Ay, Ay!"*

He laughed frankly, delightedly. *"Comme tu es naturelle, comme tu es véridique!"* (Admiring because it is so difficult for him to be real!) And he took me up at the game: *"Pénétrable, enveloppante, caressable —surréaliste!"*

In the car I take his arm. And he is delighted, but floating in his mist of moods. Life reaching him from afar, his eyes so blank. He looks like a very appealing child. He talks so much to fill the spaces of his discoordination.

I observe him wonderingly, as one looks at one's image in a mirror. As he leaves us, I think: When he gets home he will regret not having done this or that. He will think he has not pleased me; he will blush to think of the books which fell on us when we lay together (the horror of something gone wrong, the discomfort)! He will wish he had said this or that. He will forget that he did please me by observing I looked beautiful after our lovemaking (Why? But I did look transfigured, although I had felt nothing). He may regret that I offered him the opportunity to be honest and that he chose to lie. I know all this trend of thought. And I feel such compassion!

I arrived too early at Henry's, and he was out. I sat on his bed and finished the book I was reading, Maryse Choisy on [Joseph] Delteil. Then I got restless and looked over the manuscript of my "Alraune" lying on Henry's desk. And I found he had made this note: "All pictorial passages wonderful. Would make a *cinéma*. Begin with scene of gigantic fish bowl."

When he came we launched into a vigorous talk.

When I overflow in excessive emotion, my style suffers. It's got wobbly legs, that's all. It will have to learn to support the weight of my vitality. All force is window breaking. Window breaking produces oxygen, not art. I'm full of oxygen just now. Art suffers. I guess I'm still a little young.

I caricature Hugh when I should caricature my weakness. He is behaving more nobly than ever—that is what angers me. Trying not to give me a sense of guilt—receiving me with a smile when I arrived this morning for breakfast. But my will is set on my decision, and I am working for that end. I must stop being sentimental. I am disgustingly sentimental. Easily softened. When I come home Hugh has a cold. But so has Henry.

I want to become less sentimental and more humorous. I want to master my tragic sense of life, which is too prominent.

Dream at Clichy: After I have been living with Hugh many years we decide to have a church wedding. I get dressed in white, with a veil. But I observe my dress is poor. When I get to the church there is no fête. We scurry along and I discover I have not been given the usual bouquet of flowers. I am not sad, just a bit ironic. In the taxi, with the whole family, I say laughingly, "It's like a workman's wedding." Before the wedding I tried to get Henry on the telephone so that he would see me in my wedding dress.

In another dream I had to go to live in Clichy, and I was very happy.

Dream after Father's visit: Father and I are sitting on my big bed. We hear a deafening noise—so loud it is torturing. I look out of the window. I see a man about to enter the house with a heavy grass roller, with which he is going to crush me. I want to close the door of the bedroom against him, and I cannot because I am trying at the same time to close the window. Anxiety.

Distinct feeling of certain events being closer to me—real to me, really experienced—while others have a dim quality. Would distinguish between dream-quality and reality-quality. With Henry everything becomes warm and real. With Hugh things are dim and mental. With Father they are also dim, and strange besides, like something happening in water or skies. Henry I feel with my whole body— keenly, wholly, always: sex, compassion; mental, psychic. Father, Hugh, Eduardo, and Allendy are phantasmal.

Henry's new workingman's shoes. Henry's odor. It is all miraculously real. His defects, his naturalness, his hunger, his sleepiness, his pains. In two or three dreams I live with him in complete contentment. I like his woolen bedroom slippers and his thick woolen tie.

Henry is the only one who has given me human life.

NOVEMBER 7, 1933

I GOT UP YESTERDAY IN A COURAGEOUS MOOD. I HAD on my list three ordeals to face: visit to Otto Rank, reconciliation with Bernard Steele, visit to Edward Titus to ask for money. I fought with the three, wondering which one I would tackle. Decided first to bring Steele out of his jealous sulking, out of his self-interest. He was out.

Titus was in the South.

I don't remember how I found out that Dr. Otto Rank was living in Paris, on the boulevard Suchet. First of all, I had sent Henry to him, and they had a vast talk about history, literature, anthropology, Rank's *Art and Artist*—but not the analysis I felt Henry needed.

Now I impulsively decided to ring Rank's doorbell. I expected to have a difficult time explaining to the maid to let me see him. I had heard he was very busy, took very few patients, and was very expensive. My heart was pounding; my hands were cold.

By sheer accident, it was he who opened the door. "Yes?" he said in his harsh Viennese accent, wrapping the incisive, clean French word in a German crunch, as if the words had been chewed like the end of a cigar instead of liberated out of the mouth as the French do. French words are sent out to fly in the air like messenger doves, but Rank's Viennese French, or English, was always chewed, spewed.

He was small, dark skinned, round faced; but actually one saw nothing but the eyes, which were beautiful. Large, dark, fiery. With my obsession for choosing the traits which are beautiful or lovable, and wearing blinkers to cover what I do not admire or love, I singled out Rank's eyes to eclipse his homely teeth, his short body.

"Come in," he said, leading the way to his office. It was a spacious corner room, overlooking the Bois. Walls covered with books. Deep, lulling armchairs, a couch. He seemed very affable and accessible.

I see him today at three.

I also make a gesture to reconcile myself with Bradley. Several reasons: first, to discipline my exaggerated pride; second, because I want to succeed, to be published, to become independent; third, because I hate breaks and discords unless there is a big, big reason for them. Today I am still in a determined, courageous mood. I make use of it! Write a letter to Titus.

Talk with Rank. He asked me for a clear, full outline of my life and work. I told him I knew the artist could make good use of his conflicts but that I felt at the present I was expending too much energy trying to master a confusion of desires which I could not solve. That I needed his help.

Immediately I knew that we talk the same language. He goes beyond the psychoanalytical. He said, "Psychoanalysis emphasizes the resemblances, I emphasize the differences between people. They try to bring everybody back to a certain normal level. I try to adapt each person to his own kind of universe. The creative instinct is apart."

He understood the *more:* There is *more* in my relation to my Father than the desire of victory over my Mother. There is *more* in my relation to Henry than masochistic sacrifices or a need of victory over the other woman. There is—beyond sexuality, beyond lesbianism, beyond narcissism—creation, *creation.* Rank said, "What did you *produce* during the period of extreme neurosis following your affair with John? That will be interesting to me." Immediately he grasped the *core* of me; he said the stories I wrote as a child about being an orphan were not to be explained merely as criminal desire to do away with Mother out of jealousy, and Father out of an inordinate love. I wanted to create myself. I did not want to be born from human parents.

When I mentioned the psychoanalytical formulas he smiled a bit ironically, as if they were insufficient. I felt the expanse of his thought, beyond medicine into metaphysical and philosophical universes.

We understood each other with half phrases.

I said, "I don't expect you to solve my life tangibly, to tell me whether I must live with my husband, or my lover, or my Father, but to help me get to be at peace with myself."

I felt I was speaking Rank's thoughts by the swift recognition of his nod.

Rank: "Your energies must be able to flow into your work."

A.: "What I doubt, you see, is my destructive instinct. To create my life with Henry, I destroy my Father, Hugh, my Mother, and Joaquin. That is the impulse I suspect a little, although everything carries me toward Henry."

He understood so well my being tired of all the lies and deformities I am obliged to live every day, feeling the need of absolution.

The curious thing was the mood which preceded my talk with Rank.

I made this note in the train: On my way to see Rank, *je mâchonne des fourberies.* I begin to invent what I will tell Rank instead of coordinating truths. I begin to rehearse speeches, attitudes, gestures, inflections, expressions. I see myself talking, and I am sitting within Rank, judging me. What should I say to create such and such an effect?

I meditate lies as others meditate confessions. Yet I am going to him to *confess,* to get help in the solution of my conflicts, which are too numerous and which I don't succeed in mastering by writing. I prepare myself for a false comedy, like the one I played for Allendy.

Preparing to deform—and all to interest Rank, and also to interest myself, for I am vastly interested in complexities. In fact, I am going to Rank for the sport of it, not to solve, but to aggrandize, dramatize my conflicts, to see all that they contain, to seize them in full. I realize that my experience with Allendy was a new conflict added to my life, and that the old was only solved by the appearance of the new. It was misplaced. I mean that I believe I did not cease to be a masochist in the June–Henry situation, but that I balanced the pain by my interest in Allendy and my conflict with him, which removed the absolute obsession with June and Henry and gave me the necessary energy and stimulation to be strong.

I want to go on juggling. I am again at an impasse. I want too strongly to live with Henry, and I cannot do so for three primal reasons. So I shift my ground. Conflict insoluble, so I will interest myself in my exchange with Rank.

Allendy is not interested in literature, art, or artists. That is his great limitation. *"Petite fille littéraire"* does not dispose of my vital preoccupation with directions and deviations of my creative instincts. But he was the saving diversion. I needed to be diverted.

Whether this attitude before seeing Rank denoted simply a desire to embark on this as on an intellectual adventure—with a certain nonchalance, circuiting tragedy—or whether it is a form of ironic resistance to what I have felt to be a vital influence—I don't know.

But when I sat before Rank, I was as truthful as before my journal: I was natural, not too tragic, not too mental, preoccupied chiefly with saving and developing the artist because I am aware that I let my love problems engross me beyond all reason.

Confusion creates art. Too much confusion creates unbalance.

Rank immediately gave me the feeling that he is curious, alive, fond of exploration, experiment, the open road, anarchism, that he swims freely in big free spaces.

On November 8, 1933, Rank asked me to give up my journal and I left it in his hands. He delivered me of my opium.

It was a bold stroke. It stunned me. It was a violation. A few moments ago, just before dark, in the park, I had sat writing in it, writing of the lies I would tell Rank to interest him. I feared he would not find me interesting enough, and I was going to dramatize my life. I had heard he only took cases which interested him. And I had confided to the diary the lies I intended to tell. And now he wanted to take possession of all my secrets.

I had carried the diary around for years when I visited René Allendy, and he never expressed any curiosity.

Dr. Rank saw how stunned I was and added: "If you carry it around and bring it here, it is because you want to give it, you want someone to read it. And it isn't only your wish to have it read. It is your last defense against analysis. It is like a traffic island you want to stand on. If I am going to help you, I do not want you to have a traffic island from which you will survey the analysis, keep control of it. I don't want you to analyze the analysis. Do you understand?"

Recovering from the shock, I began to feel elation, a feminine elation like that of a woman who is asked to give all by a possessive man: I want your body, your heart, your soul. Dr. Rank was demanding all in one blow. I felt an elation due to a recognition of power, of mastery. Was it not power and mastery I was looking for? Did I not come because I was lost, confused, disturbed? Dr. Rank was clever to realize that the diary was the key. Give me the keys to the city, now. I always kept an island, inviolate, to analyze the analyst. I had never submitted.

I deposited the diary on his table. He was not grave or solemn,

Dr. Rank. He was very agile, quick, bright, as if this were a game of wits. His eyes shone resplendently, as if the unconscious were a clever adversary and the act of detecting it a pleasure, a superior game of chess.

"Your game, your move, Anaïs Nin."

The diary was now on the table. He will know I had intended to lie, but he will also know I was utterly truthful from the moment he opened the door.

I don't feel defeated. I feel that I have chosen a wise, courageous guide.

But that is not all he asked, that first evening. As I unfolded the maze—Hugh, Henry, Eduardo, Allendy, Father—he said, "I can't help you unless you break away from all of them, isolate yourself, until you are calm and integrated again. There is too much pressure on you."

"How can I isolate myself? You mean not live at home?"

"For a few weeks, at least, I want you to see none of them, to live alone, yes."

This was even more stunning than taking possession of my diary. I could not imagine myself persuading Hugh to let me live alone, even for a week.

Dr. Rank's eyes were still shining; he sounded so certain, so confident. I said I would try.

Already I had begun to cheat in the game of analysis. I saw that this prescription might enable me to fulfill one of my deepest desires: to live continuously with Henry and work on our books together. It was not entirely a foolish act, because I was not in a state of conflict with Henry, and together we incited each other to write. I could not envision a hotel room and Dr. Rank only.

Hugh consented to the strange demand of Dr. Rank.

Henry, who was then staying in a pimp-and-whore hotel in Montmartre, agreed to move to whatever hotel I chose. And I chose what I believed to be a modern, attractive, but not deluxe hotel, and took two adjoining rooms [at 26, rue des Marronniers]. (As it turned out later, my choice was actually a hotel in Auteuil very well known for temporary alliances, well-kept mistresses, intended to give the illusion of home. My choice was right for the situation, but it shocked my Father—who probably had very good reasons for knowing the hotel.)

Henry preferred homely surroundings. But he settled down cheerfully to work, and I to work and to visit Dr. Rank. It was then that I realized that Henry would not give me emotional support, continuity, or reinforcement when I needed it.

JANUARY 14, 1934

I FEEL EQUAL NOW TO WRITING A SKETCHBOOK with only the human essence which is always evaporating, with the material left out of novels, with that which the woman in me sees and loves, not what the artist must wrestle with. A sketchbook without compulsion or continuity.

I will never write anything [here] which can be situated in "Alraune," "The Double," or the novel. I will not give my all to the sketchbook.

In no other book I am writing now can I situate the portrait of Dr. Rank—and this portrait haunts me, disturbs me, while I am working on the novel. This portrait must be written.

Portrait of Dr. Rank: Impression of his keenness, alertness, curiosity, of his nonpreparedness. The opposite of the mechanical, automatic, ready formula. A feeling that he is going to create, that he feels at once beyond details, not progressing through them. The feeling that he considers the differences and not the resemblances between human beings; and he said in words this which I had thought. Impression of distinctive mental adventure with him. The fire he brings to it, as if he felt, as I do, the great exhilaration born of mental adventures, explorations, and bouts. He gets joy from it. This keen mental activity and joyousness immediately relieved me of that obsessive fixation with one's pain, that terrible neurotic knot which ties up one's faculties in a vicious circle.

Immediately I felt air, space, movement, vitality, joy, the joy of detecting, observing, divining, the joy of the spaciousness of his mind. The fine dexterity and muscular power. The swift-changing colors of his moods. The swiftness of his rhythm of thought, because it is intuitive and subtle.

I trust him.

I trust him with the truth, which I give so rarely. I really want to give it to him.

I sense an intelligence rendered clairvoyant by feeling. I sense an artist.

I tell him everything. He does not separate me from my work. On the contrary. He seizes me through my work.

He knows already the conflict I have been struggling with. He knows I wanted to break with my Father and with Hugh, to live courageously with Henry. He knows that I fear insanity. He knows all about the diary.

When I leave him I am dazed by his bold stroke and the acuteness of it. In one blow. I walk deprived of the diary, which is myself. He says I have given him this self to preserve, to reintegrate, and to return to me whole.

I am in his hands so completely. It is incredible. He has asked me not to write about the analysis because it would be like standing on a traffic island. He has understood so quickly the role of refuge played by the diary, the role of a personage with whom a dialogue could help me resist invasion of the self. He has understood what a shell the diary is around me, what a weapon of defense. But he has understood, too, that it contains the *truth,* and that this truth, which I feel compelled to tell somewhere, I can tell him, since I have written it in that diary he kept. I talked to Rank as I talk to my journal.

He has such a joyous smile when he makes a discovery. I want him to triumph. I feel his sympathy, a far-reaching one. I can tell him everything.

It seems to me that he immediately touched upon the vital points. The diary and my Father—the connection between them. He began to talk very subtly about the Double theme, saying more than he had said in his book, *Don Juan: Une étude sur le double*, expanding, extending, touching on the subject from a great diversity of aspects. Said first of all that I had written the diary in order to replace my Father, unconsciously imitating my Father, too, and identifying myself with him. Said any lesbian tendencies were probably more imaginative than physical, due to identification with Father. Diary then originates in the need to cover a loss, to fill a vacancy. I call the diary, little by little, a personage; then I confuse it with the shadow, *mon ombre* (my Double!) whom I am going to marry . . .

January 20, 1934

I couldn't go on. I felt rank's influence— Rank's sureness that the diary was bad for me. I knew immediately that I would show him all this, that everything is transparent for him because I wish it to be so. I also understood today that it was because the analysis was coming to an end, and because I was losing Rank, that I felt impelled to re-create Rank for myself by making my portrait of him.

As soon as I knew that I was going to see Rank on Monday I had no more desire to write.

At the same time, I am still a romantic. Not that I am contemplating Werther's suicide; I have outgrown the religion of fatal suffering. But I still need the personal expression, the direct personal expression. When I have finished writing ten pages of the very human, simple, sincere novel, when I have written a few pages of corrosive, fantastic "Alraune," when I have done ten pages of the painstaking, detective-minute "Double"—I am not yet satisfied. I still have something to say. And what I have to say is really distinct from the artist and art: it is the woman who has to speak. My world is still composed of Rank, Henry, my Father, Hugh. I am immensely interested in the kind of smile which comes to Rank's face when he makes a discovery!

It seems to me that I could write my sketchbook *after* my work, with the overflow. The *personal* and feminine overfullness. Feelings that are not for the books, not for art. All that I want, not to wrestle with, but to enjoy. My life is a lifelong series of *effort*, self-discipline, will. In the sketchbook I taste, improvise. Incidentally, when I improvise I sometimes compose.

I began with the portrait of Rank because it did not fit anywhere else. Let us try.

Rank: I have a blurred memory of vigorousness, of muscular talks. Of sharpness. I mean the contents alone are indistinct. Impossible to analyze his way of analyzing, because of its spontaneity, its unexpectedness, its daring, nimble opportunism. I have no feeling that he knows what I will say next, nor that he awaits this statement that I therefore may be suggested to make. He waits, free, ready to leap, but not holding in readiness a little trapdoor which will click at the clichéd phrase. He waits, free. And the detour of the obvious begins with the expansion into the greater, the more, the over, the beyond. Art and imagination. Always with that joyousness and alertness.

I stopped for a moment to look for the order and progression of our talks. The order made by reality. But since Rank does not believe in that literal sequence, I perceive a new order, which is the choice of events made by the salient impulse of memory—the relief created by a sense of the whole. No more stairways of calendrical exactitude.

That means the deathblow to the diary again, to any rigorous sequence.

Nonchalant perspective.

Yes. Everything is changed. There is a pre-Rank vision, and there is an after-Rank swimming. Perhaps, at last, he has made me swim in life, rather than collect aquariums! The aquariums have the stamp of stillness. A love of things so great, so clutching, it made me stand still with fear.

Avançons. Il y a de l'audace au désordre, des lacunes dans la mémoire.

What I remember is the day he discovered two things: my love of exact truth versus artistic deformations, and the fact that I was a child, a wife, and a mistress but had inadvertently skipped the woman—no woman. Child, artist, sensual being—but no woman. Sex alone did not make me a woman. Henry's passion had not made me a woman.

When Rank said this the literal, materialistic aspect of psychoanalysis in general was revealed to me, and the transcendentalism of Rank. The liberation of the sexual instinct did not create maturity, womanhood. Sex gestures did not ripen the neurotic's child soul. I had felt this so keenly when I rebelled against Allendy's urging me to accept the "five-to-seven" liaisons lightly, as a step toward a normal, nontragic view of love. To normalize myself I had to act like a normal woman, from the outward to the inner. And my nature rebelled at the falseness of this. It touched me to hear Rank talk deeply and seriously about the transformation from the inner to the outward. Restoring to sex at once its sacral and its secondary place: I mean as a gesture which springs from the core of the being, as necessary expression—the necessity of art creation in the artist—which cannot be forced, and which when forced is deprived of its effectiveness as an expression of maturity—emotional maturity.

The repercussions of this talk were magical. Suddenly I felt a great serenity. All striving and nervousness left me. It was as if he had summoned up the woman. The artist ceased to write. I was filled with a great feminine activity. I did more and more for Henry; I wanted to serve Henry, to live my deepest wish for the Thou, whoever he might be—and all I know is that he is definitely, distinctly the genius whose wife I wanted to be.

A great change in me, but no change around me. Rank divined this would happen—that the woman would not find an outlet. I can't do more for Henry, except to become his wife. I do things for him continuously, but not as a wife could. Rank doesn't need me. He is self-sufficient in his work, and cared for.

But for a few days I enjoyed my superfluous womanhood. Rank noticed the change of mood.

We talked about my excessive need of truth, my suspicion of my own imagination, the fear I had that a fact which I did not describe on the instant would immediately get deformed in my head. A great passion for accuracy because I know what is lost by perspective and art. The desire I had to be true to the immediate moment, the immediate mood. Rank questioned the validity of this. The artist, he said, was the deformer and inventor. We don't know which is the truth, the immediate vision or the later one. I told him how Henry deformed and never understood things as they were. Rank said that was the nature of the artist. Genius is invention.

Then we talked about the realism of the woman, and Rank said perhaps that was why women had never been great artists. They invented nothing. It was a man, not a woman, who invented the soul.

I asked whether the artists whose art is a false growth, an artificial excrescence bearing a relation to their own personal truth, insincere artists, were greater than the sincere ones. Rank said this was a question which he had not yet answered for himself—"I may have to write a book for you, to answer it."

This statement gave me an unnatural, immense joy. I said, "That would please me more than if I finished my own novel."

"There's the woman in you speaking," said Rank. "When the neurotic woman gets cured, she becomes a woman. When the neurotic man gets cured, he becomes an artist. Let us see whether the woman or the artist will win out. For the moment you need to become a woman."

For me, this was the most joyous moment of the analysis. Also when I felt or divined Rank, the man, behind the analyst, the warm man, compassionate, divinatory, gentle, expansive. Behind the eyes which had at first appeared analytical, I now saw the eyes of a man who had known great pain, great dissatisfaction, and who understood the abysses, the darkest and the deepest, the saddest.

It was only a flash. It was as if he, too, were enjoying the soft human moment. He knew, perhaps, that the woman would soon fade out because there was no role for her, that the woman's role was to live for a man and that this was denied me—that to live fragmented between three men was a negation of the woman. And that I would be driven back to art.

I feel as I write that I am missing the overtones. For me, the adventures of the mind, each inflection of thought, each movement, nuance, discovery is an immense source of exhilaration.

Rank has a leaping quality of mind. It is exciting to see how he corners one, how he attacks, and how he enlarges the problems like a creator who is there to add, to invent, to multiply, to expand rather than analyze into nothingness. He does not raze the ground by analysis; he explores and quickens into life, he illumines—and partly because he is not seeking a definite, static conclusion. He does not work for a determined finality of judgment, but to arouse, awaken, stimulate, enrich. I see him always as the man with very, very open eyes: "You see, you see, eh? And there is more . . ." There is always *more*. He is inexhaustible. When he shrugs his shoulders, then I know that he has dismissed the unessential. He has a sense of the essential, the vital. His mind is focused always; his understanding never wavers. Expansion. A joyous fertility of ideas. The gift for elevating incident into destiny, for making life currents flow.

I still wonder whether it is not the *presence* of Rank the man which imparts the wisdom he gives. I find it difficult to retain exact phrases. His presence, his being convey all kinds of subtle teaching. He defeats the past, its obsessive, clutching hold, more by the fact of his enthusiasm, his interest and productivity, his adventurousness in new ideas, his war against conventions, than by any simple statement. It is his livingness which sings the funeral rites! He suggests quick, vast panoramas: the cosmic, the collective, the nonegoistic! (He is, incidentally, the one extremely individualistic man who is not an egoist.)

What is most salient is Rank's gift for extracting the essence—the quintessence—of thought. His books could produce a hundred books. Yet he regrets not having written a novel—a novel, which is only distilled, diluted, inflated material!

I seduced the world with a sorrow-laden face and a sorrow-laden book. And now I am preparing to abandon this sorrow. I am coming out of the cave of my own protective books. I come out without my book. I stand without crutches. Without my great, dissolving pity for others, in which I saw deflected the shadows of an even greater self-pity. I no longer give pity, which means I no longer need to receive it.

I think of a self-portrait tonight in order to disengage my self from dissolution. But I am not interested in it, or perhaps my self is beyond resuscitation. I am spent, wasted, lost, given, empty.

FEBRUARY 1, 1934

*H*ENRY SAYS, "I DON'T GIVE A FUCK ABOUT LAW-rence, really; it is myself I am making room for, myself I am explaining."

He is installed in the velvety, carpeted, comfortable room at 26, rue des Marronniers.

I sat at the typewriter taking dictation, to help Henry file his quotations. I pondered with him the order of the [Lawrence] book. He let me try my own classification. He asked me, "Is this good?"

These days together, when I live absorbed by Henry, are right. But when we separate I feel other things pulling me away—and that hurts. Hugh's demands, Hugh's life, the house, servants, family, Father.

A litany of weariness.

To the lost self.

It was Rank who divorced me, who isolated me. Rank asked, "Is your love of Henry more than the desire to escape from your Father by seeking the opposite, by swinging away from him? Look at your relationship objectively."

There is no objectivity. There is only instinct.

Blind instinct.

I broke away from Hugh. I broke away from my Father—never from Henry. I sway but I don't move away, ever.

I changed. Nothing around me changed. I became more woman. I have remained so ever since.

Objects. House. Food. Beauty. Persons. Human beings.

Over and above this, there are men discussing, talking, talking, talking. I guess I am in a feminine rage. No better than June or Frieda.

All the harm comes from me. I sent Hugh to Allendy. Hugh sent his sisters. I sent Hugh knowing Allendy loved me. I sent Hugh's sisters knowing they would know Allendy loved me, that everywhere they would be confronted with my triumphs.

I am not blackening myself, merely trying to approximate the truth. But there are always two truths. I had intended to liberate Hugh from me (in order to be able to go to Henry), to liberate Hugh's sisters from their love of Hugh, to liberate myself of my subjection to my Father.

What I did was to conquer and defeat Allendy, to arouse the hatred of the sisters, to fall into my Father's arms, to bind Hugh more than ever to me, because he chose me again, for the second time, against his family.

FEBRUARY 4, 1934

SITTING BETWEEN HUGH AND DONALD KILLGOER, who believe in me implicitly, and listening to what they think [of Elsie's betrayal of Donald], seeing their anger, their loathing, their humiliation, and knowing I have done things a hundred times more terrible and more intelligent, more noble and more tremendous, everything on a grander scale, I want to laugh. I want to laugh. If suddenly I confessed everything, Hugh would twist his hands, as Donald did, until the bones cracked, and rave as Donald did, and curse me, and try to kill me, as Donald tried to kill Elsie, and say, "If only she had told the truth! It's the lies I can't bear, the lies and the trickeries."

I worked on three stories at once. Every day at les Marronniers, I wrote a few pages of the June–Henry novel, the final version ["Djuna"]. If in a mad, neurotic mood, obsessed, I wrote in "Alraune," adding diseased and monstrous pages. Whenever I returned from Father's, I added a few pages to "The Double," a story which Rank nurtured and inspired by his insight into the drama.* Tonight I returned from a visit to my Father and added two pages. All of them based on my incredulity, my complete lack of faith in his pretense of faithfulness because I judge him from myself. My Double cannot deceive me.

FEBRUARY 5, 1934

SITTING HERE, WAITING FOR LOUISE, AFTER WORKing four hours with Henry on the schema of his book. I said, "Draw a chart!" I am nimble and always know what to throw overboard in order not to load down one's wings. But he does not trust me as he would a man because I do not have the visible knowledge. Yet I see, I know, and we always attain beautiful heights, wrestling with the immense load of ramifications, expansions, distensions.

I reach serenity by exhaustion. Inertia of exhaustion. Fine. I lie back, waiting for the doorbell to ring, playing "Firebird." I forget the details of Donald's drama because it is similar to Lawrence and Frieda, Henry and June, Father and Mother. And Donald will end by marrying his tormentor, no doubt. I am invaded by a mature detachment. Father and his cunt hunting, like playing at life instead of living. Bah, it is meager. I seek the real stuff of life. *Profound drama.*

---

* "Alraune" was an early version of *House of Incest*, and "The Double" became the title story of the volume *The Winter of Artifice*.

FEBRUARY 6, 1934

SIX HOURS OF WORK WITH HENRY. THINKING WITH him, watching his activity. And he finds time and warmth for caresses.

So beautiful, the great tree on the chart. Henry in his soft, royal blue wool kimono, thinking, smoking, talking. I on a pillow on the floor, taking notes, absorbing, learning, watching how Henry devours Lawrence in order to give forth something which others only nibbled at. The strangely plastic, imitative, feminine nature of Henry's mind. Genius is sensitivity. And genius has a treacherous core. I expect that. At the core of my joys there is always a fear, a fear of his inevitable cruelty.

That period in the rue des Marronniers remains a kind of trial. Rank had taken my diary from me November 8. The moving occupied me at first. But once settled, every evening I wanted my diary as one wants opium. I wanted nothing else but the diary, to rest upon, as in a womb. But I also wanted to save myself. So I struggled and fought. I went to my typewriter and I wrote.

A deep struggle.

A month or so later I began the portrait of Rank in a diary volume, and Rank did not feel it was the diary I had resuscitated but a notebook, perhaps. The difference is subtle and difficult to seize. But I sense it. It consists chiefly of *not nurturing the neurotic plant*.

I entered life at les Marronniers. Work. People. No communing with the self. And now not even Rank. This I could achieve only by finding myself again, lost in my Father.

My connection with Father really terminated at Evaux. I had a foreboding of this separation when I wept more than the month's separation justified. I knew.

When we met at Louveciennes there was a malaise. We both acted (two of the same nature—deception, kindness). Father said it was the terror of being caught. I said it was seeing Maruca again every day. Rank said it was guilt.

But how to separate from Father without hurting him?

My own way was to slowly get Father to admit the malaise, slowly hint at the possible cause. But he is too long-trained a liar. He is not even honest with himself. He simply made a date with me for Evaux, in June.

I made a little scene of "You don't love me," purely a habit. Father answered in his usual eloquent way with a scene of his own habit-impelled condition of "You don't love me—don't abandon me." We wept, we kissed, and since then I have experienced not a single physical regret or tremor, or even jealousy. A kind of fatalism. No more haunting pain or guilt or confusion. I see all the differences between us, and as to the resemblances, I make literature of them. I feel hard inside, because Father is less honest than I am in the final analysis, and he is vain, vain, and such a comedian!

In my story "The Double," the tragedy becomes attenuated, and the love almost vanishes. Indifference now. A profound disillusion, really, that he is not the man among men, not he. But I cannot keep a middling course—I either love or hate him. Just now I hate him.

After spending an afternoon with Henry, I come home to dinner with Hugh, Eduardo, Eduardo's "wife," Thomas, Donald; and I begin a lively description of my afternoon at the Lowenfelses'. Mrs. Lowenfels's stomach (the baby will arrive in a month), the six temple cats, the little girl's question to her father and Henry's answer ("First you must define your terms"), the disorder, the mad talk (culled from my evening there)—and I amuse the whole group with the vividness of my description. (The baby and the little girl all make Hugh reassured.)

I also invented that Caresse Crosby, the woman editor, has a house in Fontenay-aux-Roses, where I am often asked overnight, where I can go when Hugh goes away because I can work there. And I say there is no telephone (to make it impossible for Hugh to reach me). This permits me to stay a whole night with Henry, now and then.

To amuse Father at lunch I describe life at this house like the life I would like to have had in Louveciennes (Caresse Crosby being the woman I would like to be, a rich widow and editor!). People staying there and working all day, to meet only at night for dinner. Then we read our work and plan for it, criticize each other.

I live wrapped in lies which do not penetrate into my soul. I am not warped by my lies as Father is. My lies are costumes. My soul is intact; the shell of mystery can break and grow again overnight. But I can always see the early-morning face of my acts.

I am ready, in June, to tell my Father the truth: "We are too old and wise now to go on pretending. Let us enjoy our maturity and not romanticize. You will continue to be a Don Juan until you die, because you thrive on the foam of conquest. You are made for fluidity, not for the absolute. Between us there is only narcissism, and I have grown beyond this. Let us pay each other the compliment of not lying to each other."

But I know he is not as courageous as I am. He wants to admire himself. I have grown beyond this.

One evening of hysteria in les Marronniers.

A choice between standing in the middle of the room and breaking out into hysterical weeping—or writing. I felt that I would break out in some wild, disruptive fit of blind, furious rebellion against my life, against the domination by tenderness of Hugh, the domination of my Father, my desire for a free artist life with Henry, my fear of not being physically strong enough for it, my desire to run amok. A fear of the wildness of my fever and my despair, of the excessiveness of my melancholy. A fear of madness. Then I sat at the typewriter, saying to myself: Write, you weakling; write, you madwoman, write your misery out, write out your guts, spill out what is choking you, shout obscenely. What is rebellion—a negative form of living. Crucify your Father. And it is the cursed woman in me who causes the madness, the woman with her lover, her devotion, her shackles. Oh, to be free, to be masculine and purely artist. To care only about the art.

Letter to Dr. Rank: Besides being indebted to you for a rebirth, I am indebted for enormous inspiration. I will never be able to tell you how keenly I have realized and admired the subtlety and swiftness of your perceptions, your penetration and wisdom, the far-reachingness of your sympathy. I am so profoundly grateful. And last night you triumphed completely. I had the diary in my hand and did not write in it, nor will I ever. I have put all my faith in you.

FEBRUARY 14, 1934

HENRY IS INVITED TO FATHER'S FOR LUNCH. INTERESTING encounter. Father unnatural and Henry full of natural pleasures, awe, humility. Father says, as he enters, "Here is the monster who created Anaïs, the phenomenon." Henry serves his dessert into the finger bowl, which delights Maruca. Henry is greatly moved by the house and Father's files and industriousness. Desires a home like that, an organized life.

The dreamworld is becoming my specialty. Henry has now gathered all his dreams together and is rewriting them, transforming them, expanding them as a wind-up to *Black Spring*, recapitulating the themes of the book. I watched for the times when he fell out of the dream.

Letter to Dr. Rank: I want to confess something: When I said that I was sure you would not abandon me, it was not sureness, as you thought! It was because my husband showed me there were strong sympathies between your horoscope and mine. So that today when you said so casually to drop you a line with my new address I was quite distressed. I thought, Maybe I put too much faith in astrology! Please let me know when you are well. I wish I could be of some use to you, as you were to me so greatly. Thursday I will be at 49, avenue

Victor Hugo. But I will telephone you before that for news. With best wishes.

Realizing with what fervor I lose myself in the beings I love, I am making a struggle to distinguish between myself and Henry, to separate the skeins of our work, which have fused. I must save my individuality. Love swallows in me even the artist. Is it a good sign?

Revolt of the woman artist, who, because she understands man's work and demands less than anyone, is not treated like a woman. The primitive woman, who demands a man's whole life and who hates man's work, gets all she wants. I get the love of egotists because I fit into the schemes of their creations. And I am tired of egotistic love. Tired. Tired to death. I do not ask that man should give up his work for me. I enter into the work, nourish it, sustain it, but the less I ask, the more like a fellow worker I am treated. And of this I have had enough. I have played the role wonderfully. I am always the woman men have come to when they got tired of the primitive woman. But this primitive woman who has shouted and raged and extolled her dues, destroyed the work, been contemptuous of it, this woman has always got the best part of men's lives. I get them when they wish to create, when they wish for peace and understanding and I am tired of my beautiful role. They flatter me and praise me because I am not *encombrante,* because I fit into their new scheme. And they starve the woman in me.

Dream: I arrive at the apartment we have decided to take up on the avenue Victor Hugo, and I am beginning to settle down. [The maid] Teresa is in the kitchen washing. I go to the bedroom and enter and find a man sleeping in the bed. I am immensely surprised. I leave on tiptoes so as not to awaken him. I go to the kitchen. Then two men come and apologize for not having left the apartment, saying they will do so now, and I say, very indulgently, that it is all right, that they don't need to hurry. They are very gallant with me, but I don't know who they are. One of them looks like Rank. I feel like inviting them to stay, but I am afraid of what Hugh will say. I look out of the kitchen door and see that the apartment is really a house and that it is built on top of a river. There is a beautiful flagstone path in front with flowers on it, but it is underwater and going downhill so I cannot walk on it. I am told the river has come up a little too high and covered this walk, which I now see transparent under the water and very poetic. Then I go to the studio and look out of the window. I look at the foundation of the house and observe it is very solid, although the river is rushing by. Every hour or so the house turns on its foundation, like the solarium at Aix-les-Bains, in order to follow the sun. I watch the maneuvers and wonder how it is possible to do this so neatly in a river full of boats and people swimming. My Father is sitting with me on the couch and very amorous right in front of my Mother. I see that they are beginning to be reconciled. They begin to write messages to each other on a pad. But what they write are names of people whose loyalty they question. Mother puts names down and Father shakes his head. Then he writes names down and Mother looks as if she knew he was mistaken as to their loyalty. Mother writes the word *Alazabel,* and Father says no. I am wondering when they will quarrel, but it does not happen. Father is perspiring and very natural—as natural as Henry, it strikes me. There are a lot of cats about, and the dog, Banco. I want to let the cats out, but they are afraid of the water. I think, isn't it wonderful that now I am not afraid to live in a house right over the water, with the journals and everything, when before I would have minded.

Association: *Alazabel* is the name of a member of the Aguilar Quartet, who are friends of Father's. House on water resembles the castle seen in Touraine built in middle of river rushing by, which gave me anxiety when I saw it. I imagined it would be swept away. Cats and dog at home, I used to fear, would climb on me. Yesterday I was planning to invite Don to stay with us, to lessen expense of the apartment, and because he is so young and lonely.

Rue des Marronniers. Room on the court. Intermittent music from a phonograph below playing "Please," and from the conservatoire. The woman next door blows her nose as into a trumpet. Big typewriter. Henry's map on drawing board of "World of Lawrence." Jung's book, Sumner on folkways, Thomas Mann's *Magic Mountain*, Father's machine for cutting pages and cards, the file case with the three hundred cards we did together, Henry and I. Henry's alarm clock. When he is in a two-in-one mood he works in my room and sleeps with me. When he is an independent mood, he sleeps in his room and he goes to the café after midnight, when I feel sleepy. He does not drink. He is taking care of his health, adapting himself to a slower rhythm. He talks to himself as he writes. He is illogical and contradictory. But all the little things get lost in the large expanse of our life together. Everything is enlarged in fine broad sweeps and curves and rhythms. There is a magical continuity and depth. It is the deep living most people look for in vain. Everything else is small, fragmented, not profound (Henry said this). I lose in the vastness my own little fears, little moods, little difficulties, hitches. I can stand this bigger life and I give to it my *biggest* self.

MARCH 4, 1934

VISITED HUGH, WHO TREATED ME LIKE A NEW AND precious mistress. We came to an important decision: to keep Louveciennes, to live in it from April to October, to shut it and live in Paris from October to April.

The fear of losing Louveciennes has been a great torment to me. Louveciennes, the symbol of *creativity in life*. Home. A basis for life and creation. *Un foyer*. Dream of living there with Henry and drawing everybody there. Dreams which I am determined to realize.

MARCH 6, 1934

*I*FINISHED THE NOVEL. IT NEEDS ONLY LITTLE touches and Henry's corrections. A thin novel has come out of a thousand pages of diary writing. The diary contains much that art eliminates. Will see what becomes of "The Double," which is the experience which followed Henry-and-June episode. It is less in the diary and more in literature. *Allons voir.*

Richard Osborn writes Henry: The other day I went to the movies and saw Kay Francis in *Mandalay*, and she seemed just like Anaïs: tall and languid and beautiful, with startled eyes and a deep, passionate soul, a fine lisping voice, direct, shy, honest, and yet how subtle; the kind of woman that can put a man's guts back in place after they've spilled out seemingly irrevocably.

Henry and I have now created a world, but nobody else fits in it but Rank. Henry is sick of Lowenfels, sick of everybody. When I first met him he did not care if a friend did not fit into his world, because he was less conscious of this world. It had not yet been born.

MARCH 8, 1934

*I*BREAK DOWN UNDER CRITICISM. COWARD. CAN'T bear it. Think then that Henry is disappointed and that my book is rotten. No self-confidence. Just an immense terror—complete demoralization. My greatest weakness. Hell.

Next day break up the whole book and make a different plan. I yearn to be delivered of this book. It is devouring me.

MARCH 11, 1934

*M*ADE A GREAT CHANGE—A DARING CHANGE. Invented a complete scene with Henry which I call "the breakdown of narcissism."

MARCH 12, 1934

*E*MERGENCE OF THE TIGRESS. AS I RODE TO FATHER'S house I knew I would explode and that I would not let him go to Spain without informing him that I had abandoned him—to precede him—to take the joy out of his silly little cunt chasing, to make him suffer before he made me suffer.

The two tigers. Giving him the railroad tickets he ordered through Hugh, I say ironically, "Don't show Maruca this, as the travel agent writes you there are no compartments for *two* on this train."

I don't care about the pain in it all. I think only of the book I will write, the most difficult, most terrible book. Instead of writing in the diary I rush and add four pages, reporting our dialogue coldly, accurately. Noting coldly, coldly, everything. Not caring. I sit here and turn the radio on—jazz. Deep down I care, but I don't want to. I want to drown pity. I feel hard and full of cruelty. Immense cruelty. I want to telephone Father and let him hear the jazz and say to him, "Here I am. I have been living a few blocks away from you, with Henry. Under your nose." Under Allendy's nose. Under everybody's nose. Now I have become the tigress. I will make men suffer. I write my book, then, observing everything. No wasted emotion. No neuroses. Art. Hardness, the impersonal! I want to write the vilest book on incest—stark, real.

I can see very clearly now the monster in myself. Too much sweetness in the June–Henry novel. Not enough demoniac spirit of treachery, which drives me. Cruelty is necessary.

But how mine comes down like lightning. I pounce on people so unexpectedly. Nothing ever prepares them. Volcanoes. Nothing prepared Father for my hardness today. He thought me more terrible than he had ever been—but I know it is not so. He is a tiger, too—and his sensitivity and tears—all weakness, like mine.

Self-assertion—unjust—cruel—necessary. I must be true to myself. There is a savage in me—there is a primitive woman—there is a savage—no pity. I had to erupt. I don't care if Father is sick. He gets sick to call for pity. He works to the bone for glory, vanity, titles, admiration—*not* to protect Maruca or to pay his way in life, because then he might deny himself the hairdresser coming to the house, the doctor coming to the house for infections, the Chrysler, big tips—while Maruca deprives herself of everything. He works oh-so-hard to travel full luxury in Pullman and to stay at the Ritz—sickening. No sense to his life, no deep directive. Just form, show, style, externals.

How I taunt Father. Bitterly. Directly. Cruelly.

MARCH 16, 1934

BATTLE WON ONLY FOR MYSELF. FINAL PARTURItion. Nascence of difference between Father and me, therefore birth of my own isolated individuality. Father failed me. When he got ill after our scene, when he let me come with pity, when he came down with a tragic, theatrical air to say, "In front of Maruca I wish to prove that I ordered a double compartment," thus missing completely the great issue between us. All the rest he failed to see. He took refuge in Maruca's image of him as a simple, loyal, truthful, honest man. He said before her, "What hurt me is that you should call me a liar!" In front of Maruca, when he knows what he is! The bland, hypocritical angel.

But I was at the end of my fighting spirit. Out of despair, frustration, hopelessness, I began to sob hysterically—had to leave them—stood before an open window gasping for air. Then he came, the puerile being, weeping feebly, with his feminine, whining voice that I dislike so. And we were reconciled. I gave up; I wept. We were reconciled while I parted from all my hopes, my desire for an absolute and honest relationship. He wants gay lies. He is weak and puerile. He talks another language. I sought a match again—and found only differences.

I am resigned, tired, detached. Tired of everything. Have been sick and feverish. Life has no savor. Only the savor of disillusionment. I can't taste Henry, nor this house, nor my work. Henry, too, is so sandlike. Nothing to build. Nowhere, nowhere can I build a strong, strong human relation. Henry is a wanderer, no husband. One cannot build with him. He is "treacherous at the core." He must be.

Therefore—the diary—the self—loneness—singleness. To hell with human relationships.

As I write my novel, I rejoice that it is an avenue of escape from all of them. Escape. Flight.

The *scene* always falls into the same pattern—the pattern of my destiny. I make it appear that I am suffering from the poverty of love. The fact that I am deceiving, betraying, never occurs to me. I am only aware of the other's treachery. I am cast into a mold of receiving pain—can't escape it. Yet I can give pain. I need only reveal everything to Hugh, to my Father, and to Henry. Yet I am not tempted to do this.

Rank! I miss Rank terribly. He is so kind, so understanding, so solid, so serious.

MARCH 27, 1934

GROWN OLD, A BIT WEARY, A BIT IRONIC. DEFLA-
tion. Emptied myself in the novel, and I know
already that I am not satisfied and that I am going to write a better
book. Feeling less God in man than I supposed; the need of a nonhuman
god, self-dependence. Yet I can't sleep with the nonmythological personages like Don. When I let him go to Milan without giving him
what he wanted, this handsome and magnetic boy, I knew then I could
only be possessed by mythological beasts—artists, magicians, poets.

Now that I know there will be nothing deep between Father and
me, I am weary of *all* life. I seem to have come to a standstill. The
only avenue is art. Books and more books. But not introspection.

Dream: Joaquin, or Hugh, falls off a horse. He is brought to me
all cut up on a silver dish. It is a chicken. I look at its legs, head,
wings, all separate, and I say, "It isn't possible he should have died."
The dish is taken away.

Someone says, "He is still breathing."

Dream: Rank and I are listening to a phonograph. He suddenly
takes hold of the needle wheel and he himself guides it over the disk,
forcibly, scratching—and I admire his forcefulness. He says, "It will
give much better music." I let him make love to me and feel very
happy. But suddenly I draw away and look at myself in the mirror:
I have a beard.

Eduardo's interpretation: Record is like destiny, turning fatal-
istically. Rank *interferes* with destiny, like a god, alters it.   Then I
want to submit to him. But I see I am a man. I wish to be a man in
order to be able to do the same thing.

Notes: Henry's speech on how he will contain less and less good for me.

Feeling of pity for Mother. I become woman, individual, and then *friend* of my parents, not child. Understanding of Mother, pity, sympathy. Because I'm separate now. No more need of *fighting* for independence. Friendship.

Friendship with Eduardo.

Arguments with Henry over his criticisms. I fight, but reasonably. We always get somewhere, and he is always right!

I have *less love* for Henry—or is it maturity? I *care* less. I watch him with a little irony, a little sadness. I'm terribly sad, at bottom. Detached. Weary. Passive. Indifferent.

The *other* book is ready in my head. It will be called *Don Juan and His Daughter*.

All entries of *complaint* due to health. Health, of course, the son-of-a-bitch, fails me always. Bad moods; yellow color; no savor—pay no attention to me.

MARCH 28, 1934

*I*MPORTANT DATE: HENRY AND I RETURN TO OUR original plan—to be our own publishers, our plan made in the Louveciennes garden.

Kahane has failed, in business as well as in true loyalty and faith in Henry. Bradley has called Henry the *poète maudit* and has lost interest in him.

Rather than see him frustrated again (and it won't be once—every book he writes will again present the same problem), I'm going to break my neck and get him published. He and I—alone—against the world. Lowenfels, being just another writer with his eyes on me as a fructuous source, had to be eliminated. Henry's instinct, too, is to beware of Lowenfels. And above all, symbolically, he must stand alone.

Only I will go all the way with him. Deep down, he wants independence. And I want to give it to him. I want him free and strong.

A closed corporation, he said. He and I—one. We danced together, we shouted, we laughed. We felt so free. We're so furious to see everybody balking, squirming, with their eyes on gain alone: money. They all worry about the money, fear of risk. How right it is that Henry and I should address the work directly.

As soon as Henry felt free again, he regained courage and ambition.

The only way my intuition always goes astray is that I'm jealous of *every* woman. I imagine *every* woman to be the one who will steal my loves—all my loves! In that I'm blind as a bat!

Easter Sunday—Louveciennes. Came down to earth with my usual absolutism and excess. The house. Dirty and neglected. Began to clean it from top to bottom, from attic to cellar. Earthy and domestic. Hands dirty and spoiled. But every closet and nook and corner tidy, clean. Great healthy joy and exuberance. No thoughts. Food. Order. Organization. Filing. Care. Work with the hands. As proud of my house as of my writing. Getting ready to look at my book with fresh eyes, for final touching up.

Feeling very martial and terrorized by effect of my self-assertion. Love for Hugh turning into hatred. Can't bear his proximity, his defeats, his desire of me. Need independence.

Finished with hypocritical sweetness. Finished *worshiping* man— all men. No longer the slave woman.

Full of strength, like the strength of my scarred hands.

APRIL 15, 1934

*T*OUCHING ONLY THE SALIENT POINTS NOW. FIN-ished analysis and desolate to no longer have Rank to talk with. Miss him, his intensity, alertness; feel so attached to him.

Immediately invited him to dinner here with Henry. A disappointing evening, with cold, snippy, frostbitten Mrs. Rank cutting everybody's wings. But Rank talked like his books (a characteristic sincerity between his talk and writing). Henry, as usual, broke down the tension and softened the atmosphere with his enjoyment of the food.

I adore Henry more than ever. He is the man who has never misused his will—no twisting or forcing, but letting himself grow and willing only creation (Rank's theme of the *volonté du bonheur*). I will describe Henry again in my next novel. Always Henry.

Need of diary again, only for contact with truth. Only occasional contacts. I have given myself to the illusion. I live within my work.

Planning a trip to London for Henry's books.

On April 7, I mailed my manuscript to W. A. Bradley.

Very little introspection. One week a month I am definitely and completely insane, but aware of it. Insanely sensitive, insanely jealous, and so desperate with disillusion that I crave drugs and drink. But I drift along. And one morning I awake sane, for no reason.

My house is in edifying order. I have been throwing out ballast, manuscripts, copies, old letters, to feel light and in possession of little.

Poor Mother, with her dark, instinctive love. She alone has suffered—not Father. He is not whole enough to suffer.

Hugh did Rank's horoscope before meeting him. Absolutely accurate.

Cable from Rebecca West: "Look forward very much to seeing you. Writing."

APRIL 22, 1934

*J*EALOUSY AS A DEFINITE MALADY. BECAUSE MA-
ruca is powerfully attracted by Henry, I imag-
ine Henry responding. For a day and night I am tortured, obsessed. I
go to Henry. He receives me in bed, ready for me to slip in with him.
Says Maruca is a halfwit. Immediately my fears are dispelled.

I come home to a big dinner, and I can live through the evening
gaily, softly. In the middle of the dinner I smile to remember Henry's
caresses.

All my happiness is in his hands. I am entirely dependent on him.
It is terrifying, and beautiful, and tragic.

He has moved to the heart of the city, out of rebellion against the
dullness of Auteuil.

I spent the night in the ugly room he likes for its ugliness. Visiting
squalid, morbid streets with him. He falls asleep asking, "Are you all
right? Are you warm?" Barely awake in the morning, we embrace
closely.

I have breakfast with Henry at the café in front of Métro Cadet,
where I met Allendy!

I go to London, alone, for Henry, and also to escape from Henry,
because I want to keep alive in me the necessary independence to
preserve his. I have never been as courageous or as great in any of my
loves!

APRIL 25, 1934

O N THE WAY TO LONDON. ON THE WAY TO ALL kinds of realizations.

Before I leave, I strike a cruel blow at Father, letting Maruca inform him that I am trying to separate from Hugh in order to marry Henry. Telling Maruca all my love for Henry, with the knowledge that she will tell Father. I wrote him a vague farewell letter about the failure of our dream.

Before I left, I also won Kahane by a marvelous speech, and he will publish Henry's *Tropic of Cancer*—only, I pay for the printing. I was full of courage, determination, and eloquence.

In the crest of this courage I visited Sylvia Beach, Anne Greene, Rank. Rank applauded me. He said, talking about this old pattern I still live by, the pain pattern, that I might finally kill it off by my book on Father.

I get on with all kinds of people now, demanding nothing but a sort of human spark.

I don't frighten ordinary people off anymore, but, *par contre*, I frighten myself, because the only way out of the victim role is to make others the victims. I see myself using and deceiving Hugh, as June used to deceive Henry. I see myself victimizing my Father because he victimized me.

But I move on. I don't stop to judge. I board a train merely because I'm full of visionary schemes for Henry and for myself. I must look for a man called Cecil Wilson, who appeared in a dream to serve me. I dreamed the number of my next lottery ticket, 1912 N.

Maruca, the angel, hates me. I arouse bad instincts, fear, jealousies.

I sit on a camp stool, second-class rear deck, tenderly watched by a young English sailor, and I telegraph my journal a few headlines. I dream that Rebecca West and I will love each other.

I carry in a music holder Henry's "Self-Portrait" (*Black Spring*), and his manuscript on Lawrence, and the memory of a very amorous parting. The ugly, beautiful room, freezing temperature, but a warm bed and warm hands and Henry's jealousy of what will become of the "perpetual silkiness" in London.

Joaquin can't read my novel for jealousy of Henry. Maruca tells me Father is in a terrible mood; Hugh clings, and Henry clings; Rank is tender; Allendy's memory holds good; Eduardo is yellow with jealousy: "I won't pay my rent to you, Anaïs, because I can't bear to think my money is going to Henry."

I have an emotional tapeworm. Never enough to eat.

Well, there is London to be devoured.

A P R I L 2 7 , 1 9 3 4

*E*VERYTHING ACCOMPLISHED. WENT WITH BEATING heart to Rebecca West's palatial home. The hall porter threw a rug under my feet as I came down from the high-perched London taxi as from a camel's back.

Empire-style salon. Stately and cold, with vast bay windows overlooking London.

Rebecca West enters *en coup de vent,* mobile, flashing eyes—"Oh, you look like a Romanian princess!"—and bombards me with questions while we are sitting before an electric hearth fire. Such brilliant, intelligent fawn eyes. Pola Negri without beauty and with English teeth, tormented, with a strained, high-peaked voice which hurts me. We meet on only two levels: intelligence, humanity. I like her full mother's body. But everything dark is left out. She is deeply uneasy. She's intimidated by me. Excuses herself for her hair being messy, for being tired.

Dainty, formal lunch with her nineteen-year-old son. I'm a little frozen by the *encaustique* and the *grand monde* atmosphere, which I detest. Yet she's real, when she doesn't talk. When she doesn't talk she glows, fox and mother with earthy hands, dressed vividly in the wrong shade of green, in a beautifully decorated house which does not reflect any particular individual soul.

I expose my mission. I talk about Henry's books.

Rebecca West begins by inviting me to dinner to meet people—an American editor, an English playwright, the niece of Somerset Maugham.

When I arrive, Rebecca appears to me like a sumptuous woman of the Renaissance in her black velvet dress with garlands of silver and her very, very full breasts, square décolletage. As she gets up, she drops her handkerchief before me and says, "I drop my handkerchief before you. That's an homage to you, isn't it?"

The fire in the chimney is real now. The two other women are highly decorative. It is Maugham's niece, and not Rebecca West, who talks much and dizzily and breezily, with malicious eyes and a fruity mouth. I am charmed by her liveliness, and she dedicates to me her champagne mood. Talk is polished and full of that "you-know-I-don't-really-care-one-way-or-another" nonchalance which I detest, but that night I enjoyed everything, as I enjoyed the pink ice and pink biscuits, knowing the pinkness was meant to be decorative and added nothing to the vitamins. Rebecca West feels and acts as I did in the pre-Rank epoch, a little abstracted, a little uneasy, wanting to shine exclusively, yet too timid deep down to do so, nervous and talking far less well than she writes. I felt such sympathy for her, yet I could not show it, because once when I said, "No, I won't come to see you right after you come back from the dentist with a tooth extracted, because you'll be tired," she winced, touched her hair with a gesture of distress and answered: "Do I look as frightful as all that?"

She telephoned her agent, Mr. Peters. She telephoned Jonathan Cape. I took the manuscripts to Peters. She had no time to read them.

Today I will spend the afternoon with her. Then I must go, because my supply of courage is running low. To be alone in London (I refuse to see anyone of no real interest to me). To eat alone. All that hurts me a little. The men persecute me with attention and I feel tempted sometimes. Adventure. Everything fell a little short of my inflated imaginings.

Saturday. Lunch with Rebecca. Her son there. More and more disillusioned by her sexlessness, her domesticity, and her last book, on St. Augustine. I don't know why such people and their writings leave me starved. I get a kind of starvation pain, emotional and mental, too. Perhaps more emotional, not intellectual. It is life I want—not ideas. When I give her my novel, it is Rebecca West the emotional woman I want to touch.

It is quite possible that it is my emotional and sensory life which Henry has aroused, and that I refuse purely intellectual food. I find myself walking the streets as Henry does, fascinated by houses, windows, doorways, by the face of a bootblack, by a whore, by the dreary rain, by a gaudy dinner at the Regents Palace, by Fitzroy's Tavern. Only the watchfulness of the men cuts my wings, because I feel I could be easily swayed and I don't want a banal adventure. Or maybe I'm just a coward. My imagination runs amok, but I can't yield to the passerby's interest.

Naturally, Rebecca West admired Henry's book on Lawrence and passed over *Black Spring* in silence.

The last evening brought life.
Rebecca came alone. I had just finished reading her book. In the taxi we talked tumultuously and abruptly.
"What kind of education have you had?" she asked me.
"Very bad," I answered. And told her about my early life.
R.: "So have I."
A.: "But I always thought of you as marvelously cultured!"
R.: "I made myself. My father disappeared when I was nine, abandoned us."
She, too! A deluge of questions. She was about to get to the university when her health broke down. She was poor. She was an actress. She wrote criticism. She ran away from home with a man.
The dinner at Ivy's became unreal. I felt moved and unsettled. Didn't talk well, but we understood each other.
Rebecca wrote in her book for me: "Love to Anaïs Nin." And apologized for being so familiar, whereas it was the very spontaneity in her which fascinated me.

A new Rebecca appeared to me that night, and I was thankful for that desire in me to see people naked and true which divests them of their social, conventional aureole and delivers them to me devoid of poise and divine with emotion.

Her past and mine created one of those arrowlike routes, and in one instant we stood where it takes others years to stand.

Parting, we kissed with great affection. Her flashing, fawn, intelligent eyes glowing. Her Irish voice low now.

I left London too soon. Having touched a height, I feared. True, my money was finished; true, I had seen the people I had to see for Henry; but truer still that I obeyed a flight motif. Fear of tiring Rebecca, of disillusioning her. There you are.

She caused me the greatest surprise I have ever had concerning my writing. She said, in the middle of the dinner, "What baffles me is that you should come to London with two manuscripts by Henry Miller, when you're so much better a writer than he is—so much more mature."

I was mute with surprise. I protested feebly. It stunned me. No. She must be prejudiced. No, no. She's wrong.

And she had only glanced over my novel—which I had finally given her, when I saw that she was my friend, felt her to be so.

And now I sat there and I felt she didn't want to hear about Henry Miller.

And I felt, too, that Henry would never forgive me for this—if he knew. I realized, suddenly, that Henry would not want me greater. That it would kill his love.

It was to him I returned Sunday night, playing tricks on everyone by letters, etc., to stay with him.

And he received me joyfully, desirously. He had been improving *Tropic of Cancer*, realizing its defects humbly, working laboriously.

When I tell Hugh and Eduardo what Rebecca said, they say, "Naturally." But I don't believe them. They hate Henry.

And Rank, what will Rank say about Henry as a thinker? Why did Rank ask me one day, "Why has Henry written about Lawrence, and you had written about Lawrence? A curious coincidence."

His question offended me, because it skirted a doubt, a mad doubt which comes to me sometimes: The best pages of his "Self-Portrait" are derived from "Alraune." Only more power always, a masculine expansion. But we both imitate each other. Hell. All of us imitate each other.

I was set off by Rimbaud, wasn't I?

The question is, How great a writer is Henry?

I haven't done enough for him, then, if he still is raw, immature, rough hewn, uneven, faulty.

MAY 4, 1934

NO GOOD. I CANNOT REWRITE MY CHILDHOOD BE-cause I have already written it. So I had the idea, while talking with Henry, of translating volume one of the diary [begun in 1914 in French] into English. Present volume one, and then, twenty years later, the recent story of the Double in diary form.

I'm facing my greatest technical problems.

Encouraged by Mrs. Bradley's glowing admiration of volume one.

Horace Guicciardi said, "Must say your book gripped me. I had to finish it even though I didn't like the subject. 'Mandra,' of course, is you. She dominates the book even though you tried to efface her. The man is unreal, blurred—he is only important because he is the man you love. One gets terribly interested in the mentality of Mandra. It's a very feminine book, the logic of emotion."

I walk the streets happy, meditating my new book.

I tease Henry for filling my head with streets. I think about streets. I am letting myself live. I want to know many people, possess a map of realities as Henry possesses his maps of Paris and Brooklyn.

It is I who have taught Henry that streets in themselves are of no interest but need to be alchemized with some drama, some emotion. It is I who awakened the man who walks through these streets—no more anonymous maps, but maps of reality, matter, form, and significance.

Hugh, feeling my independence, goes to Rank and gives himself up to his care.

MAY 14, 1934

*R*ESTLESS. LOOKING AGAIN FOR INTENSITY, FEVER, turmoil. Everything seems to move too slowly. Exchange with Rebecca West impossible. Like June, she thrives on cables and telegrams.

I see many people. I crave sensation again. I imagine. I desire. I am full of immense curiosities.

Whenever I feel sadness about Father, I write. When I yearn for him, I write. When I feel regrets, I write.

MAY 18, 1934

I BROUGHT DOWN THE CURSES OF THE GODS. IT HURT me tremendously [to get] Rank's statement, after reading Henry's book on Lawrence: *"Where* is Henry in all this?"

I realized I was finally blinded by Henry's giantism, his long speeches, his accumulation of notes, his enormous quotations, etc. It is a tragedy, because Henry is his own victim, and he has deceived himself as well as me. We have lived on an immense illusion. He did say once, "I wonder whether I am saying anything?"

Of course, I am not yet persuaded that Henry has produced nothing. That Rank judges the contents, and Rebecca the art failure, still leaves an uncreated, unformulated being who is struggling to be born, and whom I have not yet given birth to.

This is all the more tragic to me because it comes at the same time as the discovery that I carry in my womb the seed of Henry's child. I became pregnant five or six weeks ago. I discovered it positively two days ago. I know it is Henry's child, not Hugh's, and I must destroy it. I have experienced the most terrible mixture of emotions—pride to be a mother, a woman, a complete woman, the love of a human creation, the infinite possibilities of motherhood. I have imagined this little Henry, desired it, refused it, weighed it against love (it is a choice between the child and Henry). I have been sad, elated, hurt, bewildered. I have hated the idea of destroying a human life. I have watched the transformation of my body—the swelling of the breasts, the weight of the womb, the feeling of being pulled downward, of a growth, of a transformation. I have desired the serenity in which alone a child can be born. Now, at this critical moment of my life, I cannot have it. Henry doesn't want it. I can't give Hugh a child of Henry's.

When Henry and I have failed to bring forth works of art, we create a child. It overwhelms me, it ties me to him, it terrifies me. He treats me with awe and tenderness. But he remains an ego. He remains the child himself who does not wish a rival. And I stand at a mysterious *carrefour,* hesitant, killing the child only out of love for Henry and for Hugh.

I am awed, and all devilry and passion are stilled. No longer the virgin, the sterile artist woman, the mistress, the diabolical half-human woman—the full bloom of woman. To be killed. In my imagination I have lived through motherhood. I still regard it as an abdication, as an abnegation, as the supreme immolation of the ego. I am offered this at the time when I am most awake to myself as an artist, as a solitary, unmated woman.

Why unmated? Where is Henry? Henry seems to be becoming the child. The self-destructive, immature child who must play so much, sleep so much, drink so much, and stay in the street, irresponsible and unconscious.

Oh God, oh God, oh God.

Night. I refuse to continue to be the mother. I have been the mother of my brothers, of the weak, of the poor, of Hugh, of my lovers, of my Father. I want to live only for the love of man, and as an artist—as a mistress, as a creator. Not motherhood, immolation, selflessness. Motherhood, that is solitude again, giving, protecting, serving, surrendering. No. No. No.

Rebecca has failed to understand Henry—to see beyond the chaos, beyond the struggles. She has only passed an aesthetic judgment. The antiliterary quality of Henry's work has offended her. She has not understood that he has a great deal to say. I understand everything imperfect, everything uncrystallized, everything half-born. I accept imperfection. I do not prefer Rebecca's grace and elegance. I think her remarks are inadequate, like a frivolous woman's phrases before a great catastrophe.

And anyway, I don't care. If I am blind, let me remain blind. The only thing which is important is to love, not to criticize. Criticism is death.

MAY 19, 1934

WHAT I HAVE BEEN CONCEALING FROM MYSELF IS my strange, ideal attraction for Rank. Always a subtle undercurrent—always a peculiar understanding. Blindly, blindly I lived. Today he forced me to reveal myself. Last night I had a dream of a passionate kiss. I went to him thinking only of the kiss. And he divined everything. Why had I said, "My child will be born in December, and he may be like you"?

So many moments when we looked at each other without talking, disturbed. The night I came away feeling that he loved me (the day I became woman under his eyes). I forgot all this. But I dreamed that if a child would not be right for Henry and me, a child could live in Rank's home, because Rank is a father, a lover, and a creator. Henry is a lover, a creator, and a child—not a father, not a husband. Rank forced me to formulate my imaginings. A child of Henry's blood, but like Rank. A child which must be destroyed because of Henry. A child I had desired symbolically. I teased Rank about my becoming pregnant because of his psychoanalysis. Pregnant and fecundated by Rank—I don't know. I am all confusion. I trembled. I desired. I felt his love. I am happy. I am blind. It is he who asked me, "And where do I stand with you?"

The child, being only a symbol, is unnecessary. Something had to flower between us—Henry made it flower. Rank stood by, but our minds intermingled. He gave me great joys in a world different from Henry's. I went to awaken Henry this morning with lilacs. He was inundated with tender joy. He kissed me so gently. We sat on the terrace of a café, having breakfast. And I was full of my dream, and full of that strange, strange awe and joy which move me whenever I split and fragment and my road opens into two. I don't know. It may be only a mirage.

Tuesday. Persecution by Hugh, trying to assert his will over mine, trying to force me to keep the child, surprised by my determination, angered that I should not bow and obey. So he used astrology, and for two days he tried to oppress me by dark prognostications. He destroyed my courage, he, Eduardo, and Earle, the French astrologer. I resisted; I went to the *sage-femme,* but full of forebodings. And the instrument she needed she did not have—not small enough for me— so the treatment was postponed. But now the persecution of the French Catholic doctors, the conflict with myself, and the morbid conferences between Hugh and Eduardo during two long holidays have finally crushed me. I feel depressed.

Today I see Henry, and I feel such a growing weariness toward his constant, irrepressible bohemianism—movies, cafés, billiards, movies, cafés, streets, streets, movies, cafés—continuous round. Very little work, and no *recueillement.*

Rank comes to fill a want, a craving—a response to my seriousness, my intensity. Perhaps not a lover, but a much-needed companion.

With Hugh, everything is dissolving. Now that his love for me is no longer neurotic, he can stand alone. He could bear my departure. And I am a prisoner of material necessity. Craving liberty, but not to become Henry's wife, because he is creative only in one form—in everything else, in life, in surroundings, in repose, in fun, he is the destroyer, the element of dissolution.

M A Y   2 5 ,   1 9 3 4

*T*ALK WITH RANK, A STRANGE, DISTURBED, FENCING talk, like two people leaning over a precipice. He sees I will no longer answer his analyst's questions. But I see, too, that he makes no attempt to detach me from him as he should if he felt we were caught in a psychoanalytical spell. Does he believe the enchantment is real? Both of us seem to enjoy the suspense, this absence of gestures.

The psychoanalytical spell! Or reality? I ask Eduardo, because I want to talk about Rank. I want to hear myself saying, "I am falling in love with Rank." Eduardo makes this diabolical statement: "You are a kind of victim to an immense psychoanalytical drama. These analysts—Allendy, Rank—who have not lived, they see you so wonderful, so alive, so interesting; they cannot remain analysts, they get caught, they look for their redemption in you, for life in you, they make use of the gift which comes to them, they have not the courage to refuse it. You seek always an analyst, because they are the highest type of men—nearest to God. It is your destiny. You are a victim, and yet a joyous victim. You love redeeming others."

Yes, not a *victim,* because I had been staying with Henry two days when I went to see Rank. I left Henry at his typewriter to go and see Rank. When I returned to Henry I was full of a terrible joy, like the days I returned from Artaud's embrace or from Allendy's. A terrible joy to be deceiving—full of the ecstasy of a new love and of another, darker feeling of diabolical enjoyment. Henry and I playing chess. His face and his hands always, to me, so tender, fleshy. I see him always as tender-skinned flesh, as I see no one else.

We were playing chess, and I was thinking of Rank, not as flesh, no. Thinking of *another* penetration, *another* infiltration, *another* fusion.

If Henry is not the greatest writer alive, what does it matter? We lived; we worked; we created an illusion, a life. I would not suffer even to discover he was no writer at all. He is a human being. He is what he is. I no longer believe in achievement, in the future, but in being. Being. Today. Joy. Human life. Honestly, immortality doesn't bother me. I am nearsighted. I'm a woman. I forgive Henry in advance. It was my illusion, my invention. I will always invent life. It needs it.

MAY 26, 1934

*H*ENRY ALONE CREATES AN AMBIENCE FOR ME, A *physical climate* in which I thrive. It is like the sun. I am enslaved by this climate as one is by earth. Soil and sun. But I am still hungry for other things; there is the mental climate, the dream climate. Henry touches them now and then, but he remains fundamentally earthy.

MAY 27, 1934

*V*ISITS TO THE *SAGE-FEMME.* TEA PARTY IN THE garden for Louise, who wears a gold band on her hair, and gold earrings.

There was also Madame de Montagu, who may be, some day, Hugh's mistress. I am pushing him away. She is pretty, timid, sensitive, and very much impressed by the astrologer. She is studying astrology.

Henry, in the Hôtel Havane, is writing about dung, ulcers, chancres, disease. Why?

André [de Vilmorin] sat in the sun, and his profile was shadowed on the back of the chair. Louise ran forward and said, "Let me kiss your shadow!"

Only shadows! I was not content with kissing shadows! I demanded flesh. I demanded flesh, and the flesh consummation destroys ghosts. The detestably *curative* property of sheer living!

Rank. I don't want to think about Rank. I sit here like a plant, and I dream of gestures because I am so weary of ghosts. Shadow kissing. That means blood like the juice of a rubber plant, and early death, and insanity.

I am no longer insane. I will not be haunted. I will kiss Rank. *Et tout s'évanouira—tout fondra.*

M A Y 3 0, 1 9 3 4

O N TUESDAY I DECIDED TO BECOME AN ANALYST, TO become independent, to support Mother, Joaquin, and Henry.

I fussed and fretted to obtain my new hyacinth blue dress from the cleaner. I would go to Rank the next day in my new dress because he was going to kiss me. I went to sleep full of dreams, energies, desires. I got up vibrant, courageous, impulsive. I rushed to Rank.

I couldn't talk. I got up from my chair, and I knelt before him and offered my mouth. He held me tightly, tightly; we couldn't speak.

He made me come back to talk about my work. It was hard to talk. I can't think or work. Oh, God, I know no joy as great as the moment of rushing into a new love, no ecstasy like that of a new love. I swim in the sky; I float; my body is full of flowers, flowers with fingers giving me acute, acute caresses, sparks, jewels, quivers of joy, dizziness, such dizziness. Music inside of one, drunkenness. Only closing the eyes and remembering, and the hunger, the hunger for more, more, the great hunger, the voracious hunger, and thirst.

JUNE 1, 1934

TODAY *HE* WAS NOT SHY. HE DRAGGED ME TOWARD the divan and we kissed savagely, drunkenly. He looked almost beside himself, and I could not understand my own abandon. I had not imagined a sensual accord.

He awoke from his distracted air with this naive question: "Have you ever—has it ever been like this before—you can tell me." And he looked away as one expecting to be hurt. I said, "No, everything is different." What was he thinking, of my other lovers? And how true that it is different; everything is *always* different.

We awake from our intoxication, and he talks then, so subtly. He is tricky and subtle.

His hand is thrust out, directly, and he clutches my cheek, or my neck, not gently—hard. And I like the hardness. I like the animal thrust forward.

I am far away from all, from Henry, from everything. I am under a spell.

While he talks I feel this dark-skinned. mythological animal so potent, not human looking, but animal, with the ugliness of earth, the solidity, and the sinewyness, and the mind so agile and abysmal. He fascinates me; he is dark, and he is old. He is older than I.

Strange. He talked about totality and partiality. No one could live totally—there was no absolute. To live, one must balance emotion and creation; he had learned that. It did not mean not loving, not giving one's self. In balance, too, there was the whole giving. The strong one could make a whole out of the two portions. Everything extreme meant death; art had saved me when I gave too much emotion. Emotion would save me from too much art. He knew that he had not been able to live on only one of them.

"They nourish each other," I said.

I knew, too, he was talking for us, because this time I was looking for a still-closer marriage of ideas, closer than with Henry. A wild quest. Rank's own quest. Immediately, our bouts of ideas sprang up, too. I have to give him an analysis of his methods. But I told him I didn't want to think just now. I had been discovering the soft bloom of life.

"Good," he said, "then you approach your new work in a state of semiopposition. Fine. That means it won't swallow you up. It will be a protection. And your work will be a protection against emotion. But there won't be any conflict, because your work is in harmony . . . in harmony."

"With you," I said.

And then I knew Henry could have swallowed me up—and that I would not be swallowed up any longer. And that I didn't want to die in the misery and drabness Henry chooses to live in—that I want to live, to live.

I came out of Rank's place. The sun was warm. I just walked, walked along the Bois, tasting, retasting, remembering only the emotions. "It was for me you wore this new dress—you never wore it before?"

I walked, I walked, but before me the world tottered and trembled like a view from an airplane in the movies.

I was walking along the same road I had walked through one winter night when I desired John, when I strained and craved the impossible, when I struggled to *imagine* realization, when I kissed only the air and shadows, and when the emptiness of my life crushed me as soon as I sat in the lamplight, as soon as I faced reality.

Today I was walking loaded with overfullness.

And the next day I received a tender, wistful letter from Father: "You idealized me—you expected too much—I am only a poor little musician. Where are you? It is neither your fault nor mine. I have been haunted by your eyes."

With this letter in my pocket, I arrive at Henry's room, and he opens his arms. He kisses me as if I were new. He has been hating the world, hating people, and so loving me all the more. He clings. He makes plans for our future life. He will work so much better when he has me there. I will have my "office," but near him.

Solitude, isolation cease to be unbearable when we are together. We are less alone.

The clash of a newborn conjunction with Rank. This divine tenderness with Henry. We are playing billiards together and he cannot bear it when I lose. His blue eyes are innocent and sad. He makes me feel his solitude, and the refuge that I am for him. The mother.

My Father's letter is in my bag. The wheel is turning. I am spinning. My Father arrives in a few days. I have not yet ejected the unwanted child. I lie in bed, and I want to sleep because the fullness is too much for me.

I write fantastic pages for "Alraune" on the dancer without arms (Helba Huara), on the faces of snowdrops, on shadow kissing; and I read about the golem avidly, with terror.

JUNE 4, 1934

WHAT HAS MADE OUR DAYS DRAB, HENRY'S AND mine, is that he is rewriting *Tropic of Cancer* for its publication. He is immersed in a past self, he is trying to recapture the mood he was in when I first met him, and both he and I felt then that perhaps the new Henry was all a fiction, that *Black Spring* and the book on Lawrence had never existed. We were oppressed by the drab past, the life of a newspaperman, life with puny Fred and dirty Wambly Bald, the love affairs without love, the whores, and the bidets. And Henry instinctively had chosen to live in a room I hate (to re-create the past too), chosen almost to be and feel as before. And I revolted inwardly. The ugliness of the room, the flabbiness of the day, no swoops and flights, and Henry working little, monotonously, without exuberance.

We discovered this the other day. And when I saw that he was aspiring to something else, desiring to come out of this mire, I was happy.

Funny, our dreams. I still imagine myself helping Henry's creation. Deep down, I have not lost faith, though my exaltation is subdued. I feel no bitterness about the perspiring, the labor, the effort I gave to Henry's book on Lawrence. Patience, patience.

JUNE 6, 1934

AFTER DREAMING ALL NIGHT OF AN ORGY WITH Henry, I went to him and found him depressed and desirous. He had refused other times to resort to perverse ways of love, but today, after much teasing and many unsatisfactory games (I cannot at the present indulge in real lovemaking) he forgot himself and I swallowed his sperm for the first time.

I had to powder myself quickly afterward to arrive in time at Rank's.

Half-stretched on the couch, we talked, and all the magic continued. He said, "You are an unknown woman for me. Everything I knew before about you I have forgotten, or it does not serve me."

"Yes, I am a new woman."

"And I feel we must not seek to know too much."

I feel that, too. I feel we are in possession of the bloom, the fragile summer bloom. We must not touch it—it is so new and delicate.

What we do not want to touch is the past, or the past me.

"You do not think of me as diabolical, then; you do not fear me? You do not intend to analyze me away, as a mirage?" I asked.

"However you may have acted before—I don't know—I don't feel you will do it with me. I won't let you."

I laughed. I liked his "I won't let you."

"I have been looking for a name for you," I said.

"I, too," said Rank, "and I can only think of *YOU*. When I say *YOU,* you stand before me."

But the past did intrude. I said, "My Father is arriving tomorrow. Hold me tight, hold on to me."

Then Rank said wistfully, "I see you need me yet, but I don't mind."

"Yes, I suppose I would not have had all this courage if I had not leaned on you a little."

He was sad that I should need him. Perhaps it makes him doubt my love. But then I said, "I could say to you wistfully, reproachfully, 'And you, you don't need me. I have always desired to be needed.' "

"I could need you too much," said Rank.

"I wanted to call you by the name of the creator of Alraune— except that I do not intend to be altogether Alraune to you . . ."

Suddenly he kissed me, kissed me voraciously. And he made me lie under him and we kissed until we forgot ourselves again, but he knew we had to stop, yet we couldn't, and in our drunkenness I found myself drinking his sperm, too. And he threw himself over me and whispered, wildly, in my hair: "You! You! You!" It was like a cry of surprise, of worship, of joy, of ecstasy.

I came away with the manuscript of one of his books, and I saw Henry again. I said to Henry, "A woman should be nourished with nothing but sperm." And we talked psychoanalysis. And Henry said, "Get independent soon so we can begin our new life soon, soon."

JUNE 10, 1934

MY FATHER ARRIVES AND AS I MOVE FORWARD TO kiss him, passing beyond the ticket agent, he says severely, "It is forbidden, you know."

And I smile to see I have no emotion—no feeling for this stiff inhuman schoolteacher. None. My liberty, my joys, even my unexpected and incongruous motherhood—everything so rich, and my poor Father like a mummy, a dried-up soul, with all his medicines, hydrotherapy, and functional materialism. And his woman's sensitiveness. Sensitiveness, that's not feeling.

Oh, I'm free! I'M FREE.

So I forget all about him. The next day I go to Rank. So human; so human and tender and passionate.

Much later, a lunch with Father. He tries to discourage me and frighten me about my work, and I end by riveting his interest, playfully, showing how quickly I am sailing away from all dependence; no need of him, either, which must be a relief to him, as he continues to enjoy his luxury.

So I rush to Henry for the night and we go to the movies and I begin to see the areas of emptiness in Henry, the maps of Paris, the dictionaries and the inventories, so I console myself with the fat, meaningful contents of Rank, who looks like a sad crab. All life is strangely lacking. Rank lacks beauty, so the night before, while dancing with Turner, I begin to quiver and be tremulous. I close my eyes as he gets more and more like a feline vice, and I go home drunk and singing, after having danced like a Negro to amuse everybody, with complete abandon.

My life is very much like the jazz I am listening to, only *en profondeur,* and I am wondering what secret sorrow I am trying to forget by turning around so dizzily. It seems that since Father returned I have lost a little of my joy and he is like a thorn in my side.

The wheel and the jazz and the dizziness. Rank and his profundity, his nimbleness, his understanding. Henry and his fountain spurts of gaudy livingness, like the insensate eddies of traffic. Everything has a slightly shabby color today because through my life there runs the poison of Father's gloom, and he is the great abortionist—not the *sage-femme* I have to see almost every day.

Why has the diary come to life again?

JUNE 11, 1934

WHEN I RESPONDED TO TURNER'S EMBRACE A FEW hours after having been with Rank, the full diabolical compulsion of my whole life became monstrously clear. Not love, but revenge, or love and revenge always mixed; yet I do not use my treacheries to make men suffer. I never betray my treacheries. They are only for me, like a secret and poisonous knowledge.

I said to Eduardo, "I betray men because men are treacherous. Think if I had wholly given myself to my Father, how I would be suffering now; and as it is, look what I am suffering for what I did give to an unworthy materialist and dry-souled Don Juan."

And Henry—look how Henry betrayed June and would not hesitate to betray me at any moment that it pleased him.

Will Rank be another victim, or do I love him? I am like a whore who gives herself but remains full of anger and contempt and bitterness.

I don't know. I feel possessed again, and evil. I feel truly diabolical.

Eduardo tells me a fable: "The beauty and the beast. You always choose a beast because you are not sure of your beauty, so you go around ringing doorbells with your beast, and everybody is startled by the contrast and says, 'Look at the beauty and the beast,' and then you are pleased."

Was Henry the beast, and was I pleased to be admired at his expense and as his victim? ("You are superior to Henry." "You are too good for Henry." "You are a better writer.")

Diabolical again. I wanted Rank to protect Henry, and Rank now dislikes Henry. Everybody turns against Henry when they see me serving him.

Oh, God, there is absolute confusion in me. I don't know what I am. I carry a demon in me, I feel that. Two truths, always.

JUNE 12, 1934

AFTER THIS MOMENT OF DARKNESS, I BEGAN TO dream again. I was going to see Rank, to see Him; I was going to see Him, I wanted to see Him. Everything is blurred, but I am so certain in my blindness. Him! Today I awake with joy, a joy I feel only for him, and as soon as I am in his room, it is like a place of deep magic. And every time we sit near each other we are mowed down by the same desire for closeness.

He said exactly what I felt: "I have such a strange feeling of living through something *unconscious*. When I try to think about you, I can't. I can't relate you to anything I know, to analysis, to ordinary life, to reality. It is all like a dream, elusive. I just went out and walked, because you had talked about desiring to go out with me and walk."

Through the confusion of his words I sensed his mood, exactly like mine: Music, mystery. No words. No thoughts.

"Like a warm dream, a warm and passionate dream, but a dream," I said.

I came out and waited for Hugh, sitting in the little park in front of Rank's house. I sat in the sun, like a mute plant, breathing and growing in joy.

Hugh tortures me, Henry uses me, Father is cruel; but I have this jeweled tower with Rank, an island remote and paradisiacal.

"With your help, I will be able to keep the balance this summer between analysis and living," Rank said.

Strange (or not strange, because I was inspired, perhaps) that during these days I was able to write for him some ten pages of a summary of the effect of his theories, or attitude, on me—and that he was pleased with them, praised the way I expressed it, the way I got at the core of the matter. It is a cool, direct, compact set of notes—issued out of languid dreams and physical joy.

I like the pleasure I give him; I like giving him the marvelous.

The dream prolonged and carried into life, that is what I feel. My life is truly orchestral.

JUNE 14, 1934

WHAT IS HAPPENING IS THIS, AS EDUARDO AND I discover: I have been living out an angel pattern—but only externally. Internally diabolical. As my novels come out I reveal the devil. Even simple Guicciardi says, "It is clear that the apparently quiet Mandra runs the whole show in the book." Slowly I am being discovered. But I deny this revelation and say to Hugh, "What is in the novel is a lie. What I seem to you is the truth."

Occasionally, I would like to live out the devil, when I see how devils are loved (since my great preoccupation is how to become more and more loved).

When Father and Hugh torment me—out of jealousy—I retort and defend myself with cruelty, *but only in self-defense.*

I do not want to be a masochist any longer, and there is no way out of masochism but by sadism. Eduardo knows only a positive extreme will satisfy me.

Impasse.

Art. Slowly, by art, I will fuse the two women.

JUNE 18, 1934

SOUGHT OUT AND OBTAINED PEACE WITH MY Father—a beautiful truce, or perhaps the entering into a new plane. Aired and explained and confessed and made him sincere, too. He accuses me of being overfeminine. I confessed my hypersensitivity. He said, "We loved each other as no two people ever loved each other. Yet we continue to be lovers, but the kind of lovers who wait for each other forever. For six months I have not touched a woman—I couldn't after you. Yet I understand your returning to Henry—you are too rich, too full of life—that doesn't hurt me—no, that doesn't hurt me." (But his voice broke.)

He swore about his faithfulness. I question nothing. I realize I have the *génie du doute*—so I don't know.

Peace.

Then I went to Henry, and I was tender, passionate, amusing. He passionate, and childlike, too. "Once I have put my faith in someone—it is for good. I never believe that you will hurt me." But he comes out with an understanding of my occasional feeling of being injured (usually imaginary), which shows the older, wiser Henry.

Unbroken continuity, yet for four days I could not, would not see him, after seeing Rank.

I question nothing.

I go to Rank today and he asks at last, "What about Henry?"

I am honest. I say, "The exterior changes in the life come slower than the inner changes." And I do not excuse myself.

Henry played at being a philosopher, a wise man, and a prophet for me and for himself. It is Rank who is the philosopher. Rank says, "You will be able to make a better synthesis of my philosophy than anyone, because you do not intellectualize."

Henry is the child and will not grow older than he is with me at his best moments. The world will never see him at his best moments because the world is not an amorous, believing woman. No one but a woman in love ever sees the maximum of men's greatness.

It is perhaps true that I run the whole show, always, but that I am also run by my show, that I pay with faith and illusion, that the show exists because of my faith.

JUNE 20, 1934

COPY PAGES OF VOLUME FORTY FOR FATHER NOVEL. Read Rank's manuscript. Wonderful, profound stuff. Wait for hatching of an egg, which is delaying. Accept Anne Green's invitation to dinner. Eduardo tells me I am his "anima" and offers to support me if I abandon everybody and just write. Father is happy and loving. I promised to become, in the future, the Amazon he believed me to be. The gardener is cutting up old boxes, old shutters, old doors for the water furnace so we will not have to buy coal, but I have paid Kahane the first five thousand francs for the publication of Henry's book.

I am preparing to leave Louveciennes in September, perhaps never to see it again. Hugh has accepted that I should have a little office for my work where I will live alone from Monday to Friday night. On Friday I will join him. He accepts everything. I have a certain loving way of asking. As Henry asks me for all kinds and manner of concessions, whims, gifts.

The garden paths are snowed under with withered blossoms. The *sage-femme* admires me warmly, and Turner trembles when I shake his hand. Mother and I are close and intimate; and Joaquin watches me, as usual, as if I were a flickering flame, and we have such whimsical talks about his Dominican discipline of life.

JUNE 21, 1934

TO LIVE SYMPHONICALLY: TO RUSH TO HENRY IN the morning with his rent money, read his pages, get kissed; to rush to Father for a walk in the Bois with tenderness and whimsicalness, to receive his kiss on my neck, like his first kiss in Valescure, and to hear him say, "I am so happy now that we are engaged again"; to read to Rank and feel how suddenly, in the middle of a phrase, he feels impelled to kiss me, and how violently he kisses me, stirring me instantly. Motif of kisses and desire and drunkenness of the blood.

To live symphonically: Writing for Rank; writing "The Double"; writing "Alraune"; writing the diary.

To think more of the future, of the little place I will have in the same house with Henry—the colors of it, the idealized vision I have of it which reality will have to conform to. Surrounded by men, by people, swimming in life.

JUNE 30, 1934

I HAVE FOUND *LOVE*—I HAVE FOUND LOVE, LOVE, equal love! I am blessed, blessed with ecstasy, with a new ecstasy, a new kind of love, a new man, a new world. I dream. I close my eyes and I dream, and I feel his passion, I see him white with passion, I see the trembling of his mouth. I see him returning to the room after being called away and suddenly pushed toward me, pushed, a force I feel the impact of. I can't walk beside him without him clutching me. Tumult, tumult, ecstasy, blindness. "I can't let you go. You!" And he makes plans for our running away to the country for one night.

We talk sometimes, we talk, and suddenly he leans over and I close my eyes; I close my eyes because when he puts his hands on my breasts I am dizzy.

We had to talk one day as of old, because I got tied in a knot with the past. I tried to push the past away too quickly, too violently. It came back to strangle me. Then I fought off my need of him as an analyst and as a human being. I refused to use him. He was glad of this, glad of the effort I made—but it was enough to have wanted not to need him. Then we fell into a more natural rhythm. He did analyze; we did talk. I told him (the most miraculous sincerity for me) how I stood with Henry—the truth: "What remains strong is my desire to protect him. Predominant. I evade nights with him; I feel him a child only." Everything. And when it was all over, we dropped into our drunkenness again.

He said, "You see, there is no danger in our talking, analyzing, philosophizing, because this is always the strongest, this always wins out." And he closes his eyes too, with a great interior ecstasy.

A day. I awake and write a preface for Henry's book. I translate. I copy for "The Double." I write Father. I rush to Paris, to Rank. I rush to the bakery and buy pastry for Henry and run down to Mother's apartment, where I have installed him. I am radiant with joy. It sets him on fire. He had not been able to work. He is inert and sleepy, and awakes when he sees me. On the way, the concierge stopped me to tell me all about her little son, who will be a painter someday.

After tea, I run out to the *sage-femme,* leaving Henry dancing around my preface, which pleases him. At the *sage-femme*'s I ask for the size of her little girl's feet to get her sandals because she is leaving for the beach.

I rush back to have dinner with Henry, and we go to the movies, but all the time I am dreaming, dreaming of the strong, strong caresses and the miracles of differences, how life can continue to produce new savors, new caresses, new phrases, new ecstasies. He says, "With you one goes so far away from reality that it is almost necessary to buy a return ticket. I am afraid never to come back here."

We laugh about the return ticket.

J U L Y   4 ,   1 9 3 4

NOT TONIGHT, NOT TOMORROW NIGHT, BUT THE next night Rank and I will be together for a night. We are going to run away. He wants to take me away. He has no need of the city, of cafés, only the need to be with me, in the country. We cannot talk when we are together; we dream, drown in feelings.

J U L Y   7 ,   1 9 3 4

O H ,   M Y   J O U R N A L ,   I   H A V E   F O U N D   T H E   O N E   W H O loves in the way I love! I have found the one who loses himself into me as I lose myself in my love. I have found such fullness as only religion brings, exaltation of such a supreme kind that it is a religion. That is all I wanted, this equality and fullness. How often I desired someone who would love me with the divine attentiveness, the continuous exaltation I gave Henry—because that was the absolute, the oneness. I sought that, that impossible, desperately, hungrily. I accepted Henry as one accepts human life. But that exaltation, intensity, gravity, that impossibility came to me when I had accepted human life.

I feel that I am like a St. Theresa of love, that no one knew the exaltation, the mystical fervor, the destructive wholeness of my love. How it burned me, devoured me. And all this can go to Rank. He wants it; he gives it; he feels as I do—he gives.

The word *love* is not enough. We are both ill with our joy; we are truly dying of joy. We are broken, feverish.

All those who tried to make me renounce the impossible, accept the realities of love, its limitations! I possess it. I am possessed by it. For the first time, I am incapable of enjoying Henry, incapable of thinking of anyone but Rank—I'm full of him. I awake thinking of him. His selflessness. We live for each other. We break down obstacles. We love in a way everybody believes impossible. We love impossibly. And I am overwhelmed, dazed. The inner ecstasy is tremendous, terrifying. The certainty, the completeness. *My* love, not me. He is not me, he is the Other, but it is my love he gives me—a unique, strange formula—a love nobody understood, a love that was called neurotic, romantic. He knows it.

I have believed in love, but in an unanswered love, and by "unanswered" I mean not answered *in the same language*. Henry loves in *his* way. I thought my Father would love in my way, but it was not so. But Rank, he loves to death, he loves selflessly, he loves.

The night before our night together, I couldn't sleep. I was feverish. All day I prepared myself, consumed with impatience, by the visions of my imagination, by the burning of my blood. The hour came and I sat in a café waiting for him. He came, looking very ill. He said, "We cannot go away. I got up out of bed to tell you. I'm very sick. Are you very angry? I have been tortured all day, thinking about you. Are you angry?"

"Angry? God, no. You're sick, you're sick, that is all I'm worrying about. And you came out. You shouldn't have come out. It may hurt you. You must go home. Can I come with you—see you a little while?"

He asked me to come in a little later. When I arrived and he lay on his couch and I sat beside him, I saw he was trembling with fever. "You. I was too excited. I am so ashamed, so anxious."

I understood him so well. I remembered when the intensity with Henry made me ill, beforehand, with nervousness, expectation, tenseness. I told him all this. We had been waiting too long.

"I wanted you too much," he said. "The waiting has been unbearable. I couldn't sleep all night." And then, in an accent I have never heard, in a tone which was like a caress, he said a word I hate, and instantly it became a beautiful word: "Darling."

Again this morning, over the telephone, with his whole body and soul: "Darling!" and he makes me tremble. He is getting well. He will be well for Tuesday, when Hugh goes to London.

I didn't want Henry. I didn't enjoy Henry. I only want *him*. I am not afraid of the terrible wholeness, the terrifying way I have of loving. I have not yet learned not to believe.

To Father: I am going to study French again, I promise you; but for the moment I want not to write, but rather to make music. Deep down, my adored Papa, you would have been very unhappy with a woman like me, because I am an excitable person who only understands life lyrically, musically, in whom feelings are much stronger than reason. I am so thirsty for the marvelous that only the marvelous has power over me. Anything I can't transform into something marvelous, I let go. Reality doesn't impress me. I only believe in intoxication, in ecstasy, and when ordinary life shackles me, I escape, one way or another. No more walls.

You are able to come to terms with both. You find time for the marvelous (Valescure, Evaux-les-Bains), as well as for ordinary life (like our poor winter). I always choose the moon, even for breakfast. But I don't put up with the humdrum aspects of life. Overboard with all the banality of this world. Such thinking leads straight to extravagance—no, not to eccentricity, but always to great strides in seven-league boots. I am going to try. If that produces broken eggs, will you come and take care of me?

Equilibrium? An impossible dream for me, *Padre-amor*. For I was born under the sign of Saint Theresa and the great depraved courtesans. One or the other. Mysticism of the earth or of heaven, but always the extremes.

So much for the stars. Don't be sad, Papa. Astrologically I am kin to Bergson, George Sand, Saint Theresa, and Rimbaud. So you see, instead of fleeing to Africa to escape madness, as Rimbaud did, I devote myself to the madness of others and am becoming as well behaved as possible so as not to distress you. But tell me, tell me that you love me as I am. Relieve me of the weight of your idealism, which thought me someone else. I am sorry to have disappointed you, but just as I am, I love you as no daughter has ever loved her father.

July 13, 1934

*H*UGH LEFT ON TUESDAY, AFTER TELLING RANK nothing could persuade him that I was anything but the woman he believes me to be, and painting for Rank an incredibly naive portrait of my fundamental innocence. At the very hour when he boarded the train, I was in Rank's arms. We could not wait for Louveciennes, for solitude. I yielded completely to an ardor which I thought would extend to the deepest roots of sensual expression. My exaltation, like an immense rainbow-colored cloud, was punctured by irony: *Une éducation sexuelle reste à faire.* He needs an education in sex. But like a creator, I measured the material and found it good: all the elements of sensuality there, potency, vibrancy, impetuousness. Only expertness lacking. My cloud did not wither. We fell into a dream and made our plans for the next night.

Louveciennes. Heat. House cool and dark. The glow of color and sun. We lie on the bed. Too swift, he is too swift, and so unaware of the woman's response; but the love is immense, the abandon to love, the selflessness. We fix dinner gaily, all alone. He is joyous. Our conversation is far from brilliant. Closeness. He seeks it constantly. We drink champagne and put peaches in it, as the Viennese do. The evening is soft, like flower petals. We are like plants, eating, laughing, swaying. Poetry all around us. None in his language. We fall half-asleep. The window is wide open on a beauty which hurts me. He is snoring. My dreams, like a breathing, pour out of the room, where a man is snoring. Restless dreams unfed. But when I want to leave he clings to me: "Don't go away. Don't leave me. I want you. Where are you? You!" I lie there dreaming, waiting. From his body emanates an intense fervor. But I want to be alone.

Finally, I whisper, "I must go and sleep in the other room. I feel uneasy here. I can't sleep."

"Why, why?" he murmurs.

"Someone might come in the morning." (I was thinking dimly of that morning Hugh returned so early.)

He let me go.

I went to Eduardo's room (he was away) and went to bed.

Human life. Would I ever accept human life? The poison of my dreams. I was almost asleep when he came, calling me. "I can't sleep," he said. "What you said about the morning awoke me completely." We laughed. I went to his room. I sat on the edge of the bed. I didn't tell him about Hugh's return that morning, as it would have made him anxious. I said I had vague fears about sleeping in the same room, here, in the house. He understood this. We talked. We laughed. He made me lie beside him. Then a wave of desire caught him again and he took me passionately without arousing me. For him it was all wonder. I loved only his love of me. It is easy for me to be caressing and to yield to fervor. For him it was all wonder: the breakfast in the garden early in the morning, the peace and the joy I give, the expansion and the naturalness. His happiness gave me happiness. There was only the dream in me withholding, the dream in me weeping and ironizing. He had the short-stepped walk of Dr. Caligari. His naturalness was different from Henry's.

He was busy all day.

I went to Henry. Henry had been inert, listless, moody. Painting watercolors, not writing, living somnambulistically. Blocked like Eduardo. And withdrawn.

We began to argue over nothing, irrationally, meaninglessly. But suddenly I realized it was a disguised scene of jealousy. The tears came to my eyes. I felt an immense distress. All our talk only meant, *You are abandoning me; I feel you are abandoning me,* from Henry's cold blue eyes. And we talked like that—chaotically, stupidly, blindly; but I knew what we were saying to each other. He was so much like Eduardo is when I torment him.

We were reconciled over nothing. Henry held me close. He came to me, and I enjoyed him, and felt again exactly as if no other man had ever penetrated me or possessed me. Only Henry.

I met Rank for dinner. His joyousness is vulgar. He makes puns and talks foolishly. No divine joy, but jokes. He could not come to Louveciennes because his wife was telephoning him. He took me in a taxi to St. Cloud so that I could take my train there. We kissed in a taxi. It is easy to kiss when a candle light has been lit between two people, a current. Disillusionment does not snuff out everything instantly. It has to burn itself out. Besides, I love a tragic philosopher with a great well of Jewish love and soulfulness. His daily self, his vulgar self, *le pain quotidien,* is always a little stale. I suffer from a hunger for the marvelous.

There was no train for two hours. I walked down the St. Cloud hill. Would I go tonight and take drugs? Would I drink myself unconscious? Would I plunge into darkness? Oh, the bitterness in my mouth. And then a cry, a cry. I called out, "Henry! Henry!" Walking down the hill, yearning for Henry. Was he lost? Had I lost him? Pushed him away?

I rushed in a taxi to his place. He was out. I took the key from the concierge. I got into his bed. I read. I waited. At midnight, I heard the door downstairs open for the tenth time, but I knew it was he. A quiet Henry, surprised, perhaps knowing deep down—happy. I told him a lot of lies. It didn't matter. With his feeling he knew. We fell asleep holding each other. We awoke holding each other. Everything was as before. We sat down and worked together at my preface for his book. And Henry miraculously resuscitated. A new man. Everything clicked again. He said, "I'm awake again." He didn't say, "because you are back." But we knew. He had said, "You tormented me with jealousy."

He wanted immediately to write. He was all alert and happy. He is coming to Louveciennes tonight. Hugh is coming home Sunday night. Rank's wife returned last night, so he is imprisoned.

Until Henry hurts me, betrays me, I am his—I really tried to free myself so many times.

On the morning Rank and I were leaving Louveciennes, I got a letter from my Father.

July 16, 1934

SUNDAY NIGHT I RECEIVED HUGH WITH PRETENSES. Monday morning I awoke ill because I didn't want to go to the Psychological Center, didn't want to become an analyst. But I went for Rank's sake.*

As I walked in the sun to the Cité Universitaire I fell into a Greek mood—the life of the body blossoming full in the fragrance of philosophy. In the conference room, fifteen female schoolteachers and three interesting, dynamic men: Rank, dolorous, black eyed, soft handed; Hilaire Hiler, big, loud, and overflowing, like Erskine; [Dr. Harry] Bone, high browed, laughing eyes, American poise.

Pause at the end of the first conference, which was like the droning of a bee.

The discussions are pragmatic, dull, like all American craft talk. They are not interested in ideas. Rank looms too big, with his immense cosmological books, his nonconformism, his subtlety. I can look at him now for a moment as the brilliant philosopher and the dangerous enemy of Freud. We are entering together into our nontragic epoch. But there, at the bottom of his black, black eyes, it lies, and at the bottom of mine—but today we are laughing. I am laughing. I have discovered humor, enjoyment.

At the end of the session Bone walks straight up to me and introduces himself, talks, asks me to help him raise the level of the discussions, looks ironic, amusing, smart.

Rank had asked me to wait for him. "Are you free? We'll have lunch together. Meet me in half an hour at the Café Porte d'Orléans."

He comes scurrying. Orders chicken. I'm not sick anymore. He

---

* Dr. Rank had established the Psychological Center at the Fondation des Etats Unis, Cité Universitaire, across from the Parc Montsouris, to hold a seminar between July 15 and August 31, mostly for American psychiatric social workers.

tells me to be careful of Bone—he's too smart. Bone has quickly sensed that I, at least, don't bore Rank. Bone had stopped me on the way out: "Why don't you have lunch here at the school?" The chicken is wonderful, and I'm laughing.

Rank takes me to a lovely house near the Parc Monceau.

I have no excuse now not to enjoy myself. Rank has become a stirring lover. It is just that I am holding back now, faithful to Henry. Enjoying the embraces and the caresses. Playing the eternal comedy. Spasm only for Henry. Mysterious expression of faithfulness, to withhold the orgasm, as the whores do. So wonderful not to be timid anymore. There was a time when I was frozen with timidity, trembling, heart and body iced with fear. Love as an ordeal. Now everything is spontaneous, and only the last secret lock keeps closed, for the One, like the whore.

I accept life as it is, the ugliness, the inadequacies, the ironies, for the sake of joy, for the sake of life. It is a comedy. It is slightly ridiculous and, at best, the most passionate is full of homeliness. The homeliness. That which my Father repudiated at the cost of naturalness. There will always remain enough tragic days. Today I laughed, caring less, letting others care. Shifting the burden.

Now. I ask Rank many questions. He buries his head on my breast and says, "I can't think when you are here." He only expresses himself in a wordless, blind, unconscious love. He melts into me, but he disregards my appearance, color, details. It is all a dark oneness—a dimness again—undramatized, unexteriorized, the unformulated. I am sex—clearly, to him, sex adorned with the other things. The image he wants is that of the mistress. He approves that I don't want children—he abhors the mother image. I am glow and color and senses and wine, and that satisfies me, unphrased as it is—no Artaud phrases! He loves me with his senses. He feels me. Talk is secondary.

July 21, 1934

LREADY THERE IS A GREAT CHASM BETWEEN THE Rank the world sees and mine.

I owe to Rank's love this great exaltation, just as Henry owes to my love his most powerful creative ascensions. I look at his wide mouth with immense gratitude. I am living in a dream of warmth and lightness.

July 23, 1934

EMINAR YIELDS NOTHING. BUT I MEET RANK afterward, and he cannot wait for the ceremony of lunch. He drives me to the house. He throws himself on me. He engulfs me. He bites me savagely.

And then we have lunch in the room with the curtains drawn. Lunch with champagne and laughter. I say to him, "You have a gift for living."

"But I never used it," he answers, "never used it until now."

And after lunch we lie down again and he desires me, and we sink into a long orgiastic feast of caresses.

What deep inner, secret fortress do I still keep closed against him, and why? His passion arouses all the outer realms of my being, but it does not make me wholly his. I am thinking of Henry.

I get sick this morning. Hugh goes to Dinard, but I cannot have Henry because I have not the strength. I have to lie here alone. I love life, and it always kills me—physically. Talk with Eduardo, and this is uncovered: I feel that I am June to Rank. He loves me with his senses. I can destroy him. He loves the June side of me, the dangerous, rebellious, perverse side. I have enslaved him and have not become a slave to him (by my frigidity). I do not wish to create with him. That he has done alone, before me. I rather enjoy seeing that he is destroying his own creation (undermining psychoanalysis, from which he lives). He talks in the school for me, not for the others, and this talk is disruptive and baffling to the others. I could warn Rank, but Rank wants to live. I am joy, the body, expansion, and danger, movement, color. He craves a kind of suicide after having seen the ultimate error of all philosophies and systems of ideas. He is afraid of the truths he has discovered. They do not help to live. He has met me and he has lost his head. It is obvious to everyone when I come into the room that he no longer listens to the others. He tears the telephone away from his secretary when I telephone. He leaps out of the classroom window to meet me. I am aware of the joy I feel in this triumph. Since I cannot have God, says Eduardo, I will have the analysts, whom the world considers as godlike men. As victories. As I took my Father. But I don't give myself to them. I keep myself. How far can I be June to Rank?

Eduardo and I observe that I have never gone to the very end of my perversities. I did not take drugs with June. I conformed to Henry's image of me as the opposite of June (but occasionally Henry gets perverse and says, "When you live with me I will make you go to the end of things." And that means, "To be the June in me").

Being the mother to Henry, I could not be June.

Now, about the end: I did not go to the end with June and Henry. I stopped somewhere and I wrote the novel. The novel is the *aboutissement*.

I did not go to the end with my Father in an experience of destructive hatred and antagonism. I created a reconciliation, and I am writing a novel of hatred.

Henry went to the end with June. Can he write a novel? He is forty-two and lived with her eight years, and did not write about her.

Will I go to the end with Rank? What stops me? I say health. But it is creation. Do I arrest myself on the brink of destruction and self-destruction in order to catalyze all into art?

I want to live out the June in me.

Eduardo had sent me to his analyst as his anima. I, as a woman, will get the love he wants from the analyst, the love his feminine self wants. This is my own interpretation of his influencing me into psychoanalysis while knowing what would happen.

I said today, "Should I go to Jung now and get another scalp?" Scalps, and not cure, but more life and love. Slaves. Eduardo worships Jung. He knows Jung, too, would become human with me. And if I wrote the novel of these men's ideologies and the drama of their temptation by me—they are the priests, and I am Thaïs. Only I don't know what stops me from being June. The novel-writing compassion, or a weaker body?

I got sick today so as not to continue living. Otherwise Henry would be here, and tomorrow the school, and Thursday Rank, and Friday the trip to Dinard, and so on. Or was it the champagne? Anyway, I have a sense, not of tragedy, but of high, perverse comedy. Power.

Eduardo and I keep turning the colored ball. I write the novels, perhaps, more to supply the deficiencies of life itself. The novel was better than taking drugs. It was my superior drug. Where life turns into an arid valley, I stop.

Hatred of Father. War with Father. Futile waste of emotions. Better to write the "Double" book.

Life with Henry. Satisfying, and therefore I write no novel. I can only make a life portrait of him.

The idea of living out the June in me, the half of me I so quickly recognized in June, strongly appeals to me.

Rank's passion is like an intoxicant. To live only for the intoxicating moments of life. I turn on the music and my blood begins to dance again.

Music.

I have read part of Rank's technique book. I said to him, "I'm falling in love with your books. Are you jealous?"

"That depends on how far they take you away from me."

Yes, there are two Ranks. Rank the philosopher and psychologist, and Rank the human being. The human being has only one quality: the power to love. It is what I want. I want wine.

The equivalents I find for wine and drugs are so potent, and they give life, not death.

The psychologist writes, "Frigidity: one of the typical expressions of an attempt at partialization carried too far . . ."

But how beautifully I enact "totality." I am moved and responsive with every particle of flesh and nerve. I play only a partial comedy. The warmth stays in me. I am branded enough. I give enough to remember and to yearn later.

So, biologically, I express my final holding back from Rank. Loving only partially.

"This would then give the definition that pleasure is a result of a successful partialization."

AUGUST 1, 1934

I LEFT FOR DINARD THAT FRIDAY ABSOLUTELY worn-out, amazed, amazed by Rank's sensuality, moved by it. He is so voluptuous and instinctive. A dim, fleshly life in that room. And then Henry; and then, in Dinard, gambling, winning; and then return to Rank and his appetite, and again almost surfeited with love.

A dim, unformulated world—like Hugh's—no words. I'm sinking again into twilight, nebulousness. Rank, like Hugh, is losing himself in my flesh and giving his soul. And I'm sinking, too. I don't think; I don't talk. Eduardo is the only one who sees and knows what it is all about. I live in a dream. A dream full of people, of love, of sensations.

I awake only to the most trivial pains—to imagined injuries, a slight offense from someone—and then I rush back to Hugh's vast, protective wings, when I feel that even at the highest peak of my life I can still be hypersensitive and invent injuries.

Obscurely, mysteriously, I enact for Rank all the gestures of my passion for Henry, aggrandizing the illusion of his complete possession of my senses; gestures and words repeated but unreal.

I have lost the desire to write.

August 2, 1934

DEPRESSION. EXHAUSTION. WHEN I CAN'T SEE RANK I miss him. His intensity, his gravity, his darkness, his wordlessness. A world of somnolence. I have descended into the impulsive, the instinctual. Yet Rank is quick and alive. He baffles me; he draws me, as Hugh did. Caverns.

I have suddenly ceased fighting Hugh. I feel close to him. He will never enter life, clarity, expression. Analysis has made him ascend into astrology, develop up there. In life he is just as absent, dim, joyless, slow, late, forgetful, nebulous. I let him be.

Our room on the rue Henri Rochefort, near the Parc Monceau. A quiet house where a pretty woman takes one up in the elevator without looking at one, and without asking questions. The little foyer, the room, the bathroom as on French prints. We telephone for lunch, and it is served in the foyer while we lie naked in bed, smoking. We hear the champagne cork exploding. The maid has disappeared. It is all like a game, and I am laughing and hungry. He eats quickly, and I eat slowly, like Henry. His big dark eyes have a heavy way of turning in their sockets. He seems to be looking over the rim of his own eyes, chin down. They are heavy and sad, like the wide mouth. We did not finish our champagne. We did not finish our cigarettes. His body is all flames again, from head to toe. Now he prolongs, prolongs, tastes to the full. It is hot when we awake. We take a bath together. He tells me that when he was a boy he liked to catch fish with his hands, his hands alone. And he did catch them. I get into the bathtub with my wristwatch on and laugh. It is all twilight because it is all feeling. We talk with caresses. We lie silent, but he buries his head on my breast. And he grunts with pleasure. Like a dark animal.

How flesh touching flesh generates a perfume, and the friction of words only pain and division. To formulate without destroying with the mind, without tampering, without killing, without withering. That is what I have learned by living, that delicacy and awe of the senses. That respect for the perfume will become my law in art.

It is the poet affirming himself because of the struggle against psychoanalysis.

A U G U S T   4 ,   1 9 3 4

I SIT NEXT TO A SENSUAL HILER, WHO HAS ASKED me to be his mistress, and if not his mistress, his analyst, and if not his analyst, would I smoke *kief* with him?

In eight weeks I will be living close to Henry. Always Henry. I would like to smoke with Hiler once, lie with him, because he looks so much like John. I would also like to enslave Bone completely, he who trembles when I approach him. He awaits it.

But I spend my free evenings with Henry and respond only to his caresses.

And yearn to see Rank and be caressed and enveloped by him. We have planned to be in London at the same time.

I have made my peace with Hugh, accepted his limitations in life, in wakefulness. I feel tenderness.

Realizing my human fulfillment completely and accepting my spiritual, mental loneliness. Possessing my own soul alone, here in the journal.

Cannot repair my novel yet. Have finished translation of volume one [of the diary] into English. Planning trip to London, where we are invited by the president of the bank. We will see Rebecca West. Planning my life in October.

Henry said, "When we live together I won't let you run around like that anymore."

AUGUST 7, 1934

JE BRÛLE. I AM BURNING WITH ALL MY DESIRES —all the dreams, all the sensations imaginable. Ideas, too.

I talked for the Bradleys yesterday like a torch; humor and lightness of touch, too (what a metaphor!). Talked abundantly.

And today I spend a few hours with Henry. I yearn for Rank tremendously at the same time. I see him at the school. We cannot meet. A physical hunger. I am caught, caught. I am aware of terrific egoism, that my vanity, conceit are increasing with my strength. Everything magnified by this expansion of myself. *Tant pis.* I amuse others, inspire them; those things cannot be done without a fat *I!*

Henry rereads my novel and falls in love with me anew. Says he would not change anything about me if he could. Has been weeping and laughing over the book. We hunt for our future home together.

And Rank flits by in the lens of my imagination while I am with Henry. Rank, swift and small and tense, and dark and passionate, like another part of Henry himself, one of Henry's faces, a double. I feel a strange correlation there; a half of Henry has split off and loved me.

My breasts are full and heavy; the shadows gather in between them. I have plenty of love to give—plenty, plenty. I am burning, burning like Joan of Arc.

"Thus psychology has become finally the worst enemy of the soul" (Rank).

Bradley thinks I am perhaps not old enough to tackle my big theme (Father story). Suggests I write a life of somebody as a preparation. I would like to be the Queen in *Alice in Wonderland* and shout crisply, "Off with his head!" But when he added later, "I have difficulty in speaking now—I am not used to my false teeth yet," I tore up the death decree. Although there were two serious crimes against him. He put Blanche Knopf up as arbiter of my novel and now tells me nonchalantly that she is absolutely without intelligence.

Listening to violin and dreaming of Rank's caresses tomorrow.

Dream: After talk with Eduardo about my feeling of being like a mother toward him, of being [my aunt] Tía, I come to see Tía. I find that her body has been cut off below the shoulders, above the breasts, and nailed down to a low platform on small wheels. Her face is vivid and handsome. I kneel down to speak to her, trying to pretend I notice nothing abnormal, but overwhelmed by anxiety and horror and the feeling that it is *me* this is happening to. I am wondering how she can be alive, since she has no heart, and how she can eat and digest. Suddenly Tía gets hysterical. She tugs and spills over like a scarab, with the platform in the air. Someone picks her up and places her right. I notice the effort has made her perspire and her dress shows wet around the neck.

This dream haunted me for days, and the vividness and realism of it were unforgettable. Rank: "The influence of the dream upon reality is just as great and apparently much more significant than the influence of reality on the dream."

The passion which Rank brings to me is contagious. I lose myself in it, each time more. It sweeps me away. The room glows with it. I am getting caught in his vibrancy. It is all flesh and silence. Yet I do not have his fears. He fears that it might not last, that I might run away from him. He feels lost and is beginning to fear the intensity.

He knows now that life is contained only in these two or three hours; he plunges into them. He is lascivious, voracious. When he awakes, talks, it is the other. I get disentangled, isolated again. I have less tenderness, less sympathy than I had for Henry after the passion. Almost none. Just that sensual response. No desire to give, no wild illusion. Yet when I beg him to let me be free of the school, he says only, "I will miss you," and because I think of him alone in that school, among the handful of Americans, I am going tomorrow, to see this little, unhappy man's eyes light up, to give him pleasure. But I hate the school as I hate the world, as I hate society, as I hate all but my own individually created world with my few, selected inhabitants.

AUGUST 10, 1934

*I*DISCOVERED DRAB REALITY, THE MEANING OF Lawrence's and Henry's railing and raving about the disintegration of the world (these were but words for me). Doom! The pessimism of Hugh, of men, the concrete anxieties of men losing power and money. I saw the tottering, the exodus of Americans, the changes and havocs brought by the world conditions. Individual lives shaken, poisoned, altered. The struggle and instability of it all. I was overwhelmed. It hurt me for a day. And then, with greater, furious, desperate stubbornness, I continued to build my individual life as if nothing were happening. I refuse to share the universal pessimism and inertia. I put on blinders, wax in my ears. I am one who will be shot while dancing.

Dancing. Rank and I alone in the studio of Chana Orloff, which he borrowed. We sink into savagery. Drunk. His fieriness is exasperating me. Rank envelops me, envelops me altogether, although when we awake from our physical closeness I awake free of him. It is my body he is laying siege to. It is my body which goes to him as it might be impelled to walk into flames. I go where there are flames.

Everybody is watching me burn. I asked once which one would be the *dark* Double, Father or I? It is I. He is living ascetically, and watching me, fascinated. *"Feux d'artifice,"* he says. I know I make him laugh, now, with my letters full of verve, and I make his blood run faster. He can no longer put any lids on me. Nobody can put lids on me. Not even the despair of the world.

Rank's eyes. They fill all the silences. His sense of completeness. I love giving him that, like the emotion of abandon Henry gave me. How sweet, too, the loss of one's self.

When we awake, move, talk, the wholeness splits into layers. There are layers on which we don't meet. His understanding is infinite, like a sea, but I sail alone on it. He is everything, immense but not personified, palpable except in love. Grand stretches of silence, of the unlived, the nonhuman. Suddenly he becomes distinct and formulates an idea about Henry's book on Lawrence, about women's psychology. It is sharp and acute. And then he oscillates, and totters again head and all, into the forest of my breasts, hair, legs. *Il veut se perdre, se noyer en moi.* He wants to lose himself, to drown himself in me.

I said good-bye to the school (exactly as I did when I was sixteen and I walked out of Wadleigh High). What is it I salvage from commonness, from the staleness of such places, people? My individual world.

AUGUST 11, 1934

I VISIT HENRY, WHO HAS PUT ALL HIS HOPES ON our life together. I take quinine to rush the delivery of the Easter egg. I reward Hugh for having been charmingly pedantic last night, winningly whole and sincere. When I am alone all day now I am not happy. Then all the insanities, the obsessions, the broodings return and assail me.

Sunday. This is my drug and my vice. This is the moment when I take up the mysterious pipe and indulge in deviations. Instead of writing a book, I lie back and I dream and I talk to myself. A drug. I turn away from reality into the refracted, I turn events into vapor, into languid dreams. This driving, impelling fever which keeps me tense and wide-awake during the day is dissolved in abandon, in improvisation, in beatitude and contemplation. I must relive my life in the dream. The dream is my only life. I seek in the echoes and reverberations the transfiguration which alone keeps wonder pure. Otherwise all magic is lost. Otherwise the man who ensorcells my body shows himself only by his deformities, and the homeliness becomes rust, rust falling on the articulations which should crack only under the weight of pleasure.

My drug. Covering all things with the mist of smoke, deforming and transforming as the night does. All matter must be fused this way for me through the lens of my vice, or the rust of living would slow down my rhythm to a sob.

AUGUST 14, 1934

I AM FALLING IN LOVE WITH RANK. I CANNOT LIVE without seeing him. It is a hunger, an unbearable hunger. I rushed to him today. It is like touching fire. He makes me terribly happy. Somewhere, deep down, deep down in darkness, we are close. I lie there and ask myself why he makes me so happy.

Rank gives me that most elusive of all realities, the reality of love, of active, explosive love. Love overwhelms him, hurts him as it does me, plows him; he almost sobs with the joy of abandon, the ecstasy of a caress. A caring so immense that it breaks him.

June said, and knew as well as I, that this is not Henry's way of loving. And she craved this, too. It is a feminine love, exalting, engrossing, absorbing, almost fantastical, abnormal. In this well of sameness, of equality of temperature, there is a rest from doubt and anxiety, there is a joy so rare, so rare. Caring. All feeling, all selflessness, all abandon, beyond one's self, far beyond all selves. The statues [in Chana Orloff's studio] are all around us, bulging pregnant women all, round flesh, ripe breasts, maternity, abundance.

I look up at the white ceiling, Rank's head on my breasts (they are real breasts now, full and heavy). Rank is talking about his despair. He may be forced to go to America. He cannot earn a living here. He hates to go. What are we going to do? I feel bruised, and a great, great pain. I suggest other solutions. I help him make plans. All our joy is in lying body to body. We don't want letters, talks, ideas. We have nothing to create together. His creation is accomplished. He wants to live. Resurrected in the flesh. And the pressure of reality is terrible.

I have clung to my "child," the Egg. I have taken longer than any woman to abort. I have baffled the *sage-femme*. Conception, because of the introversion of the matrix, was really impossible, yet it happened. Abortion should have taken two weeks. It has taken me four months. I have loved the feeling of growth in me, the physical well-being, the richness, the connection with the earth, the whole physical experience of pregnancy. I have dreams: Of a woman throwing a baby into the sea, and I furious with her. Of crippled babies I tried not to look at. Hatred of destruction. This seed in me, I have loved.

Consciously, I made my decision and carried it out. Unconsciously, I preserved the illusion. The stomach swelling, the feeling of expansion, of fullness.

I begin a letter to my Father and I am stopped by sobbing. Frustration and despair. He is no *Father*. I love an image of him which does not exist. When he is away this image begins to obsess me. I know that when he is near it is just misery.

I am not feeling well. Dana Ackeley came, a friend of Hugh's father. A voice just like John's, and exactly the same way of saying my name, so that when he said, "Anaïs, this lunch is good," it was as if he were showering red carnations on me. I am nothing but a sea of sensations, rudderless with feeling.

A U G U S T 1 5 , 1 9 3 4

I SEE HENRY IMAGINING AND CREATING OUR LIFE together, excited and wide-awake, planning how to sell his books, how much he will work; to see his joy at having "sex, a home, and food, and the best sex!"—gives me joy. He is tender and jealous, too. "Did you tell Rank it was our home?"*

I have not told Rank. I would have liked best of all to live alone. I am again not doing exactly what I *want* to do. And tenderness for Henry wins over everything. I am caught. If I could only forget Rank and become absolute again. All Henry's—blindly, fanatically. I am always getting bound up. I do not belong to myself at all! And all is well. Love is a divine slavery. I love. I love. I love. I couldn't leave Henry either. I could not live without Henry. Nor without Rank.

A U G U S T 2 1 , 1 9 3 4

I FEEL FOR RANK A REAL PASSION—A PHYSICAL blind hunger. Everything around the moment when we lie together is not as important as that fiery collision. I had wanted that so much, that darkness and intensity, that instinctive,

---

* Anaïs Nin had rented a studio at 18, Villa Seurat as her "office" and a place for Henry Miller to live.

purely passionate flow. We can't talk; we can't separate even to talk. He said, "Precisely because I have finished my creation without you, I can love you as a woman"—just a woman. Passion. No talk. No creation. No mother. No communion. No tenderness. Just collision and intoxication, conjunction and a physical hunger which nothing can appease.

Then he says, "I have never laughed so heartily in my life as I have with you." He has poured all his joyousness into me, his new joys. Laughed—in the Eskimo way? (The Eskimos say, in their strange language, "They laughed together"—meaning they made love.)

When we talked about social psychology and the double, I asked him why we only remember Robinson Crusoe on his island, whereas two-thirds of the book is really about Crusoe's travelings after he left the island. "But don't forget Friday," said Rank. (Friday we usually meet. Friday is my night out; a week and two months from Friday, he expects me in New York.) "Crusoe could bear his desert island because of Friday."

AUGUST 22, 1934

I AWOKE IN THE EARLY DAWN AND TALKED TO Hugh: "My definition of art is an act of human love. If I write a synthesis of Rank's work it will be about his life, not an intellectualization, but a dramatization." Fortunately, Hugh was half-asleep, and anyway, as Rank put it, Hugh's double, or other self, does not know at all what the other half thinks or does. In one half of himself he knows all I am doing; the other half does not know. These two halves never meet or communicate. So there is no realization, no crystallization.

Rank comes, talking about life. He talks about this love we don't call love, this love beyond love as we know it, immense, boundless, cosmic, not individualized, painless, limitless, selfless, but a level of flowingness I never knew before, nor he. I don't know where we live, but it is the biggest and highest world I have known.

"I denied myself life before, or it was denied me—first by my parents, then Freud, then my wife." His entrance into life is a beautiful spectacle.

Suddenly we are talking about dancing—Salome—which he would prefer to see me do rather than analysis, because it is closer to life. He hears how I had made an engagement with La Joselita to dance again at Easter, which I did not keep because I discovered I was pregnant. The child kept me from dancing, and then, the night before last, I wanted to dance to lose it—a savage dance!

Rank talks about dancing, dancing. So the current of life is so strong, so powerful, that I accept it and turn my back on art.

Allendy sends for me. He is sad, depressed. He feels he is dying. He feels he is losing me. He reaches out for me, begs, entreats, struggles. Says he feels he failed with me as a man, wants another chance. Two more chances. Loves me. "*Ma petite Anaïs*—it was you who made me perverse. Invited me, with all your imagination. I played for you a role, and I wasn't at ease. I didn't do it well."

"I don't want playing," I said.

"Well, let me be myself, then, and win you over again. You gave me a feeling of inferiority."

I wanted to laugh.

Dream: Going to my Father with my face tattooed, with needles stuck on it, for handsomeness. Feel very handsome. But when I come home and look in the mirror and take the pins off, my face falls apart in triangular pieces, shattered. I rush to my Mother: "What shall I do?" She very simply takes out a comb and begins combing my hair, which is silver-white, saying, "It will be all right in a moment. This is all you have to do."

A UGUST 27, 1934

*M*Y LIFE WILL ALWAYS BE A TRAGEDY. NOW I AM in Louveciennes with Henry, packing books for our home, making plans, filing our manuscripts, and thinking all the while of Rank, yearning for his love, hoping Henry will not desire me. I don't really want to live with Henry, yet I have made this life myself. Today I want to live *alone,* because I love too many men.

It is Henry now who clings, who is jealous, but is he not being given what his egoism calls for? A half love.

Tuesday. Saw a doctor, who discovered the *sage-femme* has accomplished nothing. I have to be operated on, and the child is six months old, and alive and normal. It will be almost a childbirth. It will take over a week. I had begun to feel so heavy, and there were slight tremors inside of my womb. I look down and see the round white stomach. My breasts are full of milk, a milk that is not yet sweet. As I walk up the hill toward Rank I think of the child. I could give it away to Mother, and that might deliver Joaquin. But otherwise it would be nothing but a fetter. It does not belong in my life with Henry; it does not belong with Rank, who has a child and too many burdens already; it does not belong to Hugh because it is not his child and could only cause him sorrow. It belongs nowhere. I am a mistress. I have already too many children. There are too many men without hope and faith in the world. Too much work to do, too many to serve and care for. Already I have more than I can bear. I am trying to give to Hugh, to Henry, and to Rank.

When I got to Rank he was sad and brooding. He is being pushed to go to New York, offered plenty of money and a job. He has debts. But he wants to stay here. "How can I go there and just work, without living? My life is here with you. I don't want to go. I never wanted success. Now less than ever."

These conflicts, which he helps others to solve, he must solve alone. I cannot help him. It is not a question of six months or a year, but of an indefinite time. Why don't I come with him as assistant?

I would follow him anywhere.

I know I want to go with him. I love his sadness, his tenacity, his caring. We could face New York together, work together. "If I could be happy in my life," said Rank.

AUGUST 29, 1934

AFTER SEEING RANK SO SAD, ONLY FOR AN HOUR, I suddenly felt a great distress, an immense distress. Hugh was not arriving from London until midnight. I telephoned Henry, who was at the Lowenfelses', asking him to join me. He was slow and hesitant. It hurt me. I hung up brusquely. I went to Louveciennes. But this morning I went to him, meaning to call him a monster and remembering, for some unknown reason, the Henry who, while his wife was being operated on, was fucking a Negress on the table. His callousness. But the "monster" had left the Lowenfelses' last night all upset, had looked for me in several cafés, had come home at ten and waited for me, had a headache from worry, and looked quite ravaged. All my feelings about his imagined cruelty vanished. He would not let me have lunch with the Lowenfelses. He was terribly anxious about the abortion, terribly tender. But I would not let him take me. I was thinking of Rank, whom I was meeting at three.

Rank and I went to the boulevard Suchet apartment, which is empty. And we were overwhelmed with sadness. It stifled our desire. His going to London for four days seemed like a foretaste of his departure for America.

All night, neither one of us had slept.

I was awake, thinking I could not bear life without him, that again I had thrown myself into a purely physical passion and it was becoming love, a slavery, a whole. Not just the hour of possession. And pain and seriousness came with love.

I don't understand.

The violence of my feeling for Rank is almost terrifying.

When he left, I wandered through the place, restless and nervous. I occupied my hands. I thought how strange it was that Rank was living a block away when I lived on the boulevard Suchet, when my life was so empty and so tragic. He was living and working where I often passed in my walks, in those walks I took desiring John and imagining John kissing me. Memories. The life in Suchet. The explosion of color and dancing, together with the starvation of soul and senses.

The place was lovely. I prepared the bed to receive the doctor tomorrow. I was glad of the soothing, glad of the decor in which the Princess was going to abort.

I sat in the studio, talking to my child. I told my child he should be glad not to be thrust into this black world in which even the greatest joys are tainted with pain, in which we are slaves to material forces. He kicked and stirred. So full of energy, oh, my child, my half-created child that I will thrust back into the *néant* again. Back into obscurity and unconsciousness, and the paradise of nonbeing. I have known you; I have lived with you. You are only the future. You are the abdication. I live in the present, with men who are closer to death. I want men, not a future extension of myself into a branch. My little one, not born yet, I feel your small feet kicking against my womb. My little one, not born yet, it is very dark in the room you and I are sitting in, just as dark as it must be for you inside of me, but it must be sweeter for you to be lying in the warmth than it is for me to be seeking in this dark room the joy of not knowing, not feeling, not seeing, the joy of lying still and quiet in utter warmth and darkness. All of us forever seeking again this warmth and this darkness, this being alive without pain, this being alive without anxiety or fear or aloneness. You are impatient to live; you kick with your small feet, my little one, not born yet; you ought to die. You ought to die before knowing light or pain or cold. You ought to die in warmth and darkness. You ought to die because you are fatherless.

You and I, my journal, alone, with the bottles of medicine, in the sumptuous bedroom. Hugh has gone to get medicine. The German doctor has been here. While he operates we talk about the persecution of the Jews in Berlin. I help him wash the instruments. I wear the "charm" which Rank gave me. I dream of him. In this same room, a few years ago, I suffered from the emptiness of my life. Now I am suffering from an overabundance! I got up so gaily, as if I were going on a voyage. I am so happy, no amount of physical pain can cower me. Life is full of wonder, even when I see the bloodstained rags. I thought this morning of how Henry greeted me once: "Here is the Princess Aubergine." And I telephoned him this morning: "Come and visit the palace of the Princess Aubergine, where the Prince Aubergin will be born." And an hour later I was opening my legs to instruments. The doctor said I could not have a child without a Caesarian operation. I am too small. I was not built for maternity. I am surrounded with so much love that it makes me weep.

You are a child without a father, just as I was a child without a father. You are born of man, but you have no father. This man who married me, it was he who fathered me. I could not bear it that he should take care of another and that I should be an orphan again. This care is the only care I have known. With everybody else it was I who did all the caring. I nursed the whole world. When there was a war I wept for all the wounds inflicted, and wherever there was injustice I struggled to return life, to re-create hope. The woman loved and cared too much. And inside of this woman there was still a child without a father, a child who did not die when it should have died. There was still the ghost of a little girl forever wailing inside, bewailing the loss of a father. This man who married me, he took care of her, and now, if you came, you would take him for a father and this little ghost would never let me alone. It would knock at the windows; it would cry at every caress he gave you. You are also the child of an artist, my child unborn. And this man is not a father; he is a child, he is the artist. He needs all the care, all the warmth, all the faith for himself. There is no end to his needs. He needs faith, indulgence, humor. He needs worship. He needs to be the only one in the world we created together. He is my child, and he would hate you. And if he did not hate you, he would hate your sickness, your wailing, and the woman who bore a child. I must nourish his creation and his hopes with all I have. He would cast you aside. He would run away from you, just as he ran away from his wife and his other little girl, because he is not a father. He feels awkward before a human child with needs. He does not understand the needs of others. He is too full of his own hunger. You would be abandoned, and you would suffer as I suffered when I was abandoned by my father, who was not a father but the artist, and the child. It would be better to die, my child, unborn; it would be better to die than to be abandoned, for you would spend your life haunting the world for this lost father, this fragment of your body and soul, this lost fragment of your very self. *There is no father on earth*. The father is this shadow of God the Father cast on the world, a shadow larger than man. This shadow you would worship and seek to touch, dreaming day and night of its warmth and of its greatness, dreaming of it covering you and lulling you, larger than a hammock, as large as the sky, big enough to hold your soul and all your fears, larger than man or woman, than church or house, the shadow of a magic father which is nowhere to be found—it is the shadow of God the Father. It would be better if you died inside of me, quietly, in the warmth and in the darkness.

Hugh drove us to the *clinique*. I was shaved and prepared for the major operation. I felt resigned, and yet, deep down, terrified of the anaesthetic. Remembrances of other anaesthetics. Feeling of oppression. Difficulty in breathing. Anxiety. Like a birth-trauma dream. Suffocation. Fear of death. Fear of yielding to eternal sleep. Fear of dying. But I lay smiling and making jokes. I was wheeled to the operating room. Legs tied, raised, the pose of love, in an operating room, with the clatter of instruments and the smell of antiseptic, and the voice of the doctor, and I trembling with cold, blue with cold and anxiety.

The smell of ether. The cold numbness trickling through the veins. The heaviness, the paralysis, but the mind still clear and struggling against death, against sleep. The voices growing dimmer. The incapacity to answer. The desire to sigh, to sob, to murmur. "*Ça va,*

madame; ça va, madame? Ça va, madame, ç a v a m a d a m e ç a v a-
m a d a m e . . . ." The heart beats desperately, loudly, as if
about to burst. Then you sleep, you fall, you roll, you dream, dream,
dream; you are anxious. Dream of a drilling machine drilling between
your legs, but into numbness. Drilling. You awake to voices. Vomiting.
The voices growing louder: *"Ça va, madame? Elle vomit. Faut-il lui en
donner encore? Non. C'est fini."* I weep. The heart, the heart is pressed
and weary. Breathing so difficult. My first thought is to reassure the
doctor, so I say, *"C'est très bien, très bien, très bien."*

I lie in my bed. When I see Hugh, I weep. I come back from
death, from darkness, out of fear, an absence from life.

The doctor waits anxiously. At ten o'clock, he examines me again,
probes me, hurts me. Exhausts me. The next morning, he has to operate
again.

I have talked with Hugh about my fear of anaesthetic. He has
urged me not to fight it, to let go, to think of it as a drug, as a forgetting.
Had I not always wanted drugs, wanted to forget?

For the second time I yield to the ether. I yield to sleep. I resign
myself to die. And the anxiety is lessened. I let myself go.

It is shorter this time. The awakening is less heavy with anxiety.
I had worn a towel, like a nun, so as not to wet my hair.

I felt that if Rank would only come everything would be well. But
he was in London. Toward eight o'clock I had several spasms of pain.
The doctor thought it would happen. He sent for a nurse. I made
several fruitless efforts. He tormented me with his hands. I only ejected
the balloon which he had placed inside of me during the operation. It
was punctured and therefore ineffectual. He was in despair, tried to
urge me to labor. I labored fruitlessly until midnight. I was exhausted.
Then he began to prod me with his instruments. I was at the end of
my endurance. I begged him only for a rest, just to let me sleep for a
few hours. I could not bear any more. He let me.

I slept fitfully and called out to Rank, called him with all my being.
In the morning, the doctor came and said he would let me rest all
day. Early in the morning I had asked Hugh to telephone Rank to
come. And as soon as he had done this, I was relieved. Rank said he
would be in Paris that evening.

I combed my hair; I powdered, perfumed myself, painted my

eyelashes. I sent for Henry. He came, looking haggard and desperate: "Oh, Anaïs, Anaïs, what torture. God, I don't know what to say, but I love you, I love you." We embraced. Hugh came. Eduardo.

At six o'clock Rank came. And this joy I felt was so terrible, so immense. All this love calling me back to life. He came. Overflowing with love. I was illumined. I revived. I felt his strength.

Sunday evening.

At eight o'clock I was taken to the operating room. I lay stretched on a table. I had no place to rest my legs. I had to keep them raised. Two nurses leaned over me. In front of me stood the German doctor with the face of a woman and eyes protruding with anger and fear. For two hours I had been making violent efforts. The child inside of me was six months old, and yet it was too big for me. I was exhausted; the veins in me were swelling with the strain. I had pushed with my whole being, I had pushed as if I wanted this child out of my body and hurled into another world. "Push, push with all your strength!" Was I pushing with *all* my strength? All my strength? No. A part of me did not want to push out the child. The doctor knew it. That is why he was angry, mysteriously angry. He knew.

A part of me lay passive, did not want to push anyone, not even this dead fragment of myself, out into the cold, outside of me. All of me which chose to keep, to lull, to embrace, to love, all of me which carried, preserved, and protected, all of me which imprisoned the whole world in its passionate tenderness, this part of me would not thrust the child out, nor this past which had died in me. Even though it threatened my life, I could not break, tear out, separate, surrender, open and dilate and yield up a fragment of a life like a fragment of the past; this part of me rebelled against pushing the child, or anyone, out into the cold, to be picked up by strange hands, to be buried in a strange place, to be lost.

He knew—the doctor. A few hours before, he loved me, adored me, served me. Now he was angry. And I was angry, with a black anger, at this part of me which refused to push, to kill, to separate, to lose. Push! Push! Push with all your strength! I pushed with anger, with despair, with frenzy, with the feeling that I would die pushing, as one exhales the last breath, that I would push out everything inside of me; and my soul with all the blood around it, and the sinews with my heart inside of them would choke, and my body itself would open and smoke would rise, and I would feel the ultimate incision of death.

The nurses leaned over me and they talked to each other while I rested. Then I pushed until I heard my bones cracking, until my veins swelled. I closed my eyes so hard I saw lightning and waves of red and purple.

There was a stir in my ears, a beating as if the tympana had burst. I closed my lips so tightly the blood was trickling. My legs felt enormously heavy, like marble columns, like immense marble columns crushing my body. I was pleading for someone to hold them. The nurse laid her knee on my stomach and shouted, "Push! Push! Push!" Her perspiration fell on me. The doctor paced up and down angrily and impatiently: "We will be here all night. Three hours now." The head was showing, but I had fainted. Everything was blue, then black. The instruments seemed to be gleaming before my closed eyes. Knives sharpened in my ears. Ice and silence.

Then I heard voices, at first talking too fast for me to understand. A curtain was parted; the voices still tripped over each other, falling fast like a waterfall, with sparks, and hurting my ears. The table was rolling gently, rolling. The women were lying in the air. Heads. Heads hung where the enormous white bulbs of the lamps hung. The doctor was still walking, the lamps moved, the heads came near, very near, and the words came more slowly.

They were laughing. One nurse was saying, "When I had my first child I was all ripped to pieces. I had to be sewed up again, and then I had another, and had to be sewed up, and then I had another."

The nurses talked. The words kept turning, like on a disk. They kept saying over and over again that the bag would not come out, that the child should have slipped out like a letter in a letter box, that they were so tired with so many hours of work. They laughed at what the doctor said. They said there was no more of that bandage, it was too late to get any. They washed instruments, and they talked, they talked, they talked.

"Please hold my legs! Please hold my legs! Please hold my legs! PLEASE HOLD MY LEGS!" I am ready again. By throwing my head back I can see the clock. I have been struggling four hours. It would be better to die. Why am I alive and struggling so desperately? I could not remember why I should want to live. Why *live?* I could not remember anything. I heard women talk. I saw eyes bulging out, and blood. Everything was blood and pain. What was it to *live?* How could one feel to *live?*

I have to push. I have to push. That is a black point, a fixed point in eternity. At the end of a long, dark tunnel. I have to push. A voice saying, "Push! Push! Push!" A knee on my stomach, and the marble of the legs and the head too large, and I have to push. Am I pushing or am I dying? The light up there, the immense, round, blazing white light, is drinking me. It drinks me. It drinks me slowly, sucks me into space; if I do not close my eyes it will drink all of me. I seep upward, in long icy threads, too light, and yet inside there is a fire, too, the nerves are twisted, there is no repose from this long tunnel dragging me, or from me pushing myself out of the tunnel, or from the child being pushed out of me and the light drinking me. If I do not close my eyes, the light will drink my whole being, and I will no longer be able to push myself out of the tunnel.

Am I dying? The ice in the veins, the cracking of the bones, this pushing in blackness with a small shaft of light in the eyes like the edge of a knife, the feeling of a knife cutting the flesh, the flesh somewhere tearing as if it were burned through by a flame—somewhere my flesh is tearing and the blood is spilling out. I am pushing in the darkness, in utter darkness. I am pushing, pushing until I open my eyes and I see the doctor, who is holding a long instrument which he swiftly thrusts into me, and the pain makes me howl. A long animal howl.

"That will make her push," he says to the nurse. But it does not. It paralyzes me with pain. He wants to do it again. I sit up with fury and I shout at him, "If you do that again I won't push. Don't you dare do that again, don't you dare!" The heat of my anger warms me; all the ice and pain are melted in the fury. I have an instinct that what he has done is unnecessary, that he has done it because he is in a rage, because the needles on the clock keep turning, the dawn is coming, and the child does not come out and I am losing strength, and the injections do not produce the spasm. The body—neither the nerves nor the muscles do anything to eject this child. Only my will and my strength. My fury frightens him, and he stands away and waits.

These legs I opened to joy, this honey that flowed out in the joy —now the legs are twisted in pain and the honey flows with the blood. The same pose and the same wetness of passion, but this is dying and not loving.

I look at the doctor pacing up and down or bending to look at the head, which is barely showing. The legs like scissors, and the head barely showing. He looks baffled, as before a savage mystery, baffled by this struggle. He wants to interfere with his instruments, while I struggle with nature, with myself, with my child, and with the meaning I put in it all, with my desires to give and to hold, to keep and to lose, to live and to die. No instrument can help me. His eyes are furious. He would like to take a knife. He has to watch me and wait.

I want to remember all the time why I should want to live. I am all pain and no memory. The lamp has ceased drinking me. I am too weary to move even toward the light or to turn my head and look at the clock. Inside of my body there are fires, there are bruises, the flesh is in pain. The child is not a child; it is a demon lying half-choked between my legs, keeping me from living, strangling me, showing only its head, until I die in its grasp. The demon lies inert at the door of the womb, blocking life, and I cannot rid myself of it.

The nurses begin to talk again. I say, *"Let me alone."* I put my two hands on my stomach and very softly, with the tips of my fingers, I drum, drum, drum, on my stomach, in circles. Round and round, softly, with eyes open in great serenity. The doctor comes near and looks with amazement. The nurses are silent. Drum, drum, drum, drum, in soft circles, in soft, quiet circles. "Like a savage," they whisper. The mystery.

Eyes open, nerves quiet. I drum gently on my stomach for a long while. The nerves begin to quiver . . . a mysterious agitation. I hear the ticking of the clock . . . inexorably, separately. The little nerves awake, stir. I say, "I can push now!" And I push violently. They are shouting, "A little more! Just a little more!"

Will the ice come, and the darkness, before I am through? At the end of the dark tunnel a knife gleams. I hear the clock and my heart.

I say, "Stop!" The doctor holds the instrument, and he is leaning over. I sit up and shout at him with fury, "Don't you dare!" He is afraid again. "Let me alone, all of you!"

I lie back so quietly. I hear the ticking. Softly I drum, drum, drum. I feel my womb stirring, dilating. My hands are so weary, so weary, they will fall off. They will fall off, and I will lie there in darkness. The womb is stirring and dilating. Drum, drum, drum, drum. "I am ready!" The nurse puts her knee on my stomach. There is blood in my eyes, blood, blood. A tunnel. I push into this tunnel, I bite my lips and push. There is fire, flesh ripping, and no air. Out of the tunnel! All my blood is spilling out. "Push! Push! It is coming! It is coming!" I feel the slipperiness, the sudden deliverance; the weight is gone. Darkness.

I hear voices. I open my eyes. I hear them saying, "It was a little girl. Better not show it to her." All my strength is coming back. I sit up. The doctor shouts, "For God's sake, don't sit up, don't move!"

"Show me the child!"

"Don't show it," says the nurse. "It will be bad for her."

The nurses try to make me lie down. My heart is beating so loud I can hardly hear myself repeating, "Show it to me!" The doctor holds it up. It looks dark, and small, like a diminutive man. But it is a little girl. It has long eyelashes on its closed eyes; it is perfectly made, and all glistening with the water of the womb.

It was like a doll, or an old miniature Indian. About one foot long. Skin on bones. No flesh. But completely formed. The doctor told me afterward it had hands and feet exactly like mine, and long eyelashes. The head was bigger than the average. It was black. The child had died—strangled, perhaps, or from the operations. One more day and the tumor in its head would have infected me. I would have died. As I looked at the little Indian for a moment I hated it for all the pain it had caused me, and because it was a little girl and I had fancied it to be a boy.

It was only later that this flare of anger turned into great sadness, regrets, long dreams of what this little girl might have been. A dead creation, my first dead creation. The deep pain caused by any death and any destruction. The failure of my motherhood, of at least the embodiment of it, the abdication of one kind of motherhood for the sake of a higher one.

But all my hopes of real, human, simple, direct motherhood lying dead. The simple human flowering denied to me because of the dream, again, the sacrifice to other forms of creation. The necessity in me to produce more subtle flowerings. Nature conniving to keep me as Bilitis, as the Virgin. Nature arranging my destiny as man's woman, not child's woman. Nature shaping my body for passion alone, for the love of man. This child, which meant a simple, primitive connection with the earth, this child, a prolongation of myself, now cast off so that I would live out my destiny as the mistress, my life as a woman. This child, which meant self-sufficiency and separation from man. My child. My possession.

So wholly woman had I become that I became also the mother, the mother independent from the man she loves, with her flesh-and-blood image of the man she loves. But for man, for Henry, for love of Henry, or of my life as a woman, I killed the child. To protect Henry, to be free, I killed the child. Not to be abandoned, I killed the child. I did not give myself to the earth or to the lifelong task of nursing a child. I love man as lover and creator. Man as father I do not trust. I do not believe in man as father. I do not trust man as father. I stand by man the lover and creator. With him I feel an alliance. In man the father I feel an enemy, a danger.

This little girl, a prolongation of myself and of Henry, I reabsorbed into myself. It is to remain in me, a part of me. I gathered myself all together again. My womb did not remain dilated, open, bleeding for a selfless giving. I returned to life.

When I saw the child I thought that it looked like a diminutive Henry. The bald head, the thick, open mouth, the nose, the leanness of it, something almost nonhuman, not mental looking, a little bit monstrous. Or was the vision of Henry as my child definitely formed and associated with this creation of my flesh and blood? The womb love—a love that does not come from that flame between the legs at the petal external flowering of the womb's mouth, but from deeper beyond, inside the womb, like that little Indian who slipped out so easily, like a penis swimming in my overabundant honey.

I had sat up on the operating table to look at the child. The doctor and nurses were amazed by my aliveness and curiosity. They expected tears. I still had my eyelash makeup on. But afterward I lay back and almost fainted with weakness.

In my bed, when I saw Hugh again, I wept. He was terrified when he saw all the veins on my face cracked. We drank champagne. I fell asleep. Glory, glory of deliverance. The sleep of deliverance. Hugh had almost gone mad when he heard my screams.

Sleep. Morning toilette. Perfume. Powder. The face all well. I can see it in the long Egyptian hand mirror Hugh has given me with a poem. The rose silk jacket he bought me when I asked for an attractive hospital costume.

Rank came at eleven. We said very little. I saw Henry, Eduardo, Hugh as in a dream. Immense weakness. Henry and Hugh had suffered like primitive men, in their guts, with me. Henry said he had had terrible pains in his stomach all night.

The next day I suffered an intestinal poisoning. A bad night.

Wednesday all was well. But a new anxiety appeared. The breasts began to hurt. Henry came and announced the coming out of *Tropic of Cancer*. I said, "Here is a birth which is of greater interest to me." Henry and Rank met. I felt nothing. Just languid. Everybody was amazed by my appearance. The morning after the birth: pure complexion, luminous skin, shining eyes. Henry was overwhelmed. He was awed. He said it made him weak to see me. He was vulnerable like a woman. Weeping and trembling like a woman. Eduardo brought me an orchid. The little nurse from the Midi left all her other patients waiting to comb my hair lovingly. All the nurses kissed and fondled me. I was bathing in love, feeling languid and calm and light, too.

And then my breasts got hard with the milk. Too much milk. An amazing amount of milk from such a small person. So hard and painful.

Thursday, Rank came and he was in despair to be going to New York.

The night was a nightmare. I felt again in the grip of some dark menace. I imagined my breasts spoiled forever. Ulcers. The nurses leaning over my bed seemed malevolent to me. The way they leaned over, examined me, predicted the worst things, it affected me, frightened me.

I could not sleep. I began to think about religion, about pain. I had not yet come to the end of pain. I thought of the God I had received with such fervor at Communion and whom I had confused with my Father. I thought of Catholicism. Wondering. Where was God, where was the fervor I had as a child? I got tired of thinking. I fell asleep with my hands folded on my breasts as for death. And I died again, as I had died again other times.

I died and was reborn again in the morning, when the sun came to the wall in front of my window. A blue sky, and the sun on the wall. The nurse had raised me to see the new day. I lay there feeling the sky, and myself one with the sky, feeling the sun, and myself one with the sun, and abandoning myself to immensity and to God. God penetrated my whole body. I trembled and shivered with an immense, immense joy. Cold and fever and light, an illumination, a visitation, through the whole body, the shiver of a presence. The light and the sky in the body, God in the body, and I melting into God. I melted into God. No image. I felt space, gold, purity, ecstasy, immensity, a profound, ineluctable communion. I wept with joy. I knew everything then; I knew everything I had done was right. I knew that I needed no dogmas to communicate with Him; I needed but to live, to love, and to suffer. I needed no man or priest to communicate with Him. By living my life, my passions, my creation to the limit, I communed with the sky, the light, and with God. I believed in the transubstantiation of blood and flesh. I had come upon the infinite through the flesh and through the blood. Through flesh and blood and love, I was in the Whole, in God. I cannot say more. There is nothing more to say. The greatest communions come so simply. But from that moment on I have felt my connection with God, an isolated, wordless, individual, full connection which gives me an immense joy and a sense of the greatness of life, the elimination of human time and boundaries. Eternity. I was born. I was born woman. To love God and to love man supremely, and separately. I was born to a great quietude, a superhuman joy above and beyond all my human sorrows, transcending pain and tragedy. This joy I found in love of man and in creation, completed in communion.

The doctor came, examined me, could not believe his eyes. I was intact, as if nothing had ever happened to me. I could leave the clinic. It was a soft summer day. I walked with joy at having escaped the great mouth of the monster.

At five o'clock I left for Louveciennes. The day was soft and lulling. I sat on a deck chair in the garden. Eduardo took care of me. I dreamed and rested.

The walk through the forest. Rank desiring me and tortured not to be able to touch me. The dinner out in the garden. Rank touched my knees under the table. We were both drunk and hungry.

Louveciennes. Henry came Monday. He found me beautiful. My rhythm is slow. I am resisting entering life again, pain, activity, conflicts. Thursday I go to the studio Henry and I chose together. Henry is joyous. Everything is beginning. The day is soft but perishable, like a sigh, the last sigh of summer, heat and foliage. Soft and sad, the end of summer, leaves falling. And my love for Henry dying softly and gently, without drama, my love seeming to sleep, or to die?

SEPTEMBER 17, 1934

HENRY IS HAPPY AND SECURE AND FINALLY EN-slaved. "You don't know, Anaïs—while you were in the hospital, I couldn't eat and I couldn't sleep. I almost went crazy. I felt your pains in my stomach. I lay in bed and my whole body ached when I thought of you."

And I am moving away. I don't feel his joy. I don't feel the studio.

It is all a dream. I worked there; I hammered, I cleaned, I gave orders, I made lists.

I felt weak, languid. As we walked down the street in the dying softness, I listened to his voice and tried to remember what it once made me feel. It seemed to me that I was simply very weary of loving, that I was turning and resting in those who loved me. I tried to remember. How I let things die their slow seasonal deaths and cannot hasten any act of destruction. I cannot tell Henry I do not love him anymore. I do not believe that I do not love him anymore.

The next day, in the studio closet, while cleaning, I found a photograph of Artaud, who had lived there. Artaud, who feared so much the *envoûtements,* the spells, and the demoniac evil wrought by sticking pins into a photograph. I hung it up for fun at the head of our bed and made Henry laugh. Henry was sad because he had insulted his editor. "I destroy all your work." The sun poured into the studio. Henry was laughing at my fantasies of Artaud. I thought of Rank leaving for New York.

SEPTEMBER 19, 1934

RANK AND I MET AT BOULEVARD SUCHET. WE CAressed violently, struggled to find our joys again. But it was all darkened by the pain of separation. In talk we tried to find the constructive element of his trip. I felt an immense distress because lately I had only thought of my lover, not of *Dr*. Rank. Not of his philosophy, but of his caresses. But now, now, when I would be deprived of him, could I live with his books, his creation?

We began to laugh, to laugh at "Dr." Rank. His eyes laughed. He told me about a humorous book he wanted to write on Mark Twain. "The suicide of the double." We struggled against tragedy with humor.

SEPTEMBER 21, 1934

*H*ENRY AND I WORKED IN THE STUDIO. I HAD LUNCH with Louis Andard and his wife. Then I met Rank, and all our humor had vanished.

I went with Teresa to the studio, to clean. I came late. Intending to stay there all night because Hugh was in Switzerland. But Hugh suddenly sent a message he was arriving at midnight. Henry and I had dinner together. His disappointment made me sad.

SEPTEMBER 23, 1934

*M*OTHER ARRIVED, DISAPPOINTED THAT I HAD NOT had the child, not caring much about me or my suffering, urging me to try again.

At three I met Rank, but I was in a dark, dangerous mood. Rebellion against our destiny, hating him for the feelings he aroused in me, desiring to hurt him, betray him, forget him, desiring destruction because he was forced to leave me. I was looking out of the window, angry and rebellious, and the tigress fully awakened. But when I saw him walking toward the apartment so quickly, so intensely, I melted completely. Still, while I was combing my hair I did say, "Tonight I am sleeping in my studio for the first time." And I saw that I had hurt him. My studio. Montparnasse. Henry.

At the studio I cooked dinner for Henry, and we sat down and wrapped and addressed copies of his book. He was gentle and tender. And then he began to dance savagely around the studio, crowing,

"Coquelicot! Coquelicot!" And laughing and joking about this new name for his Sir Thomas, he took me. We woke up to the sun, to late breakfast, and to housework.

The Andards took me to their house in Sèvres.

S E P T E M B E R   2 7 ,   1 9 3 4

I SPENT THE DAY IN PARIS. SAW A *VOYANT* WHO read all that was on my mind. Predicted a trip to America. (I discovered afterward that "telepathy" was the way Freud had interpreted clairvoyance, palm reading, etc., and this had also been *my* explanation.)

At five o'clock I happened to telephone Hugh. Rank had telephoned Hugh, early in the morning, that it was absolutely necessary for him to see me. When I telephoned Rank, he asked me to come right away.

I rushed to him. He had been restless, terribly nervous, all night and all day. And then it was all unleashed, his suffering, his jealousy of Henry. I myself, the last time we had been together, had felt a need of truth and had told him about not being happy in the studio, not desiring this move, and had asked him: Did he want me to give it up?

And he, he knew the studio meant Henry. He could not bear it. We had long ago ceased to talk about Henry. But I cannot lie to Rank.

He said he had not wanted to be possessive. He had wanted to let me solve my own life. To be objective, to be *Dr.* Rank. But he couldn't. And I loved so much his imperiousness, his madness, his impulsiveness—it moved me. His suffering, like mine over Henry. His impatience. I see all the time in him this immense, overwhelming caring which I gave to Henry and which makes the other almost mute by its very power. Only, I am not mute with Rank. I get on fire. I answer with all my being.

And the next day came the climax. He broke through the shell of my frigidity. I abandoned myself to an absolute love. Climax. Three hours of drunkenness and talk and tumult. The lover in him is the most fiery and moving I have known.

In the evening we met again for dinner at his place. Dr. Endler, Chana Orloff, and he and I, glowing with the most absolute joy.

Henry seems now so old, so burned away.

Mrs. Guiler lives in Louveciennes, has a maid, eats breakfast in bed, eats the pheasants killed by Lani and Louis Andard, listens to the radio, gives orders to the gardener, pays her bills with checks, sits by an open fire, copies the diary and translates the first volume, dreams by the window, gets restless to be away from Louveciennes.

Mrs. Miller peels potatoes, grinds coffee, sweeps, markets, wraps books for Henry, walks down the cobblestone street, which seems Italian, drinks out of chipped cups, uses the worn linen not needed in Louveciennes, repairs the phonograph, takes the bus, talks a great deal, takes long naps with Mr. Miller, smokes a great deal, and objects secretly to the invasion of people walking in and out of the place. Stupid people.

Anaïs is caught by Rank's love and wants to go to New York with him.

Rank can only bear the idea of New York because I have promised to go there. He will struggle to keep me there. He asked me if my religion helped me. I said it somehow eliminated the human conception of time. Enlarged it. I feel two months are short in the span of eternity.

The days of sad moods. We feel there is nothing left for us to do but eat each other up completely. "But even then," we say, laughing, "I'm afraid we could not digest our problem."

In boulevard Suchet, where we meet, there are all the flowers I had received during my illness, withering away in the fireplace. I often look at them and secretly desire to be back in the days of my convalescence, the moment of quietude, beatitude, before the stronger, more vivid life presented its steely, inexorable elements again.

O C T O B E R   6 ,   1 9 3 4

O N MONDAY, OCTOBER 1, MRS. MILLER PACKED A
valise and went to 18, Villa Seurat after lunch-
ing with Mother and Joaquin and a walk with Joaquin through the
Bois—a lean, serious, tender Joaquin inspired by a stay with Manuel
de Falla—and after sitting at the Café Marignan with Henry, Fred,
Mr. and Mrs. Andard, discussing the possibility of Andard publishing
Fred's book, which I gave him to read.

Fred, Henry, and Mrs. Miller had dinner together. A grateful Fred.
Friends again because Andard, reading Fred's book, believes Fred loved
me and is touched by Fred's description of me. He says that it is mostly
because I am in it that he loves the book.

Henry exulting in his studio, the cooking, the restfulness, the good
feeling it gives him.

The next morning I leave Villa Seurat to telephone Rank and
Hugh. Rank tells me to come and see him because he has news for
me—good news. I rush over in a taxi. He is exultant because Chana
Orloff was impressed with me, my head and my body, and wanted to
do a sculpture of me immediately. She had raved about my beauty
and intelligence, and Mrs. Rank had joined in. Rank was pleased,
excited. I at first held back, in self-defense. I had been the victim, as
well as the favorite, of painters and sculptors. More posing, more
fatigue, more sacrifices, more giving. No. But only for a minute. The
enthusiasm of Rank, the powerful personality of Chana Orloff, her
talent, won me over. I liked that big, homely, forceful woman with
her obsession for maternity themes. So I promised to see her. Rank
said he would buy the sculpture. He had telephoned Hugh for the
second time, imperiously and imprudently. An impulsive, mad, unwise
Rank, making all the reckless gestures I like.

At two-thirty [on October 3], Anaïs went to meet Rank at the Parc Monceau room. She proposed the idea of spending the night en route to Le Havre with Rank, the whole night. He was being driven to Le Havre. She would travel by train, meet him somewhere. At Rouen. Plans were made.

At four-thirty, Mrs. Miller posed for Chana Orloff, who lives on Villa Seurat. Orloff came to see the studio. Mrs. Miller introduced herself as "Mrs. Miller," revealed her double life in an interesting, puzzling, vague, symbolical fashion, chuckling inwardly to be deceiving the world again, to be creating a misunderstanding, to be acting Mrs. Miller when she was preparing a flight—a change.

Chana Orloff was surprised, stimulated, interested.

At nine o'clock, Henry went to the café and my first patient arrived: Mr. Stanko, hairdresser, Communist, Jugoslavian Jew. I did a shrewd and swift investigation, found no neurosis, and told him so. That was the end of psychoanalysis, which I have been hating vigorously now, ever since I became a woman and lost my assumed intellectuality. (Rank says I am not intellectual.)

Henry returned to find Mr. Stanko and me drinking coffee together. Talk. *Voilà.* Henry had been mortally scared by a dog and looked blanched and weak.

Hugh seems anxious for me to go to New York to get away from Henry. I have told him Rank is my father. Hugh fears my studio and Montparnasse and Henry more than New York and Rank. Rank could get me a dancing job.

[O CTOBER 5, 1934]

*M*ET LOUIS ANDARD AT THE CAFÉ MARIGNAN. AN-dard, a tall, rough man of forty-seven, a novelist who has lived in India, the publisher of Maurice Dekobra. Met him on the train going to Dinard. Would not talk to him. He forced me to. A fanatical believer in the *voyant* I saw. Occupied with peace propaganda. Marked my novel in this manner: "Page 48: I would like to be that man." Talked inspiredly about the predominance of feeling in the novel when he visited me during my convalescence. Believes astrology predicted our meeting, loves me, says he will wait for me forever, will serve me, wants to give me money or anything I need, says that for him I am not complicated at all but the Anaïs of the child journal which he wept over. "After crying so much, how is it that your eyes are still beautiful? I never want you to cry again, never. You frighten me. Worry me. When I saw the moving man taking things to the studio that day in Louveciennes, I wondered whether you were happy." Chivalrous, idealistic, gentle at heart, wanting to soar; soaring awkwardly, but with a certain winsomeness.

I want to write about anything except Rank's departure. Although today he said, "After that talk with Hugh, after feeling I will see you even sooner than December, I am happy. I am so happy. It is the first time I will be happy to be going to New York. I will take rooms there for both of us, my darling, my darling." Even over the telephone, his voice caresses me and his happiness stirs me.

Sunday night we will be together all night in Rouen. I tried to write him ten letters, one for each day on the boat. I couldn't. I told him, "All I have to say to you I can only say with caresses."

He jumped. "And I, do you know what I was going to say to you? Exactly the same thing. When I'm away I think of a hundred things to say to you. When I see you I forget them all with want of you. I wake up in the night longing for you. Whenever we meet we act like drunkards! *Deux fous!*"

I posed for Chana Orloff the other day with the marks of Henry's bitings on my neck.

I cannot lie to Rank, because he knows. He knows I will not break with Henry until I go to New York.

On Thursday evening Mrs. Miller left Henry, and Mrs. Guiler came home to Louveciennes! Telephoned the plumber to fix a leak and clean the furnace, ordered coal, wrote in her diary, talked with the new Eduardo, a sparkling, easygoing, talkative, industrious Eduardo.

It was the *femme de ménage* at Villa Seurat who christened me "Mrs. Miller." *"Votre mari . . ."*

Rank said, "Hugh is your father, Henry is your husband, and I the lover."

OCTOBER 7, 1934

A STRANGE DAY. HUGH AND I WENT AT FOUR O'CLOCK to Rank's apartment. There were people there, saying good-bye. I was dressed in a russet suit (the green suit dyed) and wore a veil and felt beautiful. We were not sad, because we thought of the night coming. Everybody said good-bye. They leaned out of the window while Rank drove away. Hugh and I stood on the curb, waving. Hugh, Eduardo, and I went to the movies. Then I asked Hugh to drive me to Gare St.-Lazare because "the gang would be there to take me to a dinner for Kay Boyle," then to the studio. I was carrying in a valise the curtains for the studio—which I left at the *consigne* for the next day. I ate dinner alone and tried to finish my letter to Rank—wanting him to have at least one letter to read on the boat. I picked out some things from the journal, to make him happy. I had no desire to formulate, as I had when I loved Henry.

On the train I dreamed. When he saw me at the station he leaped toward me, he kissed me passionately. It seemed to me that he was loving me in the way I had loved Henry, with all that leaping flamingness of gestures.

For hours that night we kissed, caressed, lay entangled, soldered.

I gave him the ring my Father gave me. I cast off the tie with my

Father. He wanted to give me the ring Freud had given him. He wanted to cast off his father.

We saw the dawn.

Smiling, we separated at the station, but I felt the pain of his going away physically, like my own flesh tearing.

In the train, I read Mark Twain because he loves it, for no other reason.

I arrived at the studio worn-out. Felt so strongly the meaning-lessness of my life with Henry. Whatever is reduced to tenderness ought better to die.

OCTOBER 21, 1934

*H*OME FRIDAY, SATURDAY, AND SUNDAY. WORK. OIL-ing and repairing the home machine. Writing letters. Directing the repairs. Preparing to leave Hugh and Eduardo in comfort, Teresa to her nebulous housekeeping; carrying in my valise a bedspread for the studio—for there, too, I must continue the illusion. I cannot leave that place unfinished and make Henry feel that he will be uprooted again, because he dreams of a refuge. He smothers me with love, praise, kisses, tenderness. Does he know I am leaving him?

Illusion of love for Hugh and Henry. Eduardo knows the truth. I spent Friday morning writing my love again. With Hugh I make a budget to see when I may leave. I make most of my preparations discreetly, quietly; the noise and flare of my departure would cause pain.

Hugh buys me a rich Indian shawl because he loved me in one when some people from Bombay loaned me one for an evening we spent with them.

The *voyant* (or my unconscious!) called Hugh "*une nature tributaire qui ne peut rien faire seul*" (an accessory by nature who can't do anything by himself). We joke about this "unconscious" idea, and I tell Eduardo he should see the *voyant* in order that I may know what he is really thinking!

Rank wants me as "the dancer." He wants the color, the odor, the illusion, and the gaudiness. We talked about it. He had been tempted to give me a job as his assistant, to keep me near him. I was tempted to take it, to be near him, protected. But it isn't a relationship of collaboration we want—no ink and paper and ideas and labor. I am outside of his intellectual life. (He keeps saying I am not intellectual.) Thus a new image and a new me are formed by his desire, out of elements lying dormant in me for several years, and I take up again the dancing so tragically abandoned—the actress.

I sit at the table with the Indian shawl over my head, eating figs and dates, which I really love. My only dread is my timidity and nervousness.

Love is the axis and breath of my life. The art I produce is a by-product, an excrescence of love, the song I sing, the joy which must explode, the overabundance—that is all!

So joyous that I stick a fork into my hair in lieu of a Spanish comb, and talk about the odor of the stage when I haven't really smelled it yet! But just to hear Manuela del Rio say, "Monday at eleven at the Studio Pigalle, Place Pigalle"—to rehearse some of my old dances. Sewing black lace on the Maja dress, giving Henry my paper, because I do not intend to write books for the present.

When I get old I'll write a minute and subtle relativity novel—relativity in relations, the alchemy between human beings.

[O CTOBER 24, 1934]

*T*HOUGH I LIE TO BOTH HENRY AND HUGH, THEY *feel* my going away. Hugh punishes me by depriving me of money, Henry by taking refuge in his work. A scene with Henry revealed to me that I could not bear to push him away entirely. When it was a question of his coming to New York with me, I thought I could lose him better there, that I could leave him with his friends in a country where he would always be taken care of. But he seemed to feel that New York meant staying there permanently. He dreaded it. He wanted to stay in the studio, his home. He wanted to remain fixed, to work in peace and serenity. He didn't want to be set rolling again, didn't want to be uprooted. He was very unhappy when I told him. And I was amazed that I could play this strange comedy of telling Henry it was absolutely necessary for me to go to New York with Hugh, when I was going for Rank. Watching Henry suffer. Watching him despair. And also, in a moment of fear, I saw him think of Lillian Lowenfels as one who would lend him money to go to New York. He had observed her desire to protect him. I saw all the extent of his weakness, of his yieldingness, of his parasite nature; saw all this and felt the pain of losing him altogether, felt jealousy of Lillian taking care of him, felt the last pullings and tearings and apartness, and could not accept it absolutely. Suffered for a few days, darkly, deeply; became all nerves, and fear, and tight with pain.

Relieved only when Henry and I, simultaneously, decided he would stay in the studio while I went to New York and I lied about the length of my stay there so as not to alarm him; I said it would be only two months. When I felt I would not have to separate from Henry absolutely, I felt lighter.

None of this affects or alters my love of Rank, which seems beyond and above all this—something powerful and so fixed that nothing can prevent me from going to him.

So many conflicts. Scenes with Hugh, who got hysterical the other night, weeping: "I can't bear it, I can't bear your leaving me. Don't leave me." He is only going to New York in January. I will have a month with Rank alone. I am growing desperately impatient.

In a valise I put my new, lacy underwear, which Hugh bought me because underwear arouses great perverse feelings in him. I let him buy the most beautiful and the most expensive underwear, which he made me put on, and then he caressed me. Took me in a state of keenest excitement, I thinking all the while of Rank enjoying me, seeing me. And I bought a marvelous black coat and dress, beautiful, for Rank, for New York, for my new life.

And I packed already the manuscripts of "Alraune," and "The Double," and a new diary book. I mail Him a photograph of myself, in the Hindu shawl, the only successful one taken by Brassaï, for New York and the mythical plan of dancing—against which I rebelled one night out of panic, out of fear of the public, fear of facing the world, a real fit of terror before public life. *Toujours la musique de chambre seulement.*

In the studio I realize I am not happy with Henry *as his wife.* Perhaps because I no longer love him. But more because when he feels me there as his own he reveals his irrationality, manias, contradictoriness, the wayward, the *mad* in him. He is so difficult, so illogical, that I must constantly yield to his fancies in every little thing. I get tired of his constant talking, his long-winded arguments over ideas which are so useless because he has no attitude to unify them. I get so tired of his insulting people, his primitive "naturalness," and his sleepiness. He sleeps twelve and fourteen hours a day; he writes nothing but letters; he eats erratically, lives erratically.

As I ride back and forth in the trolley from Villa Seurat to our new apartment at 41, avenue de Versailles, I write in my head constantly, seeking to transpose, to objectify what in life oppresses me unbearably, and above all the pressure of my conflicts.

Pulled so many ways. Furious that I can dance with Turner and feel a sexual upheaval because I feel, as we dance, that he has a tremendous erection. That I can be sensuously stirred by his languid eyes and sensuous, Venusian mouth, and by his desire.

Not stirred but bored by Andard, who makes love to the little girl of the child's diary and talks about my purity—vehement but boring.

Mellow talks with an indulgent, secretly admiring Father. As the sex problem dies, our understanding grows. In coolness always.

I wrote Rank about the *musique de chambre.* He writes me, "I am not so sure you will like my possessiveness, because I begin to feel jealous of your dancing—after your letter this morning!" (My first letter, where I exalted dancing.) Already he has been feeling jealous of my past—of all I have given to others!

I write today, "Strange, what you write me about the dancing. Almost at the same moment I was writing you something about it, which must have pleased the possessive YOU. Nothing more productive of magic than simultaneous thought. Because it makes one learn to live in the present. How else, or why else, live in the present, when nobody catches up with you or is there to answer?"

Turner tells me I have been on his mind for years. First he found me proud, then strange and perhaps a drug addict and indifferent; then suspected me of lesbianism. Thought of me as so entangled with loves, inaccessible. Said that at the Guicciardis' I gave him the feeling of great "illusion," a feeling he believed dead in him. Last night I liked the mouth open and shivery, the tongue all ready to flicker.

Oh, my love, Rank, my love, hold me, keep me.

I make an accomplice of Joaquin, who brings me Rank's letters and cables. But he makes me go to mass, Sunday, and it all seems drab and literal and not connected with my mystical trance. Eduardo points out, however, that I have received no other visits from God, no more signs of mystic communication, thinking I may revert to dogma and ritual in quest of a new religious ecstasy. No. But I am sad not to receive any more signs from my God. Will I fall back on man again, adore and serve and worship man? Is God jealous, and does He, too, want me all to himself, and is *this* the tangle which will take me to Jung?

Why look so far?

NOVEMBER 2, 1934

HENRY HAS FALLEN UNDER THE SPELL OF A RE-markable old man [Aleister Crowley] who is fantastic and psychic, a painter gone mad in Zurich, who talks as I write in "Alraune," all in symbols, and who is continuing or accentuating my fantastic and poetic influence on Henry. Henry is so mellow, so receptive, so emotional, and shows such a strange worship of me now. I have been living again close to him. Realizing I still love his relaxed, animal warmth, the content he exudes, his power to keep me on earth. This old man came to see us but refused to look at me. Said I was a mystic, a powerful animal, thousands of years old, just a light, incandescent, awe inspiring; that I ensorcelled men's souls and that he did not dare look into my eyes. That before he met me he had a dream of me encased in a temple, with the letter *U* underneath. Saw my photograph in the Hindu shawl. Said to Henry, "See, the eyes of the mystic. She is suspended over life. She has the voice of one going away. Nirvana." He addressed Henry and never looked at me.

And Henry, at night, in bed, slipped his hand softly between my legs, around my buttocks, and said: "Who would think that a woman with such luminous eyes, a vestal virgin, could have such a round ass, and such a burning cunt, such an electric bush right here." And we plunged into a frenzied fucking as of old, Henry whispering obscenities hoarsely, and I, too—I with a voice I never have, like an animal's.

Groaning and panting there, two warm bodies, moaning and breathing heavily. Joy. I love him, and I love Hugh, and I love my dark little Rank waiting for me.

I am conscious of a new power which expresses itself wholly through my eyes—a new mystical power—a strength which I have been feeling ever since the mystical trance. I am not afraid of ascension. I am in life. I am alive. But I can leave life. I do not die. I travel. I float. I come back.

But Eduardo says, "You will practice black magic instead of white if you do not collaborate with religion. If you insist on standing alone."

Or I may go mad.

NOVEMBER 7, 1934

I MAILED HIM A LETTER TUESDAY MORNING. I HAD lunch with Henry. Fell back into the old rhythm of a melting indulgence for all his defects, his boorishness, his crudeness, his lack of understanding, his imitativeness. I realize how he borrows, copies, appropriates, steals. I know him—fully. Yet I look at him indulgently, humorously, wisely.

It is my work—this.

To make, or create, the man you love, but not a forced, false "him"—to discover his true self, slowly, by love and divination—accepting his limitations. I did not try to make a bourgeois out of Henry, or a man of power. Henry, only *more* Henry. And why it is, I don't know, but I am doing that to Rank, too. "You understand the *You* in me." He speaks of his newborn Self. Of never having talked about his Self to anyone else. Of no longer being *Dr.* Rank.

So. Peace and joy with Henry. Pretending to be miserable about leaving, acting regrets which I do not feel, which are not as strong as my desire to be with Rank.

Peace with Hugh by satisfying his perversity, his secret love of my coldness to him; wistfulness, looking back to a past empty for me but still strong in him. Hugh—my victim, the giver.

I, buying what I need ruthlessly, without qualms. Buying for my new life. Egoistically, selfishly. *Taking*—accepting.

Marcel Duchamp. Book of his *notes*—sketches for a book never written. Symbol of the times. Henry said he would like to have his letters published. I said, "Yes, pre-posthumous letters." We laughed.

Rank had said, "Someday Henry will discover he is not a genius. Then he will blame you."

I tell Henry I am forced to go to New York. For a moment I hated his passivity. Wished him active, like Rank. He takes everything lying down. He weeps, and writes despairingly. But he could not act. Could not act against Hugh or Rank, or for himself, or against June. Can only write violently, curse, and fuck whatever woman comes his way. This great passivity has made all things in me flower. This great effervescence of moods which I look for, his livingness, his yieldingness to life. I love its physical expression of repose, nonchalance, looseness, easygoingness. The will which only expresses itself in a negative way, opposing the Other. How one can love the physical manifestation of a defect. But how I needed that looseness. How it untied, unknotted, unleashed me, how it oiled me, de-mentalized me, softened me. Henry made me great gifts.

NOVEMBER 8, 1934

SCENE WITH ANDARD WHEN I ATTEMPT TO TELL him there is no hope whatsoever. And he turns white, shakes, and trembles. And I sit there so cold, pretending to feel. I don't feel anything at all. But he is profoundly affected. He pleads, entreats, speaks of his life being finished, of suffering. *"Je ferais des folies pour vous, ma petite Anaïs."* I'd commit crimes for you . . .

Do I *enjoy* this, causing pain? No. I am contracted; I want it to be over quickly. I breathe with relief when I leave him. Once a week he had been taking me out in his car.

NOVEMBER 10, 1934

*I*F I HAVE NOT GONE MAD THESE DAYS WITH ALL that has happened to me, I never will.

Rank's nerve-racked letters; Hugh's cruelties with money; Henry's childlike irresponsibility, his weakness, struggles to launch his book against the timorousness of Kahane; Father's eczema and his bitter mouth; Joaquin's cool, religious coziness; Mother's concern with last, before-she-dies love, and the pathetic way she asks me for advice; Hugh's new furies and obsessive jealousy and the sexual scenes of his perversities and my coldness; Rank calling me; my Father waiting for signs of fatigue and wisdom in me.

Meeting with Abbé Alterman, whom I wish to seduce to deprive Joaquin of his faith and keep him from becoming a monk—the talk with him; the thoughts of Thaïs; the purchase of a severe black costume of wool and heavy braid, like a voluptuous nun.

Cables to Rank: "Sailing Nov. 15th for audition with you"—and not with Balanchine, the ballet master; the reflection of Turner and of meaningless sensuality; the knowledge that after Rank I will have lived all I want to live, have all I want of love and life and desire, the joys of mysticism and creation; that I have lived through the deepest dramas of existence, fully; that I want to dream later, cease to live for myself, which I have not the courage to do because all the feelings of others affect me, because I am not cruel enough, and everyone, even the one I appear to send away empty-handed, seems to take away with him a piece of my flesh and my strength.

Whirlpool and whirlwind visits to painters and writers with Henry. Movie, *Of Human Bondage*, where the woman explodes with hatred—sexual hatred of the poetic, dolorous man who adores her—and is betrayed by him.

Last lie to Hugh, who finds Rank's letter in my bag, where fortunately there is no question of *my* love, only of his, so I say with great calm, "Of course he loves me, but that's nothing. So does Turner, so does Andard, so does Harvey, so does everyone I meet these days."

"Why does he call you *'darling'*?"

"Well, I showed you Andard's letter the other day. He, too, thought he could call me 'darling' after seeing me once on the train."

So calm, so general. Everybody, it is true, belongs now to my new power. Harvey (Dorothy Dudley's husband) wrote an inflamed letter to Henry about me. I make light of it. And I yearn for Him, desperately, wondering how much there will be left of me after this struggle to live for myself, which is so difficult, so difficult, so wearing. It is what *I want* against the happiness of Father, Hugh, Joaquin, Eduardo, Henry. A terrible algebra, always.

After Rank, I will live only for others, which is my joy.

Psychoanalysis did save me, because it allowed the birth of the real me, who is religious. I may not become a saint. But I am very full and very rich, and I have a great deal to write about. I will be glad of a little peace and a little careful remembering. I cannot install myself definitely in human life. It is not enough. I must climb dizzier regions.

Psychoanalysis did save me from death. It allowed me to live, and if I leave life it will be of my own volition, as not containing the absolute. But how I still love the relative, the cabbage and the warmth of a fire, and a fine collection of earrings, and Haydn on the phonograph, and the laughter with Eduardo, and the jokes on Mae West, and the new black wool costume with enormous sleeves and the sensual slit from throat to breast, and the bracelet and necklace of blue stone, set with stars, and the new underwear, and the new black velvet kimono, and the trunk drawer full of Henry's *Tropic of Cancer*, with my preface, and Rank's last letter, and the telephone ringing all day, and Turner's sensual voice requesting, and Emilia's short abortion of two hours, which I would not have exchanged for my superb adventure.

Love.

And the Abbé Alterman saying, *"Vous êtes une âme très disputée."*

BIOGRAPHICAL NOTES

ALLENDY, DR. RENÉ FÉLIX *(1889–1942):* French psychoanalyst; author of numerous works, including *Les théories alchimiques dans l'histoire de la médecine,* 1912; *La psychanalyse,* 1931; *Capitalisme et sexualité,* 1932. In 1926, with Freud's protégée Princess Marie Bonaparte, he became a founding member of the Paris Psychoanalytic Society. Interested in alchemy, astrology, and mysticism, he was close to the surrealist movement and initiated several dream-film projects. His wife, Yvonne, served as treasurer of Antonin Artaud's Théâtre Alfred Jarry in the late 1920s. Anaïs Nin became Dr. Allendy's patient in May 1932. He also analyzed Eduardo Sanchez and Hugh Guiler.

ANA MARIA: Daughter of Anaïs Nin's aunt Anaïs Culmell and of Bernabé Sanchez; younger sister of Eduardo.

ANDARD, LOUIS: French politician and publisher of popular authors like Maurice Dekobra; at various times he expressed an interest in the writings of Alfred Perlès, Henry Miller, and Anaïs Nin.

ARTAUD, ANTONIN *(1896–1948):* French poet, essayist, stage and screen actor (notably as Marat in Abel Gance's film *Napoléon,* 1926, and as the monk Massieu in Carl Dreyer's *La passion de Jeanne d'Arc,* 1928), director and creator of the "Theater of Cruelty." For many years he was a patient and protégé of Dr. Allendy, who introduced him to the Guilers in March 1933. After their first meeting, he presented Anaïs Nin with a copy of his *L'art et la mort* (1929) and with pages of his stage-work-in-progress, *Heliogabalus, ou l'anarchiste couronné.* Hugh Guiler briefly supported Artaud's theatrical experiments.

BACHMAN, RUDOLF: Austrian refugee in France who solicited help from Anaïs Nin and Henry Miller by telling them about his adventures as a vagabond.

BALD, WAMBLY *(1902–1989):* Chicago-born journalist who, from October 1929 to July 1933, reported the goings-on among the English-speaking colony in France in a weekly gossip column, "La vie de Bohême," for the Paris edition of the Chicago *Tribune.* A collection of these columns, *On the Left Bank,* appeared in 1987.

BONE, DR. HARRY: American psychologist who studied and worked at Dr. Otto Rank's Psychological Center in Paris during the summer of 1934.

BOUSSIE—HÉLÈNE BOUSSINESCQUE: French educator and translator who met the Guilers in 1926 and introduced Anaïs Nin to various aspects of French intellectual life.

BRADLEY, WILLIAM ASPENWALL *(1878–1939):* American poet and translator who settled in France after World War I and became a literary agent. With his French-born wife, he established a literary salon at their elegant apartment on the Ile St. Louis, which attracted many American and English writers and publishers.

CROSBY, "CARESSE"—MARY PHELPS JACOB *(1892–1970):* Widow of Harry Crosby (1898–1929), American playboy, poet, and publisher of the Black Sun Press. She continued her husband's publishing activities and entertained many writers and artists at Le Moulin du Soleil, the Crosbys' country estate near Ermenonville, about an hour's drive from Paris.

CROWLEY, ALEISTER *(1875–1947):* English writer, painter, and magician; self-proclaimed saint of his own Gnostic Church. His *Confessions* appeared billed as the memoirs of "the most notorious magician, satanist, and drug cultist of the twentieth century."

DAVIDSON, MR.: American businessman in France, client of Hugh Guiler.

DELIA: Friend of Maria and Joaquin Nin.

DOROTHY: Friend of Eduardo Sanchez; became a patient of Dr. Allendy.

DUCHAMP, MARCEL *(1887–1968):* French artist, dadaist, whose painting *Nude Descending a Staircase,* first exhibited in New York in 1911, served Anaïs Nin as a symbol of her own sense of fragmentation.

EDUARDO SÁNCHEZ *(1904–1990):* Cuban-born amateur scholar, astrologer, one-time actor, Anaïs Nin's beloved cousin and first intense romantic interest (see *The Early Diary of Anaïs Nin, 1920–1923; 1927–1932).* He came to Paris in 1930 and lived at times with the Guilers at their rented house in Louveciennes. He introduced Anaïs Nin to psychoanalysis, after having been analyzed himself in New York in 1928 by a pupil of Dr. Otto Rank, and encouraged her writing, especially her interest in D. H. Lawrence. (See also *Anais: An International Journal,* Volume 9, 1991.)

EMILIA: Longtime Spanish maid in the Guiler household whom Henry Miller insisted on calling "Amelia."

ETHEL GUILER: Hugh's younger sister, who visited her brother and his wife in France on several occasions, though her parents initially disapproved of his marriage to Anaïs Nin.

FATHER *(Padre, Papito)*—JOAQUIN J. NIN Y CASTELLANOS *(1879–1949):* Cuban-born Spanish pianist, composer, musicologist, author of *Pour l'art,* 1908, and other writings. He left his wife, Rosa Culmell, and their three children (Anaïs, Thorvald, and Joaquin) in 1913 and eventually married one of his pupils, Maria Luísa Rodriguez. Until their reunion in Louveciennes, Anaïs Nin had seen her father, whom she called "the Problem" in her early diary, only once, in

December 1924, when she first returned to France after her ten-year exile in the United States.

FRAENKEL, MICHAEL *(1896–1961):* Lithuanian-born American bookseller and writer. He settled in Paris in the 1920s to live off his investments and pursue a literary life. Under the Carrefour imprint he published some of his own work and that of his friends at the St. Catherine Press in Bruges, Belgium. Among other properties, he owned the house at 18 Villa Seurat where Henry Miller (who turned Fraenkel into the "Boris" of *Tropic of Cancer*) found temporary shelter in 1930 when he was down-and-out in Paris. In August 1934 Anaïs Nin rented a studio in the same building to serve as her "office" and as a home for Henry Miller.

FRANKENSTEIN, DR.: American psychiatrist who attended Dr. Rank's seminar for psychiatric social workers at the Cité Universitaire.

FRED—ALFRED PERLÈS *(1897–1991):* Austrian journalist and writer. Worked for the Paris edition of the Chicago *Tribune* until the demise of the paper in 1934. He met Henry Miller and his wife June on their first European trip in 1928. He helped Miller to survive his early, difficult days in Paris in 1930, and from March 1932 to late 1933 the two shared a two-room apartment at 4 avenue Anatole France in Clichy, on the northern outskirts of Paris. He portrayed Anaïs Nin as "Pietà" in *Sentiments limitrophes,* his "novel-souvenirs," which, together with another work written at the time, *Le Quatuor en ré majeur,* was reissued in France in 1984.

GUSTAVO DURÁN: Young Spanish intellectual and music student living in Paris. Recalled to active military duty, he distinguished himself as a commander on the Loyalist side in the Spanish Civil War.

HARVEY, HARRY: American expatriate, married to the writer Dorothy Dudley who, during the 1930s, covered the French literary and artistic scene for various U.S. publications.

HENRY MILLER *(1891–1980):* American author who took up writing "seriously" in 1924 but did not publish his first book, *Tropic of Cancer,* until 1934. After six frustrating years in New York, where his second wife, June Edith Smith, a former taxi dancer, provided most of their precarious livelihood, Miller left for Europe in 1930. His struggle to survive alone in Paris provided the raw material for the book he was working on when he met Anaïs Nin and her husband in December 1931. Hugh Guiler helped Miller to find a teaching job in Dijon in February 1932, but the job proved short-lived, and Miller returned to Paris where, in March 1932, he and Anaïs Nin became lovers. His stay in Dijon triggered a lifelong correspondence (*Henry Miller: Letters to Anaïs Nin,*

1965; *A Literate Passion: Letters of Anaïs Nin and Henry Miller, 1932–1953,* 1987), and the initial course of their intimate relationship is charted in the volume *Henry and June: From the Unexpurgated Diary of Anaïs Nin,* first published in 1986.

HILER, HILAIRE *(1898–1974):* American artist, musician, raconteur, and, briefly, co–owner–manager of the Jockey Bar in Paris in the 1920s. At his studio in the rue Broca, he gave art lessons to Henry Miller, and he became interested in the ideas Dr. Otto Rank presented in his book *Art and Artist.*

HUGH (HUGO) PARKER GUILER *(1889–1985):* Born in Boston, he spent his childhood on a sugar plantation in Puerto Rico, where his father worked as a design engineer. His Scottish parents sent him to be educated in Scotland at the age of six, first at Ayr, in Halloway, then at the Edinburgh Academy. After graduating from Columbia University in 1920, with degrees in literature and economics, he signed up as a trainee with the National City Bank. He was assigned to their Paris branch in December 1924, where he became a specialist in the trust department. He met Anaïs Nin, then eighteen, at a dance at his parents' home in Forest Hills, New York, in 1921, and they were married in Havana, Cuba, in March 1923. The story of their courtship and marriage is covered in great detail in the three volumes of *The Early Diary of Anaïs Nin, 1920–1923; 1923–1927; 1927–1931.*

HUNT, HENRI: French businessman, married to Louise de Vilmorin.

JOAQUIN NIN-CULMELL: Anaïs Nin's younger brother, born in Berlin in 1908. He studied piano and composition at the Schola Cantorum and the Paris Conservatory, and privately with Alfred Cortot, Richard Viñez, and Manuel de Falla. He lived with the Guilers at the house in Louveciennes until, in October 1931, he and his mother moved to an apartment in Paris.

JOHN ERSKINE *(1879–1951):* American educator, pianist, best-selling novelist *(The Private Life of Helen of Troy,* 1925). He was Hugh Guiler's literature professor at Columbia University and later befriended Guiler and his young wife, Anaïs Nin. In 1928 he and his wife and children visited the Guilers in France and Anaïs Nin became infatuated with Erskine. Though the relationship never developed, it precipitated the first major crisis in Anaïs Nin's marriage; she attempted to deal with the experience in her eventually abandoned "John" novel.

JOLAS, EUGENE: Editor of *transition,* an influential "little magazine" published in Paris, intermittently, since 1927.

JUNE EDITH SMITH (ALSO KNOWN AS JUNE MANSFIELD): Born Juliet Edith Smerth in Austria-Hungary in 1902, one of five children of a Galician family that emigrated to the United States in 1907. At the age of fifteen, she dropped out of her Brooklyn high school to become a taxi dancer. In 1923, working at Wilson's Dance Hall on Broadway, she met Henry Miller, who was married, had a five-year-old daughter, and worked as personnel manager for Western Union. She married Miller the following year, after he had obtained a divorce from his first wife. Miller quit his job and for the next six years they led an adventurous, precarious life on the margins of society, which provided much of the raw material for Miller's later writing. In 1930, she encouraged Miller to go to Europe by himself to write, promising him financial support which never arrived. She met Anaïs Nin in December 1931, on one of her brief visits to Paris, and again when she returned, for the last time, in October 1932. She divorced Miller in Mexico in December 1934.

KAHANE, JACK *(1887–1939):* Born in Manchester, England, he left the family textile business to become a writer in Paris in the 1920s. Author of a number of pseudonymous "naughty" novels for the English-speaking tourist trade, he set up the Obelisk Press in 1930 to publish his own and other books that had been or might be banned by English and American censorship.

KILLGOER, DONALD: A young Scotsman who briefly stayed with the Guilers at Louveciennes and became a patient of Dr. Allendy.

KRONSKI, JEAN: June Miller's name for a disturbed young woman she took under her wing in Greenwich Village in 1926. Claiming to be an orphan, a poet, and an artist, Jean eventually moved in with the Millers at their Henry Street apartment. Miller dealt with this ménage à trois in a novel, *Lovely Lesbians,* later entitled *Crazy Cock,* which he brought with him to Paris and eventually cannibalized for other books. Committed to a mental institution, Jean is supposed to have taken her own life in the early 1930s.

LALOU, RENÉ: French critic, writer, and literary historian who tried to develop a systematic approach to criticism in reaction to dadaism, surrealism, and other -isms.

LOWENFELS, WALTER *(1897–1980):* American poet and writer who, with his wife Lillian, lived in Paris during the 1920s and early 1930s. Some of his work was published under Michael Fraenkel's Carrefour imprint. He appears as "Jabberwhorl Cronstadt" in *Tropic of Cancer.*

MARIA (MARUCA) LUÍSA RODRIGUEZ: Music student, daughter of a Cuban cigar manufacturer, who became Joaquin Nin's second wife.

MIRALLES, ANTONIO FRANCISCO (PACO): Spanish dancer with whom Anaïs Nin studied between 1927 and 1929, and who once asked her to elope with him.

MOTHER—ROSA CULMELL DE NIN *(1871–1954):* Soprano of Danish-French ancestry. She met and married the young musician Joaquin Nin in Cuba in 1902 and went to live with him in France, where her first child, Anaïs, was born in 1903. In 1914, after her husband had deserted the family, she took her three children to New York. She supported herself by taking in boarders in a brownstone on Manhattan's West Side and by acting as a "mail-order" buyer for her Cuban family and friends. She eventually returned to France, with the support of Hugh Guiler, to enable her son Joaquin to continue his musical studies. For several years she and Joaquin lived with the Guilers in Louveciennes.

NELLIE—COMTESSE DE VOGÜE: French aristocrat and society woman interested in the arts. Involved in a magazine project with writer Edmond Jaloux, she planned to translate and publish some of Anaïs Nin's writings.

NESTOR DE LA TORRE: Young Spanish painter, friend of Anaïs Nin's brother, Joaquin.

ORLOFF, CHANA: Russian-born sculptor with a studio in Villa Seurat. Friend and patient of Dr. Otto Rank.

OSBORN, RICHARD: Young lawyer and frustrated writer from Connecticut who worked with Hugh Guiler at the Paris office of the National City Bank. He supported Henry Miller during his early, penniless days in Paris and served as the inspiration for "Van Norden" in *Tropic of Cancer*. He introduced Miller to the Guilers, late in 1931, by promising Miller a free meal in Louveciennes.

PAULETTE: A French girl Alfred Perlès installed at the apartment in Clichy in June 1932, until, about a month later, her mother reclaimed her as a fifteen-year-old runaway.

RANK, DR. OTTO *(1884–1939)*:   Austrian psychoanalyst (born Otto Rosenfeld) who, from 1905 to 1924, belonged to the inner circle of the psychoanalytic movement as the protégé and designated "son" of Sigmund Freud. He served as secretary of the Psychoanalytic Society of Vienna and editor of its publications until his pioneering study *The Trauma of Birth* precipitated a break with Freud and his contentious orthodox followers. In 1926 Rank, with his wife and daughter, moved to Paris, where he continued to practice until his move to the United States in 1934. By then he had published most of his major works, including *Don Juan et son double, Art and Artist,* and *Das Inzest Motif in Dichtung und Sage (The Incest Motif in Poetry and Myth)*. Between July 15 and August 30, 1934, he conducted a special seminar for American psychiatric social workers, the "Psychological Center," at the American Foundation of the Cité Universitaire in Paris.

SCHNELLOCK, EMIL *(1891–1960)*:   American graphic artist and teacher who graduated together with Henry Miller from Brooklyn's P.S. 85 in 1905. Miller called him his "oldest friend" in America and his *Letters to Emil* (edited by

George Wickes, 1989) contains the full text of Miller's lengthy letter about June referred to in these pages.

STEELE, BERNARD: American-born editor, co-owner of the Paris publishing firm Denoël & Steele, which published the work of Dr. René Allendy and Antonin Artaud as well as many avant-garde and surrealist writers.

TERESA: Spanish maid who replaced Emilia in the Guiler household when the latter left to get married.

THORVALD NIN (1905–1991):   Anaïs Nin's younger brother, who became an engineer and spent most of his life in Latin America.

TÍA ANAÏS: Rosa Culmell's sister, married to Bernabé Sanchez.

TITUS, EDWARD: Polish-born publisher and husband of Helena Rubinstein. He established a bookstore and a press, "At the Sign of the Black Mannikin," on the Left Bank in Paris, which published Anaïs Nin's first book, her "unprofessional" study of D. H. Lawrence, in 1932. Between 1929 and 1932, Titus also edited and published the literary magazine *This Quarter*, which featured the first English translation (by Titus) of a section from Rank's *Art and Artist*, and a famous special issue on the surrealists, edited by André Breton.

TROUBETSKOIA, PRINCESS NATASHA: Russian emigré painter and decorator who met Anaïs in 1929 and painted several portraits of her. She allowed Anaïs Nin to use her studio in Paris as a meeting place and a mailing address.

TURNER, MR.:   American businessman in Paris, client of Hugh Guiler.

VILMORIN, LOUISE DE (1902–1970):   French aristocrat and writer. Though married at the time to Henri Hunt, she remained deeply attached to her two brothers, André and Roger. She met Anaïs Nin in November 1931 and later served as the model for "Jeanne" in some of Anaïs Nin's fiction, notably the story "Under a Glass Bell."

WEST, REBECCA—PEN NAME OF CICILY ISABEL FAIRFIELD (1892–1983):   British writer and journalist, author of numerous books, including the novels *The Return of the Soldier*, 1918, and *The Judge*, 1922; a critical study, *Henry James*, 1916; and a biography, *St. Augustine*, 1933. After a ten-year extramarital relationship with the writer H. G. Wells, whom she bore a son in 1914, she married banker Henry Maxwell Andrews in 1930. She became well known as an ardent feminist and a prolific writer.

ZADKINE, OSSIP: Russian-born sculptor who met June Miller and her friend Jean Kronski on their solo visit to Paris in 1929 and later welcomed Henry Miller and Anaïs Nin to his studio.

I N D E X